Drug Absorption

INTERNATIONAL Conference on Drug
1st
Absorption (1979: Edinburgh, Scotland)

# Drug Absorption

Edited by
*L.F. Prescott and W.S. Nimmo*

ADIS Press
New York · Tokyo · Mexico · Sydney · Auckland · Hong Kong

# Drug Absorption

The Proceedings of the International Conference on Drug Absorption,
Edinburgh, September, 1979

National Library of Australia
Cataloguing-in-Publication entry
International Conference on Drug Absorption,
Edinburgh, 1979
  Drug absorption: proceedings . . .

  Index
  Bibliography
  ISBN 0-909337-30-6

  1. Pharmacology — Congresses. 2. Drug metabolism —
Congresses. I. Prescott, L.F., joint ed. II. Nimmo
W.S., joint ed. III. Title

615'.7

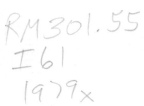

ADIS Press
404 Sydney Road, Balgowlah, NSW 2093, Australia.

Printed in Hong Kong by Cameron Printing Co. Ltd.

# Preface

This book records the proceedings of an International Conference on Drug Absorption which was held in Edinburgh in September 1979. The Conference was conceived and organised with the object of bringing together scientists from different disciplines with a common interest in drug absorption. Despite its importance in clinical practice, pharmacy, pharmacology, toxicology and drug development, there has been no recent comprehensive review of the subject. The major emphasis of the Conference was on absorption from the gastrointestinal tract and topics included the effects of physiological and pharmaceutical factors, disease, food and other drugs and novel drug delivery systems as well as practical aspects of bioavailability assessment and regulatory agency requirements. We are most grateful to the many distinguished speakers who took part in this Conference and to those who participated in the discussions which are included in this book in edited form. We are also indebted to the pharmaceutical companies who generously supported the Conference, to our colleagues on the local and international advisory committees and of course, to our publisher.

We hope that the interest shown in this meeting will lead to further inter-disciplinary collaboration and to a better understanding of the many problems of drug absorption.

*L.F. Prescott*
*W.S. Nimmo*
Edinburgh 1979

v

The International Conference on Drug Absorption was held at the Assembly Rooms, Edinburgh, September 26 to 28, 1979.

## Advisory Committee
L.F. Prescott (UK) *(Chairman)*
T.B. Binns (UK)
C.T. Dollery (UK)
F. Gross (FDR)
G. Levy (USA)
M. Rowland (UK)
J. Sjogren (Sweden)

## Local Organising Committee
L.F. Prescott *(Chairman)*
R.N. Boyes
G.H. Draffan
R.C. Heading
W.S. Nimmo
A. Pottage
M.D. Rawlins
I.H. Stevenson
I.P. Sword

# Contributors

Contributions are listed alphabetically by the first-named author. Numbers in parenthesis indicate the pages on which the authors' contribution begins.

*D.J. Back, M. Bates, A.M. Breckenridge, F. Crawford, A. Ellis, J.M. Hall, M. MacIver, M.L'E. Orme, I. Taylor and P.H. Rowe* (p.80). Department of Pharmacology and Therapeutics, Liverpool University, Ashton Street, P.O. Box 147, Liverpool L69 3BX, UK

*Gilbert S. Banker and V.E. Sharma* (p.194). Industrial and Physical Pharmacy Department, School of Pharmacy and Pharmaceutical Sciences, Purdue University, West Lafayette, Indiana 47907, USA

*Arnold H. Beckett* (p.133). Department of Pharmacy, Chelsea College, University of London, Manresa Road, London SW3 6LX, UK

*Bjorn Beermann* (p.238). Department of Medicine and Clinical Pharmacology Laboratory, Serafimerlasarettet, S-112 83 Stockholm, Sweden

*A.G. de Boer and D.D. Breimer* (p.61). Department of Pharmacology, Subfaculty of Pharmacy, University of Leiden, The Netherlands

*Dennys Cook* (p.324). Drug Research Laboratories, Health Protection Branch, Health and Welfare, Ottawa, Canada

*D.S. Davies, K.F. Ilett and C.F. George* (p.73). Department of Clinical Pharmacology, Royal Postgraduate Medical School, Ducane Road, London W12 OHS, UK

*C.T. Dollery* (p.339). Royal Postgraduate Medical School, Ducane Road, London W12 OHS, UK

*C.F. George, A.G. Renwick and D. G. Waller* (p.278). Faculty of Medicine, University of Southampton, Medical and Biological Sciences Building, Bassett Crescent East, Southampton SO9 3TU, UK

*Milo Gibaldi* (p.1). School of Pharmacy, University of Washington, Seattle, Washington, USA

*Peter Goldman* (p.88). Division of Clinical Pharmacology, Beth Israel Hospital, 330 Brookline Avenue, Boston, Massachusetts 02215, USA

*J.P. Griffin* (p.334). Medicines Division, Department of Health and Social Security, Finsbury Square London EC2A 1PP, UK

*Takeru Higuchi* (p.177). Department of Pharmaceutical Chemistry, The University of Kansas, 2065 Avenue 'A' — Campus West, Lawrence, Kansas 66044, USA

*William I. Higuchi, N.F.H. Ho, J.Y. Park and I. Komiya* (p.35). College of Pharmacy, University of Michigan, Ann Arbor, Michigan 48109, USA

*P. Johnson* (p.342). Hoechst Pharmaceutical Research Laboratories, Walton Manor, Walton, Milton Keynes, Buckinghamshire, UK

*Stanley A. Kaplan* (p.144). Department of Pharmacokinetics and Biopharmaceutics, Hoffmann-La Roche Inc., Nutley, New Jersey 07110, USA

*A. Karim and D.L. Azarnoff* (p.313). Research and Development Division, G.D. Searle and Co., P.O. Box 5110, Chicago, Illinois 60680, USA

*J. Koch-Weser and P.J. Schechter* (p.217). Center de Recherche Merrell International, 16, rue d'Ankara, Strasbourg Cedex 67084, France

*Gerhard Levy and K.M. Giacomini* (p.115). Department of Pharmaceutics, School of Pharmacy, State University of New York at Buffalo, Amherst, New York 14260, USA

*P.J. Neuvonen* (p.228). Department of Clinical Pharmacology, University of Helsinki, Paasikivenkatu 4, SF-00250 Helsinki 25, Finland

*Walter S. Nimmo* (p.11). Department of Anaesthesia, University of Glasgow, Western Infirmary, Glasgow, UK

*R.L. Parsons and J.A. David* (p.262). Section of Clinical Pharmacology, Academic Department of Medicine, Royal Free Hospital, Pond Street, London NW3, UK

*Michael D. Rawlins* (p.331). Department of Pharmacological Sciences, (Clinical Pharmacology), Wolfson Unit of Clinical Pharmacology, The University, Newcastle upon Tyne, UK

*Sidney Riegelman and R.A. Upton* (p.297). School of Pharmacy, University of California, San Francisco, California, 94143, USA

*Malcolm Rowland* (p.285). Department of Pharmacy, University of Manchester, Manchester M13 9PL, UK

*Hitoshi Sezaki, S. Muranishi, J. Nakamura, M. Yasuhara and T. Kimura* (p.21). Faculty of Pharamaceutical Sciences, Kyoto University, Sakyo-Ku, Kyoto, 606, Japan

*D.G. Shand* (p.100). Division of Clinical Pharmacology, Duke University Medical Center, Durham, North Carolina, USA

*J.E. Shaw and S.K. Chandrasekaran* (p.186). ALZA Corporation, 950 Page Mill Road, Palo Alto, California, CA94304, USA

*John Sjogren* (p.205). Department of Pharmaceutics, AB Hassle, Fack, 2-43120 Molndal, Sweden

*I.H. Stevenson, S.A.M. Salem, K.O'Malley, B. Cusack and J.G. Kelly* (p.253). Department of Pharmacology and Therapeutics, University of Dundee, Ninewells Hospital, Dundee DD1 9SY, UK

*F. Theeuwes* (p.157). ALZA Research, 950 Mill Road, Palo Alto, California, CA 94304, USA

*L.A. Turnberg* (p.6). University of Manchester School of Medicine, Department of Medicine, Hope Hospital, Eccles Old Road, Salford, UK

*Harmut Uehleke* (p.123). Federal German Health Office, Department of Toxicology, Thielallee, 88-92, D-1000 Berlin 33 (West)

*T. Zysset and J. Bircher* (p.108). Department of Clinical Pharmacology, University of Berne, Murtenstrasse 35, CH-3010 Bern, Switzerland

# Contents

# 1

# Limitations of Classical Theories of Drug Absorption

*Milo Gibaldi*

School of Pharmacy, University of Washington, Seattle, Washington

Almost 80 years ago, Overton (1902) demonstrated that a number of organic compounds penetrate cells at rates roughly related to their lipid/water partition coefficients. Some 35 years later, the importance of lipid solubility in the intestinal absorption of foreign organic compounds was recognised by Hober and Hober (1937). A report by Travell in 1940 gave the first indication that the gastrointestinal epithelium is selectively permeable to the undissociated form of a drug and that the pH at the absorption site and the dissociation of the drug, as well as lipid solubility, are important factors in the absorption of weak organic electrolytes. Travell noted that large doses of strychnine in the pyloric-ligated stomach of the cat produced no toxic effects when the gastric contents were very acidic, but were fatal when the stomach contents were made alkaline. She concluded from these and other observations that the absorption rate of alkaloids was dependent on the concentration of undissociated drug.

## 1. The pH-partition Hypothesis

It was undoubtedly these reports, among others, that stimulated the brilliant quantitative experimental efforts of Shore et al. (1950), Hogben (1957, 1959) and Schanker et al. (1957, 1958, 1959) which culminated in the classical pH-partition hypothesis of drug absorption. The beautiful simplicity of this concept of gastrointestinal absorption is reflected in the title of Hogben's (1960) review of this work, 'The first common pathway'.

Today, with the clarity of hindsight, we recognise the limitations of the pH-partition hypothesis and view it more in terms of a first approximation rather than as a unifying hypothesis. This is as science should be and in no way diminishes the enormous contribution of this research to our understanding of drug absorption.

## 2. Virtual Intestinal pH

The first limitation of the pH-partition hypothesis was discovered during the initial work. The lowest $pK_a$ of an acidic drug consistent with very rapid intestinal absorption was about 3, while the corresponding highest $pK_a$ for a basic drug was about 8. If intestinal fluid pH is assumed to be 6.6, this means that the necessary proportion of non-ionised to ionised drug is 1:6000 for acids but only 1:16 for bases, which is unlikely if the idea of passive absorption is valid. Hogben et al. (1959) therefore proposed the concept of a hypothetical or 'virtual' intestinal pH, possibly located at the surface of the intestinal epithelial boundary, that is lower than luminal pH. Assuming a virtual pH of 5.3, the ratio of non-ionised to ionised drug needed for rapid absorption is 1:3000 for both an acid of $pK_a$ 2.8 and a base of $pK_a$ 7.8.

The idea of surface pH is not new to the colloid chemist but whether it applies to intestinal absorption is debated. Some believe that the difference between the virtual pH and the luminal pH is, at least in part, the result of the important but incorrect assumption of the pH-partition hypothesis that only the non-ionised form of a drug can be absorbed. Although organic anions or cations appear to cross the intestinal epithelium much more slowly than their corresponding non-ionic species, they do cross the barrier. Moreover, considering that at the pH of the intestine a significantly greater fraction of an acid drug may exist in the ionised than in the nonionised form, the contribution of ion absorption may not be trivial. Crouthamel et al. (1971) calculated that at pH 6.1, the absorption of sulphaethidole ions accounts for 43 % of the total absorption of the drug from the rat intestine.

Another, perhaps more important, factor that contributes to the observation of a virtual pH, is the existence of unstirred water layers adjacent to the intestinal epithelium (Wilson et al., 1971; Wilson and Dietschy, 1972). Winne (1975) has demonstrated that an unstirred layer can influence absorption kinetics in the following manner:

1) The apparent permeability coefficient of a passively transported substance is reduced and

2) The permeation of a weak electrolyte is reduced and the inflection point of the pH-absorption curve is shifted to the right for acids and to the left for bases.

## 3. Residence Time and Surface Area

Since the absorption of ions is assumed to be negligible, the pH-partition hypothesis seems to suggest that the absorption of weak acids should be optimal at the low pH of the stomach. This conclusion however could not be supported by experimental observations. For example, Siurala et al. (1969) found that the rate of appearance of salicylate in plasma was much more rapid after intraduodenal than after intragastric instillation of aspirin in human subjects. These workers came to the same conclusion after studying warfarin absorption in human volunteers (Kekki et al., 1971). Classical absorption theory simply does not consider the two principal factors that determine the site of drug absorption: residence time and surface area. In general, the residence time of a drug in the stomach is much shorter than in the small intestine and the absorptive surface area of the stomach is substantially smaller than of the small intestine. Studies in the rat with barbitone and sulphaethidole suggest that the absorptive surface area of the small intestine is 10 to 15 times that of the stomach (Crouthamel et al., 1971). As a result of the limited absorptive surface area in the stomach, among other considerations, we often find that gastric absorption contributes little to the overall absorption of a drug. Beermann et al. (1971) observed that only 15 % of a dose of digitoxin was absorbed in healthy volunteers by the time that the test solution had passed the stomach. Clements et al. (1978) determined, by means of a sophisticated pharmacokinetic analysis of both gastric emptying and plasma concentration data, that the gastric absorption of paracetamol (acetaminophen) in adult subjects was negligible.

## 4. Gastric Emptying Time

Many drugs are not absorbed significantly until they reach the small intestine and since intestinal absorption is often a rapid process, we sometimes find that gastric emptying rather than permeation is the rate-limiting step in gastrointestinal drug absorption. Heading et al. (1973) observed highly statistically significant correlations between gastric emptying half-life in convalescent hospital patients and the time to maximum plasma concentrations of paracetamol after an oral dose as well as with the maximum plasma concentrations. Clements and co-workers (1978) found in certain subjects under certain conditions that the apparent first-order absorption rate constant for paracetamol as determined from plasma concentration data, was actually the first-order rate constant for gastric emptying. A large number of investigations, many of which are reviewed by Nimmo (1976), have shown that various factors which promote gastric emptying, including co-administration of metoclopramide, tend to increase the rate of drug absorption, whereas factors that delay gastric emptying, including the co-administration of drugs with anticholinergic effects, tend to decrease the rate of drug absorption.

## 5. Absorption of Solid Dose Forms

The principal limitation of classical absorption theory is that it was developed for drugs in solution whereas most oral medications are given as solid dosage forms. The pioneering work of Edwards (1951), Nelson (1957, 1959), Levy and Hayes (1960) and Levy (1961), which has been extended to many drugs by countless investigators, has clearly shown that when a drug is given in a solid form, in almost every instance, dissolution rather than permeation is the rate-limiting step in the overall absorption process. The pH conditions needed to promote the dissolution of weak electrolytes are exactly the opposite of the conditions needed to promote the permeation of such drugs across lipid membranes — i.e. an increase in pH increases the dissolution of a weak acid drug but also increases dissociation and thereby decreases permeation across lipid barriers. This reverse dependence has given rise to several apparent contradictions to the pH-partition hypothesis which are easily explained from dissolution theory. For example, Kekki et al. (1971) reported that the gastrointestinal absorption of warfarin, a weak acid, is decreased rather than promoted when the pH of the luminal fluids decreases. Pottage et al. (1974) found that the absorption rate of aspirin after oral administration was considerably faster in patients with achlorhydria than in normal subjects. The relatively poor dissolution of weak acid drugs at low pH, along with considerations of surface area and residence time, contributes to the fact that gastric absorption of drugs is usually of little consequence.

## 6. Gut and First-pass Metabolism

At the time Brodie and his colleagues were constructing a largely conceptual framework for drug absorption the idea of gut metabolism was largely a biochemical curiosity and first-pass metabolism had rarely been considered. We now know that these metabolic processes sometimes play a predominant role in determining the amount of unchanged drug that reaches the systemic circulation after oral administration. It is well recognised that drugs with high hepatic extraction ratios, including most β-blockers, analgesics and tricyclic antidepressants, may be substantially metabolised during absorption because virtually all of the blood draining the gastrointestinal tract must pass through the liver before reaching the other tissues in the body. Hency the amount of drug actually reaching the systemic circulation may be far less than the administered dose (Gibaldi et al., 1971; Rowland, 1972). Other drugs appear to be substantially metabolised by enzymes in the intestinal epithelium during absorption in addition to (Iwamoto et al., 1972; Conway et al., 1973) or instead of (Mearrick et al., 1975) those in the liver. Again, the consequence is reduced bioavailability.

Because they are poorly permeable, poorly soluble or administered in slowly releasing dosage forms, some drugs may reach the large intestine in relatively large amounts and be subject to considerable metabolism by intestinal microflora, resulting in bioactivation or inactivation (Scheline, 1974; Boxenbaum et al., 1974; Goldman, 1978).

Although the study of drug absorption has become very complicated, the excellent scientists selected for the programme before us will undoubtedly unravel many of these complexities.

## References

Beerman, B.; Hellstrom, K. and Rosen, A.. Fate of orally administered ³H-digitoxin in man with special reference to the absorption. Circulation 43: 852 (1971).

Boxenbaum, H.G.; Jodhka, G.S.; Ferguson, A.C.; Reigelman, S. and MacGregor, T.R.: The influence of bacterial gut hydrolysis on the fate of orally administered isonicotinuric acid in man. Journal of Pharmacokinetics and Biopharmacy 2: 211 (1974).

Clements, J.A.; Heading, R.C.; Nimmo, W.S. and Prescott, L.F.: Kinetics of acetaminophen absorption and gastric emptying in man. Clinical Pharmacology and Therapeutics 24: 420 (1978).

Conway, W.D.; Singhvi, S.M.; Gibaldi, M. and Boyes, R.N.: The effect of route of administration on the metabolic fate of terbutaline in the rat. Xenobiotica 3: 813 (1973).

Crouthamel, W.G.; Tan, G.H.; Dittert, L.W. and Dolusio, J.T.: Drug absorption iv. Influence of pH on absorption kinetics or weakly acidic drugs. Journal of Pharmaceutical Sciences 60: 1160 (1971).

Edwards, L.J.: The dissolution and diffusion of aspirin in aqueous media. Transactions of the Faraday Society 47: 1191 (1951).

Gibaldi, M.; Boyes, R.N. and Feldman, S.: Influence of first-pass effect on availability of drugs on oral administration. Journal of Pharmaceutical Sciences 60: 1338 (1971).

Goldman, P.: Biochemical pharmacology of the intestinal flora. Annual Review of Pharmacology and Toxicology 18: 523 (1978).

Heading, R.C.; Nimmo, J.; Prescott, L.F. and Tothill, O.: The dependence of paracetamol absorption on the rate of gastric emptying. British Journal of Pharmacology 47: 415 (1973).

Hober, R. and Hober, J.: Experiments on the absorption of organic solutes in the small intestine of rats. Journal of Cell Composition and Physiology 10: 401 (1937).

Hogben, C.A.M.: The first common pathway. Federation Proceedings 19: 864 (1960).

Hogben, C.A.M.; Schanker, L.A.; Tocco, D.J. and Brodie, B.B.: Absorption of drugs from the stomach II. The human. Journal of Pharmacology 120: 540 (1957).

Hogben, C.A.M.; Tocco, D.J.; Brodie, B.B. and Schanker, L.S.: On the mechanism of the intestinal absorption of drugs. Journal of Pharmacology 125: 275 (1959).

Iwamoto, K. and Klaasen, C.D.: First-pass effect of morphine in rats. Journal of Pharmacology and Experimental Therapeutics 200: 236 (1972).

Kekki, M.; Pyorala, K.; Justala, O.; Salmi, H.; Jussila, J. and Siurala, M.: Multicompartment analysis of the absorption kinetics of warfarin from the stomach and small intestine. International Journal of Clinical Pharmacology 5: 209 (1971).

Levy, G.: Comparison of dissolution and absorption rates of different commercial aspirin tablets. Journal of Pharmaceutical Sciences 50: 388 (1961).

Levy, G. and Hayes, B.A.: Physico-chemical basis of the buffered acetylsalicylic acid controversy. British Medical Journal 262: 1053 (1960).

Mearrick, P.T.; Graham, G.G. and Wade, D.N.: The role of the liver in the clearance of L-dopa from the plasma. Journal of Pharmacokinetics and Biopharmacy 3: 13 (1975).

Nelson, E.: Solution rate of theophylline salts and effects from oral administration. Journal of Pharmaceutical Sciences 46: 607 (1957).

Nelson, E.: Influence of dissolution rate and surface on tetracycline absorption. Journal of Pharmaceutical Sciences 48: 96 (1959).

Nimmo, W.S.: Drugs, diseases and altered gastric emptying. Clinical Pharmacokinetics 1: 189 (1976).

Overton, E.: Beigrage zur allgemeinen muskel - und nerve physiologie. Pflugers Archiv fur die gesamte Physiologie des Menschen und der Tiere 92: 115 (1902).

Pottage, A.; Nimmo, J. and Prescott, L.F.: The absorption of aspirin and paracetamol in patients with achlorhydria. Journal of Pharmacy and Pharmacology 26: 144 (1974).

Rowland, M.: Influence of route of administration on drug availability. Journal of Pharmaceutical Sciences 61: 70 (1972).

Schanker, L.S.; Absorption of drugs from the rat colon. Journal of Pharmacology 126: 283 (1959).

Schanker, L.S.; Shore, P.A.; Brodie, B.B. and Hogben, C.A.M.: Absorption of drugs from the stomach II. The rat. Journal of Pharmacology 120: 528 (1957).

Schanker, L.S.; Tocco, D.J.; Brodie, B.B. and Hogben, C.A.M.: Absorption of drugs from the rat small intestine. Journal of Pharmacology 123: 81 (1958).

Scheline, R.R.: Metabolism of foreign compounds by gastrointestinal micro-organisms. Pharmacological Review 25: 451 (1973).

Shore, P.A.; Brodie, B.B. and Hogben, C.A.M.: The gastric secretion of drugs. A pH partition hypothesis. Journal of Pharmacology 119: 361 (1950).

Siurala, M.; Mustala, O. and Jussila, J.: Absorption of acetylsalicylic acid by a normal and atrophic gastric mucosa. Scandinavian Journal of Gastroenterology 4: 269 (1969).

Travell, J.: The influence of the hydrogen ion and concentration on the absorption of alkaloids from the stomach. Journal of Pharmacology 69: 21 (1940).

Wilson, F.A. and Dietschy, J.M.: Characterisation of bile acid absorption across the unstirred water layer and brush border of the rat jejunum. Journal of Clinical Investigation 51: 3015 (1972).

Wilson, F.A.; Salee, V.L. and Dietschy, J.M.: Unstirred water layers in intestine: rate determinant of fatty acid absorption from micellar solutions. Science 174: 1031 (1971).

Winne, D.: The influence of unstirred layers on intestinal absorption. Excerpta Medica International Congress 391: 58 (1975).

# 2

# Gastrointestinal Drug Absorption — Anatomical and Physiological Considerations

*L.A. Turnberg*

University of Manchester School of Medicine

In this short review only a few aspects of gastrointestinal structure and function will be considered. Those which have particular relevance to drug absorption will be stressed.

## 1. Gastric Function

Two aspects of gastric physiology are particularly relevant; these are gastric acid secretion (Konturek, 1974) and gastric emptying. The stomach is capable of secreting hydrochloric acid to a pH of about 1. Secretion is stimulated via the vagus nerve in response to the central stimuli due to the thought, sight and smell of food. Direct stimulation by the hormone gastrin follows its liberation from the antral mucosa in response to mechanical stimulation by food in the antrum and chemically in response to amino acids present there. In the fasting state, little acid is secreted and that secreted in response to food is partially buffered by the meal, thus intragastric pH rarely drops below 3. In some diseases, the pH may be lower than this from time to time.

## 2. Mucosal Protection

Gastric mucosa has to protect itself from acid peptic digestion and recent observations have indicated the possibility that the surface epithelium may secrete bicarbonate which is involved in this 'cyto-protective' effect (Garner and Heylings, 1979). It has been proposed that bicarbonate secreted from the surface epithelium enters the basal aspects of the mucus which coats the mucosa. Hydrogen ions diffusing slowly through the mucus meet the bicarbonate and are neutralised, a pH gradient being established across the mucus. Thus the pH at the mucosal surface is neutral or alkaline. Direct measurements of the pH at the surface confirm that it is slightly alkaline (Williams and Turnberg, 1979). It has been shown that gastric mucosal bicarbonate secretion is inhibited by non-steroidal anagesics, which inhibit prostaglandin synthesis, and is stimulated by certain prostaglandins and this may explain 'cyto-protective' effects (Garner and Heylings, 1979). It is interesting to reflect on the 'partition hypothesis' which proposes that weak acids, such as acetylsalicylic acid, are absorbed only in the undissociated form. Gastric acid pushes the equilibrium between dissociated and undissociated acetylsalicylic acid over towards the undissociated side and hence encourages absorption. Since we now know that the absorbed drug would have to cross an alkaline barrier, and there become undissociated, it would appear that this hypothesis has to be re-examined.

## 3. Gastric Emptying

Gastric emptying rate must influence the shape and height of drug absorption curves. Factors which influence gastric emptying (Hunt and Knox, 1968) include the size of food particles and the presence of lipids. Fluid and small particles empty relatively quickly while larger particles are held back at the pylorus until they are broken down by antral muscular activity to the correct size to be allowed through the pylorus. Lipids are believed to empty more slowly than aqueous solutions. Receptors in the duodenal mucosa for the osmolality and acidity of material emptied from the stomach into the duodenum exert a negative feedback effect on gastric emptying (Hunt and Knox, 1969). This allows osmotic and pH equilibration to occur at a regulated rate within the upper intestine. Account has to be taken of these factors when drug absorption is being considered.

## 4. Digestion

Digestion and absorption is the province of the small bowel. Peptides, fats and carbohydrate as well as acid present in the duodenum stimulate the release of gastrointestinal hormones from the duodenal mucosa. These then evoke a coordinated activity of the gall bladder and pancreas so that bile and pancreatic juice containing enzymes as well as bicarbonate enter the duodenum to mix with the meal. The bicarbonate neutralises gastric acid and creates the correct pH for proper activity of pancreatic enzymes particularly lipase which splits the majority dietary fat, triglyceride. Proteolytic and amylolytic enzymes split protein and carbohydrate into small oligo peptides and oligo saccharides respectively.

### 4.1 Fat

The intraluminal phase of fat digestion is of interest and bile salts play a vital role in this. Bile salts are sterols produced from cholesterol in the liver. They are amphipathic, that is they have a lipid soluble portion and a water soluble portion and have the features of detergents. When present in a suitable concentration, bile salts congregate together so that their lipid soluble portions face inwards and their water soluble polar groups face outwards into the watery solution (Heaton, 1972). These molecular aggregates are called micelles and it is into the centre of these that many highly insoluble lipids become dissolved. Since micelles are very small compared with emulsion droplets, they are capable of transporting small numbers of lipid molecules across the hostile watery environment of the duodenal contents to the lipid membrane of the mucosa. Fatty acids, (liberated by the activity of pancreatic lipase), cholesterol and fat soluble vitamins all require micelles for their proper absorption. It is conceivable that some drugs, particularly those which are sterol in form, also require micelles.

The enterohepatic circulation of bile salts allows their very efficient utilisation (Hoffman, 1977). They are predominantly absorbed in the terminal ileum and recirculate via the portal circulation to the liver ready for re-secretion. The whole bile salt pool circulates twice during each meal on average so that the whole pool can be used 6 or 8 times a day. Interruption of this circulation, as for example by surgical removal of the ileum for Crohn's disease, results in a profound loss of bile salts into the stool and an inadequate bile salt concentration for micelle formation in the upper intestine. Such a situation results in malabsorption of fat.

Although lipid soluble drugs may not require bile salts directly, the large luminal lipid bulk phase in which these drugs will be dissolved will interfere with their proper absorption. Relatively small amounts of drugs will be available to come into contact with the mucosal epithelium if they remain in this lipid bulk phase. Thus any cause of malabsorption of fat can interfere with lipid soluble drug absorption.

## 5. Absorption

Turning now to the absorptive process, we should consider the physiochemical properties of substances which determine their ability to pass the intestinal membrane. Lipid soluble materials pass across the lipid mucous membrane relatively easily and do not require any specific transport process, since they dissolve in the membrane and pass into the cells. Water soluble substances on the other hand pass across with some difficulty. They pass not through the lipid but rather through water filled channels which are thought to exist in the epithelium.

These pores are of limited size and hence molecular size or diameter becomes important. On average the bigger the molecule the less it is likely to pass across. Since the pores are believed to be electrically charged, the electrical charge on the molecule will also have an influence on the rate of transfer. Thus highly charged molecules tend to get across with greater difficulty than neutral, or uncharged molecules. Many compounds are partially soluble in water and partially soluble in lipid and the 'partition coefficient' which is related to their degree of solubility in these two phases will influence their rate of absorption. Finally there is a group of compounds for which specific active transport mechanisms are available and these are transferred across the membrane irrespective of their physiochemical attributes.

In the intestine, there is an enormous reserve capacity for absorption which resides in its length and the fact that its surface area is enormously increased by foldings and by the finger-like villi. Each epithelial cell is itself covered with innumerable micro-villi which also increase its surface area. The terminal stages of digestion of peptides and small carbohydrate chains occurs here and there are specific absorptive processes for the aminoacids and monosaccharides.

## 6. Salt and Water

It is of interest to consider the normal processes for the absorption of salt and water (Turnberg, 1978) because these may be relevant to the absorption of water soluble drugs. Of interest is the observation that a high proportion of the salt and water which is absorbed passes between the epithelial cells rather than through them. Adjacent cells are joined together by so-called 'tight junctions' and the weight of evidence suggests that the majority of the water which is absorbed passes through these tight junctions (Frizzell and Schultz, 1972). The pores through which water soluble materials pass are believed to exist in the tight junctions and these are probably rate-limiting. In the jejunum at least, a high proportion of small ions such as sodium, are likely to pass through this route too, relatively smaller amounts passing through the cells. There is good evidence to suggest that the water filled channels in the jejunum are about twice as large as those in the ileum and this is reflected in differences in behaviour of these two regions of the intestine (Fordtran et al., 1965). A large proportion of a meal is absorbed in the jejunum and the free permeability of this wide pored region of the intestine caters for the rapid movement of salt and water which is absorbed along with the meal here. This free permeability also allows for the rapid adjustment of osmotic pressures across the mucosa so that luminal contents rapidly becomes isosmolar with interstitial fluid on the other side of the mucous membrane. In the ileum and colon the mucosa is much less permeable having smaller pores, and here specific active transport processes for sodium and chloride ensure that luminal contents become further dehydrated. The ileum does not rely on the rapid absorption of food stuffs to stimulate the absorption of salt and water. Hence the development of more specific active transport processes. In the colon too, active transport of electrolytes occurs and the colon very effectively dehydrates its luminal contents.

In diseases in which the free permeability of the jejunum becomes impaired, as for example in coeliac disease, it is clear that absorption of drugs which are water soluble and rely on this permeability, may be impaired. In coeliac disease too, a variety of other defects have been described since there is a diminution of brush border enzyme activity and terminal digestion of carbohydrate and peptide as well as lipid absorption become impaired. The absorption of drugs may well be affected by this combined defect.

A 'microclimate' is believed to exist immediately adjacent to the surface epithelium in which the pH is slightly acid compared with luminal contents. A pH of about 4.5 may be achieved here and it has been postulated (Blair and Matty, 1974) that this could influence drug absorption by affecting the dissociation of weak acids or weak bases rendering them more or less liable to absorption according to whether they are more or less dissociated at this particular pH. This interesting possibility has been examined but to date no strong evidence in favour or against this proposal has been demonstrated.

## References

Blair, J.A. and Matty, A.J.: Acid micro-climate in intestinal absorption. Clinics in Gastroenterology 3: 183-198 (1974).

Fordtran, J.S.; Rector, F.C.; Ewton, M.F.; Soter, N. and Kinney, J.: Permeability characteristics of the human intestine. Journal of Clinical Investigation 44: 1935-1944 (1965).

Frizzel, R.A. and Schultz, S.G.: Ionic conductances of extra-cellular shunt pathway in rabbit ileum: influence of shunt on transmural sodium transport and electrical potential differences. Journal of General Physiology 59: 318-346 (1972).

Garner, A. and Heylings, J.R.: Stimulation of alkaline secretion in amphibian isolated gastric mucosa by 16, 16 dimethyl- $PGE_2$ and $PGF_{2a}$: an explanation of the cytoprotective activity of prostaglandins. Gastroenterology 76: 497-503 (1979).

Heaton, K.W.: Bile Salts in Health and Disease, p.24-41 (Churchill Livingstone, Edinburgh 1972).

Hoffman, A.F.: The enterohepatic circulation of bile acids in man; in Baumgartner (Ed) Clinics in Gastroenterology, vol. 6, p.3-24 (Saunders, Philadelphia 1977).

Hunt, J.S. and Knox, M.T.: Regulation of gastric emptying; in Code (Ed) Handbook of Physiology, vol. 4 p.1917-1913 (American Physiological Society, Washington 1968).

Hunt, J.N. and Knox, M.T.: The slowing of gastric emptying by nine acids. Journal of Physiology 201: 169 (1969).

Konturek, S.J.: Gastric secretion; in Jacobson and Shanbour (Eds) Gastrointestinal Physiology, p.227-264 (MTP, Lancaster 1974).

Turnberg, L.A.: Intestinal transport of salt and water. Clinical Science and Molecular Medicine 54: 337-348 (1978).

Williams, S.E. and Turnberg, L.A.: Studies of the 'protective' properties of gastric mucus: evidence for a 'mucus-bicarbonate' barrier. Gut 20: A922-923 (1979).

## Discussion

*L.F. Prescott* (Chairman): Whatever the significance of the pH of gastric contents for drug absorption it is important to recognise that achlorhydria is quite common, particularly in the elderly.

*L.A. Turnberg*: I am sure you are right; 30 to 40 % of people over the age of 65 have either relative or absolute achlorhydria with is asymptomatic of course. I do not think that acid is terribly relevant to drug absorption however.

*J.A. Blair* (Birmingham): You mentioned that the gastric mucosa had a layer of mucus on one side of which was an aqueous solution of pH 2 or pH 3 depending upon acid secretion, while bicarbonate was secreted on the other side. Have you been able to measure this very considerable difference in hydrogen ion concentration?

*L.A. Turnberg*: We have measured it directly with micro pH probes and can demonstrate a pH gradient. The pH next to the epithelial cell is around 7.

*J.A. Blair:* You spoke of small inorganic solutes passing through the tight junctions of the intestinal epithelium by virtue of water flow induced by osmotic pressure gradients, but you did not specify how these gradients were created. Some would speak of them being created by a specific transport process for the sodium ion. Can other solutes such as glucose create these osmotic gradients?

*L.A. Turnberg*: Yes. Very little happens to a simple isotonic solution of saline placed in a human jejunal lumen. It is absorbed very very slowly indeed. If you add glucose or aminoacids or any other actively transported solute, then you stimulate tremendously the absorption of sodium and water. It is only when you stimulate unidirectional movement across the epithelial membrane, by glucose for example, that you create an osmotic gradient which then stimulates the movement of water.

*D.W.T. Piercy* (Berkhamsted): Is there any indication of a difference in the unstirred layer, or of sodium transport at these tight junctions?

*L.A. Turnberg*: I think that the unstirred layer is relatively unimportant in resisting the transfer of small water soluble solutes like sodium. It is much more important for lipid soluble materials in micelles.

# 3

# Gastric Emptying and Drug Absorption

*Walter S. Nimmo*

Department of Anaesthesia, University of Glasgow

The stomach is not an important site of drug absorption. The established belief of the pH partition theory that weak acids are significantly absorbed from the stomach, has not been confirmed by more recent studies and many deviations from the predicted results of this theory have been reported. For example, phenobarbitone ($pK_a$ 7.2) and pentobarbitone ($pK_a$ 8.1) are weak acids and should be more rapidly absorbed from the stomach than from the small intestine. The reverse is true, however, and in a study in rats (Magnussen, 1968), more than twice as much was absorbed by the small intestine in 10 minutes than was absorbed from the stomach in 1 hour (fig. 1). This difference simply reflects the complex nature of the overall process of absorption and it is likely that the much greater surface area of the intestinal mucosa relative to that of the gastric mucosa more than compensates for the potentially reduced rate of absorption per unit area of intestine (Levine, 1970). The absorption of ethanol, which is independent of pH, was also much more rapid from the small bowel than from the stomach as predictably was promethazine, a basic drug.

Similar results have been obtained in human subjects for aspirin and warfarin (Siurala et al., 1969; Kekki et al., 1971). Thus the rate of gastric emptying markedly influences the rate at which drugs are absorbed irrespective of whether they are acids, bases or neutral compounds (Levine 1970).

Other evidence of the fallibility of the pH-partition theory as applied to gastric absorption is shown in a study of aspirin absorption in normal subjects and achlorhydric patients. An increase in the pH at the absorption site should decrease the absorption of a weak acid since the proportion of unionised drug is decreased. The reverse is true, however, and aspirin was absorbed more rapidly than normal in achlorhydric patients. The most likely explanation for this enhanced absorption is the increased solubility of aspirin in the achlorhydric stomach (Pottage et al., 1974). Paracetamol (acetaminophen) has been used as a model drug for absorption studies since it is a weak acid ($pK_a$ 9.5) that is largely unionised in both gastric and intestinal fluids. Its rate of absorption is largely independent of pH changes and is directly related to the rate of gastric emptying (Heading et al., 1973; Nimmo et al., 1975a).

Gastric emptying and paracetamol absorption were measured simultaneously in healthy volunteers. After an overnight fast, each subject received 400ml of orange juice containing 20mg/kg paracetamol and non-absorbable radioactive isotopic

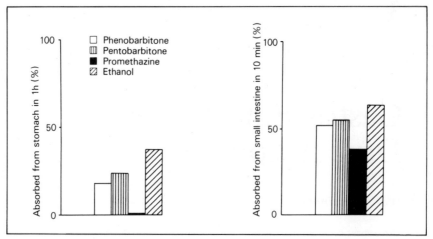

*Fig. 1.* Comparison of absorptive capacity of stomach and small intestine in rats (data from Magnussen, 1968).

marker for the emptying measurements. Gastric emptying was measured by continuously scanning the subject's abdomen and blood was taken for estimation of plasma paracetamol (fig. 2). A good correlation between the rate of paracetamol absorption and the rate of gastric emptying was obtained and when emptying of the stomach was inhibited by diamorphine, paracetamol absorption was similarly inhibited (fig. 3) [Nimmo et al., 1975a; Prescott et al., 1977].

It is possible to construct a pharmacokinetic model in which the gastrointestinal tract is represented by 2 compartments — one for the stomach and one for the small intestine. Using this model in a variety of clinical situations such as Crohn's disease, coeliac disease or after the administration of narcotic analgesics, it is possible to calculate the first-order rate constant for drug transfer from the intestinal lumen into the systemic circulation (Clements et al., 1978). The mean half-time for transfer was consistently less than 7 minutes even after narcotic administration, confirming that gastric emptying is the rate-limiting step for paracetamol absorption.

It seems probable that the rate of drug absorption and, in turn, the onset of pharmacological response are often directly related to the rate at which drugs pass from the stomach to the intestine. It follows that any factor which influences the rate of gastric emptying will influence the rate of absorption and onset of action of an orally administered agent.

## 1. Physiological Control of Gastric Emptying

A variety of physiological factors are involved in the control of gastric emptying rate (table I) [Nimmo, 1976]. Food is one of the major factors modifying drug absorption, partly by its influence on gastric emptying rate (Melander, 1978). Liquids are emptied from the stomach more rapidly than solids (James, 1957; Dozois et al., 1971) and the volume and osmotic pressure of a drug solution are important determinants of the rate of absorption because of their influence on gastric emptying rate

*Table I.* Factors influencing gastric emptying rate

a)  Physiological
        Food
        Gastric distension
        Osmotic pressure
        Posture
        Sleep
        Personality trait

b)  Pathological
        Trauma and pain
        Myocardial infarction
        Gastrointestinal disease
            pyloric stenosis
            Crohn's disease
            coeliac disease
        Gastric surgery
        Metabolic disease

c)  Pharmacological
        Anticholinergics
        Narcotic analgesics
        Antihistamines
        Tricyclic antidepressants
        Aluminium hydroxide
        Metoclopramide
        Anticholinesterases
        Alcohol

(Hunt and Pathak, 1960; Hunt and Knox, 1968). Gastric distension is the only physiological stimulus known to accelerate gastric emptying (Hunt and Knox, 1968).

There is good evidence in rats, that drugs are more rapidly absorbed and are more toxic when given in a large volume of dilute solution than when given in a small volume of concentrated solution. This is due to more rapid gastric emptying (Borowitz et al., 1971).

The physiological role of gastrointestinal hormones in influencing gastric emptying is uncertain but posture affects the rate of paracetamol absorption presumably by influencing gastric emptying rate (Nimmo and Prescott, 1978). In healthy volunteers, mean plasma paracetamol concentrations at 15 minutes and 30 minutes in supine subjects were only $0.18 \pm 0.18 \mu g/ml$ ($\pm$ SE) and $7.8 \pm 3.1 \mu g/ml$ respectively and $12.5 \pm 4.8 \mu g/ml$ and $20.8 \pm 3.3 \mu g/ml$ in ambulant subjects. Plasma concentrations after 45 minutes did not differ in the 2 groups. Patients who take tablets while in bed on their left side will be likely to have delayed absorption and it is obvious that the position of subjects must be taken into account in drug absorption studies.

## 2. Pathological Influences on Gastric Emptying

A variety of diseases both gastrointestinal and non-gastrointestinal seem to modify the rate of gastric emptying but there is little data to demonstrate conclusively the effect of disease and many reports are anecdotal or merely a hypothesis. In only a few situations have gastric emptying measurements been carried out (Nimmo, 1976).

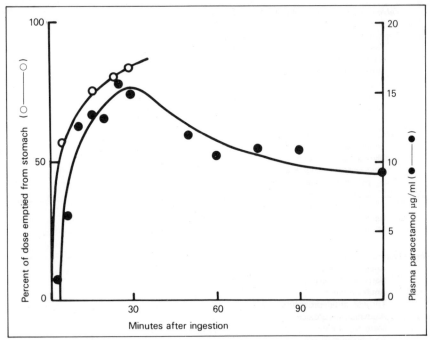

*Fig. 2.* Simultaneous measurements of gastric emptying rate and plasma paracetamol concentrations in a control subject given 20mg/kg of paracetamol orally in solution (from Prescott et al.,
1977 with permission).

However, trauma and pain delay gastric emptying and drug absorption (Zaricznyj et
al., 1977). It was claimed that migraine delayed gastric emptying and reduced the rate
of aspirin absorption. Delay in absorption correlated with the severity of the headache
and gastrointestinal symptoms at the time of treatment (Volans, 1974). Increasing
pain and distress during labour slightly delays paracetamol absorption presumably by
delaying gastric emptying but this delay is insignificant compared to that observed in
patients who had received pethidine (fig. 4). In early labour paracetamol absorption
was rapid and indistinguishable from that in healthy non-pregnant controls. Thus
delayed gastric emptying observed in women during labour is probably largely due to
the administration of narcotic analgesics (Nimmo et al., 1975b).

Similar results have been obtained from a study of mexiletine absorption in
patients following myocardial infarction (Pottage et al., 1978). Mexiletine absorption
was delayed and possibly incomplete following administration of a narcotic analgesic.
Only slight delay was observed in patients who had sustained a myocardial infarction
but had received no analgesia. This delay in drug absorption produced by narcotic
analgesics was described by Hercule Poirot in his first case, 'The Mysterious Affair at
Styles'. He recognised that narcotic analgesics delayed the absorption of the fatal dose
of strychnine (Agatha Christie, 1920).

Not surprisingly, gastric emptying is delayed in pyloric stenosis and one example
of the consequence of this condition is given in the report of a woman with rheumatoid arthritis and pyloric stenosis: 61 enteric coated aspirin tablets were recovered
from her stomach (Harris 1973). In Crohn's disease and coeliac disease, there is probably a delay in gastric emptying which results in altered drug absorption. The effects

of gastric surgery on emptying are complex but well described. However, there is little data on the consequences for drug absorption.

Gastric emptying is influenced by a variety of metabolic conditions such as diabetes mellitus, thyroid disease, hepatic coma and hypercalcaemia. One example is the increased rate of paracetamol absorption in thyrotoxic compared to euthyroid and hypothyroid patients (Forfar et al., in press).

## 3. Drugs and Gastric Emptying

Many drugs influence gastric emptying rate and in turn modify the rate of absorption of another orally administered drug (Nimmo, 1976). For example anticholinergics, antihistamines, tricyclic antidepressants, phenothiazines, narcotic analgesics and antacids containing aluminium hydroxide delay gastric emptying. Metoclopramide, anticholinesterases, sodium bicarbonate and cigarette smoking have been shown to accelerate gastric emptying.

For drugs which are normally absorbed rapidly and have a short biological half-life, changing the rate of gastric emptying will change the rate of absorption and may produce either enhanced drug effects or therapeutic failure.

Propantheline prolonged the mean half-life of gastric emptying from 25 to 152 minutes producing an associated delay in the absorption of paracetamol: the mean time to reach peak concentrations was prolonged from 70 to 160 minutes. Conver-

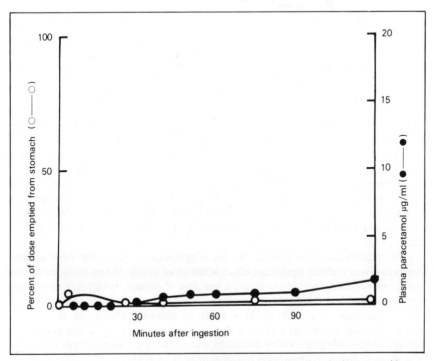

*Fig. 3.* Gastric emptying rate and plasma paracetamol concentrations in the same subject as in figure 2 studied 30 minutes after 10mg of diamorphine intramuscularly (from Prescott et al., 1977 with permission).

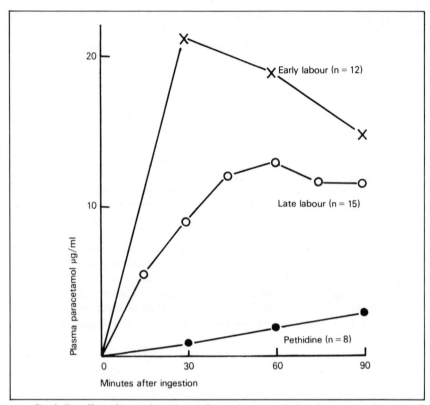

*Fig. 4.* The effect of increasing pain and distress in women during labour on the absorption of paracetamol compared with the effect of pethidine (150mg intramuscularly). On each occasion, after a 4 hour fast, each patient received 1.5g paracetamol with 200ml of water.

sely, metoclopramide accelerated gastric emptying and significantly increased the rate of paracetamol absorption (Nimmo et al., 1973). Only the rate of paracetamol absorption was changed. The amount of drug absorbed was not influenced by the modification of gastric emptying rate.

Propantheline or atropine and metoclopramide have been shown to retard and accelerate, respectively, the absorption of tetracycline (Nimmo, 1973); pivampicillin (Gothoni et al., 1972); propranolol (Castleden et al., 1978); mexiletine (Wing et al., 1979); diazepam (Gamble et al., 1976) and alcohol (Finch et al., 1974; Gibbons and Lant, 1975).

Metoclopramide was effective by the intravenous or oral route whereas propantheline was without significant effect when given orally. When metoclopramide was given to healthy volunteers before a test dose of ethanol, the ethanol absorption was accelerated and the degree of sedation was significantly greater than in control studies (Bateman et al., 1978). In a study of diazepam absorption in patients, metoclopramide accelerated diazepam absorption and narcotic analgesics delayed its absorption (Gamble et al., 1976). Similarly, a magnesium aluminium hydroxide mixture delayed diazepam absorption (Greenblatt et al., 1978).

When metoclopramide (10mg intramuscularly) is given simultaneously with a narcotic analgesic, it fails to reverse the narcotic-induced delay in paracetamol absorption and gastric emptying (Nimmo et al., 1975a). However, naloxone largely reverses this inhibition (Nimmo et al., 1979).

Decreased gastrointestinal motility is not necessarily associated with reduced drug absorption. For example, propantheline increased the effective time available for dissolution and absorption of digoxin tablets and increased the amount absorbed, while metoclopramide had the opposite effect (Manninen et al., 1973). These results could not be reproduced when the digoxin was given in solution. Similar results have been obtained for hydrochlorothiazide (Beermann and Groschinsky-Grind, 1978), nitrofurantoin (Jaffe, 1975) and riboflavine (Levy et al., 1972).

Slow or delayed gastric emptying may produce erratic absorption and therapeutic failure if a drug is metabolised or degraded in the stomach. For example for levodopa, methyldigoxin and penicillin, the amount of active drug available for absorption is reduced when emptying of the stomach is delayed (Prescott, 1974).

In conclusion, gastric emptying rate influences the rate of absorption of most orally administered drugs and factors influencing gastric emptying will in turn influence the rate of drug absorption. Usually rapid gastric emptying results in rapid drug absorption and vice versa unless the drug is slow to dissolve or be absorbed. Changes in gastric emptying do not usually affect the amount of drug absorbed unless the drug is metabolised in the stomach when delayed emptying may result in reduced bioavailability and therapeutic failure or if the drug dissolves slowly in the gastrointestinal tract when delayed emptying and gastrointestinal transit may increase bioavailability.

# References

Bateman, D.N.; Kahn, C.; Mashiter, K. and Davies, D.S.: Pharmacokinetic and concentration-effect studies with intravenous metoclopramide. British Journal of Clinical Pharmacology 6: 401-407 (1978).

Beerman, B. and Groschinsky-Grind, M.: Enhancement of the gastrointestinal absorption of hydrochlorothiazide by propantheline. European Journal of Clinical Pharmacology 13: 385-387 (1978).

Borowitz, J.L.; Moore, P.F.; Yim, G.K.W. and Miya, T.A.: Mechanism of enhanced drug effects produced by dilution of the oral dose. Toxicology and Applied Pharmacology 19: 164-168 (1971).

Castleden, C.M.; George, C.F. and Short, M.D.: Contribution of individual differences in gastric emptying to variability in plasma propranolol concentrations. British Journal of Clinical Pharmacology 5: 121-122 (1978).

Christie, Agatha: The Mysterious Affair at Styles, p.174 (Pan, London 1975).

Clements, J.A.; Heading, R.C.; Nimmo, W.S. and Prescott, L.F.: Kinetics of acetaminophen absorption and gastric emptying in man. Clinical Pharmacology and Therapeutics 24: 420-431 (1978).

Dozois, R.R.; Kelly, K.A. and Code, C.F.: Effect of distal antrectomy on gastric emptying of liquids and solids. Gastroenterology 61: 675-681 (1971).

Finch, J.E.; Kendall, M.J. and Mitchard, M.: An assessment of gastric emptying by breathalyser. British Journal of Clinical Pharmacology 1: 233-236 (1974).

Forfar, J.C.; Pottage, A; Toft, A.D.; Irvine, W.J.; Clements, J.A. and Prescott, L.F.: Paracetamol pharmacokinetics in thyroid disease. European Journal of Clinical Pharmacology (in press).

Gamble, J.A.S.; Gaston, J.H.; Nair, S.G. and Dundee, J.W.: Some pharmacological factors influencing the absorption of diazepam following oral administration. British Journal of Anaesthesia 48: 1181-1185 (1976).

Gibbons, D.O. and Lant, A.F.: Effects of intravenous and oral propantheline and metoclopramide on ethanol absorption. Clinical Pharmacology and Therapeutics 17: 578-584 (1975).

Gothoni, G.; Pentikainen, P.; Vapaatalo, H.T.; Hackman R. and Bjorksten, K.A.: Absorption of antibiotics: Influence of metoclopramide and atropine on serum levels of pivampicillin and tetracycline. Annals of Clinical Research 4: 228-232 (1972).

Greenblatt, D.J.; Allen, M.D.; MacLaughlin, D.S.; Harmatz, J.S. and Shader, R.I.: Diazepam absorption: effect of antacids and food. Clinical Pharmacology and Therapeutics 24: 600-609 (1978).

Harris, F.S.: Pyloric stenosis: hold up of enteric coated aspirin tablets. British Journal of Surgery 60: 979-981 (1973).

Heading, R.C.; Nimmo, J.; Prescott, L.F. and Tothill, P.: The dependence of paracetamol absorption on the rate of gastric emptying. British Journal of Pharmacology 47: 415-421 (1973).

Hunt, J.N. and Knox, M.T.: Regulation of gastric emptying; in Handbook of Physiology (American Physiology Society, Washington 1968).

Hunt, J.N. and Pathak, J.D.: The osmotic effects of some simple molecules and ions on gastric emptying. Journal of Physiology 154: 254-269 (1960).

Jaffe, J.M.: Effect of propantheline on nitrofurantoin absorption. Journal of Pharmaceutical Sciences 64: 1729-1730 (1975).

James, A.H.: The physiology of gastric digestion. Monograph of the Physiological Society (Arnold, London 1957).

Kekki, M.; Pyorala, K.; Mustala, O.; Salmi, H.; Jussila, J. and Siurala, M.: Multicompartment analysis of the absorption kinetics of warfarin from the stomach and small intestine. International Journal of Clinical Pharmacology 5: 209-211 (1971).

Levine, R.R.: Factors affecting gastrointestinal absorption of drugs. Digestive Diseases 15: 171-188 (1970).

Levy, G.; Gibaldi, M. and Procknal, J.A.: Effect of an anticholinergic agent on riboflavin absorption in man. Journal of Pharmaceutical Sciences 61: 279-280 (1972).

Magnussen, M.P.: The effect of ethanol on the gastro-intestinal absorption of drugs in the rat. Acta Pharmacologica et Toxicologica 26: 130-144 (1968).

Manninen, V.; Apajalahti, A.; Melin, J. and Karesoja, M.: Altered absorption of digoxin in patients given propantheline and metoclopramide. Lancet 1: 398-401 (1973).

Melander, A.: Influence of food on the bioavailability of drugs. Clinical Pharmacokinetics 3: 337-351 (1978).

Nimmo, J.: The influence of metoclopramide on drug absorption. Postgraduate Medical Journal 49 (Suppl. 4): 25-28 (1973).

Nimmo, J.; Heading, R.C.; Tothill, P. and Prescott, L.F.; Pharmacological modification of gastric emptying: Effects of propantheline and metoclopramide on paracetamol absorption. British Medical Journal 1: 587-589 (1973).

Nimmo, W.S.: Drugs, diseases and altered gastric emptying. Clinical Pharmacokinetics 1: 189-203 (1976).

Nimmo, W.S.; Heading, R.C.; Wilson, J. and Prescott, L.F.: The reversal of narcotic induced delay in gastric emptying and drug absorption by naloxone. British Medical Journal 2: 1189-1190 (1979).

Nimmo, W.S.; Heading, R.C.; Wilson, J.; Tothill, P. and Prescott, L.F.: Inhibition of gastric emptying and drug absorption by narcotic analgesics. British Journal of Clinical Pharmacology 2. 509-513 (1975a).

Nimmo, W.S. and Prescott, L.F.: The influence of posture on paracetamol absorption. British Journal of Clinical Pharmacology 5: 348-349 (1978).

Nimmo, W.S.; Wilson, J. and Prescott, L.F.: Narcotic analgesics and delayed gastric emptying during labour. Lancet 1: 890-893 (1975b).

Pottage, A.; Campbell, R.W.F.; Achuff, S.C.; Murray, A.; Julian, D.G. and Prescott, L.F.: The absorption of oral mexiletine in coronary care patients. European Journal of Clinical Pharmacology 13: 393-399 (1978).

Pottage, A.; Nimmo, J. and Prescott, L.F.: The absorption of aspirin and paracetamol in patients with achlorhydria. Journal of Pharmacy and Pharmacology 26: 144-145 (1974).

Prescott, L.F.: Gastric emptying and drug absorption. British Journal of Clinical Pharmacology 1: 189-190 (1974).

Prescott, L.F.; Nimmo, W.S. and Heading, R.C.: Drug absorption interactions; in Grahame-Smith (Ed) Drug Interactions, p.45 (Macmillan, London 1977).

Siurala, M.; Mustala, O. and Jussila, J.: Absorption of acetylsalicylic acid by a normal and an atrophic gastric mucosa. Scandinavian Journal of Gastroenterology 4: 269-273 (1969).

Volans, G.N.: Absorption of effervescent aspirin during migraine. British Medical Journal 4: 265-269 (1974).

Wing, L.M.H.; Meffin, P.J.; Grygiel, J.J.; Smith, K. and Birkett, D.J.: The effect of metoclopramide and atropine on the absorption of orally administered mexiletine. British Journal of Clinical Pharmacology 9: 505-509 (1979).

Zaricznyj, B.; Rockwood, C.A.; O'Donoghue, D.N. and Ridings, G.R.: Relationship between trauma to the extremities and stomach motility. The Journal of Trauma 17: 920-930 (1977).

## Discussion

*S.A. Kaplan* (Nutley, New Jersey): Since fluid can distend the stomach and therefore alter gastric emptying, would you comment on the use of solutions as a standard for assessing oral absorption?

*W.S. Nimmo*: To study the effect of changes in gastric emptying on absorption a solution may be best because you avoid the problem of tablet dissolution.

*S.A. Kaplan*: Regulatory agencies are trying to promote the use of oral solutions as standards for assessing bioavailability when drugs cannot be mimicked by tablets.

*W.S. Nimmo*: I agree. You cannot equate absorption from solutions and absorption from tablets.

*L.F. Prescott* (Chairman): Other important points to consider include the volume of the solution, its temperature, pH and flavour etc. It is a very complex subject. Agreement must obviously be reached if drug solutions are to be used as bioavailability standards.

*M. Rowland* (Manchester): Dissolution can be a rate limiting step. Do you have any information regarding the relative dissolution rates of solid particles in the stomach compared with the intestine? If solid particles are not dissolved in the stomach, then they have to be dissolved in the intestine. I am curious to know the relative rates of dissolution.

*W.S. Nimmo*: No. Most of our work was done with paracetamol in solution.

*S. Riegelman* (San Franciso): We noticed that the composition of the solution had a marked effect on the absorption of theophylline given in a constant volume. Addition of sugar, or syrup seriously affected absorption. Indeed, aminophylline from a rapidly dissolving distintegrating tablet can be absorbed faster than from a solution. So there are clearly complicating factors.

*L.F. Prescott*: Effervescent preparations are popular and in our experience absorption from such solutions is very rapid.

*P. Johnson* (Milton Keynes): We must not make the naive assumption that a perfect solution in a test tube will remain as such inside the body. A drug may come out of solution as soon as it enters the stomach and if aggregation occurs, absorption could be far worse than with any well designed solid dosage form.

*D.S. Davies* (London): We looked at the effects of metoclopramide on alcohol absorption and found that the time to peak concentrations was dependent upon the temperature of the solution. At 37°C, absorption was much more rapid than at room temperature.

*H.S. Fraser* (Barbados): You referred to impaired paracetamol absorption in certain situations but the data could also infer high first-pass metabolism.

*W.S. Nimmo:* We showed only delayed absorption and never decreased absorption. The total 24-hour urinary recovery was always the same.

*H.S. Fraser*: First-pass metabolism of paracetamol could still explain the very low plasma concentrations with delayed absorption, as in the case of the narcotics. The total amount finally absorbed would be the same.

*L.F. Prescott*: There is undoubtedly some first-pass metabolism of paracetamol and this is probably dose dependent. By altering the rate of absorption you could alter the systemic availability. As judged by the areas under the plasma concentration-time curves, changes in the first-pass metabolism of paracetamol are unlikely to be important.

*J. Bircher* (Berne): Can optimal conditions for very rapid absorption now be defined?

*W.S. Nimmo*: To produce rapid gastric emptying the drug should be given in a large volume of warm, isotonic, slightly alkaline solution with the subject fasting and ambulant. Metoclopramide may also be given.

*B.O. Hughes* (London): Morphine and phenothiazines are frequently used in terminal care and gastric emptying may be delayed. Metoclopramide will not reverse this. Can you suggest something which will?

*W.S. Nimmo*: Naloxone will reverse the effects of narcotics on gastric emptying but this might defeat the purpose.

*A. Melander* (Malmo): We should not generalise about gastric emptying, at least in relation to food. The rate of absorption of drugs such as phenytoin and atenolol is enhanced by food which presumably should delay gastric emptying.

*W.S. Nimmo*: Is it not that motility is increased by food so that dissolution is increased?

# 4

# Absorption of Polar Acids and Bases

*Hitoshi Sezaki, Shozo Muranishi, Junzo Nakamura, Masato Yasuhara and Toshikiro Kimura*

Faculty of Pharmaceutical Sciences, Kyoto University

The classical concept of drug absorption based on lipoid theory (Collander, 1945) is generally applicable to many organic compounds, and the parabolic relationship between absorption parameters and the logarithm of the oil/water partition coefficient has been established (Hansch and Fujita, 1964; Houston et al., 1974, 1975; Wood et al., 1979).

As a first approximation, the pH-partition theory (Shore et al., 1957; Hogben et al., 1959) still forms a useful basis for the gastrointestinal absorption of polar organic ions despite the fact that some of the conditions resulting from the application of this theory have been criticised (Smolen 1973; Winne, 1977).

Some new aspects of the absorption mechanism of polar drugs, that is, highly ionised, poorly lipid soluble low molecular weight organic ions, as well as the contribution of this new approach to drug development, will be discussed. The absorption of polar drugs which obey the lipoid theory but have very poor intrinsic absorbability will be discussed first and then the absorption of drugs which do not follow the classical lipoid theory, but have selective transport mechanisms.

## 1. Non-lipophilic Poorly Absorbable Polar Drugs Obeying the Lipoid Theory

From the standpoint of overall absorption, it is known that poor lipoid solubility of a drug or its ionic moiety is largely counterbalanced by the large absorptive surface of the small intestine and the residence time within the digestive tract (Levine, 1970). Thus, despite relatively low lipoid solubility, significant absorption may occur from the intestine under normal conditions. However, certain polar drugs have been described as 'poorly absorbable' (table I). The highly polar nature of these compounds is associated with very poor intrinsic absorption from the human intestinal lumen. Absorption is not only poor but also erratic with consequent fluctuation in pharmacological effects.

*Table I.* Examples of poorly absorbable drugs

| | |
|---|---|
| Bromphenol blue | Gentamicin |
| Carbenicillin | Heparin |
| Cefazolin | Phenol red |
| Cromoglycate | Tobramycin |
| Cytarabine | Tubocurarine |

## 1.1 Nature of Poor Absorbability

Poor absorbability is an inherent property of the drug molecule and it is a characteristic of the interaction between the drug molecule and the biological membrane or cellular components which impede subsequent drug transport to sites from which it can be removed by the circulation. Studies performed with the microvillus membrane of intestinal epithelial cells and the components of the cells lying on the surface of the lumen have made it possible to investigate the nature of absorption-limiting factors involved at every step of drug transport across the epithelial barriers. One experimental model is shown in figure 1 (Nakamura et al., 1976a, 1976b). Net absorption of phenol red and bromphenol blue from the small intestine of rats was 1.2 and 2.4 % respectively, indicating poor absorption.

Differences in the absorbability of these dyes were then investigated by binding studies performed with various membrane components. It was found that the poor absorbability of phenol red was mainly due to its intrinsic low affinity for the intestinal mucosa while that of bromphenol blue was due to slow penetration through the lipid bilayer although the dye could rapidly bind to the brush borders, probably in the glycocalyx region. Marked reduction of bromphenol blue binding to brush borders was observed after digestion with proteolytic enzymes, but no such effect was found with phenol red.

Localisation of the absorption site as observed in bromphenol blue may sometimes be desirable for polar drugs which have a local effect on the gastrointestinal tract. One such example is shown in figure 2. This polar compound is a newly developed anti-ulcer drug with low toxicity. After oral administration, the drug is rapidly taken up by the stomach and high levels of radioactivity are found only in the gastric wall up to 8 hours after administration (Ono et al., 1976). Similar selective uptake by the gastrointestinal tissue was reported in guinea pigs for loperamide, an orally active anti-diarrhoeal compound (Van Neuten et al., 1979).

## 1.2 Modification of Absorption Characteristics

Several methods for improving the absolute bioavailability of poorly absorbed drugs have been reported (table II). Some of the absorption promoters increase permeability thus making drug molecules more readily accessible for clearance from the absorption site. The extent and duration of the effects of such promotors depend not only on their effective luminal concentration but on various other factors such as physicochemical state, method of formulation, absorbability, metabolism, structure of absorbing surface, and metabolic activities of absorbing cells.

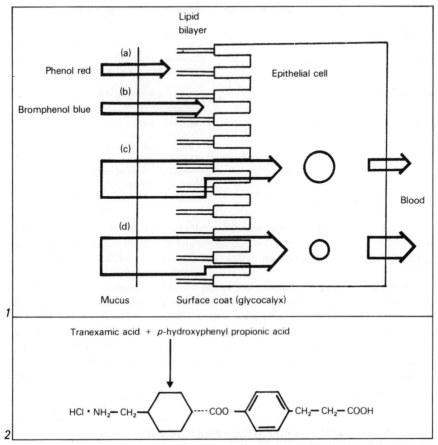

*Fig. 1.* Intestinal absorption of dyes: (a) phenol red; poor absorbability due to its low affinity for intestinal mucosa and poor lipid solubility. (b) bromphenol blue; ability to bind to brush borders but with poor transference. (c) dyes such as bromthymol blue; extensive binding to brush borders and intracellular components. (d) dyes such as methylene blue; extensive binding to brush borders but less intracellular accumulation.

*Fig. 2.* A newly developed polar drug for gastric ulcer.

For example, polar chelating agents such as ethylenediamine tetra acetic acid (EDTA), in small amounts, increase the transfer of poorly absorbable compounds by altering the integrity of the absorptive membrane (fig. 3) [Tidball, 1971]. On the other hand, lipophilic chelating agents such as enamines (e.g. phenylglycylethyl acetoacetate) may modify the membrane surface during their translocation by depleting cementing substances such as calcium ions (Murakami et al., 1979), thereby enhancing the absorption of poorly absorbable drugs.

Surfactants and mixed micellar components are also critical determinants of the rate and extent of absorption. In proper amounts, partial but selective solubilisation of membrane components is attained. However, their action depends largely on their physicochemical characteristics and effective concentration per unit area of the absorptive membrane (Kaneda et al., 1974). Unlike most synthetic polyoxyethylene derivatives (POE) which are the least absorbable, mixed micelles possessing a

*Table II.* Methods of improving the absolute bioavailability of poorly absorbable drugs

| Method | Example |
| --- | --- |
| Chemical | Lipophilic prodrugs |
| | Introduction of carrier function |
| Pharmaceutical | Entrapment in liposomes |
| | Ion-pair formation |
| (Addition of absorption promoters) | Synthetic surfactants |
| | Oils and their degradation products |
| | Lipid-bile salt mixed micelles |
| | Chelating agents |
| | Membrane channel former |
| | Methylxanthines |

nutrient-like composition such as monoglycerides or unsaturated fatty acids and bile salts readily penetrate the absorptive membrane and induce a transient increase in the permeability of poorly absorbable drugs (Tokunaga et al., 1978; Muranishi et al., 1979).

Other interesting membrane-active agents tested by Nakamura et al. (1979) are methylxanthines and the absorption of phenol red and bromphenol blue is increased by pretreatment with theophylline and caffeine. Changes in membrane permeability were observed at least 30 minutes after removal of the methylxanthines. Also the disappearance of phenol red and bromphenol blue from luminal perfusate was significantly increased after pretreatment with isoprenaline (isoproterenol) which produces intracellular accumulation of cyclic adenosine monophosphate (AMP) by activation of adenyl cyclase.

## 2. Non-lipophilic Polar Drugs which do not Conform to the Lipoid Theory

Although many questions concerning poor absorbability of non-lipophilic polar drugs mentioned in the previous section still remain to be answered, the general principle of the lipoid theory can be applied to those drugs. There are other compounds, however, which are absorbed very rapidly despite their low partition coefficient at physiological pH. This group includes benzoic acid derivatives and some aminopenicillins.

### 2.1 Benzoic Acid Derivatives

#### 2.1.1 Absorption of p-Aminobenzoic Acid

*p*-Aminobenzoic acid (PABA) is a representative non-lipophilic polar drug which does not obey the lipoid theory (Yasuhara et al., 1978a, 1978b). The physicochemical properties of PABA and its major metabolite, *p*-acetoamido-benzoic acid (Ac-PABA) are shown in table III. Although both compounds are almost completely ionised and possess very low partition coefficients at pH 6.5, the absorption rate is very high.

To investigate the anomalous absorption of PABA, the pH-profile of the absorption rate of PABA from the rat small intestine was compared with its physicochemi-

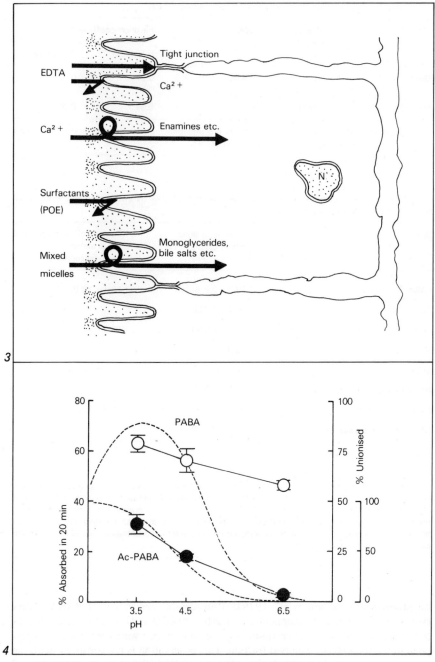

*Fig. 3.* The effect of some absorption promoters on intestinal absorption.

*Fig. 4.* pH-profiles of absorption rate from the small intestine and the fraction of unionised PABA and Ac-PABA. The continuous lines represent the absorption rate and the broken lines the theoretical fraction unionised. Results of absorption experiments are expressed as the mean ± SD of at least 3 experiments.

*Table III*. Physicochemical properties of PABA and Ac-PABA

|  | Molecular weight | pK | Partition coefficient[1] | |
|---|---|---|---|---|
|  |  |  | n-butanol | chloroform |
| PABA | 137.14 | 4.85 | 0.27 | 0.02 |
| Ac-PABA | 179.18 | 2.41 4.28 | 0.34 | 0.00 |

1   Drugs (0.1mmol) were dissolved in pH 6.5 phosphate buffer solution and the partition coefficients to organic solvents were determined at 37°.

*Table IV*. Disappearance of drugs and appearance of their N-conjugates in the intestinal lumen in the *in situ* loop experiment

| Drug | Percent of dose which disappeared | Percent of dose appearing in lumen as N-conjugate |
|---|---|---|
| PABA | 59.0 ± 2.9 (6) | 22.1 ± 1.2 (6) |
| Ac-PABA | 10.4 ± 2.8 (4) |  |
| PAS | 28.8 ± 3.0 (4) | 23.2 ± 2.0 (4) |
| N⁴-acetyl-PAS | 3.0 ± 2.1 (4) |  |
| Sulphisoxazole | 26.1 ± 2.7 (4) | 1.8 ± 0/5 (4) |
| N⁴-acetylsulphisoxazole | 1.5 ± 0.9 (6) |  |
| Sulphadimethoxine | 45.0 ± 3.4 (4) | 0.6 ± 0.6 (6) |
| N⁴-acetylsulphadimethoxine | 17.2 ± 3.5 (4) |  |

Drugs (0.1mmol) were dissolved in pH 6.5 isotonic sodium phosphate buffer solution and 5ml were injected into the small intestinal loop. Free and total amines were determined and the amount of N-conjugate was obtained by subtracting free amine from the total amine. At this concentration, the main metabolic pathway of the drugs is acetylation in the rat small intestine. Results are expressed as the mean ± SD. Number of experiments is shown in parentheses. Period of absorption experiment was 5 minutes.

cal properties (Yasuhara et al., 1979a). Considerable absorption of PABA occurs even at pH 6.5, when the compound is largely ionised (fig. 4). The profile of absorption is inconsistent with the partition characteristics which were confirmed to correspond to the theoretical unionised fraction. This observation is not consistent with the pH-partition theory alone. On the other hand, the pH-profile of the absorption rate of Ac-PABA correlated well with the partition characteristics and the theoretical uionised fraction. At pH 6.5, almost all of the PABA and Ac-PABA is ionised and both have similar partition coefficients. Nevertheless, a marked difference in the intestinal absorption is clearly established. This phenomenon was observed in the small intestine but not in the large intestine. The pH-profile of absorption from the large intestine corresponded to the theoretical unionised fraction (fig. 5) and the ionised form of the drug was poorly absorbed. These results indicate a specific absorption mechanism for PABA in the small intestine at pH 6.5.

When PABA was instilled into the small intestinal loop, a significant amount appeared in the lumen as Ac-PABA, having been acetylated in the epithelial cells. A significant fraction of the original drug in the lumen was later excreted as N-conjugates (table IV) Yasuhara et al., 1978b.

There was more extensive conjugation of benzoic acid derivatives than sulphonamides and also a good correlation between the excretion of N-conjugate into the intestinal lumen and the intestinal mucosal N-acetyltransferase activity. The anionic absorption of acetylated drugs was markedly slower than that of the parent drugs although molecular weights and partition coefficients are similar.

To clarify further the specific mechanisms of PABA absorption in the small intestine, modification of the brush border membrane by mercurial compounds has been attempted. Bihler and Cybulsky (1973) showed that short pretreatment with low concentrations of mercuric chloride strongly inhibited sugar transport at the luminal surface without affecting the internal concentration of sodium and potassium ions. The effect of mercuric chloride pretreatment on absorption of PABA and its metabolite is shown in table V. The absorption of PABA at pH 6.5 was significantly inhibited, while the absorption of Ac-PABA and sulphanilamide was unaffected. A similar effect was observed with p-chloromercuribenzene sulphonate (PCMBS), which is thought to penetrate cell membranes very slowly (Yasuhara, 1979b). These results suggest that protein and sulphhydryl groups within the brush border membrane are involved in the absorption of PABA from the rat small intestine.

Evidence supporting the selective absorption of PABA from the rat small intestine is summarised in table VI. Recent investigations (Turnheim and Lauterbach, 1977) indicate that the small intestinal epithelial cells play a unique role in the excretion of some monoquaternary ammonium compounds. In the case of Ac-PABA excretion into the intestinal lumen from the cells, a counter transport phenomenon was observed by Yasuhara et al. (1979c) using isolated brush border membrane vesicles. Measurement of radio-labelled compounds released from pre-loaded brush border membrane vesicles demonstrated that in spite of its slow absorption characteristics, Ac-PABA was released faster than PABA and D-glucose. The addition of non-radiolabelled Ac-PABA in the outer medium accelerates this release, indicating that a counter transport phenomenon plays a role (fig. 6).

### 2.1.2 Effect of Taurine on the Absorption of Some Salicylates

Some amino acid-like compounds were found to enhance the rate of absorption of some salicylates not only from the intestine but also from the stomach (Kimura et al., 1979b).

The primary absorbing site for most orally administered drugs is the small intestine, but a unique role of the stomach was demonstrated with these polar drugs. Taurine enhanced the absorption of aspirin from the rat stomach and small intestine but not from the large intestine (table VII) [Kakemi et al., 1962]. The enhancement of aspirin and o-ethoxybenzoic acid absorption (but not salicylamide) was sodium ion-dependent (table VIII). Modification of the relatively impermeable gastric mucosal membrane by safe endogenous compounds like taurine may hold considerable promise for future drug development.

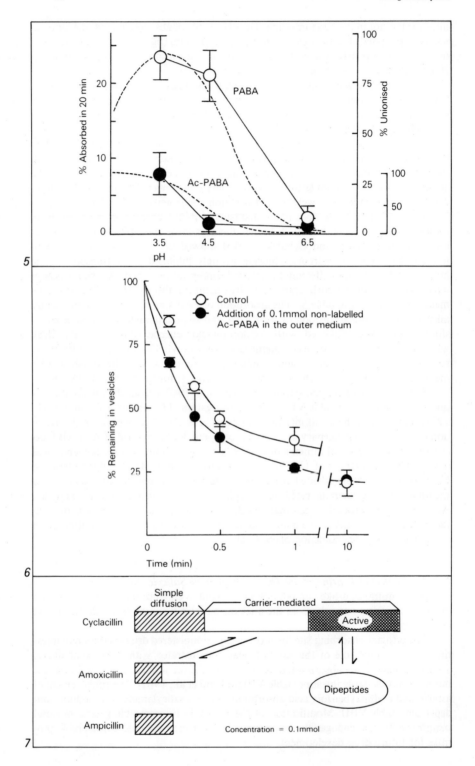

*Table V.* Effect of pretreatment with mercuric chloride on the absorption of drugs in the *in situ* loop experiments

| Drugs | Concen-tration (mmol) | Pretreatment | Percent absorbed in 5min |
|---|---|---|---|
| PABA | 0.1 | Buffer | 52.1 ± 2.5 (4) |
| | | Mercuric chloride 1mmol | 41.0 ± 3.2 (4)** |
| | | Mercuric chloride 3mmol | 36.8 ± 3.6 (4)*** |
| | 1.0 | Buffer | 51.1 ± 2.5 (4) |
| | | Mercuric chloride 1mmol | 40.1 ± 3.9 (4)** |
| Ac-PABA | 0.1 | Buffer | 9.9 ± 0.8 (3) |
| | | Mercuric chloride 1mmol | 11.3 ± 1.9 (6) NS |
| Sulphanilamide | 0.1 | Buffer | 35.0 ± 3.2 (4) |
| | | Mercuric chloride 1mmol | 36.7 ± 1.4 (4)NS |

The small intestine was perfused with the pretreatment solution for 2 minutes and washed with 20ml of isotonic buffer solution. Then, the absorption experiment was carried out at pH 6.5 for 5 min. Results are expressed as the mean ± SD with the number of experiments in parentheses. **$p < 0.01$; ***$p < 0.001$; NS not significant; Student's *t*-test.

*Table VI.* Evidence supporting selective absorption of PABA from the rat small intestine

1. At pH 6.5, completely ionised but good intestinal absorption
2. Specific to small intestine (not large intestine)
3. PABA transfer rate: forward flux > backward flux
4. Uptake against a concentration gradient (*in vitro*)
5. Uptake inhibited by 2, 4-dinitrophenol and mercurial agents *(in vitro)*
6. Absorption inhibited by mercurial agents (brush border membrane alteration)
7. Addition of surfactants: absorption of PABA (decreased), Ac-PABA (increased)
8. Secretion of Ac-PABA from the epithelial cell to the intestinal lumen

*Fig. 5.* pH-profiles of absorption rate from the large intestine and the fraction unionised. Key and results expressed as in figure 4.

*Fig. 6.* Release of radio-labelled Ac-PABA preloaded in the brush border membrane vesicles, suggesting the existence of specialised transport mechanisms in the excretion of Ac-PABA from the intestinal epithelial cell into the lumen.

*Fig. 7.* Proposed absorption mechanisms of aminopenicillins from the rat small intestine.

*Table VII.* Effect of taurine on regional specificity of aspirin absorption

| Site of absorption | pH | Percent absorbed (1h) | |
|---|---|---|---|
| | | control | taurine 1mmol |
| Stomach | 1.1 | 34.7 ± 0.9 (3) | 41.4 ± 1.7 (4)*** |
| | 4.0 | 30.4 ± 1.4 (9) | 39.2 ± 1.6 (8)** |
| | 6.5 | 15.6 ± 1.2 (4) | 23.6 ± 2.6 (4)* |
| Small intestine | 6.5 | 42.1 ± 1.0 (8) | 50.7 ± 0.7 (6)*** |
| Large intestine | 6.5 | 7.7 ± 0.6 (3) | 8.1 ± 0.8 (4) |

Method: stomach, loop with 4ml of drug solution; small intestine, recirculation with 40ml of perfusion solution; large intestine, recirculation with 20ml of perfusion solution. Results are expressed as the mean ± SD followed by the number of experiments in parentheses. *$p < 0.05$, **$p < 0.01$, ***$p < 0.001$, compared with each control.

*Table VIII.* Significance of sodium for the effect of taurine on drug absorption from the rat stomach[1]

| Drug | Adjuvants | Percent absorbed (1h) | |
|---|---|---|---|
| | | sodium chloride medium[2] | mannitol medium[3] |
| Aspirin | None | 34.3 ± 0.3 (5) | 35.4 ± 0.2 (3) |
| | Taurine (1mmol) | 41.4 ± 0.5 (4) | 33.0 ± 1.2 (3) |
| | Ouabain (1.5mmol) | 32.0 ± 1.3 (3)) | |
| | Taurine (1mmol) + Ouabain (1.5mmol) | 34.0 ± 1.2 (4) | |
| O-Ethoxybenzoic acid | None | 33.9 ± 1.2 (3) | 33.8 ± 0.8 (4) |
| | Taurine (1mmol) | 49.2 ± 1.9 (4) | 31.6 ± 1.4 (4) |
| Salicylamide | None | 31.8 ± 1.2 (5) | 31.2 ± 1.2 (3) |
| | Taurine (1mmol) | 43.4 ± 1.4 (6) | 41.0 ± 1.8 (4) |
| Sulphanilic acid | None | 1.4 ± 0.1 (4) | 0.3 ± 0.0 (3) |
| | Taurine (1mmol) | 1.4 ± 0.1 (4) | |

1   Results are expressed as the mean ± SD with the number of experiments in parentheses. Concentration of drugs = 1mmol.
2   0.1N HCl containing 0.1M NaCl, pH 1.1.
3   0.1N HCl containing 0.2M mannitol, pH 1.1.

## 2.2 Absorption of Aminopenicillins

The aminopenicillins, ampicillin, amoxicillin and cyclacillin, are always ionised, the zwitterion being the dominant species at the pH of the small intestine (Purich et al., 1973) and yet they are significantly absorbed.

The small intestinal absorption of amoxicillin and cyclacillin in the rat is a saturable process (Kimura et al., 1979a, 1979c). In addition, the absorption of amoxicillin was greater than that of ampicillin and this does not fit with their relative per-

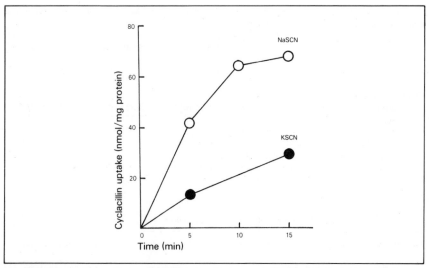

*Fig. 8.* Specific entry of cyclacillin in the reconstituted system of liposomes. In sodium ion containing medium, cyclacillin enters rapidly into liposomes. Sodium ion dependency is better demonstrated as sodium ion movement as induced by the addition of the lipophilic anions SCN⁻, moving in the same direction.

meability through an artificial lipid membrane (table IX). These data indicate carrier-mediated transport.

The effect of mercurial treatment on the absorption of aminopenicillins was studied. The absorption of amoxicillin and cyclacillin from the rat small intestine was significantly inhibited, while that of ampicillin was not affected at all. This suggested that protein and sulphydryl groups participate in the absorption of amoxicillin and cyclacillin, but not ampicillin.

Mutual inhibition of amoxicillin and cyclacillin absorption was observed suggesting a common carrier system for the two pencillins (table X). Addition of L-phenylalanylglycine and glycylglycine significantly reduced the absorption of cyclacillin although no correlation could be demonstrated between the absorption of cyclacillin and that of amino acids. It is known that dipeptides are actively absorbed through a specific transport pathway different from that of amino acids (Matthews, 1975). The absorption of amoxicillin was affected by none of these peptides and amino acids suggesting that the common carrier system for cyclacillin and dipeptides is not operative for amoxicillin. Thus the transport mechanism from the rat small intestine of the 3 aminopenicillins can be summarised as in figure 7. It seems quite possible that cyclacillin is absorbed by at least 2 carrier-mediated systems, one which can be blocked by amoxicillin and the other by dipeptides. Simple diffusion also occurs. *In vitro* experiments show that cyclacillin is actively transported across the mucosal membrane of rat small intestine while in contrast, neither amoxicillin nor ampicillin can be transported against a concentration gradient. This is in agreement with the results of other investigators (Dixon and Mizen, 1977; Miyazaki et al., 1977; Tsuji et al., 1977, 1978). We have also observed sodium ion dependency in the absorption of cyclacillin (fig. 8).

*Table IX.* The apparent partition coefficients of aminopenicillins and their permeability rate constants for the artificial lipid membrane

|                                     | Ampicillin            | Amoxicillin           | Cyclacillin           |
|-------------------------------------|-----------------------|-----------------------|-----------------------|
| Apparent partition coefficient[1]   | 0.00                  | 0.01                  | 0.02                  |
| Permeability rate constant          |                       |                       |                       |
| Absorption simulator[2]             | $5.47 \times 10^{-5}$ | $8.36 \times 10^{-5}$ | $2.45 \times 10^{-4}$ |
| Liposome[3]                         | $9.45 \times 10^{-4}$ | $8.66 \times 10^{-3}$ | $1.91 \times 10^{-2}$ |

1 pH 6.5 isotonic phosphate buffer-chloroform, at 37°.
2 Sartorius absorption simulator. In cm min$^{-1}$.
3 Composed of phosphatidylcholine-cholesterol-dicetylphosphate (80:20:5). In min$^{-1}$.


*Table X.* Inhibition of the absorption of aminopenicillins[1]

| Penicillin  | Inhibitor             | mmol | Percent absorbed in 1h        |
|-------------|-----------------------|------|-------------------------------|
| Ampicillin  | None                  | 0.1  | $9.7 \pm 1.1$ (4)             |
|             | Amoxicillin           | 1.0  | $10.5 \pm 2.1$ (4) NS         |
|             | L-Phenylalanylglycine | 5.0  | $10.5 \pm 0.2$ (3) NS         |
| Amoxicillin | None                  | 0.1  | $15.4 \pm 2.2$ (4)            |
|             | Cyclacillin           | 1.0  | $9.6 \pm 2.4$ (4) $p < 0.02$  |
|             | Glycine               | 5.0  | $15.2 \pm 1.3$ (3) NS         |
|             | Glycylglycine         | 5.0  | $14.9 \pm 2.2$ (4) NS         |
|             | L-Phenylalanylglycine | 5.0  | $15.0 \pm 0.6$ (3) NS         |
| Cyclacillin | None                  | 0.1  | $67.3 \pm 5.4$ (4)            |
|             | Amoxicillin           | 1.0  | $42.0 \pm 9.2$ (3) $p < 01$   |
|             | Glycine               | 5.0  | $64.7 \pm 4.2$ (3) NS         |
|             | Glycylglycine         | 5.0  | $48.2 \pm 5.0$ (3) $p < 0.01$ |
|             | L-Phenylalanylglycine | 5.0  | $38.8 \pm 8.6$ (3) $p < 0.01$ |

1 Results are expressed as the mean $\pm$ SD with the number of experiments in parentheses. NS: not significant; Student's *t*-test.


The active transport system for cyclacillin has been reconstituted in the liposome system made from egg yolk lecithin and Triton X-100-solubilised rat intestinal brush border membrane protein fraction, as evaluated by Kimura et al., (1979a, 1979c).

It is evident that facilitated diffusion contributes to the amoxicillin transport, a mechanism also shared by cyclacillin. Absorption also occurs by carrier-independent diffusion through lipoidal regions of the intestinal boundary and is closely related to permeability characteristics observed in the artificial lipid membranes. No evidence for carrier-mediated transport of ampicillin could be found.

## Acknowledgement

The research studies included in this report was supported in part by grants from the Ministry of Education, Japan. The authors acknowledge the secretarial assistance of Miss Kazuko Horiuchi.

# References

Bihler, I. and Cybulsky, R.: Sugar transport at the basal and lateral aspect of the small intestinal cell. Biochimica et Biophysica Acta 298: 429-437 (1973).

Collander, R.: The permeability of Nitella cells to non-electrolytes. Physiologica Plantarum 7: 420-445 (1945).

Dixon, C. and Mizen, L.W.: Absorption of amino penicillins from everted rat intestine. Journal of Physiology 269: 549-559 (1977).

Hansch, C. and Fujita, T.: $p$-$\sigma$-$\pi$ analysis. A method for the correlation of biological activity and chemical structure. Journal of the American Chemical Society 86: 1616-1626 (1964).

Hogben, C.A.M.: Tocco, D.J.; Brodie, B.B. and Schanker, L.S.: On the mechanism of intestinal absorption of drugs. The Journal of Pharmacology and Experimental Therapeutics 125: 275-282 (1959).

Houston, J.B.; Upshall, D.G. and Bridges J.W.: A re-evaluation of the importance of partition coefficients in the gastrointestinal absorption of anutrients. The Journal of Pharmacology and Experimental Therapeutics 189: 244-254 (1974).

Houston, J.B.; Upshall, D.G. and Bridges J.W. Further studies using carbamate esters as model compounds to investigate the role of lipophilicity in the gastrointestinal absorption of foreign compounds. The Journal of Pharmacology and Experimental Therapeutics 195: 67-72 (1975).

Kakemi, K.; Sezaki, H.; Morisaka, K. and Nakamoto, Y.: Absorption of aspirin derivatives from the gastrointestinal tract and effect of taurine. Yakuzaigaku 27: 232-237 (1962).

Kaneda, A.: Nishimura, K.; Muranishi, S. and Sezaki, H.: Mechanism of drug absorption from micellar solution. II. Effect of polysorbate 80 on the absorption of micelle-free drugs. Chemical and Pharmaceutical Bulletin 22: 523-528 (1974).

Kimura, T.; Endo, H.; Yoshikawa, M.; Muranishi, S. and Sezaki, H.: Carrier-mediated transport systems for aminopenicillins in rat small intestine. Journal of Pharmacobio-Dynamics 1: 262-267 (1979a).

Kimura, T.; Kim, K. and Sezaki, H.: Effect of taurine on the gastrointestinal absorption of drugs. Presented at the Symposium of the Research Society for Sulfur-containing amino Acids (1979b).

Kimura, T.; Kobayashi, H.; Muranishi, S. and Sezaki, H.: Mechanism of the absorption of water-soluble drugs from the gastrointestinal tract. Absorption of $\beta$-lactam antibiotics from the rat small intestine. Presented at the 11th Symposium on Drug Metabolism and Action of the Pharmaceutical Society of Japan (1979c).

Levine, R.R.: Factors affecting gastrointestinal absorption of drugs. The American Journal of Digestive Disease 15: 171-188 (1970).

Matthews, D.M.: Intestinal transport of peptides. Physiological Reviews 55: 537-608 (1975).

Miyazaki, K.; Ogino, O.; Nakano, M. and Arita, T.: Intestinal absorption mechanism of ampicillin derivatives in rats. I. Intestinal absorption of ampicillin derivatives. Chemical and Pharmaceutical Bulletin 25: 246-252 (1977).

Murakami, T.; Tamauchi, H.; Nakai, J.; Yamazaki, M. and Kamada, A.: Studies on absorption promoters. IV. Mechanism of the rectal absorption enhancement by enamine absorption promoters. Proceedings of the 99th Annual Meeting of the Pharmaceutical Society of Japan: 563 (1979).

Muranishi, S.; Muranushi, N. and Sezaki, H.: Improvement of absolute bioavailability of normally poorly absorbable drugs: inducement of the intestinal absorption of streptomycin and gentamicin by lipid-bile salt mixed micelles in rat and rabbit. International Journal of Pharmaceutics 2: 101-111 (1979).

Nakamura, J.; Yoshizaki, Y.; Yasuhara, M.; Kimura, T.; Muranishi S. and Sezaki, H.: Mechanism of the absorption of water-soluble dyes from the rat small intestine. Chemical and Pharmaceutical Bulletin 24: 683-690 (1976a).

Nakamura, J.; Yoshizaki, Y.; Yasuhara, M.; Kimura, T.; Muranishi, S. and Sezaki, H.: Role of membrane components, glycocalyx and lipids in absorption of water-soluble dyes from the rat small intestine. Chemical and Pharmaceutical Bulletin 24: 691-697 (1976b).

Nakamura, J.; Takamura, R.; Kimura, T.; Muranishi, S. and Sezaki, H.: Enhancement effect of methylxanthines on the intestinal absorption of poorly absorbable dyes from the rat small intestine. Biochemical Pharmacology 28: 2957-2960 (1979).

Ono, K.; Okazaki, O. and Saito, T.: Metabolism of 4-(2-carboxyethyl) phenyl trans-4-aminomethylcyclohexane carboxylate hydrochloride (DV-1006), a new antiulcer drug. I. Absorption, distribution, excretion and metabolism in rats. Pharmacometrics 12: 269-277 (1976).

van Neuten, J.M.; Helsen, L.; Michiels, M. and Heykants, J.J.P.: Distribution of loperamide in the intestinal wall. Biochemical Pharmacology 28: 1433-1434 (1979).

Purich, E.D.; Colaizzi, J.L. and Poust, R.I.: pH-partition behavior of amino acid-like $\beta$-lactam antibiotics. Journal of Pharmaceutical Sciences 62: 545-549 (1973).

Shore, P.A.; Brodie, B.B. and Hogben, C.A.M: The gastric secretion of drugs: a pH-partition hypothesis. The Journal of Pharmacology and Experimental Therapeutics 119: 361-369 (1957).

Smolen, V.F.: Misconceptions and thermodynamic untenability of deviations from pH-partition hypothesis. Journal of Pharmaceutical Sciences 62: 77-79 (1973).

Tidball, C.S.: The nature of the intestinal epithelial barrier. The American Journal of Digestive Diseases. 16: 745-767 (1971).

Tokunaga, Y.; Muranishi, S. and Sezaki, H.: Enhanced intestinal permeability to macromolecules. I. Effect of mono-olein-bile salts mixed micelles on the small intestinal absorption of heparin. Journal of Pharmacobio-Dynamics 1: 28-38 (1978).

Tsuji, A.; Nakashima, E.; Kagami, I.; Asano, T.; Nakashima, R. and Yamana, T.: Kinetics of Michaelis-Menten absorption of amino-penicillins in rats. Journal of Pharmacy and Pharmacology 30: 508-509 (1978).

Tsuji, A.; Nakashima, E.; Kagami, I.; Hongo, N. and Yamana, T.: Effect of dose-concentration on the absorption of amoxicillin and ampicillin from the rat intestine. Journal of Pharmacy and Pharmacology 29: 707-708 (1977).

Turnheim, K. and Lauterbach, F.O.: Absorption and secretion of monoquaternary ammonium compounds by the isolated intestinal mucosa. Biochemical Pharmacology 26: 99-108 (1977).

Winne, D.: Shift of pH-absorption curves. Journal of Pharmacokinetics and Biopharmaceutics 5: 53-94 (1977).

Wood, S.G.; Upshall, D.G. and Bridges, J.W.: Further consideration of the existence of an optimal partition coefficient for intestinal absorption of foreign compounds. Journal of Pharmacy and Pharmacology 31: 192-193 (1979).

Yasuhara, M.; Kobayashi, H.; Kimura, T.; Muranishi, S. and Sezaki, H.: Absorption and metabolism of p-aminobenzoic acid by rat small intestine in situ. J. of Pharmacobio-Dynamics 1: 122-131 (1978a).

Yasuhara, M.; Kobayashi, H.; Muranishi, S.; Sezaki, H. and Kimura, T.: Absorption and metabolism of p-aminobenzoic acid by rat intestine in vitro. J. of Pharmacobio-Dynamics 1: 114-121 (1978b).

Yasuhara, M.; Kobayashi, H.; Kurosaki, Y.; Kimura, T.; Muranishi, S. and Sezaki, H.: Comparative studies on the absorption mechanism of p-aminobenzoic acid and p-aceto-aminobenzoic acid from the rat intestine. Journal of Pharmacobio-Dynamics 2: 177-186 (1979a).

Yasuhara, M.; Yoshino, T.; Kimura, T.; Muranishi, S. and Sezaki, H.: Effect of surfactants on the absorption of p-aminobenzoic acid from the rat intestine. Journal of Pharmacobio-Dynamics 2: 251-256 (1979b).

Yasuhara, M.; Kurosaki, Y.; Kimura, T.; Muranishi, S. and Sezaki, H.: Mechanism of gastrointestinal absorption of water-soluble drugs. XV. Secretion of p-acetoaminobenzoic acid into the intestinal lumen. Proceedings of the 99th Annual Meeting of the Pharmaceutical Society of Japan: 559 (1979c).

## Discussion

*A. Melander* (Malmo): There may be other drugs which are absorbed by active transport. We have carried out studies with phenytoin in the rat using the closed segment technique and it seemed to be absorbed not only by passive diffusion but also by active transport. Phloridzin, which inhibits glucose transport, also inhibited phenytoin absorption.

*M. Rowland* (Chairman): I believe that Professor Lauterbach would like to make a few comments on the absorption of quaternary ammonium compounds and strong organic acids.

*F. Lauterbach* (Bochum FDR): We used isolated guinea pig mucosal preparations in a flux chamber. With *N*-methylscopolamine, permeation from blood to the luminal side is far greater than in the reverse direction. However, under anaerobic conditions, diffusion rates are the same in both directions. The same holds true for strong organic acids such as β-naphthol orange. Permeation from the luminal to the blood side is strictly correlated with the permeation of inulin which is an example of permeation through aqueous pores. Again, the transport of β-naphthol orange is much higher from blood to lumen and not correlated with inulin except under anaerobic conditions. Active secretory systems have also been demonstrated for cardiac glycosides and there is reason to believe that these transport systems are reversible and involved in the absorption of these drugs.

# 5

# Rate-limiting Steps and Factors in Drug Absorption

*William I. Higuchi, Norman F.H. Ho, Jung Y. Park and Izumi Komiya*

College of Pharmacy, The University of Michigan

One approach to studying drug absorption has been investigated mainly with the *in situ* rat intestinal model [the modified Doluisio method (Ho et al., 1977, 1979) and the 'through-and-through' perfusion method (Komiya et al., in press)] but this should also be applicable to other species including man. Examples will be presented of this approach in studying some of the rate-limiting steps and factors in drug absorption (fig. 1, table I).

The influences of the flow down the gastrointestinal tract, aqueous boundary layer, biomembrane permeability and gut reserve length will be emphasised. We will discuss some of the parameters which define and quantify membrane transport behaviour and, within the framework of this approach, how some formulation factors may be handled.

Figure 2 is a diagram of the model for simultaneous flow and drug absorption at nonsteady-state in the intestinal tract. The basic differential equation describing the kinetics (Ni et al., 1979a,b) is:

$$\frac{\delta\,C\,(x,t)}{\delta t} = \alpha\,\frac{\delta^2\,C\,(x,t)}{\delta\,x^2} - \beta\,\frac{\delta\,C\,(x,t)}{\delta x} - \gamma\,C\,(x,t) \qquad \text{Eq. 1}$$

$$(x \geqslant 0,\ t \geqslant 0)$$

where

$C\,(x,t)$ = concentration at any distance x in the small intestine and time t

$\alpha$ = longitudinal spreading coefficient, $cm^2/sec$

$\beta$ = linear flow velocity, $cm/sec$

$\quad = Q/\pi r^2$

$Q$ = bulk flow rate, $cm^3/sec$

$r$ = radius of the intestinal lumen, cm

$\gamma$ = absorption constant, $sec^{-1}$

$\quad = 2\,P_e/r$

$P_e$ = effective permeability coefficient, $cm/sec$

*Table I.* Rate-limiting factors in drug absorption

*Biological Considerations*
1.   Stomach emptying

2.   Intestinal tract
     a)  flow down the tract
     b)  aqueous boundary layer ('unstirred layer')
     c)  blood flow (sink vs non-sink)
     d)  biomembrane (nature of)
     e)  metabolism (membrane or lumen)
     f)  reserve length (intestine is not a 'well-mixed' compartment)
     g)  microclimate pH

*Physicochemical Considerations*
1.   Transport properties of the drug molecule
     a)  lipophilicity (determines permeability of the biomembrane)
     b)  $pK_a$ (determines the ratio of charged to uncharged species)
     c)  molecular size and shape (determines diffusivity in aqueous pores and in aqueous boundary
         layers)

2.   State of dispersion and formulation factors
     a)  binding (including absorption and micellar phenomena)
     b)  solubility
     c)  dissolution rate
     d)  release from dispersed systems (e.g., micro-encapsulated systems)
     e)  chemical stability

This situation may apply to an idealised simulation experiment, an animal model experiment or the *in vivo* human study.

We have introduced the differential equation here for two reasons. Firstly it is the most general statement of events within the intestine representing comprehensively and concisely the mass balance relationship for the solute. Secondly, this equation is mathematically solvable for various situations yielding relationships useful in experimental design and data analysis. For the moment, however, the primary purpose for presenting this equation is that it facilitates the description of what goes on in the intestine during simultaneous flow and absorption.

The three terms in equation 1 represent contributions to the drug concentration change with time in any segment of the intestine. In the fluid flow term, $\beta$ is the linear velocity of flow. It is equal to the volume flow rate, Q, divided by the cross-sectional area ($\pi r^2$) of the intestine treated as a circular cylinder of radius, r. In the perfusion-type rat intestine experiment, we have employed Q values in the range, 0.2 to 4.0ml/min, which correspond to the range of $\beta$ values of approximately 1.6 to 32cm/min for a rat intestinal radius of 0.20cm. Soergel (1971) suggests that, in the human, volume flow rates of the order of 2ml/min are reasonable estimates of the 'natural' intestinal flow of fasting subjects. Since r is of the order of 1.0cm for the human small intestine, a Q value of 2ml/min corresponds to a $\beta$ value of about 0.6cm/min.

The $\gamma$ in the absorption term of equation 1 is directly related to the permeability coefficient for the drug and, in turn, $P_e$ may be a function of the location in the intestine (e.g., duodenum, jejunum or ileum). It is also a function of the properties of the drug molecule — polarity, $pK_a$, molecular size and shape, etc. Less well known is that $P_e$ may be a function of $\beta$ (or Q). This interesting relationship comes about when the aqueous boundary layer (the unstirred layer) is important in determining the rate of drug absorption. As will be seen, this is the case when the solute is sufficiently lipophilic and the membrane permeability coefficient, $P_m$, is large compared to $P_{aq}$, the transport coefficient for the aqueous boundary layer.

Finally, we have the longitudinal spreading term in equation 1 with its characteristic coefficient, $\alpha$. Preliminary theoretical studies (Ni et al., 1979a) have revealed that longitudinal spreading might not be very important (as far as drug absorption patterns are concerned), for example, in the steady perfusion of a *solution* in the rat intestine when the intestinal length is sufficiently long and *only* molecular and eddy (turbulent) diffusion is important in solute flow and absorption. Longitudinal spreading, however, may be very important in systems such as powder suspensions where flow of the particles, for different reasons, may significantly lag behind the flow of the solute in solution. Furthermore, with suspensions, drug absorption patterns may depend upon longitudinal spreading because of the nonlinear nature of suspensions. For example, the extent of spreading of a suspension bolus may determine the effective area for absorption (at least initially) if the dose is sufficiently high. If, then, the solubility is low ( $< 0.10\,mg/ml$), the spreading or the lack of it may greatly influence the rate of drug absorption. Spreading due to flow retardation of particles that slowly release drug might be important, in the design of sustained release systems.

$\alpha$ may be studied directly using nonabsorbable markers (i.e., $\gamma = 0$). Influences of particle size and density, for example, of suspensions upon $\alpha$ might be studied in this way. It should be possible to separate the factors associated with the particulate nature of suspensions from those associated with only molecular and eddy diffusion processes by comparison of $\alpha$ values with those obtained with non-absorbing solutes.

The intestine is considered as a long cylindrical tube with the concentration of the drug decreasing with x (eq. 1). The reserve length may be defined (Ho et al., 1979; Ni et al., 1979a, 1979b) as the length of the intestine remaining after absorption has been completed (mathematically, it is easier to take some arbitrary criterion such as the length of the intestine remaining after absorption is 95 % complete). It is clear that the reserve length may be directly related to bioavailability where drug absorption is the limiting factor.

Equation 1 and the subsequent reserve length concept is founded on the existence of a time-dependent concentration gradient as the drug in the fluid flows down the small intestine, i.e., the intestine is longitudinally not a well-mixed compartment. This intuitive premise is well supported by human studies. Soergel (1971) followed the appearance of a bolus of a nonabsorbable marker in the jejunum and ileum (70 and 140 cm from the infusion tip positioned at the ligament of Treitz) to measure flow rates in fasted and nonfasted humans. Sharply defined parabolic concentration-time curves were observed from aspirated samples in the jejunum and ileum. In a classical study Borgstrom et al. (1957) employed a liquid test meal and found that glucose, protein and fat were completely absorbed within 100 cm of the jejunum which indicates a reserve length of about 200 cm for an average small intestinal length of 300 cm.

## 1. Recent Investigation of Factors Limiting Drug Absorption

Figures 3 and 4 illustrate the two types of *in situ* system that we have studied.

### 1.1 Through-and-through Intestinal Perfusion Method

Komiya et al., (1979) investigated the interplay of flow rate, aqueous boundary layer, membrane permeability, solute lipophilicity and length of intestinal segment.

Figure 5 illustrates the situation appropriate for the 'through-and-through' rat intestinal perfusion experiments. The physical model is described by

$$\frac{C\,(l)}{C\,(O)} = \exp\left(-\frac{2\pi rl}{Q} \cdot \frac{P_{aq}}{1 + P_{aq}/P_m}\right) \qquad \text{Eq. 2}$$

where
$C\,(l)/C\,(O)$ = fraction of drug unabsorbed in the intestinal segment
$\quad r$ = radius, cm
$\quad l$ = length, cm
$\quad Q$ = flow rate, $cm^3/sec$
$\quad P_{aq}$ = permeability coefficient of aqueous boundary layer, cm/sec
$\quad P_m$ = permeability coefficient of membrane, cm/sec

The fraction absorbed is

$$FA = 1 - C(l)/C\,(0) \qquad \text{Eq. 3}$$

The equations are applicable here when a constant concentration of drug is steadily perfused at $x = 0$ into an intestinal segment of length, $l$. Selected steroids were employed as test solutes in this particular study and flow rates of 0.2 to 4.0ml/min were utilised with rat jejunal segments of various lengths. The factor,

$$\frac{P_{aq}}{1 + P_{aq}/P_m}$$

in equation 2 is equal to $P_e$ within the $\gamma$ term of equation 1. There are two limiting situations. When $P_m$ is much greater than $P_{aq}$, we have aqueous boundary layer-controlled absorption and equation 2 becomes

$$\frac{C\,(l)}{C(0)} = \exp\left(-\frac{2\pi rl}{Q} \cdot P_{aq}\right) \qquad \text{Eq. 4}$$

When $P_{aq}$ is much greater than $P_m$ we have membrane-controlled absorption; thus

$$\frac{C\,(l)}{C(0)} = \exp\left(-\frac{2\pi rl}{Q} \cdot P_m\right) \qquad \text{Eq. 5}$$

Figure 6 illustrates some typical results of the fraction not absorbed, $C(l)/C(0)$, with progesterone. Figure 7 shows results of similar experiments for both progesterone and hydrocortisone for different intestinal segment lengths and where the steady-state (or the plateau) values of $C(l)/C(0)$ are plotted. The approximate semilogarithmic relationship seen here between $C(l)/C(0)$ and intestinal length is in good accord with equation 2.

In figure 8 the fraction absorbed within the jejunum segment is correlated with the lipophilicity of steroids ranging in 2.5 orders of magnitude in log partition coeffi-

*Table II.* Permeability coefficients and effective thicknesses of the aqueous boundary layer as a function of flow rate and surface roughness of the small intestine of the rat

| Flow rate $Q$, ml/min | Linear flow velocity $\beta$, cm/min | Permeability of boundary layer, $P_{aq} \times 10^4$ cm/sec | Effective boundary layer thickness[1] $\delta$ microns | Estimate[2] of $\delta$ r | Estimate[2] of $\delta$/h |
|---|---|---|---|---|---|
| 0.247 | 2.47 | 1.13 | 708 | 0.39 | 1.18 |
| 0.494 | 4.85 | 1.68 | 476 | 0.26 | 0.79 |
| 1.28 | 12.57 | 1.96 | 408 | 0.23 | 0.68 |
| 2.14 | 21.02 | 2.31 | 346 | 0.19 | 0.58 |
| 4.213 | 41.39 | 3.78 | 212 | 0.12 | 0.35 |

1  Effective thickness of aqueous boundary layer:

$$\delta = \frac{D_{aq}}{P_{aq}} = \frac{8 \times 10^{-6}}{P_{aq}}$$

2  Radius of intestinal lumen r = 1800 microns and villus height h = 600 microns.

cients for n-octanol/water. Differences in absorption are dominated by the effect of flow rate on the residence time (i.e. the time it takes to displace the volume of solution within the intestinal segment) more than that on the mass transfer coefficient. After factoring out the mass transfer constant, $P_e$, one observes the correlation with lipophilicity (fig. 9). At high partition coefficients, $P_e$ becomes constant as predicted. The plateau represents the aqueous diffusion layer-controlled region and the permeability of the aqueous boundary layer is flow rate dependent. For solutes possessing low lipophilicity, $P_e$ is determined more by $P_m$ than by $P_{aq}$ and consequently their absorption is less flow rate dependent (fig. 10). Progesterone shows a straight line dependence upon flow rate while the $P_e$ value for the much more polar hydrocortisone is not significantly influenced by flow rate.

The double reciprocal plot in figure 11 shows that $P_{aq}$ for progesterone is related to the flow rate by approximately a 0.44 power dependence over a 17-fold range of flow rate. For laminar flow in a smooth straight tube, the expected power dependence is 0.333 (Levich, 1962).

In table II, the aqueous boundary layer thicknesses ($\delta$, calculated using the Nernst approximation) are compared to the radius of the lumen and the height of the villus. Using a perfusion rate of 0.5ml/min, Winne (1976, 1979) recently estimated a lower limit value of about 500 microns for the rat jejunum based upon the appearance rate of *l*-phenylalanine in blood. This is in good agreement with our results based upon uptake data. Read et al. (1977) recently used an electrical method to estimate a value of 632 microns for the unstirred layer in healthy man. Their flow rate was 5ml/min which would correspond to an average lumen linear flow velocity, $\beta$, of around 1.6cm/min and somewhat below the lowest $\beta$ in our experiments. If the data in table II are extrapolated to a linear velocity of 1.6cm/min, the $\delta$ value would be around 840 microns for the present rat perfusion system. A further extrapolation to man is of interest. Based upon our 0.44 power dependence, an extrapolated value for $\delta$ in Soergel's study (1971) of the flow rate for a liquid meal in fasted humans would be around 950 microns for the flow rate of 2ml/min ($\beta$ value of around 0.6cm/min).

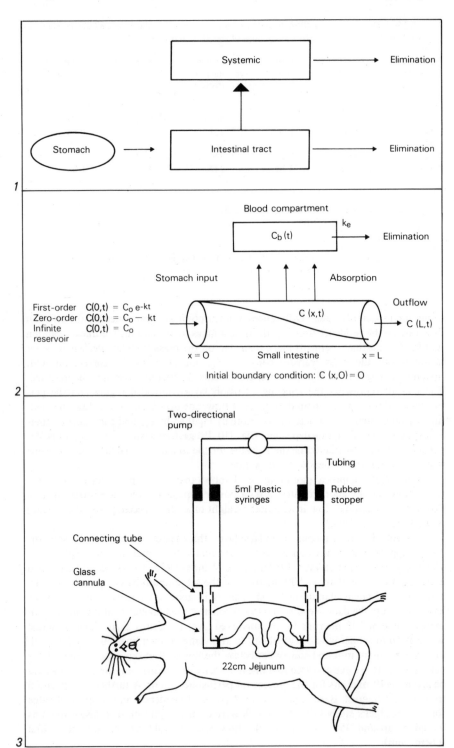

**1**

**2**

First-order   $C(0,t) = C_0 e^{-kt}$
Zero-order   $C(0,t) = C_0 - kt$
Infinite
reservoir      $C(0,t) = C_0$

Initial boundary condition: $C(x,0) = 0$

**3**

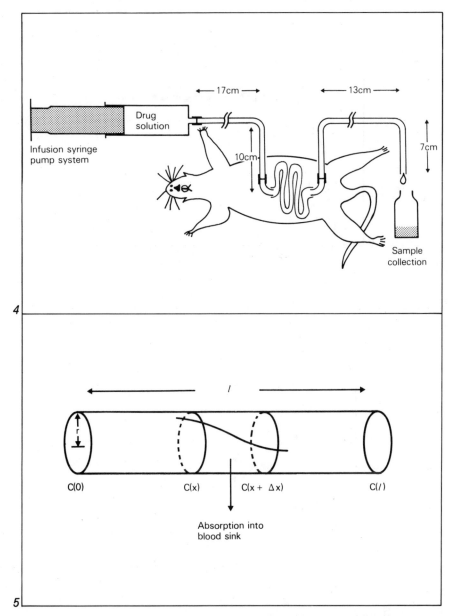

Fig. 1. The compartments relating to intestinal absorption of orally administered drugs.

Fig. 2. The model relating nonsteady-state flow, longitudinal spreading and intestinal absorption to blood level kinetics with various rates of drug input from the stomach.

Fig. 3. Modified Doluisio system for *in situ* rat intestinal absorption studies.

Fig. 4. The through-and-through *in situ* rat intestinal perfusion experiment.

Fig. 5. Physical model for the simultaneous bulk fluid flow and absorption in the intestinal tract at steady-state.

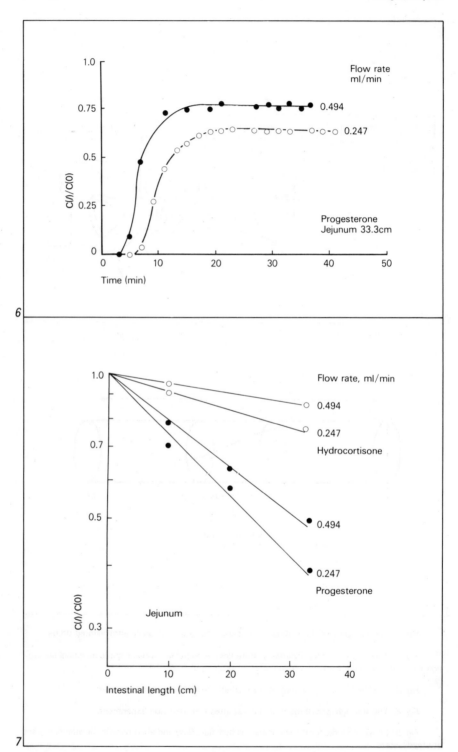

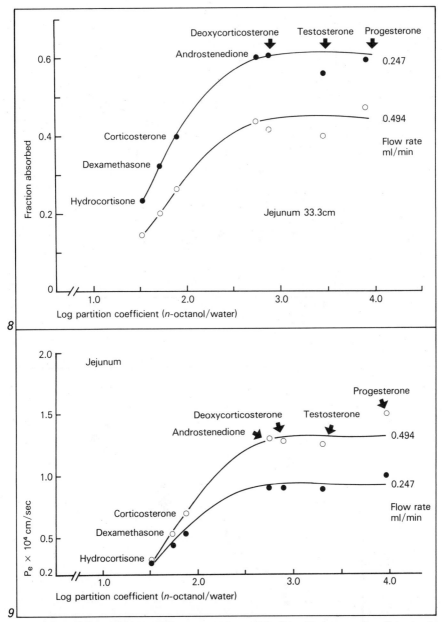

*Fig. 6.* Typical outflow-to-inflow concentration ratio profiles with time at various flow rates illustrating nonsteady and steady-states.

*Fig. 7.* Fraction of steroids remaining in various intestinal lengths as a function of fluid flow rate.

*Fig. 8.* Fraction of steroids absorbed in jejunum segment *versus* lipophilicity (*n*-octanol/water partition coefficients) as a function of flow rates.

*Fig. 9.* Correlation of *in situ* apparent permeability coefficients of selected steroids and their lipophilicity at various flow rates.

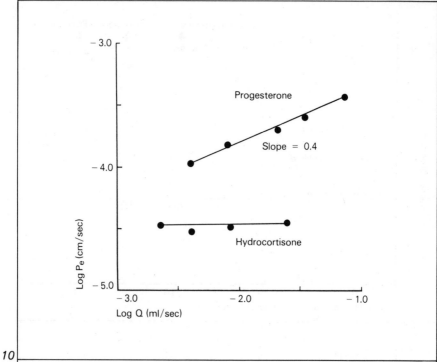

10

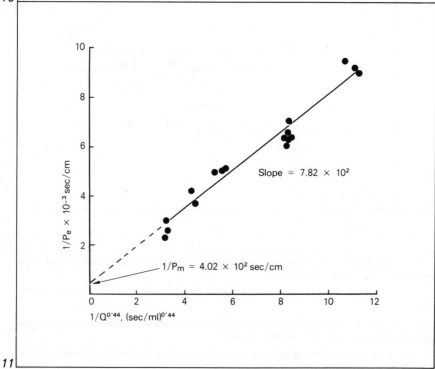

11

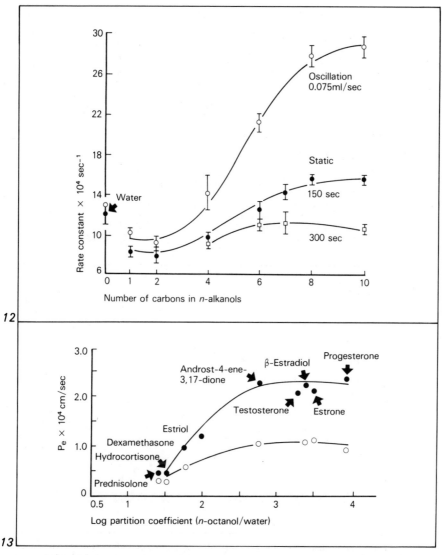

*Fig. 10.* Relationship of apparent permeability coefficient of progesterone and hydrocortisone with flow rate. The mass transport of progesterone is largely aqueous boundary layer-controlled in contrast to the membrane-controlled kinetics of hydrocortisone.

*Fig. 11.* Double reciprocal plot of the apparent permeability coefficient and volume flow rate to the 0.44 power from progesterone steady-state absorption data in rat jejunum.

*Fig. 12. In situ* first-order absorption rate constant *versus* carbon number in n-alkanol series under various hydrodynamic conditions in a 22cm length of rat jejunum. Solid lines are predicted from theory.

*Fig. 13.* Comparison of *in situ* apparent permeability coefficients of various steroids for the rat jejunum with different stirring rates in the lumen and the n-octanol/water partition coefficients. Results obtained using modified Doluisio method. Note the sigmoidal-shaped profiles. Hydrodynamic conditions: ○ static, 150 sec sampling intervals (slow stirring); ● oscillation 0.075ml/sec (rapid stirring).

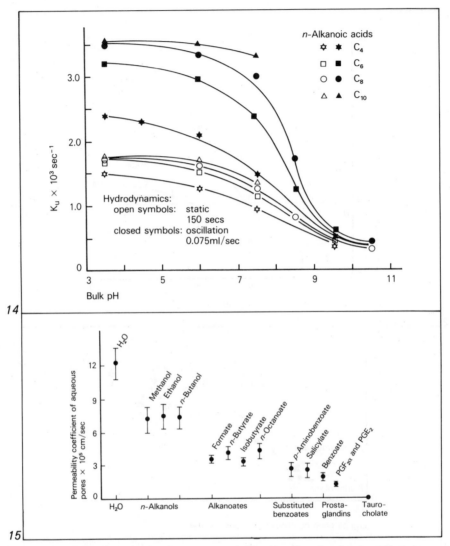

Fig. 14. First-order absorption rate constant-buffer pH profiles of n-alkanoic acid homologues (pK$_a$ 5.9) *in situ* studies carried out in 22cm rat jejunum at 37°C by the modified Doluisio method for two stirring conditions.

Fig. 15. Permeability coefficients of the aqueous pores of the rat jejunum for various hydrophilic solutes. The vertical bars are the standard deviations.

Fig. 16. Transport of progesterone in Tween 80 micellar solutions at 37°C across a 190 micron silicone polymer membrane in a rotating membrane diffusion cell system. The flux per unit area as a function of Tween 80 concentration is compared to the flux per unit area of saturated progesterone solution in water. The rotational speed is 60rpm. Two cases are shown: (a) constant progesterone with increasing surfactant concentrations and (b) saturated Tween 80 solutions. Solid lines represent theoretical predictions of the physical model and the closed circles the experimentally determined parameters.

Fig. 17. *In situ* absorption of progesterone in Tween 80 solutions in the rat jejunum at 37°C via modified Doluisio method (Hamid et al., unpublished). Solid line is best drawn line.

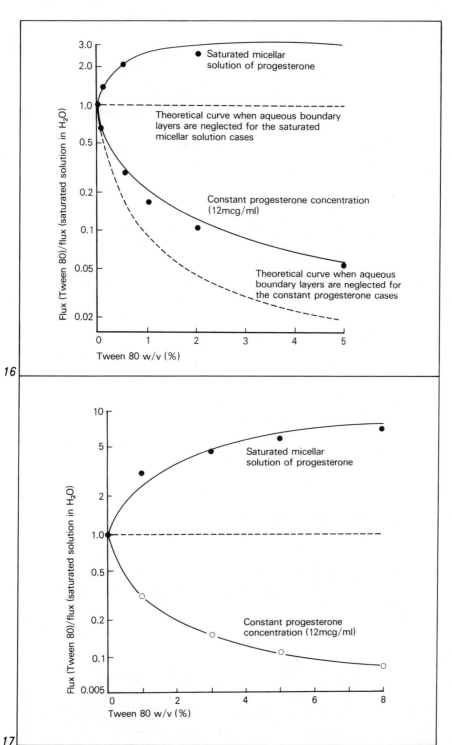

16

17

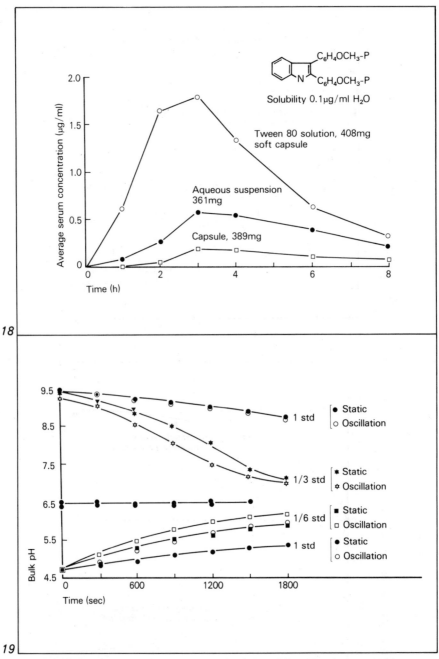

*Fig. 18.* Oral absorption of indoxole in humans (adapted from Wagner et al., 1966).

*Fig. 19.* Effect of buffer capacity and static (300sec intervals) and oscillation cases on the change in the pH of the bulk lumenal solution with time for initial buffer pH 4.5 (citrate and phosphate), pH 6.5 (phosphate) and pH 9.5 (borate) cases. Note that for the pH 6.5 case the pH remains constant for all 1/3 and 1 standard buffer capacities and the two respective hydrodynamic conditions.

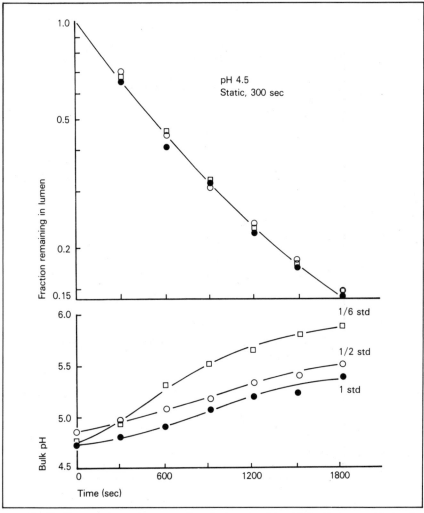

*Fig. 20.* Change in lumenal concentration of *n*-butyric acid and bulk pH change with time for the initial buffer pH 4.5 case under static, (300sec intervals) hydrodynamics and various buffer capacities.

The anatomical reserve length for absorption can be estimated on the basis of a flow rate of 2ml/min and a $\delta$ value of 950 microns. An expression for the reserve length, RL, was recently presented (Ho et al., 1979).

$$RL = L^* - \frac{0.48\,Q}{r\,P_e} \qquad\qquad \text{Eq. 6}$$

Here, $L^*$ is the effective absorbing length of the small intestine and is about 300cm in man. For a Q value of 2ml/min or 0.033ml/sec, an r value of 1.0cm and the $P_e$ value of $10^{-5}$cm/sec (based upon the $\delta$ value of 950 microns, a D of

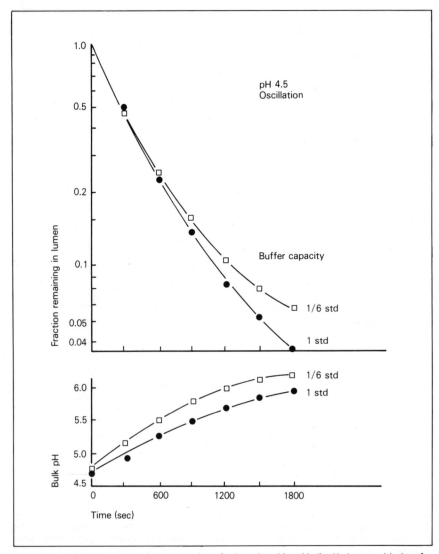

*Fig. 21.* Change in lumenal concentration of *n*-butyric acid and bulk pH change with time for the initial buffer pH 4.5 case under oscillation hydrodynamics and various buffer capacities.

$8 \times 10^{-6} cm^2/sec$, and the relationship, $P_e = D/\delta$), we obtain an RL estimate of 110cm.

While one must be very careful in extrapolating the above calculation to clinical situations, there is relatively little reserve length even under nearly optimum conditions for drug absorption (i.e., $P_m$ is very large and therefore, absorption is primarily diffusion layer-controlled). This should provide some perspective in the consideration of bioavailability. This primary implication of this calculation is that bioavailability problems may occur, i.e. the range between the best (maximum $P_e$) and the poor conditions (minimum $P_e \sim 2 \times 10^{-5}$ cm/sec) is relatively small.

## 1.2 The Modified Doluisio System

Figure 12 shows baseline studies (Desai, 1976; Ho et al., 1977) with the modified Doluisio system. The homologous series of n-alkanols studied under 3 hydrodynamic conditions clearly demonstrates the interaction among several physically relevant variables. At high carbon numbers, the rates plateau because the process becomes aqueous diffusion layer-controlled. The plateau levels differ because under continual oscillation flow conditions the boundary layer is relatively thin ($\sim$270 microns). Under static conditions with the 150-second sampling time the diffusion layer thickness is around 540 microns. When the sampling time is less frequent (300sec) and the disturbance of the solution is less, the average boundary thickness is

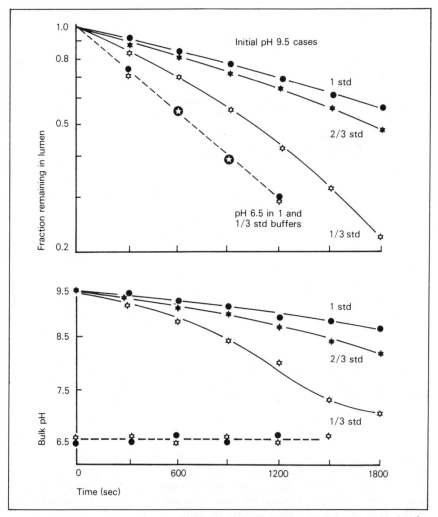

*Fig. 22.* Change in lumenal concentration of *n*-butyric acid and bulk pH change with time for the initial pH 9.5 case under static (300sec intervals) hydrodynamics and various buffer capacities. The pH 6.5 cases in various buffer capacities are included.

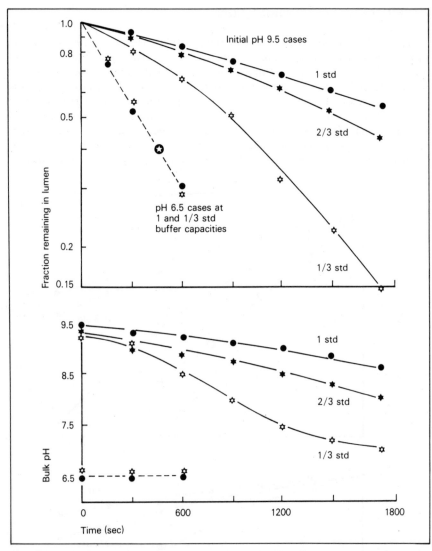

*Fig. 23.* Change in lumenal concentration of *n*-butyric acid and bulk pH change with time for the initial pH 9.5 case under oscillation hydrodynamics and various buffer capacities. The pH 6.5 cases at various buffer capacities are included.

even greater (850 microns). At intermediate carbon numbers, it is seen that the rates are strongly dependent upon the chain length and, therefore, the lipophilicity of the solute. At low carbon numbers, there is again a tendency toward plateau behaviour; however, the differences between the static rates and the oscillation rates are much smaller than at the high carbon number plateaus.

These data have been analysed by a physical model which assumes that the rate-limiting biomembrane is a two-layer barrier — an aqueous diffusion layer in series with a membrane possessing 2 parallel paths, a lipoidal pathway and an aqueous pore pathway. The model predicts a first-order disappearance of the drug in the intestinal lumen wherein the rate constant is given by

$$K_u = \frac{A}{V} \cdot \frac{P_{aq}}{1 + \dfrac{P_{aq}}{P_o + P_p}} \qquad \text{Eq. 7}$$

where

$K_u$ = rate constant, $\text{sec}^{-1}$

$A/V$ = apparent surface area to volume ratio, $\text{cm}^{-1}$

$P_{aq}, P_o, P_p$ = permeability coefficients of the aqueous boundary layer, lipid and aqueous pore pathways, respectively, cm/sec

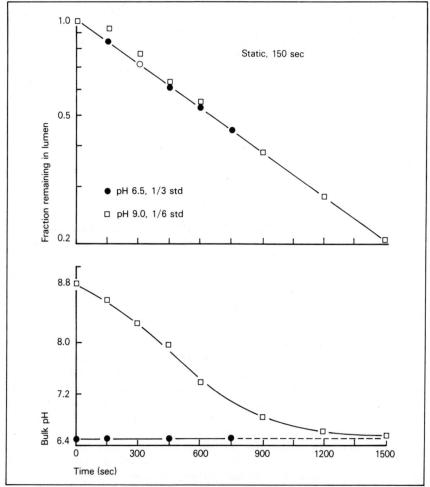

*Fig. 24.* Change in lumenal concentration of *n*-butyric acid and bulk pH change with time for the pH 6.5 and 9.0 cases under static (150sec intervals) hydrodynamics and low buffer capacities.

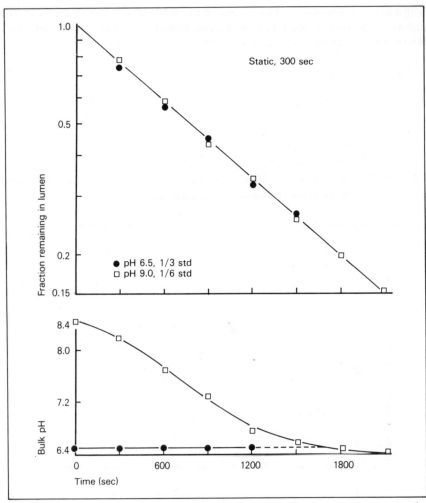

*Fig. 25.* Change in lumenal concentration of *n*-butyric acid and bulk pH change with time for the pH 6.5 and 9.0 cases under static (300sec intervals) hydrodynamics and low buffer capacities.

Hence, the membrane permeability coefficient is the sum of the permeability coefficients of the lipid pathway, $P_o$, and pore pathway, $P_p$. Only $P_o$ is assumed to depend upon the carbon number via the partition coefficient. A $\pi$ value of 0.25 (Ho et al., 1979) for a methylene group was found; the $\pi$ quantity is defined as the dimensionless free energy in the transfer of a $CH_2$ group from water into the membrane lipoidal biophase. The solid curves in figure 12 are those predicted from this theory and the agreement with the experimental data are satisfactory.

Steroid absorption studies (fig. 13) are in agreement with both the alkanol studies in the modified Doluisio system and with the steriod absorption results obtained (see fig. 9) with the flow-through perfusion system.

The homologous series of the alkanoic acids provides the opportunity to observe the simultaneous effects of polarity and solute ionisation (pH and $pK_a$ effects) on absorption. Figure 14 shows the data for 4 n-alkanoic acids at 2 flow rates as a function of pH. At high pH, the rates become relatively independent of all variables — pH, stirring rate and carbon number. At low pH there is a plateauing with decreasing pH. There is also a plateauing of the rate constant values with increasing carbon number (especially with lower flow). These results, including the rightward shifts of absorption constant *versus* lumen pH profiles with increasing carbon number and flow rate, are all in good agreement (Ho et al., 1977, 1979) with the 2-layer physical model for the biomembrane (i.e., the aqueous diffusion layer in series with a membrane with 2 parallel lipoidal and aqueous pore pathways). However, the $P_e$ expression in equation 7 had to be modified to include both dissociated and non-dissociated species. Only the non-dissociated species passes through the lipoidal pathway, whereas all species permeate the aqueous pores. Appropriately, the rate constant is:

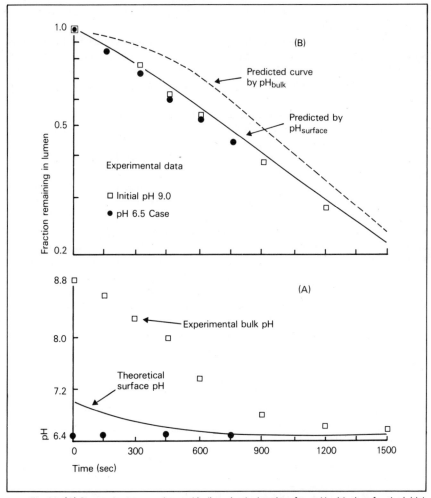

*Fig. 26.* (A) Change in the experimental bulk and calculated surface pH with time for the initial pH 9.0 case at 1/6 standard buffer capacity under static 150sec hydrodynamics. (B) Comparison of absorption profiles of *n*-butyric acid against the predictions with respect to the bulk and surface pH.

$$K_u = \frac{A}{V} \cdot \frac{P_{aq}}{1 + \dfrac{P_{aq}}{P_o X_s + P_p}} \qquad \text{Eq. 8}$$

where the fraction of non-dissociated weak acid at the membrane surface is

$$X_s = \frac{1}{1 + 10^{pH_s - pK_a}} \qquad \text{Eq. 9}$$

Here, $pH_s$ is the pH at the membrane surface and it is not necessarily the same as the bulk lumen $pH_b$. In the n-alkanoic acid studies, the buffer capacities were made deliberately large so that the bulk $pH_b$ did not change significantly during the experiment. In equation 8, the $P_p$ was assumed to be the same for both the non-dissociated and dissociated species.

Figure 15 is a plot of permeability coefficients of various solutes for the aqueous pore pathway ($P_p$). These were obtained using the Doluisio method and the model referred to above. There is a clear molecular size effect upon $P_p$. Thus, for very large molecules (for example, bile acids and steroids) the aqueous pore pathway seems to be unimportant.

We recently investigated the micelle-carrier effects in the transport of drug in the aqueous boundary layer both *in vitro* (Amidon, 1979) and *in vivo* (Ho et al., 1979). The progesterone-Tween 80 micellar system was studied in a silicone rubber membrane diffusion cell and with the modified Doluisio method. Progesterone is intrinsically a highly membrane permeable molecule.

Figures 16 and 17 show the results obtained. The flux enhancement obtained both *in vitro* and *in vivo* for saturated solutions is attributed to the micelle carrier transport of progesterone across the aqueous boundary layer and the high thermodynamic activity (free drug concentration) at the membrane surface. For unsaturated Tween 80 solutions, the rates are lower than without the solubilising agent because of the low free drug to drug-micelle concentration ratios; however, it is not as low as predicted without the carrier effect (dotted curve in figure 16). This enhancement would be expected to be most important (practically speaking) for highly lipophilic solutes of low water solubility and it probably explains the data shown in figure 18 (Wagner et al. 1966).

The intestinal absorption of micelle solubilised progesterone is consistent with the physical model predictions expressed by

$$J = \frac{1}{\dfrac{1}{P_{aq,eff}} + \dfrac{1 + k^*(SAA)}{P_o}} \cdot C_b \qquad \text{Eq. 10}$$

or

$$J = \frac{1}{\dfrac{1}{P_{aq,eff}[1 + k^*(SAA)]} + \dfrac{1}{P_o}} \cdot C_b^f \qquad \text{Eq. 11}$$

where

$J$ = total flux per unit area, mass/cm$^2$ – sec

$C_b, C_b^f$ = total and free drug concentrations, respectively, in the intestinal lumen

$k^*$ (SAA) = product of the drug-micelle equilibrium constant and surfactant concentration; equivalent to drug-micelle to free drug concentration ratio

$P_{aq,eff}$ = effective permeability coefficient of the micelle system of the aqueous boundary layer, cm/sec

$P_o$ = membrane permeability of the solute molecule, cm/sec

In turn, $P_{aq,eff}$ is related to the permeability coefficients of the micelles ($P^*_{aq}$) and the free drug ($P_{aq}$):

$$P_{aq,eff} = P^*_{aq} + \frac{P_{aq} - P^*_{aq}}{1 + k^* (SAA)} \qquad \text{Eq. 12}$$

In increasing the surfactant concentration, the micelle carriers effectively bridge the aqueous boundary layer barrier and, as can be seen, equation 11 becomes

$$J \approx P_o C_b^f \qquad \text{Eq. 13}$$

These equations and experimental findings with the micelle solubilising systems should apply in every respect to other solution systems in which the drug may exist in a complexed state or bound state in solution.

### 1.2.1 Intestinal Absorption and Microclimate pH in Modified Doluisio Systems

We have investigated the effects of changes in microclimate pH (the so-called surface pH) on the intestinal absorption of weak electrolytes. $^{14}$C-$n$-Butyric acid (pK$_a$4.9) was used at tracer concentrations as the model solution with non-absorbable buffer systems (citrates, phosphates and borates). The flow rate, bulk solution pH and buffer capacity were varied and changes in the $n$-butyric acid concentration and solution pH in the intestinal lumen with time were measured (Desai, 1976).

Figure 19 shows that the lumen pH, initially at pH 4.5 or 9.5, changes rapidly with time in low buffer capacity solutions and high stirring conditions and tends to converge eventually to pH 6.5. Solutions at pH 6.5 at all buffer strengths did not change in pH. The pK$_a$ of intestinal secretions in normal saline was found to be 6.47 which is indicative of carbonic acid (pK$_a$ 6.3). Figures 20 and 21 illustrate both the changes in lumenal concentration of $^{14}$C-$n$-butyric acid and bulk pH with time for an initial pH of 4.5 in which the buffer capacities and degree of stirring were varied. Although the bulk pH changed fairly rapidly depending upon the buffer capacity for a constant stirring condition, the semilogarithmic concentration curves are nearly linear for about 2 half-lives and then gradually depart from linearity indicating a slowing down of the absorption as the pH increases. Taken together, these data show that the absorption of $n$-butyric acid under these conditions is largely aqueous boundary layer-controlled despite the change in lumenal pH from 4.5 to 6.0 (see also fig. 14).

In figures 22 and 23 for an initial pH of 9.5, rapid changes were observed in the absorption profiles in the direction of increased absorption with decreasing lumenal pH with time. The limiting slope appears to be the same as at pH 6.5. The absorption at high pH (relative to the pK$_a$ of the weak acid) is controlled by the passage of anions across the aqueous pores; but, with decreasing pH, the absorption of non-dissociated species by the lipoidal biophase of the membrane takes on greater importance. Lastly, figures 24 and 25 give clear indications that the surface pH governs the absorption of n-butyric acid and not the bulk lumen pH. Although the lumen pH is yet quite high, the absorption curves almost immediately are the same as if the experiment was carried out at pH 6.5.

The microclimate pH at the mucosal membrane surface appears to be the result of the flux of relatively nonabsorbable buffer species from the bulk lumen to the membrane surface and the constant influx of intestinal secretion buffers (mainly bicarbonates). Rapid reactions occur at and near the membrane surface. The resulting surface pH is dynamic and changes with time. There is the concomitant flux of intestinal secretions across the aqueous boundary layer and mixing of all buffer species in the bulk lumen leading to changes in bulk pH with time, particularly, when the bulk pH is lower than or greater than pH 6.5. The rapidity in the time changes in surface and bulk pH depends upon the buffer capacity of the nonabsorbable buffers employed and the unstirred aqueous layer thickness. Here, it is assumed that the influx of secretions is constant. The equilibrium pH (i.e., $pH_{bulk} = pH_{surface}$) appears to be 6.5. While the dynamic surface pH governs the concentration ratio of non-dissociated and dissociated species, and therefore, the effective permeability of the drug across the lipoidal and aqueous pore pathways of the membrane, the overall mass transport kinetics will depend upon the relative magnitude of the diffusional rate of all drug species across the aqueous boundary layer and the effective membrane permeability rate. Accordingly, surface pH effects on intestinal absorption of weak electrolytes are significant and observable under membrane-controlled situations and not under aqueous boundary layer-controlled situations.

The mathematical description of the above physical interpretation is shown in part below [see Desai (1976) for full mathematical development]. The change in lumenal concentration with time is:

$$lnC_b = ln\, C_b\, (0) - (F(ø)t \qquad\qquad\text{Eq. 14}$$

where the rate constant, $F(ø)$, is a function of time and, for a weak acid, is expressed by

$$F(ø) = \frac{A}{V} \cdot \cfrac{1}{\cfrac{1}{P_{aq}} + \cfrac{1}{P_p + P_o\Big/\Big(1 + 10^{\,pH_s(t) - pK_a}\Big)}} \qquad\qquad\text{Eq. 15}$$

The above expression is similar to equations 8 and 9 combined except that the surface pH ($pH_s$) is a function of time. The flux of total nonabsorbable buffer species to the membrane surface is

$$J_B = P_{aq,B}\ [(TB)_b - (TB)_s]\ = O \qquad\qquad\text{Eq. 16}$$

and the flux of buffer secretions from the membrane surface to the bulk solution in the lumen is

$$J_S = P_{aq,S}\ [(TS)_s - (TS)_b] \qquad\qquad\text{Eq. 17}$$

where

J = flux per unit area

$P_{aq}$ = permeability of the aqueous boundary layer

(TB), (TS) = total nonabsorbable buffer species used (phosphate, citrate, or borate) and total secretory buffers (taken as carbonic acid and sodium bicarbonate)

b, s = subscripts denoting the bulk lumen and membrane surface locations, respectively

Without going into further mathematical details, the $pH_s(t)$ and fluxes can be calculated once the bulk $pH_b$ is known. Using the theory and experimentally determined parameters, the predicted absorption profiles of *n*-butyric acid with respect to the bulk pH and calculated surface pH can be compared with the experimentally obtained absorption profiles (fig. 26). The best agreement is seen with surface pH values.

Some *in vitro* membrane transport data is available on drug absorption from suspensions (Amidon, 1979). Studies on the perfused rat intestine are currently underway in our laboratories. It is anticipated that the longitudinal spreading $\alpha$ factor in equation 1 will be very important in many instances and a systematic investigation of the variables influencing $\alpha$ should reveal a great deal of how suspension formulations and slow release formulations may be optimised. As theory and computer simulation have advanced our understanding of the physical chemical factors influencing drug absorption, some of the familiar variation in blood level patterns caused by formulation factors can be expected to yield to systematic mechanistic analyses.

# References

Amidon, G.E.: Rotating membrane diffusion studies of micellar and suspension systems. Thesis, The University of Michigan, Ann Arbor (1979).

Borgstrom, B.; Dahlqvist, A.; Lundh, G. and Sjovall, J.: Studies of intestinal digestion and absorption in the human. Journal of Clinical Investigation 36: 1521-1536 (1957).

Desai, K.J.: Biophysical model approach to the study of intestinal transport of drugs. Thesis, The University of Michigan, Ann Arbor (1976).

Ho, N.F.H.; Park, J.Y.; Morozowich, W. and Higuchi, W.I.: Physical model approach to the design of drugs with improved intestinal absorption; in Roche (Ed) Design of Biopharmaceutical Properties Through Prodrugs and Analogs, p.136-227 (American Pharmaceutical Association, Academy of Pharmaceutical Sciences, Washington, D.C. 1977).

Ho, N.F.H.; Park, J.Y.; Amidon, G.E.; Ni, P.F. and Higuchi, W.I.: Methods for interrelating *in vitro*, animal and human studies: in Aguiar (Ed) Gastrointestinal Absorption of Drugs (American Pharmaceutical Association, Academy of Pharmaceutical Sciences, Washington, D.C. 1979).

Komiya, I.; Park, J.Y.; Kamani, A.; Ho, N.F.H. and Higuchi, W.I.: Physical model studies on the simultaneous fluid flow and absorption of steroids in the rat intestines. International Journal of Pharmaceutics (in press).

Levich, V.G.: Physicochemical Hydrodynamics, p.112-116 (Prentice-Hall, Inc., Englewood Cliffs, N.J. 1962).

Ni, P.F.; Ho, N.F.H.; Fox, J.L.; Leuenberger, H. and Higuchi, W.I.: Theoretical model studies of intestinal drug absorption V: nonsteady-state fluid flow and absorption. International Journal of Pharmaceutics (in press 1979a).

Ni, P.F.; Ho, N.F.H.; Leuenberger, H.; Fox, J.L. and Higuchi, W.I.: Relating gastrointestinal absorption and blood levels by the physical model approach. International Journal of Pharmaceutics (in press 1979b).

Read, N.W.; Barber, D.C.; Levin, R.J. and Holdsworth, C.D.: Unstirred layer and kinetics of electrogenic glucose absorption in the human jejunum *in situ*. Gut 18: 865-876 (1977).

Soergel, K.H.: Flow measurements of test meals and fasting contents in human small intestine; in Demling (Ed) Proceedings of the International Symposium on Motility of the Gastrointestinal Tract, p.81-96 (Georg Thieme Verlag, Stuttgart, 1971).

Wagner, J.G.; Gerard, E.S. and Kaiser, D.G.: The effect of dosage form on serum levels of indoxole. Clinical Pharmacology and Therapeutics 7: 610-619 (1966).

Winne, D.: Unstirred layer thickness in perfused rat jejunum *in vivo*. Experientia 32: 1278-1279 (1976).

Winne, D.: Rat jejunum perfused *in situ*: effect of perfusion rate and intraluminal perfusion rate and intraluminal radius on absorption rate and effective unstirred layer thickness. Naunyn-Schmiedeberg's Archives of Pharmacology 307: 265-274 (1979).

## Discussion

*S. Riegelman* (San Francisco): Motion pictures have been taken of the movement of radio-opaque objects in the intestinal tract and there is clearly peristaltic movement back and forth. It is not a linear flow although the net movement is downward. Could you comment on the relationship of ciliary movement at the brush border and the unstirred layer.

*W.I. Higuchi*: I agree that there is considerable back and forth movement but the spreading caused by this peristalsis would still be small, 10% or so of the length of the intestine. On the second point, the experiments were done with anaesthetised animals and so movement of the villae might have been altered. The unstirred layer that we measured is consistent with values obtained under more normal conditions.

# 6

# Rectal Absorption: Portal or Systemic?

*A.G. de Boer and D.D. Breimer*

Department of Pharmacology, Subfaculty of Pharmacy, University of Leiden

The rectal route of drug administration is quite frequently used in some European countries, whereas it is not very commonly used in the USA and others. For instance, in France in 1970, 7.5 % of all prescriptions involved preparations for rectal administration, whereas some years earlier this was only 1.1 % in the USA (Samuels Brusse et al., 1979). In principle the rectal route is a good alternative when there are difficulties with oral or other routes of drug administration, e.g. in infants, children and sick or vomiting patients. Obviously one has to make sure that drugs given rectally are indeed effective, and in this respect the dosage form is a crucial factor. Recently several critical aspects of rectal absorption and rectal dosage forms have been reviewed (De Blaey and Polderman, 1980) and biopharmaceutical factors pertaining to rectal drug administration in man have been extensively investigated (Moolenaar, 1979).

## 1. First-pass Metabolism

An interesting aspect of rectal absorption is the frequently encountered speculation that drugs will enter the general circulation without first passing through the liver. This assumption is based on the venous drainage of the rectum (fig. 1). When the drug is absorbed in the lower parts of the rectum, it may enter the lower and middle rectal (haemorrhoidal) veins, finally passing into the inferior vena cava, thereby bypassing the portal system and the liver. A drug absorbed from the upper parts of the rectum will probably be transported via the upper rectal (haemorrhoidal) veins into the portal system and will pass through the liver before entering the systemic circulation. This fraction is thereby subject to first-pass elimination in the liver. However, this anatomical situation is complicated by anastomoses between the rectal veins (fig. 1), so that a drug absorbed in the lower parts of the rectum can still enter the upper rectal veins and subsequently pass through the liver. Obviously the reverse may also be possible. Theoretically, high-clearance drugs should show a higher systemic availability following rectal compared to oral administration.

Experimental evidence concerning bypass of the liver after rectal administration in humans is scarce. Recently human experiments showed decreased systemic

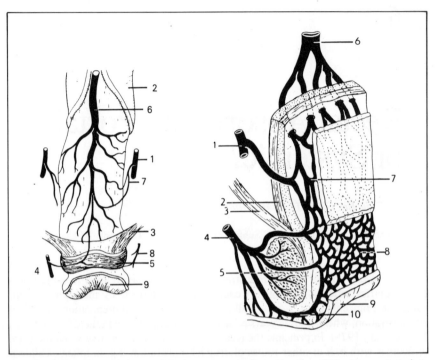

*Fig. 1.* The venous drainage of the human rectum (from Tondury, 1959 with permission). 1. Middle rectal vein. 2. Tunica muscularis: stratum longitudinale. 3. Levator ani. 4. Inferior rectal vein. 5. External anal sphincter. 6. Superior rectal vein. 7 and 8. Submucous venous plexus. 9. Skin. 10. Marginal vein and subcutaneous plexus.

availability of paracetamol (acetaminophen) following rectal compared to oral administration (Moolenaar et al., 1979) and Jonkman et al. (1979) found a similar degree of first-pass metabolism of thiazinamium methylsulphate orally and rectally. In the present investigation 3 high-clearance drugs — salicylamide, lignocaine (lidocaine) and propranolol — were administered orally and rectally to humans in order to determine the systemic availability via both routes. The latter 2 compounds were also given intravenously to determine the absolute systemic availability.

Rats do not have an anatomically well-defined rectum, and experimental evidence is lacking concerning bypass of the liver after rectal administration. Therefore salicylamide, lignocaine and propranolol were also administered orally and rectally to rats.

## 2. Methods

### 2.1 Healthy Volunteers

*Lignocaine hydrochloride* was given to 6 healthy males intravenously, orally and rectally in a balanced crossover design with at least 1 week between each study. Intravenous lignocaine was given by constant rate infusion (200mg in 60 minutes), the oral drug as 300mg in 2 gelatin capsules with 150ml tap water, and rectal drug as

300mg as an aqueous solution (5ml) by syringe. In the same panel of volunteers the oral and rectal experiments were repeated 6 months later.

*Propranolol hydrochloride* was given to 5 healthy males intravenously, orally and rectally in a balanced crossover design with at least 1 week between each study. Intravenous administration was by constant rate infusion (10mg in 60 minutes), the oral dose (80mg) was dissolved in 150ml tap water and the rectal dose (80mg) given as an aqueous solution (5ml) by syringe.

*Salicylamide sodium* was given to 6 healthy volunteers orally and rectally in a balanced crossover design with at least 1 week between each study. 500 and 1500mg doses were given orally in aqueous solution (150ml). Rectally, 500mg was given to 3 subjects as an aqueous solution (5ml; pH 10.5) and to 3 as a suspension (5ml; pH 7.0). In addition 1.5g was given rectally in aqueous solution to each volunteer (10ml; pH 10.5) by syringe.

## 2.2 Animal Studies

The same 3 drugs were used for experiments in male Wistar rats:
Lignocaine: 20mg orally and rectally; 5mg intra-arterially
Propranolol: 2.0mg orally, rectally and intra-arterially
Salicylamide: 30mg orally, rectally and intra-arterially.

The drugs were given intra-arterially through a cannula in the common carotid artery and oral solutions were given through a stomach tube. Aqueous solutions of the drugs were administered rectally through a septum (to prevent leakage) which was kept in the anus by a subcutaneous ligature. Generally the oral and rectal experiments were performed in one and the same animal, whereas for the intra-arterial experiments different animals were used.

## 2.3 Sampling and Drug Assay

Blood was sampled at regular intervals and in rats was obtained from a cannula in the jugular vein.

Lignocaine, propranolol and salicylamide were measured by gas chromatography, using solid injection and nitrogen selective detection (De Boer, 1979; De Boer et al., 1979a).

## 3. Results

### 3.1 Lignocaine in Healthy Volunteers

In figure 2 the plasma concentration curves of lignocaine for the 3 routes of administration are shown for 1 subject. The concentrations following rectal administration were substantially higher than after oral administration and in each subject the rank order of the area under the concentration curves (AUC) was intravenous > rectal > oral. The mean rectal systemic availability (defined as $AUC_{rectal}/AUC_{iv}$ corrected for dose) was 71%, versus 34% for the oral route. The elimination half-lives were the same for the intravenous and oral studies (90 min), and slightly longer after rectal administration (101 min). An equation can be derived for the calculation of the

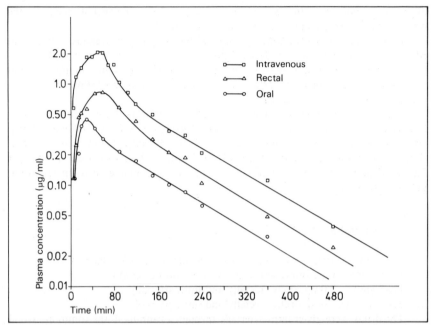

*Fig. 2.* Plasma concentration of lignocaine following intravenous (200mg), rectal (300mg), and oral (300mg) administration in a healthy volunteer.

fraction of the dose $f_{nh}$ given rectally that bypasses the liver after absorption (De Boer et al., 1979b):

$$f_{nh} = \frac{F_{rect} - F_{or}}{1 - F_{or}}$$

where $F_{rect}$ is the rectal systemic availability and $F_{or}$ is the oral systemic availability. An important assumption for the validity of this equation is that absorption via both routes is complete. This fraction was on the average just over half of the dose administered.

About 6 months after the first series of experiments with lignocaine, the oral and rectal investigations were repeated in the same panel of volunteers. The mean rectal systemic availability was now 67% versus 27% orally. In table I the fraction of the dose administered rectally that bypassed the liver on the 2 occasions is compared for each volunteer. There is good agreement between the data for each subject, but there are large differences between individuals. In any case the phenomenon of hepatic bypass of rectally administered lignocaine is quite reproducible (De Boer et al., 1979b).

Lignocaine was also administered rectally (300mg) in a fatty suppository and in slow releasing granules (De Boer et al., 1979c). The results obtained in 1 subject are shown in figure 3 and the sustained release pattern of both dosage forms is clearly demonstrated. The mean rectal systemic availability of the 2 preparations was not significantly different (49% for the suppository and 54% for the granules). These

*Table I*. The fraction of the administered dose of lignocaine which bypassed the liver after rectal absorption ($f_{nh}$) in 6 healthy volunteers; the results of 2 experiments, 6 months apart

| Subject | First experiment | Second experiment |
|---------|------------------|-------------------|
| | $f_{nh}$ (%) | $f_{nh}$ (%) |
| F.G. | 51 | 65 |
| J.O. | 75 | 85 |
| T.D. | 57 | 23 |
| T.W. | 21 | 24 |
| G.M. | > 100 | 92 |
| E.R. | 35 | 30 |
| Mean (%) | 57 | 53 |
| SD | 28 | 31 |

values are lower and more variable than those obtained with a rectal solution of lignocaine.

### 3.2 Lignocaine in Rats

The concentrations obtained by the rectal route were much higher than those achieved orally (fig. 4). The mean rectal systemic availability (with reference to intra-arterial administration) was 105% and the mean oral systemic availability was only 8%. In other words bypass of the liver of rectally administered lignocaine in rats is practically complete (De Boer et al., 1979d).

### 3.3 Propranolol in Healthy Volunteers

In figure 5 the plasma concentration curves of propranolol for the 3 routes of administration are shown for 1 subject. In this subject almost equal concentrations were obtained orally and rectally, although the rectal area under the curve was slightly greater. In 2 other subjects the concentrations achieved by the rectal route were lower and in the remaining 2 subjects substantially higher than achieved by the oral route. There was no significant difference between the mean values of the AUC ratios for the 2 routes of administration (33% orally and 40% rectally) [table II]. The mean elimination half-lives after oral, rectal and intravenous administration were similar (182, 198 and 181 minutes respectively).

Overall, these results do not clearly support the hypothesis of partial bypass of the liver with rectal absorption. It is possible that rectal absorption of propranolol is variable, whereas it is assumed to be complete when given orally (Paterson et al., 1970). It is difficult to obtain exact quantitative information on the extent of absorption if the drug is not given in radioactively-labelled form.

### 3.4 Propranolol in Rats

In figure 6 the results obtained after oral and rectal administration of 2.0mg propranolol to 1 rat are shown. As with lignocaine, the concentrations achieved by

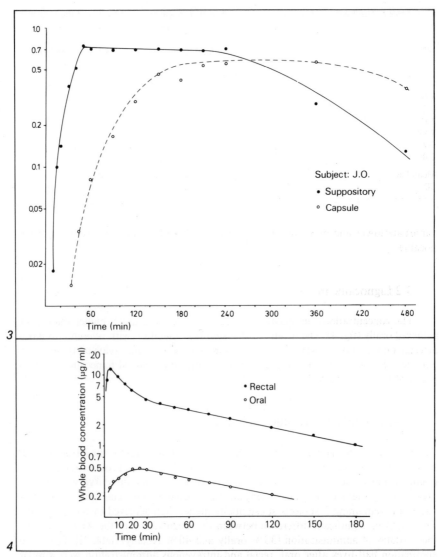

*Fig. 3.* Plasma concentration of lignocaine following rectal administration of a suppository and a capsule containing slow releasing granules with 300mg lignocaine as lignocaine hydrochloride.

*Fig. 4.* Whole blood concentration of lignocaine following oral and rectal administration (20mg) to the same rat.

the rectal route are much higher than those obtained orally. The mean rectal systemic availability (with reference to intra-arterial administration) was 101 % and the mean oral systemic availability was only 3 %, so bypass of the liver by rectally administered propranolol in rats is also practically complete. Further experiments revealed a linear relationship between AUC and dose after intra-arterial administration (dose range 0.5-2.0mg), whereas this relationship was non-linear for the rectal route (De Boer, 1979).

*Table II.* Systemic availability of propranolol following oral (or) and rectal (rect) administration of 80mg, and intravenous (iv) administration of 10mg (corrected for the difference in dose) [De Boer, 1979]

| Subjects | Propranolol availability % | | |
|----------|-------------------------------|------------------------|------------------------|
|          | $AUC^1_{or}/AUC_{iv}$ | $AUC_{rect}/AUC_{iv}$ | $AUC_{rect}/AUC_{or}$ |
| J.P.     | 13 | 43 | 325 |
| G.E.     | 36 | 26 | 74 |
| P.B.     | 28 | 54 | 191 |
| P.J.     | 57 | 37 | 65 |
| T.S.     | 29 | 42 | 144 |
| Mean     | 33 | 40 | 160 |
| SD       | 16 | 10 | 106 |

1  AUC = area under the curve.

## 3.5 Salicylamide in Healthy Volunteers

In figure 7 an example is shown of the plasma concentration curves obtained with 1.5g salicylamide in 1 subject. Contrary to the results with lignocaine and propranolol, the concentrations after rectal administration were not much lower than those obtained orally. At first a dose of 500mg salicylamide was given orally and rectally. However, the oral AUC was very low and after rectal administration salicylamide concentrations were measurable in only 1 subject. Increasing the dose to 1.5g increased the mean AUC after oral administration by a factor 34.9. The AUC after rectal administration was only 12.5% of the oral value. The mean urinary excretion of salicylamide conjugates (sulphate + glucuronide) was 82% of the oral dose and 76% of the rectal dose, which indicates comparable absorption by the two routes (De Boer, 1979). These results do not support partial bypass of the liver when this drug is given rectally, although oral salicylamide is probably extensively metabolised by conjugation in the gut wall. To what extent rectal wall metabolism plays a role in the biotransformation of salicylamide is not known.

## 3.6 Salicylamide in Rats

In figure 8 the blood concentration curves of salicylamide obtained in 1 rat following intra-arterial, rectal and oral administration are shown. The concentrations after rectal administration were considerably higher than those following oral administration, but lower than those obtained by the intra-arterial route. The mean values of the ratio $AUC_{oral}/AUC_{ia}$ and of $AUC_{rectal}/AUC_{ia}$ in 6 rats were 0.10 and 0.52 respectively. Since the time course of the concentration curves (fig. 8) suggests non-linear kinetics of salicylamide, systemic availability was also evaluated by a non-linear method. As expected the calculated absolute values of oral and rectal availability increased considerably with this method, but the ratio $AUC_{rectal}/AUC_{oral}$ remained almost unchanged. The mean rectal and oral availability was 75% and 15% respectively (De Boer, 1979). So for salicylamide considerably less drug was lost by first-pass metabolism following rectal administration, compared to the oral route.

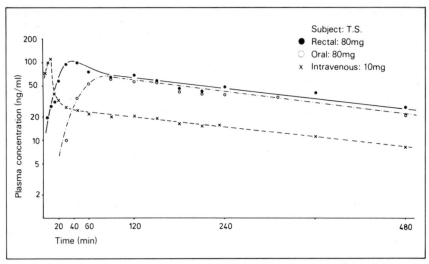

*Fig. 5.* Propranolol plasma concentrations following rectal, oral and intravenous administration
to 1 subject, showing fast rectal absorption and almost identical concentrations after oral and rectal
administration.

## 4. Discussion

These studies provide preliminary data on the systemic availability of 3 high-
clearance drugs following rectal administration to humans and rats. All 3 compounds
undergo substantial first-pass metabolism on oral administration to man (lignocaine:
Boyes et al., 1971; propranolol: Shand and Rangno, 1972; salicylamide: Fleckenstein
et al., 1976). The oral bioavailability of these drugs in the present studies was roughly
in agreement with that found by the cited investigators.

These compounds also show a considerable first-pass effect when administered
orally to rats (lignocaine: Shand et al., 1972, 1975; Nyberg et al., 1977; propranolol:
Suzuki et al., 1974; salicylamide: Barr and Riegelman, 1970).

Hepatic metabolism probably plays a major role in the first-pass removal of lignocaine and propranolol, whereas with salicylamide, gut wall metabolism is also of
importance.

In theory data on the systemic availability of a drug following 2 routes of administration should provide quantitative information on the difference in the extent
of first-pass metabolism by the 2 routes, provided that absorption is equal on both occasions. This prerequisite was not met in the present investigation with lignocaine
and propranolol since urinary excretion of unchanged drug and total metabolites was
not measured. However, the literature cited indicates nearly complete absorption of
oral lignocaine and propranolol in man. If rectal absorption were incomplete, the
relatively high systemic availability compared to oral administration indicates even
less first-pass metabolism by the rectal route.

The experiments with lignocaine in man have proved that the rectal route offers
in principle the possibility of partial bypass of the liver. The extent to which this occurred was on average slightly more than 50% and quite reproducible for each subject. On anatomical grounds (fig. 1) this bypass is unlikely to reach 100%, because if
the rectal drug solution is spread homogeneously over the entire rectum, part of the

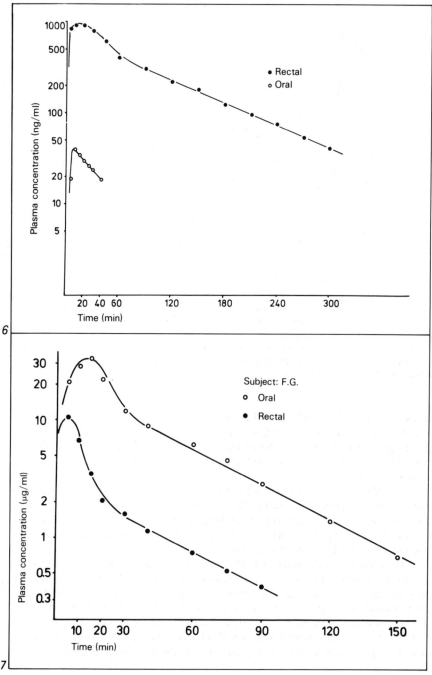

*Fig. 6.* Propranolol plasma concentrations after oral and rectal administration of 2.0mg to the same rat.

*Fig. 7.* Plasma concentrations following oral and rectal administration of 1.5g salicylamide to 1 subject.

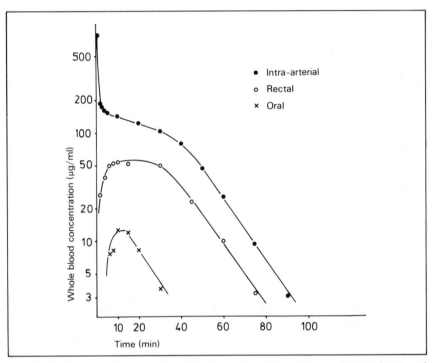

*Fig. 8.* Whole blood concentrations following oral, rectal and intra-arterial administration of 30mg salicylamide to the same rat.

absorbed drug will certainly reach the superior rectal vein and pass into the liver. The variable results with propranolol may be due to less favourable circumstances for complete absorption from the rectum than for lignocaine. It is also possible that for some reason propranolol is absorbed to a greater extent in the upper part of the rectum in some subjects.

The relatively low systemic availability of rectal compared to oral salicylamide in the volunteers is difficult to explain. Gut wall metabolism plays an important role in its oral first-pass elimination and, in addition, the results are not simple to evaluate quantitatively owing to non-linear kinetics. The drug-metabolising capacity of rectal mucosa and microflora requires further investigation.

The results obtained in rats with the 3 model compounds quite clearly demonstrate that with rectal administration a large, or almost complete, fraction of the dose enters directly into the systemic circulation. Apparently the vascularisation of the terminal part of the rat gastrointestinal tract is such that the majority of the rectal veins are not connected with the portal system, but pass directly into the general circulation. The results obtained with salicylamide also suggest the lower part of the gastrointestinal tract has low metabolising capacity compared to the upper part.

## 5. Conclusions

Rectal absorption: portal or systemic? In rats the rectal route is almost entirely systemic. In humans the rectal route is only partially systemic (lignocaine) and the extent to which first-pass metabolism is avoided is probably dependent on the drug, the dosage form, the site of absorption in the rectum and the subject (probably there are large inter-individual differences with regard to venous drainage of the rectum). It certainly cannot be generally concluded that high-clearance drugs will show higher systemic availability when administered rectally, but in principle this possibility does exist. The question as to which are the most critical factors in this respect has to await further investigation.

# References

Barr, W.H. and Riegelman, S.: Intestinal drug absorption and metabolism. II. Kinetic aspects of intestinal glucuronide conjugation. Journal of Pharmaceutical Sciences 59: 164-168 (1970).

Boyes, R.N.; Scott, D.B.; Jebson, P.J.; Godman, M.J. and Julian, D.G.: Pharmacokinetics of lidocaine in man. Clinical Pharmacology and Therapeutics 12: 105-116 (1971).

De Blaey, C.J. and Polderman, J.: Rationales in the design of vaginal and rectal delivery forms of drugs; in Ariens (Ed) Drug Design, Vol. 9, p.238-266 (Academic Press, New York 1980).

De Boer, A.G.: 'First-pass' elimination of some high-clearance drugs following rectal administration to humans and rats. Ph.D thesis, University of Leiden, 1979.

De Boer, A.G.; Breimer, D.D.; Gubbens-Stibbe, J.M.; de Koning, G.H.P. and Bosma, A.: Assay of un-derivatized salicylamide in human plasma, saliva and urine. Journal of Chromatography 162: 457-460 (1979a).

De Boer, A.G.; Breimer, D.D.; Mattie, H.; Pronk, J. and Gubbens-Stibbe, J.M.: Rectal bioavailability of lidocaine in man: partial avoidance of 'first-pass' metabolism. Clinical Pharmacology and Thera-peutics. 26: 701-709 (1979b).

De Boer, A.G.; Breimer, D.D. and Mattie, H.: Rectal bioavailability of lidocaine from a suppository and a slow release preparation in man. Pharmaceutisch Weekblad, Scientific Edition 1: 128-132 (1979c).

De Boer, A.G.; Breimer, D.D.; Pronk, J. and Gubbens-Stibbe, J.M.: Rectal bioavailability of lidocaine in rats: almost complete avoidance of 'first-pass' elimination. Journal of Pharmaceutical Sciences, in press (1979d).

Fleckenstein, L.; Mundy, G.R.; Horovitz, R.A. and Mazullo, J.M.: Sodium salicylamide: relative bioavailability and subjective effects. Clinical Pharmacology and Therapeutics 19: 451-458 (1976).

Jonkman, J.H.G.; van Bork, L.E.; Wijsbeek, J.; Bolhuis-de Vries, A.S.; de Zeeuw, R.A.; Orie, N.G.M. and Cox, H.L.M.: First-pass effect after rectal administration of thiazinamium methylsulphate. Journal of Pharmaceutical Sciences 68: 69-72 (1979).

Moolenaar, F.: Biopharmaceutics of rectal administration of drugs in man. Ph.D. thesis, University of Groningen, 1979.

Moolenaar, F.; Olthof, L. and Huizinga, T.: Biopharmaceutics of rectal administration of drugs in man. 3. Absorption rate and bioavailability of paracetamol from rectal aqueous suspensions. Pharmaceu-tisch Weekblad, Scientific Edition 1: 25-30 (1979).

Nyberg, G.; Karlen, B.; Hedlund, I.; Grundin, R. and von Bahr, C.: Extraction and metabolism of lido-caine in rat liver. Acta Pharmacologica Toxicologica 40: 337-346 (1977).

Paterson, J.W.; Conolly, M.E.; Dollery, C.T.; Hayes, A. and Cooper, R.G.: The pharmacodynamics and metabolism of propranolol in man. Pharmacologia Clinica 2: 127-133 (1970).

Samuels Brusse, F.; Bertens, A.M. and Breimer, D.D.: Het extramurale geneesmiddelengebruik door ziekenfondsverzekerden in de regio Nijmegen 1974/1975. Pharmaceutisch Weekblad 114: 385-403 (1979).

Shand, D.G. and Rangno, R.E.: The disposition of propranolol. I. Elimination during oral absorption in man. Pharmacology 7: 159-168 (1972).

Shand, D.G.; Kornhauser, D.M. and Wilkinson, G.R.: Effects of route of administration and blood flow on hepatic drug elimination. Journal of Pharmacology and Experimental Therapeutics 195: 424-432 (1975).

Shand, D.G.; Rangno, E. and Evans, G.H.: The disposition of propranolol. II. Hepatic elimination in the rat. Pharmacology 8: 344-352 (1972).

Suzuki, T.; Isozaki, S.; Ishida, R.; Saitoh, Y. and Nakagawa, T.: Drug absorption and metabolism studies by use of portal vein infusion in the rat. II. Influence of dose and infusion rate on the bioavailability of propranolol. Chemical and Pharmaceutical Bulletin 22: 1639-1645 (1974).

Tondury, G.: Angewandte und Topographische Anatomie, p.200 (Georg Thieme Verlag, Stuttgart 1959).

## Discussion

*S. Riegelman* (San Fransisco): How can you be sure that the drug remains in the lower segment of the rectum? Your data on lignocaine make me wonder whether it might have spread into the caecum. I suspect that liquid would move over a larger area than with your solid dosage form.

*D.D. Breimer*: You may be right. We would have to use dosage forms which keep the drug from spreading to answer your question.

*H.S. Fraser* (Barbados): The rectal route is reputed to be unacceptable in the UK but is this in the minds of physicians or of patients? Has a formal trial of acceptability ever been done in the UK?

*P. Johnson* (Milton Keynes): Perhaps more relevant is whether a trial of acceptability has ever been done on the Continent! Is there any evidence for the metabolism of drugs given rectally by the enzymes of the gut microflora?

*D.D. Breimer*: As far as I know, this has not been looked into properly.

*P. Goldman* (Boston): It is possible for drugs administered rectally to be metabolised by gut flora and there is a rather interesting example of this. It involves the compound laetrile which was given to a youngster for several months without incident. Then because of vomiting, it was given rectally in the same dose and proved to be lethal because cyanide was released from amygdalin as a result of the action of gut flora. Cyanide is not released in germ-free rats.

# 7

# Drug Metabolism by Intestinal Mucosa

*D.S. Davies, K.F. Ilett and C.F. George*

Royal Postgraduate Medical School, University of London and University of Southampton Medical School

The ability to eliminate potentially harmful substances from the body by metabolism represents an important defence mechanism and the intestine is the first barrier against ingested drugs and chemicals.

The drug metabolising enzymes normally associated with hepatic tissue have all been found in the intestinal mucosa of laboratory animals and man (Hartiala, 1973). Thus the a-synthetic reactions (oxidations, reductions and hydrolyses) as well as the conjugation reactions normally associated with detoxication are all catalysed by gut enzymes (table I).

In general, the specific activities of the various enzymes of drug metabolism are considerably lower in gut than hepatic tissue and this is particularly true of cytochrome P-450-dependent enzymes. Chhabra et al. (1974), found that in animals, the concentration of cytochrome P-450 in the intestine was never more than 35 % of the liver value and as low as 4 % in the mouse (table II). Benzpyrene hydroxylase activity in the intestine of most species was only a fraction of that in the liver (table III). However, pretreatment of animals with enzyme inducers can produce dramatic increases in the activities of cytochrome P-450-dependent enzymes in intestinal mucosa. Stohs et al. (1976) found that pretreatment of rats for 1 day with methylcholanthrene produced a 30-fold increase in benzpyrene hydroxylase and a 19-fold increase in ethoxycoumarin de-ethylase (table IV). Pretreatment with phenobarbitone for 3 days induced only a modest increase. Thus even if cytochrome P-450-dependent enzymes do not normally contribute significantly to the oxidation of ingested substances they may well do following the administration of inducers.

It is extremely difficult to extrapolate from enzyme activities measured *in vitro* to the quantitative importance of the gut wall in the metabolism of drugs and chemicals. In addition it is worth emphasising that extensive metabolism during the first-pass through the intestinal wall may not always be advantageous as it may render ineffective an otherwise useful drug (Dollery et al., 1971; Routledge and Shand, 1979).

Quantitative data on the role of the intestinal mucosa in the metabolism of drugs and chemicals are scarce. Curry et al. (1971) showed that more than 50 % of chlorpromazine was metabolised in the intestinal wall of the rat during absorption and suggested that this might account for the poor oral bioavailability of this drug in

*Table I.* Drug metabolising enzymes of the intestinal mucosa

Cytochrome P-450-dependent enzymes
Alcohol dehydrogenase
Monoamine oxidases (A and B)
Dopa decarboxylase
Reductases
Esterases and Amidases

Glucuronyl transferases
Sulphokinases
Methyl transferases
Acetylase
Amino acid conjugases

*Table II.* Cytochrome P-450 content in liver and intestine (Chhabra et al., 1974)

| Species | Cytochrome P-450 | | |
|---|---|---|---|
| | liver nmol/mg | intestine nmol/mg | $\dfrac{\text{intestine}}{\text{liver}} \times 100$ |
| Rabbit | 1.1 | 0.4 | 35 |
| Guinea Pig | 1.5 | 0.2 | 12 |
| Mouse | 1.1 | 0.04 | 4 |
| Hamster | 1.3 | 0.2 | 13 |

*Table III.* Benzpyrene hydroxylase activity in liver and intestine (Chhabra et al. 1974)

| Species | Benzpyrene hydroxylase activity | | |
|---|---|---|---|
| | liver | intestine | $\dfrac{\text{intestine}}{\text{liver}} \times 100$ |
| Rabbit | 2775 | 835 | 30 |
| Guinea pig | 995 | 372 | 37 |
| Rat | 3009 | 138 | 5 |
| Mouse | 1705 | 101 | 6 |
| Hamster | 579 | 33 | 6 |

*Table IV*. Effects of inducers on drug metabolising enzymes from rat intestinal mucosa (Stohs et al., 1976)

| Pretreatment | Enzyme activity (pmol/mg/min) | |
|---|---|---|
| | benzpyrene | ethoxycoumarin |
| Control | 83 | 108 |
| Methylcholanthrene (1 day) | 2425 | 1911 |
| Phenobarbitone (3 days) | 100 | 196 |

*Table V*. Pattern of metabolism of isoprenaline in isolated loops of dog gut (George et al., 1974)

| | Drug absorbed (%) | Free isopren- aline | Radioactivity in venous effluent (%) as: | | | |
|---|---|---|---|---|---|---|
| | | | free 3-OMI[1] | sulphate conjugate of iso- prenaline | sulphate conjugate of 3-OMI[1] | total metabolites |
| Saline | 2.9 | 5.0 | 20.0 | 75.0 | 0 | 95.0 |
| washed | 1.3 | 1.6 | 19.5 | 60.9 | 7.2 | 87.6 |
| | - | 4.3 | - | - | - | 95.5 |
| Mean | 2.10 ± 0.80 | 3.6 ± 1.0 | 19.8 ± 0.25 | 68.0 ± 7.0 | 3.6 ± 3.3 | 92.7 ± 2.6 |
| Salicylamide | 0.4 | 79.0 | 21.1 | 0 | 0 | 21.1 |
| pretreated | 1.0 | 74.2 | 26.5 | 0 | 0 | 26.5 |
| | 0.8 | 68.0 | 18.0 | 10.0 | 0 | 28.0 |
| Mean | 0.73 ± 0.18 | 73.7 ± 3.2 | 21.9 ± 2.5 | 3.3 ± 3.3 | 0 ± 0 | 25.2 ± 2.1 |
| Difference | | $p < 0.001$ | NS | $p < 0.01$ | NS | $p < 0.001$ |

1   3-OMI = 3-*O*-methylisoprenaline.

*Table VI*. Deamination of tyramine in isolated loops of dog gut

| Pretreatment[1] | Radioactivity in venous effluent (%) as: | |
|---|---|---|
| | tyramine | *p*-hydroxyphenyl acetic acid |
| None | 15.6 | 78.0 |
| Tranylcypromine (iv 3h) | 86.3 | 11.2 |
| Tranylcypromine (po 3h) | 58.1 | 34.8 |
| Tranylcypromine (po 24 h) | 38.0 | 57.0 |
| MD780515 (iv 3h) | 75.2 | 21.8 |
| MD780515 (po 3h) | 46.3 | 49.9 |
| MD780515 (po 24h) | 12.3 | 79.7 |

1   Tranylcypromine 11.8 μmol per kg or MD780515 5.9 μmol per kg once daily for 3 days; studies conducted 3 or 24h after last dose.

man. More recently Lasker and Rickert (1978) have shown that the intestine is an important site for the metabolism of diethylstilboestrol and Rance and Shillingford (1976) have found similar results for the metabolism of strong analgesics. The metabolism of orally administered phenol, formerly thought to occur predominantly in the liver, was shown by Powell and her colleagues (1974) to take place in the intestine.

We have established the importance of first-pass conjugation by the gut wall in limiting the oral bioavailability of a number of adrenaline-like bronchodilator drugs in dog and man. In the dog, using a loop of intestine isolated *in situ* we have been able to measure the quantitative importance of gut wall conjugation for these drugs (George et al., 1974). More recently we have used a similar experimental procedure to assess the quantitative importance of gut wall monoamine oxidase (MAO) in the metabolism of orally administered tyramine. The influence of irreversible and reversible inhibitors of MAO on gut wall metabolism of tyramine has also been studied.

# 1. Methods

## 1.1 Preparation of Animals

Dogs of either sex weighing from 16.9 to 27.3kg were anaesthetised with intravenous thiopentone sodium (25mg per kg) and pentobarbitone (25mg per kg). Each dog received intravenous phenoxybenzamine (100mg) before surgery to reduce inhibition of gastrointestinal motility. The abdomen was opened through a mid-line incision, a loop of terminal duodenum and proximal jejunum approximately 12cm in length was isolated between 2 balloon catheters and venous blood was collected from the loop as previously described (George et al., 1974).

Following irrigation with saline $^3$H-isoprenaline or $^{14}$C-tyramine was injected into the lumen of the gut loop in 10ml of saline. Isolation of the loop was checked by comparing radioactivity in the venous effluent and samples taken from the abdominal aorta. For studies of the effects of monoamine oxidase inhibitors (MAOI) on the metabolism of tyramine dogs were pretreated with 11.8μmol per kg tranylcypromine or 5.9μmol per kg MD780515 given once daily for 3 days. Both drugs were given orally in gelatin capsules or intravenously as a slow infusion over 1.5 hours. Metabolism of tyramine in the gut loop preparation was measured 3 or 24h after the third and final dose of MAOI.

## 1.2 Chemical Analysis

Total radioactivity was determined in 1ml aliquots of plasma in a Packard liquid scintillation spectrometer using Instagel scintillation fluid.

Quantitative measurements of isoprenaline, 3-$0$-methylisoprenaline and conjugated isoprenaline were made as described by Conolly et al. (1972).

Tyramine and its principle metabolite p-hydroxyphenylacetic acid (p-OHPA) were separated by high pressure liquid chromatography and quantified by liquid scintillation counting (Ilett et al., unpublished data). In all studies, tyramine together with p-OHPA accounted for more than 92% of the total radioactivity in plasma indicating the absence of any other important metabolite.

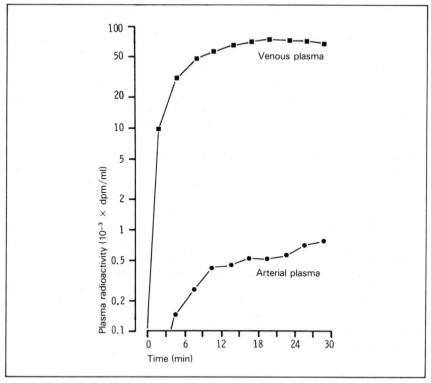

*Fig. 1.* Total radioactivity in arterial plasma or venous plasma from an isolated loop of dog gut following intraluminal administration of 50mg (50 μCi) of ¹⁴C-tyramine.


## 2. Results and Discussion

In the studies with isoprenaline and tyramine the total radioactivity in the venous effluent exceeded the activity in aortic plasma by almost 2 orders of magnitude, thus demonstrating isolation of the gut loop. Results of a typical experiment from the tyramine studies are shown in figure 1.

In dog and man the metabolism of isoprenaline depends on the route of administration (Conolly et al., 1972). Following intravenous dosing in dog and man, isoprenaline is either excreted unchanged or O-methylated; little or no conjugation of the parent drug occurs. In contrast, after an oral dose the drug is largely conjugated with sulphate and this is the dominant metabolite in plasma and urine. Intra-portal infusions of isoprenaline in dogs suggested that the site of first-pass conjugation was not the liver but the intestine.

This was confirmed by George et al., (1974) using the isolated loop of dog gut. Isoprenaline placed in the lumen of the gut loop appeared in the venous effluent largely as the sulphate conjugate (68%) with only 3.6% unchanged drug (table V). Conjugation with sulphate is limited by the supply of inorganic sulphate and this can be depleted by the administration of drugs such as salicylamide (Levy and Matsuzawa, 1967). In our studies pretreatment of dogs with salicylamide inhibited the metabolism of isoprenaline in the gut loop. Without pretreatment free isoprenaline accounted for only 3.6% of the radioactivity in the venous effluent, but this rose to 73.7% following salicylamide, whilst the sulphate conjugate fell from 68% to 3.3% (table V). The importance of this interaction was confirmed in the intact dog where pretreatment with salicylamide greatly increased the plasma concentrations and pharmacological effect of oral isoprenaline (Bennett et al. 1975).

The intestinal mucosa plays a quantitatively important role in the metabolism of isoprenaline and other adrenaline-like bronchodilator drugs and therefore contributes significantly to reducing unwanted systemic side effects when these drugs are given by inhalation in the treatment of asthma (Davies, 1979).

The exact location of the conjugating enzymes in the intestinal wall is not known but the absence of conjugated isoprenaline following intravenous administration suggests that they are not readily accessible to drug in the systemic circulation. Thus, as suggested by Routledge and Shand (1979) intestinal pre-systemic and systemic extractions need not be quantitatively the same.

We examined this problem further by measuring the effect of reversible and irreversible inhibitors of MAO on the metabolism of tyramine in the gut loop. If intestinal MAO is not freely accessible to systemically administered drug there should be a significantly different inhibition of gut wall tyramine metabolism following oral or intravenous administration of MAOIs. Further, an irreversible inhibitor should produce long-lived inhibition of gut MAO following oral dosing, whereas the effects of a reversible inhibitor should decline rapidly following absorption. We investigated these possibilities using tranylcypromine (an irreversible non-selective MAO inhibitor) and MD780515 (a reversible MAO-A type inhibitor).

In control dogs we demonstrated for the first time the quantitative importance of the gut wall in the oxidative deamination of tyramine (table VI). Only 15.6% of tyramine absorbed from the gut loop escapes deamination during its passage to the blood. Pretreatment with intravenous tranylcypromine or MD780515 caused a 5-fold increase in the availability of tyramine in the venous effluent 3 hours after the final dose of inhibitor.

Oral administration of the MAOIs had less effect (table VI). These data do not support the view that drug metabolising enzymes of the gut are not freely accessible to drugs in the systemic circulation (at least not for MAO and the inhibitors tested in these studies). At 24 hours after oral dosing with MAOIs there was considerable inhibition of tyramine metabolism by tranylcypromine but not by MD780515, thereby demonstrating the reversible action of the latter.

These studies confirm the importance of metabolism in the intestinal mucosa for the protection of the organism against ingested chemicals such as vasoactive amines. However, the question as to the equality or otherwise of intestinal presystemic and systemic metabolism of drugs such as isoprenaline remains unanswered.

## Acknowledgements

MD780515 was kindly donated by Dr P. Dostert, Centre de Recherche Delalande, Paris.

## References

Bennett, P.N.; Blackwell, E. and Davies, D.S.: Competition for sulphate during detoxification in the gut wall. Nature 258: 247-248 (1975).

Chhabra, R.S.; Pohl, R.J. and Fouts, J.R.: A comparative study of xenobiotic-metabolizing enzymes in liver and intestine of various animal species. Drug Metabolism and Disposition 2: 443-447 (1974).

Conolly, M.E.; Davies, D.S.; Dollery, C.T.; Morgan, C.D.; Paterson, J.W. and Sandler, M.: Metabolism of isoprenaline in dog and man. British Journal of Pharmacology 46: 458 (1972).

Curry, S.H.; D'Mello, A. and Mould, G.P.: Destruction of chlorpromazine during absorption in the rat *in vivo* and *in vitro*. British Journal of Pharmacology 42: 403-411 (1971).

Davies, D.S.: Pharmacokinetics of inhaled substances. Scandinavian Journal of Respiratory Disease 103 (Suppl.): 44-49 (1979).

Dollery, C.T.; Davies, D.S. and Conolly, M.E.: Differences in the metabolism of drugs, depending upon their routes of administration. Annals of the New York Academy of Sciences 179: 108-114 (1971).

George, C.F.; Blackwell, E. and Davies, D.S.: Metabolism of isoprenaline in the intestine. Journal of Pharmacy and Pharmacology 26: 265-267 (1974).

Hartiala, K.: Metabolism of hormones, drugs and other substances by the gut. Physiological Reviews 53: 496-534 (1973).

Lasker, J. and Rickert, D.E.: Absorption and glucuronylation of diethylstilbesterol by the rat small intestine. Xenobiotica 8: 665-672 (1978).

Levy, G. and Matsuzawa, T.: Pharmacokinetics of salicylamide elimination in man. Journal of Pharmacology and Experimental Therapeutics 156: 285-293 (1967).

Powell, G.M.; Miller, J.J.; Olavesen, A.H. and Curtis, G.G.: Liver as major organ of phenol detoxication? Nature 252: 234-235 (1974).

Rance, M.J. and Shillingford, J.S.: The role of the gut in the metabolism of strong analgesics. Biochemical Pharmacology 25: 735-741 (1976).

Routledge, P.A. and Shand, D.G.: Presystemic drug elimination. Annual Review of Pharmacology and Toxicology 19: 447-468 (1979).

Stohs, S.J.; Grafstrom, R.C.; Burke, M.D. and Orrenius, S.: Xenobiotic metabolism and enzyme induction in isolated rat intestinal microsomes. Drug Metabolism and Disposition 4: 517-521 (1976).

## Discussion

*D.P. Thornhill* (Salisbury, Rhodesia): What is the evidence that 90% of the inhaled isoprenaline was swallowed and how does this relate to the amount administered as the metered dose?

*D.S. Davies*: About 90% of an oral dose of isoprenaline is conjugated with sulphate, whereas there is no conjugation if it is given directly into the airways or intravenously. If it is taken by inhalation about 90% is conjugated with sulphate so quite clearly most of an inhaled dose is swallowed.

*D.P. Thornhill*: What proportion of the administered dose is absorbed by both routes?

*D.S. Davies*: The recovery of radioactivity in the urine is 90 to 95%, but the drug absorbed in the gastrointestinal tract is conjugated with sulphate before it gets into the systemic circulation and so it is inactive.

*G.H. Draffan* (Chairman): You also looked at bronchial instillation didn't you?

*D.S. Davies*: Yes, we placed the drug directly down the bronchoscope and the metabolic profile was akin to giving it intravenously although there was less methylation.

# 8

# Drug Metabolism by Gastrointestinal Mucosa: Clinical Aspects

*D.J. Back, M. Bates, A.M. Breckenridge, Francesca Crawford, A. Ellis, J.M. Hall, M. MacIver, M.L'E. Orme, I. Taylor and P.H. Rowe*

Department of Pharmacology and Therapeutics, Liverpool University

Disproportionate attention has been focused on the liver when considering first-pass metabolism, since it is evident that the gastrointestinal mucosa may well play a part. The human gut itself may metabolise a number of drugs including flurazepam (Mahon et al., 1977), salicylamide (Barr et al., 1973) and para-aminobenzoic acid (Price-Evans, 1964). Oestriol and 17β-oestradiol are also metabolised by the human gut wall, forming principally glucuronide conjugates (Diczfalusy et al., 1961, 1962). Ethinyloestradiol, the oestrogen present in most oral contraceptives, has a marked first-pass loss with a systemic bioavailability of only 42.4% (Back et al., 1979). We have examined the role of the gut wall in this first-pass effect.

## 1. *In Vitro* Studies with Human Jejunal Mucosa

### 1.1 Methods

Jejunal biopsy samples were obtained from apparently healthy relatives of patients with coeliac disease using the Quinton Hydraulic biopsy sampler. Three pieces of mucosa were taken from each volunteer to study the *in vitro* metabolism of ethinyloestradiol. Each sample was immediately placed in 450μL of Krebs-Henseleit buffer containing tritiated ethinyloestradiol (600,000dpm). The third tube also contained thiomersal (a metabolic inhibitor) as a control. Tubes were gassed with 95% $O_2$:5% $CO_2$, stoppered and then shaken in a water bath at 37°C for 1.5 hours. After incubation, the tissue was removed, blotted dry and weighed and 400μL of the buffer was extracted twice with 3ml of diethyl ether. A known proportion of the ether and the aqueous fractions were counted in scintillation fluid to ascertain the amount of drug which had become non-ether extractable (i.e. conjugated). The ether extract was also run on a thin layer chromatography (TLC) plate (silica gel) using an ethyl ace-

*Table I.* Percentage of ethinyloestradiol conjugated in test (mean of pair) and control tubes by human jejunal mucosa

| Experiment | Test | Control |
|---|---|---|
| 1 | 46.9 | 3.9 |
| 2 | 43.6 | 3.2 |
| 3 | 39.3 | 4.3 |
| 4 | 44.1 | 5.6 |
| 5 | 26.4 | 1.5 |
| 6 | 29.3 | 1.5 |
| 7 | 44.3 | 1.0 |
| 8 | 32.3 | 2.8 |
| Mean | 38.3 | 3.0 |
| SE | ± 2.6 | ± 0.5 |
| | $p < 0.001$ | |

*Table II.* Percentage of conjugates hydrolysed by incubation with sulphatase or β-glucuronidase

| Experiment | Sulphatase | β-Glucuronidase |
|---|---|---|
| 1 | 91.6 | 11.2 |
| 2 | 85.7 | 9.1 |
| 3 | 90.1 | 11.2 |
| 4 | 87.1 | 21.8 |
| 5 | 91.2 | 37.2 |
| 6 | 88.2 | 16.7 |
| 7 | 89.9 | 15.5 |
| 8 | 92.6 | 11.1 |
| 9 | 93.9 | 11.6 |
| Mean | 90.0 | 16.2 |
| SE | ± 0.8 | ± 2.8 |
| | $p < 0.001$ | |

tate:petroleum ether (3:2) solvent system. The plates were scraped in 0.5cm bands and counted for radioactive content.

The remaining aqueous fraction was divided into 3 aliquots. One was run on a TLC plate with methanol as solvent and then scraped and counted. This system separates ethinyloestradiol glucuronide from ethinyloestradiol sulphate. The second aliquot was incubated with sulphatase (5u, Sigma Chemical Co) and saccharolactone (2mg) in acetate buffer pH 5.0 (450μL) and the third with β-glucuronidase (0.8ml-Ketodase — General Diagnostics). Following a 4.0 hour incubation at 37°C, the second and third aliquots were again extracted twice with ether and the aqueous and a portion of the ether extract counted. The remaining ether extract was run on a TLC plate.

Similar experiments were performed on abnormal biopsy material from 3 patients with newly diagnosed coeliac disease and 7 coeliac patients receiving a gluten-free diet.

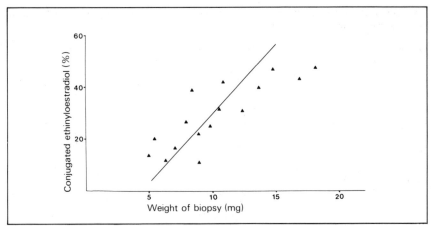

*Fig. 1.* Percentage of drug conjugated in relation to the weight of jejunal mucosa (r = 0.82 p < 0.001).

## 1.2 Results

The percentage of the drug which was non-ether extractable after incubation is shown in table I. The initial ether extract run on a TLC plate showed a single peak which corresponded to an ethinyloestradiol marker; there was no evidence of any phase 1 metabolism.

Thin layer chromatography of the aqueous portion run in the methanol solvent again only showed a single peak which corresponded to an ethinyloestradiol sulphate marker. 90% of the conjugates were hydrolysed by sulphatase and only 16% by β-glucuronidase (table II). The percentage of drug conjugated was proportional to the weight of jejunal mucosa. (fig. 1).

The results for the patients with coeliac disease were similar except that the ability of the mucosa to form conjugates was significantly reduced (p < 0.001) [table III]. The newly diagnosed coeliac patients did not differ significantly from those taking a gluten-free diet.

## 2. Measurement of Ethinyloestradiol Sulphate in Plasma

### 2.1 Methods

Oral and intravenous preparations of ethinyloestradiol and levonorgestrel were given in the middle of successive menstrual cycles in random order to 5 female volunteers aged 21 to 23 years. Oral Ovranette[1] (ethinyloestradiol 30µg, levonorgestrel 150µg) was given after an overnight fast. Ethinyloestradiol and levonorgestrel were dissolved in polyethylene glycol and ampoules containing 100µg ethinyloestradiol and 500µg of levonorgestrel were prepared separately and sterilised by Wyeth laboratories. Ethinyloestradiol (0.6ml: 30µg) and levonorgestrel (0.6ml: 150µg) were

---

1 'Ovranette' (Wyeth).

*Table III.* Ethinyloestradiol (pg) metabolised per mg of jejunal mucosa in patients with coeliac disease and apparently normal relatives

|       | Normals | Coeliacs |
|-------|---------|----------|
|       | 28.4    | 4.7      |
|       | 18.5    | 5.1      |
|       | 37.9    | 7.5      |
|       | 31.9    | 15.9     |
|       | 17.8    | 12.7     |
|       | 34.8    | 6.5      |
|       | 19.6    | 6.9      |
|       | 28.7    | 5.3      |
|       |         | 8.1      |
|       |         | 9.5      |
| Mean  | 27.2    | 8.2      |
| SE    | ± 2.7   | ± 2.5    |
|       | $p < 0.0001$ |      |

given intravenously after dilution in 10ml sterile saline. The volunteers were allowed nothing by mouth for 3 hours and serial blood samples were taken into heparinised tubes. The plasma was stored at $-20°C$ until analysis.

Plasma was analysed for ethinyloestradiol by radioimmunoassay (Back et al., 1979). Ethinyloestradiol sulphate was measured by radioimmunoassay following a 4 hour incubation of the plasma with sulphatase at pH 5.0.

## 2.2 Results

Most of the ethinyloestradiol in the plasma was in the form of ethinyloestradiol sulphate (table IV) and the ratio of sulphate conjugate to unchanged drug was almost 3 times higher after oral than intravenous administration. The area under the plasma ethinyloestradiol sulphate concentration time curve from 0 to 8 hours for the group after oral administration was 6821 ± SE 1683pg/h/ml compared with 4996 ± SE 79.8pg/h/ml after intravenous administration.

## 3. Portal Vein Study

### 3.1 Methods

The relative contribution of gut wall and liver to the metabolism of ethinyloestradiol was studied by measuring drug concentrations in portal and peripheral vein samples in a 60-year-old man in whom the portal vein had been cannulated for 5-fluorouracil therapy after surgery for carcinoma of the colon. There was no macroscopic evidence of hepatic metastases. After completion of the 5-fluorouracil therapy, a single Eugynon 50[1] tablet (ethinyloestradiol 50µg, levonorgestrel 500µg)

---

1    'Eugynon' (Schering).

*Table IV.* Ratio of area under the curve (AUC) from 0 to 8 hours of ethinyloestradiol sulphate to ethinyloestradiol after oral and intravenous administration

| Subject | Route | |
|---------|-------|---|
| | intravenous | oral |
| S.W. | 3.1 | 18.4 |
| R.K. | 8.3 | 22.4 |
| S.H. | 8.3 | 26.9 |
| H.S. | 6.9 | 13.3 |
| C.J. | 2.9 | 6.4 |
| Mean | 5.9 | 17.5 |
| SE | ± 1.1 | ± 3.2 |
| | $p < 0.02$ | |

*Table V.* Radioactivity per ml of plasma from portal and peripheral veins of a 60-year-old man given tritiated ethinyloestradiol

| Time after dosing (min) | Total radioactivity (dpm) | | Non-ether extractable radioactivity (dpm) | |
|---|---|---|---|---|
| | portal | venous | portal | venous |
| 10 | 6212 | 319 | 2927 | 282 |
| 20 | 7128 | 4912 | 6371 | 4302 |
| 30 | 5726 | 5362 | 5268 | 5132 |
| 40 | 5135 | 5136 | 4921 | 4705 |
| 50 | 4796 | 4715 | 4624 | 4144 |

containing 65μCi of tritiated ethinyloestradiol was given following an overnight fast.

Serial blood samples were taken simultaneously from the portal and a systemic vein. The total radioactivity per ml of plasma was measured. In addition, 200μL of plasma was extracted twice with 3ml of diethyl ether and the non-ether extractable radioactivity measured.

## 3.2 Results

In the first 30 minutes the total radioactivity was higher in the portal samples than in the systemic (table V). After this time (when absorption had apparently finished) the levels of radioactivity were similar. The concentrations of conjugates in this initial 30 minute period were also higher in the portal plasma suggesting that gut wall metabolism had occurred.

## 4. Effect of Ascorbic Acid Administration

### 4.1 Methods

Six female volunteers (aged 21 to 23 years) were given 'Ovranette' as in the previous study. At a similar time in the menstrual cycle, the experiment was repeated but half an hour before the dose effervescent ascorbic acid (1g) was given. Plasma ethinyloestradiol concentrations were measured as described above.

### 4.2 Results

In 4 of the women the area under the plasma ethinyloestradiol concentration time curve (AUC) increased after ascorbic acid. One woman showed no change in the AUC and one showed lower concentrations.

The mean plasma concentrations are shown in figure 2. The mean AUC values for ethinyloestradiol were 1347pg/h/ml ($\pm$ 307) and 848pg/h/ml ($\pm$ 171) with and without ascorbic acid respectively.

## 5. Discussion

The *in vitro* studies with human jejunal mucosa show that extensive metabolism of ethinyloestradiol can occur in gut wall. The major metabolite was ethinyloestradiol

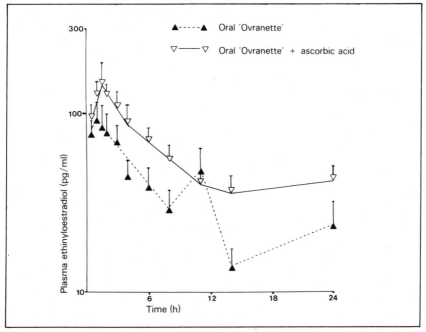

*Fig. 2.* Mean plasma ethinyloestradiol concentrations in 6 women given oral 'Ovranette' with and without ascorbic acid.

sulphate; this differs from the results found with 17β-oestradiol and oestriol in which glucuronides were formed (Diczfalusy et al., 1961, 1962). After oral dosing the AUC from 0 to 24 hours of plasma ethinyloestradiol sulphate was 18 times higher than the AUC of ethinyloestradiol. This is in agreement with previous findings (Bird and Clark 1973). After intravenous administration the AUC of the sulphate was only 6 times as high as ethinyloestradiol and this is consistent with extensive first-pass metabolism.

The concentrations of ethinyloestradiol metabolites in the portal vein compared to the systemic circulation suggest that a considerable proportion of the absorbed ethinyloestradiol had been metabolised, presumably in the gut wall. From examination of the 10 minute samples it would appear that approximately 45 % of the drug absorbed had been conjugated. The figure for the first 30 minutes, when the portal plasma still contained more total radioactivity than the systemic plasma suggests that 58 % of the absorbed drug had been conjugated. This obviously represents the major part of the first-pass metabolism of ethinyloestradiol.

There are limitations to the portal vein study in that the patient was elderly, had first undergone major surgery and had also received 5-fluorouracil. However, these factors might be expected to reduce rather that enhance gut wall metabolism.

The metabolism of ethinyloestradiol may be reduced in some women by ascorbic acid, which is also in part conjugated with sulphate (Baker et al., 1971). The gut is exposed to a large number of exogenous agents which could alter its ability to metabolise drugs, and this has important therapeutic implications.

Jejunal mucosa from patients with coeliac disease had a reduced capacity for conjugation of ethinyloestradiol, despite treatment with a gluten-free diet. Previous studies have shown that other enzymes such as α-glucosidase and alkaline phosphatase are deficient in the mucosa of coeliac patients and do not return to normal with treatment (Peters et al., 1978). The clinical significance of our observations is uncertain, but assuming that absorption is complete, a reduced first-pass effect may result in higher serum steroid concentrations.

## References

Back, D.J.; Breckenridge, A.M.; Crawford, F.E.; MacIver, M.; Orme, M. L'E.; Rowe, P.H. and Watts, M.J.: An investigation of the pharmacokinetics of ethinyloestradiol in women using radioimmunoassay. Contraception 20: 263-274 (1979).

Baker, E.M.; Hammer, D.C.; March, S.C.; Tolbert, B.M. and Canham, J.E.: Ascorbate sulfate: a urinary metabolite of ascorbic acid in man. Science 173: 826 (1971).

Barr, W.H.; Aceto, T. Jnr.; Chung, M. and Shukur, M.: Dose dependent drug metabolism during the absorptive phase. Revue Canadienne de Biologique (Suppl. 32): 31-42 (1973).

Bird, C.E. and Clark, A.F.: Metabolic clearance rates and metabolism of mestranol and ethinyloestradiol in normal young women. Journal of Clinical Endocrinology and Metabolism 36: 296-302 (1973).

Diczfalusy, E.; Franksson, C.; Lisbon, B.P. and Martinsen, B.: Formation of oestrone glucosiduronate by the human intestinal tract. Acta Endocrinologica 40: 537-551 (1962).

Diczfalusy, E.; Franksson, C. and Martinsen, B.: Oestrogen conjugation by the human intestinal tract. Acta Endocrinologica 38: 59-72 (1961).

Mahon, W.A. : Inaba, T. and Stone, R.M.: Metabolism of flurazepam by the small intestine. Clinical Pharmacology and Therapeutics 22: 228-233 (1977).

Peters, T.J.; Jones, P.E.; Jenkins, E.J. and Nicholson, J.A.: Analytical subcellular fractionation of jejunal biopsy specimens from control subjects and patients with coeliac disease; in McNicholl (Ed) Perspectives in Coeliac Disease, p.423-434 (University Park Press, Baltimore 1978).

Price-Evans, E.A.: Acetylation polymorphism. Proceedings of the Royal Society of Medicine 57: 508-511 (1964).

## Discussion

*R.I. Ogilvie* (Montreal): After oral administration, you showed a second peak which you attributed to enterohepatic circulation. This secondary peak was not seen after intravenous administration nor after oral administration with ascorbic acid. I cannot see why you would not have had enterohepatic re-circulation then. Perhaps there is some other reason, such as a change in intestinal blood flow caused by meals or activity which would alter disposition. Were these peaks related to meals or other factors?

*M. MacIver* (Liverpool): No, there was always a secondary peak in each individual following intravenous administration. These peaks were flattened out because we showed mean data. If you prevent sulphate conjugates being formed by ascorbic acid, then the glucuronide conjugates formed instead may be rapidly removed by the kidney and not excreted in the bile. You may abolish enterohepatic circulation. Unfortunately, we did not measure ethinyloestradiol sulphate concentrations after administration of ascorbic acid.

# 9

# Drug Metabolism by Gastrointestinal Flora: 3 Case Histories

*Peter Goldman*

Division of Clinical Pharmacology, Harvard Medical School

This review will be confined mainly to a discussion of 3 drugs which will serve as case histories of the possible pharmacological implications of drug metabolism by the intestinal microflora. Other reviews provide more extensive coverage of xenobiotic metabolism (Scheline, 1973), biochemical pharmacology (Goldman, 1978), and clinical implications (Peppercorn and Goldman, 1976), of the intestinal microflora.

It is obvious that orally administered drugs which are poorly absorbed will remain in the gastrointestinal tract. However, they will have little contact with the flora until they pass the ileocaecal valve. Drugs may also make contact with the flora if they are eliminated in the bile. Therefore even if administered by the parenteral route, drugs can make contact with the flora. A pathological distribution of the flora, as in the bowel overgrowth or blind loop syndrome, may also facilitate contact between drugs and the flora. Under these circumstances drugs that are ordinarily readily absorbed high in the gastrointestinal tract may still make contact with the flora and be metabolised.

The possibility that drug metabolism may occur even when drugs are not absorbed is only one difference between drug metabolism by the flora and that by the liver. The chemical transformations at both sites are also different. Reactions of the liver, particularly those dependent on the cytochrome P-450 system, require molecular oxygen. The flora on the other hand exists in an oxygen-free environment. Thus, whereas the liver tends to oxidise drugs, the flora tend to reduce them. Another contrast is that the liver carries out a variety of conjugation reactions, whereas the flora tend to nullify these by hydrolysing conjugates such as glucuronides and sulphate esters. Thus from a chemical standpoint the reactions of the flora often tend to reverse those of the liver. From a pharmacological standpoint, however, the reactions may be regarded as complementary. Thus the enterohepatic circulation of drugs may depend on the interplay between the two systems. Stilboestrol, for example, is excreted in the bile as the glucuronide and would not be re-absorbed from the intestine if the glucuronide were not hydrolysed by the flora (Clark et al., 1969).

# 1. Methods

Experience has taught us to select compounds for study that may be reduced in the body. In what has now become a fairly standardised approach, we initially compared the metabolism of the drug in germ-free and conventional rats. Germ-free rats are maintained in flexible film isolators containing 6 metabolism cages which permit separate collection of urine and faeces; conventional rats are maintained under similar conditions except that they are in the unprotected environment of the regular animal room (Wheeler et al., 1975).

When a drug metabolite is found in the urine or faeces of a conventional rat but is not detected in the excreta of a germ-free rat, the flora is provisionally assigned a role in its formation. It must be recognised, however, that there are many physiological differences between germ-free and conventional rats (Gordon and Pesti, 1971). The germ-free rat, for example, has an enormous caecum and its metabolism is slower than that of the conventional rat (Gordon and Pesti, 1971). Obviously, factors of this kind may effect drug absorption or metabolism and lead to small differences in the formation of metabolites that are not a direct consequence of the activity of the flora. Thus, we have concentrated on the metabolites present in the conventional rat that to the certainty of our analytical methods are absent in the germ-free rat.

If a metabolite is formed in the conventional rat and not in the germ-free rat, we determine whether the metabolic reaction missing in the germ-free rat can be demonstrated either in a mixed culture of caecal contents or in a pure culture of one of its predominant bacteria. The gas phase of these incubation mixtures consists of hydrogen, carbon dioxide and nitrogen from which traces of oxygen are removed by deoxy filters and then by heating to 400° in the presence of copper (Holdemann et al., 1977). Oxygen must be excluded, not only from the gas phase, but during the preparation of the bacteriological media as well. If oxygen is not excluded during autoclaving of the media, peroxides may form which will be lethal for the predominant strains of the flora. It is important to recognise that there are normally around $10^{11}$ bacteria per gram in the lower bowel and that if oxygen is not excluded and the appropriate media selected one may cultivate only $10^8$ of these bacteria. This may seem like a large number of bacteria, but they may not be the ones with the appropriate physiological and pharmacological significance. We must not attribute to the flora reactions which are found in only a negligible fraction of it.

Our basic approach then is to conduct comparative metabolic studies in germ-free and conventional rats, to determine the metabolites in the conventional rat that are absent in the germ-free rat and then to determine whether these metabolites form in physiological incubations of the anaerobic flora.

# 2. Results

## 2.1 Sulphasalazine

Clinical trials have established that sulphasalazine is effective in the prophylaxis and treatment of mild ulcerative colitis (Goldman and Peppercorn, 1975). The mechanism for this action remains unknown but the history of the development of the drug is interesting in view of recent findings concerning both the drug and the disease it is used for. The rationale for the design of the drug in the 1940's (Svartz, 1942) was that it incorporated in a single molecule an antibacterial drug and an anti-

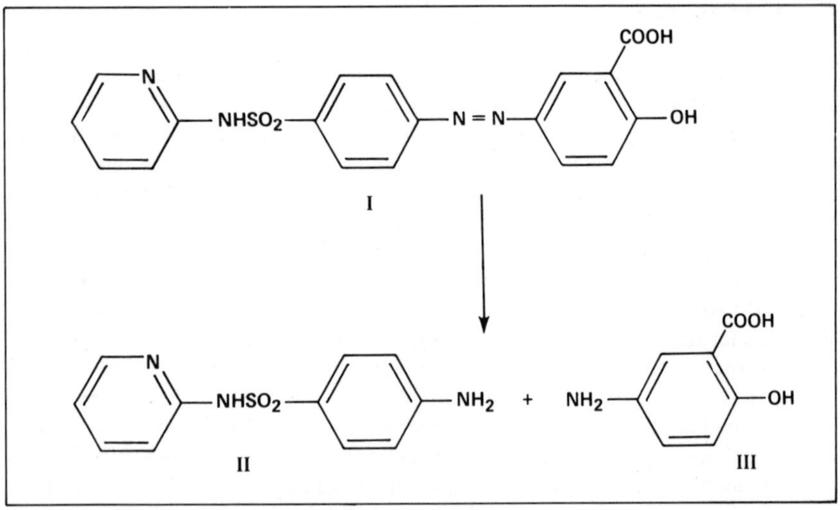

*Fig. 1.* The initial reaction of sulphasalazine (I) metabolism is reduction of the azo bond to yield sulphapyridine (II) and 5-aminosalicylate (III).

inflammatory one. Sulphapyridine and salicylate were selected to provide the 2 desired activities and an azo bond was used to join them so that structurally (fig. 1) the drug is sulphapyridine in an azo linkage to 5-aminosalicylate.

When we began our studies it was known that 5-aminosalicylate and sulphapyridine and their respective metabolites were excreted following the ingestion of sulphasalazine by either humans or rats. We reasoned that reduction of the azo bond, which seemed the logical initiation of the metabolism of sulphasalazine, might be a reaction mediated by the flora and thus we examined the fate of the drug in the germ-free rat. We found that the excreta of the germ-free rat contained only sulphasalazine and none of its metabolites, whereas only drug metabolites and none of the parent drug was recovered in the excreta of conventional rats (table I). The capacity to reduce the azo bond of sulphasalazine was widespread among intestinal bacteria. All of a dozen strains of bacteria isolated from the gastrointestinal tract of man or rat were found capable of carrying out this reaction in culture. Furthermore, germ-free rats gained the ability to reduce the azo bond of sulphasalazine when they were selectively associated with 2 strains of bacteria capable of reducing the azo bond in culture. Thus our evidence was consistent with the view that the flora is obligatory for the reduction of the azo bond of sulphasalazine (Peppercorn and Goldman, 1972).

Sulphasalazine reaches the flora in the lower bowel not because it is poorly absorbed but because it is excreted in the bile and undergoes an enterohepatic circulation (Das and Dubin, 1976). After breakdown in the lower bowel its 2 primary metabolites have different fates. Sulphapyridine appears to be almost completely absorbed and then, like orally administered sulphapyridine, is partially acetylated in the liver to be excreted almost exclusively in the urine. 5-Aminosalicylate, on the other hand, is not so readily absorbed and seems to remain within the gastrointestinal tract to be excreted in the faeces. That which is reabsorbed is partially acetylated and excreted in the urine.

It was intriguing to us that 5-aminosalicylate appeared to be selectively released in the colon, at precisely the site where its clinical activity had been demonstrated by

Table I Sulphasalazine and its metabolites in excreta of conventional and germ-free rats[1]

|  | Recovery (%) | | | |
|  | conventional rats | | germ-free rats | |
|  | urine | faeces | urine | faeces |
| --- | --- | --- | --- | --- |
| Sulphasalazine | 0[3] | 0[4] | 1.5 | 53 |
| Sulphapyridine[2] | 65 | 0 | 0 | 0 |
| 5-Aminosalicylate[2] | 55 | 27 | 0 | 0 |

1 The diet was supplemented with 1% sulphasalazine (w/w) for 24 hours and the amount of drug ingested was quantified. Measurements represent amounts excreted during the 24 hours of drug ingestion and the subsequent 48 hours.
2 Includes acetylated derivatives.
3 $< 0.2\%$.
4 $< 1.0\%$.

Table II. Distribution of metabolites after rats received either sulphasalazine or 5-aminosalicylate orally

|  | Metabolite recovered (mg)[1] | | | |
|  | sulphasalazine 0.5g (1.25mmol)/kg | | 5-aminosalicylate 0.25g (1.6mmol)/kg | |
|  | urine | faeces | urine | faeces |
| --- | --- | --- | --- | --- |
| 5-Aminosalicylate | 0 | 8.0 | 5.7 | 1.3 |
| 5-Acetamidosalicylate | 8.8 | 5.6 | 17.3 | 8.1 |

1 Either sulphasalazine or 5-aminosalicylate was administered at the doses indicated for 1 day and excreta collected for 4 days.

careful clinical trials. We reasoned that 5-aminosalicylate might be an anti-inflammatory agent and that sulphasalazine might serve merely as a vehicle for its delivery to the colon. The results shown in table II indicate the concentration of 5-aminosalicylate is higher in the faeces (which we take to indicate a high concentration in the colon) when it is given in the form of sulphasalazine than when given as 5-aminosalicylate itself. The comparison shown in table II is made with compounds administered orally. The results are virtually identical if the 2 compounds are administered parenterally (Peppercorn and Goldman, 1973), as would be expected if sulphasalazine is excreted in the bile.

Our hypothesis that sulphasalazine merely serves as a vehicle for the delivery of 5-aminosalicylate to the colon in a drug delivery system that depends on the flora has evidence both for and against it. The hypothesis can be questioned because it fails to explain the lack of effectiveness in the treatment of ulcerative colitis of the analogue of sulphasalazine which consisted of sulphadimidine instead of sulphapyridine (Baron et al., 1962). Our studies provide no reason why this analogue should not deliver 5-aminosalicylate to the colon just as effectively as sulphasalazine. However, the hypothesis gains support from the observation that 5-aminosalicylate enemas can be effective in treating ulcerative colitis (Azad Khan et al., 1977) and from our increasing perception of the pathogenesis of ulcerative colitis. Recently it has been shown that prostaglandins of the E type are elevated in the rectal mucosa and faeces of patients with active ulcerative colitis (Gould, 1976; Sharon et al., 1978) and that prostaglandin synthesis in rectal mucosa is inhibited by 5-aminosalicylate (Sharon et al., 1978). Of course this compelling evidence for the hypothesis is mitigated by the observation that prostaglandin synthesis is also inhibited by sulphasalazine itself (Sharon et al., 1978; Hoult and Moore, 1978). Thus for the time being the hypothesis that the flora serves to make sulphasalazine an effective way of delivering 5-

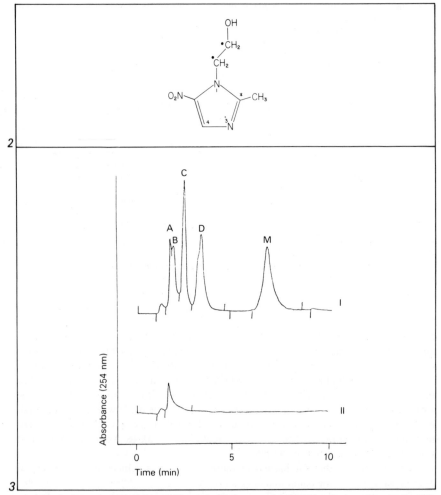

*Fig. 2.* The structure of metronidazole indicating a radiolabel either in the ethanolamine side chain (•) or at the 2-position of the imidazole ring (*).

*Fig. 3.* A high pressure liquid chromatographic record (I) showing the ultraviolet absorbing compounds (A, B, C, and D) which appear during the incubation of metronidazole (M) with rat caecal contents. Record II is of a control incubation mixture which lacked metronidazole.

aminosalicylate to the colon must remain simply a convenient means of assessing the expanding amount of evidence relating to the pathogenesis and treatment of ulcerative colitis.

## 2.2 Metronidazole

The second drug I wish to consider is metronidazole, the drug of choice in the treatment of trichomonal vaginitis and of various forms of amoebiasis as well as an important alternative agent in the treatment of both giardiasis (Anon, 1974) and some anaerobic infections (Tally et al., 1975). Recently it has been found useful in prophylaxis for colon surgery (Willis et al., 1977) and has received a clinical trial as a radiation sensitiser (Karim, 1978).

Unfortunately this useful drug increases the incidence of tumours to which laboratory mice are susceptible (Rustia and Shubik, 1972) and is mutagenic for the Ames histidine auxotrophs of *Salmonella typhimurium* (Rosenkranz and Speck, 1975). Thus metronidazole poses the dilemma of a drug with a number of useful and sometimes unique therapeutic properties which gives rise to concern because of laboratory evidence suggesting that it poses a risk of causing human cancer (Goldman et al., 1977).

We thought the actions of the flora on this drug might be interesting because of evidence which suggests that reduction of the nitro group might be involved in the toxic properties of the drug. It had been shown, for example, that an Ames mutant which lacks nitro reductase activity also lost its responsiveness to the mutagenicity of metronidazole. Mutagenicity of metronidazole for the mutant was restored, however, if the pour plate assay was supplemented with an external source of nitro reductase activity (Rosenkranz and Speck, 1975). A possible mechanism for this effect may be found in the observation that chemical reduction of the nitro group of metronidazole leads to the disruption of DNA (Knight et al., 1978). It is, of course, also known that metronidazole is particularly effective against anaerobic micro-organisms (Lindmark and Muller, 1976) and that the effectiveness of the drug seems to be related to its binding to macromolecules which occurs under anaerobic conditions (Ings et al., 1974).

The release of radioactive $CO_2$ from 2-[$^{14}C$]-metronidazole (fig. 2) indicates that the imidazole ring of metronidazole is cleaved in the rat (Ings et al., 1975). And the observation that the imidazole ring of metronidazole is cleaved during anaerobic bacterial metabolism (Edwards et al., 1975; Searle and Willson, 1976) suggested that the flora might be responsible for this reaction when it occurs in the rat.

Since the products of the anaerobic metabolism of metronidazole were unknown our first task was to characterise a metabolite of the reduction of metronidazole that might serve as a marker for the activity of the intestinal flora within the whole animal. We found that metronidazole disappeared completely when incubated with rat caecal contents and that high pressure liquid chromatography revealed a number of new products (fig. 3). N-(2-Hydroxyethyl)-oxamic acid was one of these products. When we used metronidazole radio-labelled in the ethanolamine side chain, we found this metabolite in the urine of conventional but not of germ-free rats (Koch and Goldman, 1979). Thus it appeared that the flora reduced metronidazole to this metabolite *in vivo* as well as *in vitro*. Later using 2-[$^{14}C$]-metronidazole we were able to show that acetamide is another product of the anaerobic metabolism of metronidazole (Koch et al., 1979).

*Table III.* Stoichiometry of the formation of acetamide and N-(2-hydroxyethyl)-oxamic acid[1]

| Incubation | Metronidazole consumed (%) | Metabolites formed (%) | |
| --- | --- | --- | --- |
| | | acetamide | N-(2-hydroxy-ethyl)-oxamic acid |
| 1 | 90 | 8.5 | 1.3 |
| 2 | 100 | 15.5 | 1.7 |

1  Incubation mixtures contained 5.8µmol of metronidazole together with 10.1µCi of [2-$^{14}$C]-metronidazole (to measure acetamide formation) and 10.1µCi of [1', 2'-$^{14}$C$_2$]-metronidazole (to measure N-[2-hydroxyethyl]-oxamic acid) with either *C. perfringens* (1) or caecal contents (2) in a total volume of 10ml.

*Table IV.* m-HPAA in the urine of conventional and germ-free rats[1] after the administration of levodopa or its metabolites

| Compound fed | m-HPAA (mg/72h) | |
| --- | --- | --- |
| | conventional rats | germ-free rats |
| Levodopa, 100mg[2] | 2.3 | 0.08 |
| Dopamine, 100mg | 4.0 | 0.04 |
| Dopac, 100mg | 0.3 | 0.04 |
| DL-m-tyrosine, 150mg[3] | 48.1 | 9.9 |
| m-Tyramine, 90mg[3] | 23.1 | 9.1 |

1  The compound indicated was added to the diet for 24 hours. Urines were collected for that 24-hour period and for a subsequent 48 hours and analysed for the presence of m-HPAA.
2  40mg was administered to the germ-free rats.
3  50mg was administered to the germ-free rats.

The isolation of acetamide is not surprising because, as the scheme in figure 4 indicates, acetamide is complementary to N-(2-hydroxyethyl)-oxamic acid in the sense that together the 2 metabolites account for all of the carbon and nitrogen atoms in metronidazole. However, acetamide and N-(2-hydroxyethyl)-oxamic acid each account for only approximately 2% of the metronidazole administered to conventional rats. As indicated in table III these products only account for a small fraction of the products of the complete reduction of metronidazole and thus much work needs to be done to characterise chemically the fate of metronidazole during its anaerobic metabolism. It is interesting that the anaerobic metabolism of metronidazole yields approximately 8 times more acetamide than N-(2-hydroxyethyl)-oxamic acid. Presumably some acetamide is further metabolised by mammalian enzymes to yield the radioactive carbon dioxide which Ings et al. (1975) found could account for 6% of the metronidazole administered to the rat.

One of the implications of our findings concerns acetamide. Rats fed a diet containing 2.5% acetamide developed malignant liver tumours as well as hyperplastic nodules and similar precancerous lesions (Dessau and Jackson. 1955; Jackson and

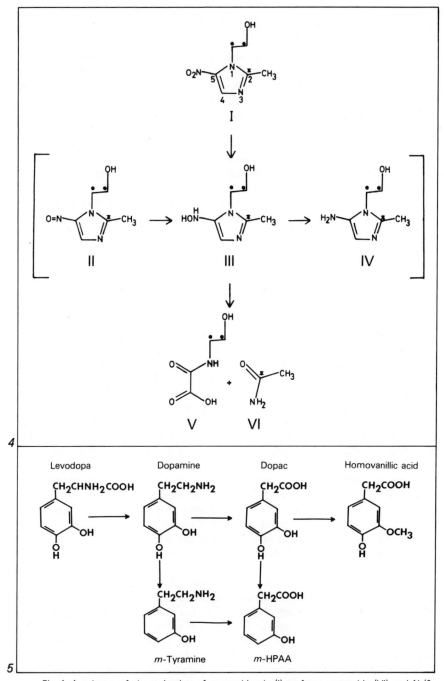

*Fig. 4.* A scheme of the reduction of metronidazole (I) to form acetamide (VI) and N-(2-hydroxyethyl)-oxamic acid (V). The proposed 5-nitroso (II) and 5-(N-hydroxy)-amino (III) and 5-amino (IV) intermediates are included in the scheme. The radiolabels are indicated as in figure 3.

*Fig. 5.* Some of the metabolic transformations of levodopa in the conventional rat.

Dessau, 1961; Weisburger et al., 1969). Thus the finding that the weak carcinogen, acetamide, is a metabolite of metronidazole provides additional indirect evidence that metronidazole is a potential human carcinogen.

The characterisation of these 2 products of metronidazole reduction allows us to speculate further about the reactive species responsible for metronidazole's mutagenicity. Our results indicate that cleavage occurs between positions 1 and 2 of the imidazole ring as well as between positions 3 and 4 (fig. 4). Cleavage of the heterocyclic ring to yield compounds that we have isolated must involve nucleophilic attack at positions 2 and 4. Of the postulated intermediates with reduced or partially reduced nitro groups shown in figure 4, only that with the electron withdrawing 5-nitroso substitute (II) should sufficiently activate the aromatic ring to facilitate attack at position 2 and 4. Such a mechanism allows for the existence of an electrophile whose presence is implied by the weak tumourogenicity of this drug. It is uncertain whether an electrophile formed by the flora will have sufficient stability and the appropriate pharmacokinetic properties to enter mammalian tissues.

## 2.3 Levodopa

Bacterial participation in the formation of some of the metabolites of levodopa was suggested by the observation that the urinary excretion of m-hydroxyphenylacetic acid (m-HPAA) and m-tyramine was diminished when Parkinsonian patients taking levodopa were also given neomycin (Sandler et al., 1971). The finding was interesting because of the suggestion of Sandler and his colleagues that the pharmacological actions of trace metabolites such as these might explain the puzzling variability in the therapeutic and toxic actions of this interesting drug.

Our studies were directed at the portion of the pathway of levodopa metabolism that contained reactions which might be due to the flora (fig. 5) and we focused particularly on dehydroxylation reactions at the 4 position of the catechol ring. Our approach was to consider the rat as a 1-compartment model and to administer the various intermediates in the metabolism of levodopa to determine their further metabolism. Table IV shows an example of this approach with regard to the appearance in the urine of m-HPAA after levodopa and several of its metabolites are administered to germ-free or conventional rats. On the assumption of a simple 1-compartment model it is obvious that the germ-free rats lack the ability to carry out the dehydroxylation at the 4 position of the catechol ring. A similar series of experiments indicated that m-tyramine did not appear in the urine of the germ-free rat following the administration of any of its metabolic precursors containing the 3, 4-catechol group (Goldin et al., 1973).

We subsequently found that the formation of m-HPAA is decreased when dopamine is administered to animals deprived of food and that this decrease correlates with the reduction in the mass of the flora in the intestinal tract (Goldman et al., 1974). The correlation between the formation of certain drug metabolites and the state of the flora suggested that the kinetics of the formation of these metabolites might be useful in helping to establish the often difficult diagnosis of a bowel over-growth or a blind loop syndrome. To explore this possibility we began to investigate the pharmacokinetics of these metabolites as they might be affected by alterations of the flora.

We created self-filling blind loops surgically in rats and 4 weeks later administered a test dose of dopamine. The metabolites appearing in the urine on the

*Table V.* The urinary excretion of metabolites after oral dopamine[1]

| Time | Metabolite | Amount excreted (mg/24h[2]) | |
|------|-----------|------------|---------|
| | | blind loop (n = 7) | control (n = 6) |
| Day 1 | Homovanillic acid | 4.1 ± 0.7 | 5.0 ± 0.5 |
| | Dihydroxyphenylacetic acid | 3.7 ± 0.4 | 5.1 ± 0.7 |
| | *m*-HPAA | 4.3 ± 0.6 | 0.24 ± 0.1[3] |
| Day 2 | Homovanillic acid | 1.0 ± 0.3 | 0.9 ± 0.3 |
| | Dihydroxyphenylacetic acid | 0.9 ± 0.2 | 0.5 ± 0.2 |
| | *m*-HPAA | 0.3 ± 0.03 | 2.7 ± 0.4[3] |

1   Dopamine (100mg) was administered by gastric intubation and urine collected thereafter for 2 consecutive 24-hour intervals.
2   Values are mean ± SE.
3   Difference between rats with blind loops and control rats statistically significant by the Student's *t*-test (p < 0.01).

*Table VI.* The urinary excretion of sulphapyridine following oral sulphasalazine[1]

| Urine collection period (h) | Sulphapyridine excreted (mg)[2] | |
|------|------------|---------|
| | blind loop (n = 8) | control (n = 10) |
| 0-6 | 0.79 ± 0.18 | 0.26 ± 0.03[3] |
| 6-24 | 0.9 ± 0.10 | 1.0 ± 0.10 |
| 24-48 | 0.26 ± 0.01 | 0.48 ± 0.06[3] |

1   Sulphasalazine (10mg) was administered by gastric intubation and urine was collected thereafter for the intervals shown.
2   Values are mean ± SE.
3   Difference between rats with blind loops and control rats statistically significant by the Student's *t*-test (p < 0.01).

following 2 days were quantified (Peppercorn et al., 1976). As noted in table V the urinary excretion of *m*-HPAA is more prompt in rats with blind loops than in the sham-operated controls. A similar observation was made in rats given a test dose of sulphasalazine. Table VI indicates that sulphapyridine appears more promptly in the urine of rats with blind loops than in that of sham-operated controls.

The results of these studies have now been applied to man. Sulphapyridine is excreted more promptly than normal following a test dose of sulphasalazine in patients with jejunal diverticula (Thithapandha 1978), and thus drugs metabolised by the flora may have a role in diagnosing abnormalities of the gastrointestinal flora.

## Acknowledgement

The following colleagues participated in these studies: Bernard B. Beaulieu, Jr., John H. Carter, Ewan J.T. Chrystal, Ronald L. Koch, Martha A. McLafferty, Mark A. Peppercorn, Frances B. Soderberg, Larry A. Wheeler, and Margo N. Woods and were supported mainly by grants R01CA 15260 from the National Institute of Health.

## References

Anon: Drugs for parasitic infections. Medical Letter of Drugs and Therapeutics 16: 5 (1974).

Azad Khan, A.K.; Piris, J. and Truelove, S.C.: An experiment to determine the active therapeutic moiety of sulphasalazine. Lancet 2: 892-895 (1977).

Baron, J.H.; Connell, A.M.; Lennard-Jones, J.E., et al.: Sulphasalazine and salicylazosulphadimidine in ulcerative colitis. Lancet 1: 1094-1096 (1962).

Clark, A.G.; Fischer, L.J.; Millburn, P.; Smith, R.L. and Williams, R.T.: The role of gut flora in the enterohepatic circulation of stilboestrol in the rat. Biochemical Journal 17-18 (1969).

Das, K.M. and Dubin, R.: Clinical pharmacokinetics of sulphasalazine. Clinical Pharmacokinetics 1: 406-425 (1976).

Dessau, F.I. and Jackson, B.: Acetamide-induced liver cell alterations in rats. Laboratory Investigation 4: 387-397 (1955).

Edwards, D.I.; Cye, M. and Carne, H.: The selective toxicity of antimicrobial nitroheterocyclic drugs. Journal of General and Applied Microbiology 76: 135-145 (1975).

Goldin, B.R.; Peppercorn, M.A. and Goldman, P.: Contributions of host and intestinal microflora in the metabolism of L-dopa by the rat. Journal of Pharmacology and Experimental Therapeutics 186: 160-166 (1973).

Goldman P.: Biochemical pharmacology of the intestinal flora. Annual Review of Pharmacology and Toxicology 18: 523-439 (1978).

Goldman, P.: Ingelfinger, J.A. and Friedman, P.: Metronidazole, isoniazid and the threat of human cancer; in Hiatt, Watson and Winston (Eds), Cold Spring Harbor Conference on Cell Proliferation, Vol. 4, p.465-474 (Cold Spring Harbor Laboratory, 1977).

Goldman, P. and Peppercorn, M.A.: Drug therapy: sulfasalazine. New England Journal of Medicine 293: 20-23 (1975).

Goldman, P.; Peppercorn, M.A. and Goldin, B: Metabolism of drugs by microorganisms in the intestine; in Floch (Ed) Third International Symposium of Intestinal Microecology. American Journal of Clinical Nutrition.

Gordon, H.A. and Pesti, L.: The gnotobiotic animals as a tool in the study of host microbial relationships. Bacteriological Reviews 35: 390-429 (1971).

Gould, S.R.: Assay of prostaglandin-like substances in faeces and their measurement in ulcerative colitis. Prostaglandins 11: 489-297 (1976).

Holdemann, L.V.; Cato, E.P. and Moore, W.E.C.: Anaerobe Laboratory Manual, 4th ed. (The Virginia Polytechnic Institute and State University Anaerobe Laboratory, Blacksburg, 1977).

Hoult, J.R.S. and Moore, P.K: Sulphasalazine is a potent inhibitor of prostaglandin-hydroxyde-hydrogenase: Possible basis for therapeutic action in ulcerative colitis. British Journal of Pharmacology 64: 6-8 (1978).

Ings, R.M.J.; McFadzean, J.A. and Ormerod, W.E.: The mode of action of metronidazole in *Trichomonas vaginalis* and other micro-organisms. Biochemical Pharmacology 23: 1421-1429 (1974).

Ings, R.M.J.; McFadzean, J.A. and Ormerod, W.E.: The fate of metronidazole and its implications in chemotherapy. Xenobiotica 5: 233-235 (1975).

Jackson, B. and Dessau, F.I.: Laboratory Investigation 10: 909-923 (1961).

Karim, A.B.M.F.: Prolonged metronidazole administration with protracted radio therapy: a pilot study on response of advanced tumors. British Journal of Cancer 37 (Suppl. III) 299-304 (1978).

Knight, R.C.; Skolimowski, I.M. and Edwards, D.I.: The interaction of reduced metronidazole with DNA. Biochemical Pharmacology 27: 2089-2093 (1978).

Koch, R.L.; Chrystal, E.J.T.; Beaulieu, B.B. Jr. and Goldman, P.: Acetamide: a metabolite of metronidazole formed by the intestinal flora. Biochemical Pharmacology (accepted May 1979).

Koch, R.L. and Goldman, P.: The anaerobic metabolism of metronidazole forms N-(2-hydroxyethyl)-oxamic acid. Journal of Pharmacology and Experimental Therapeutics 208: 406-410 (1979).

Lindmark, D.G. and Muller, M.: Antitrichomonad action, mutagenicity and reduction of metronidazole and other nitroimidazoles. Antimicrobial Agents and Chemotherapy 10: 476-482 (1976).

Peppercorn, M.A.; Amnuay, T.; Fromm, D. and Goldman, P.: Detection of bacterial overgrowth by analysis of drug metabolites. Gastroenterology 70: 926, part 2 (1976).

Peppercorn, M.A. and Goldman, P.: The role of intestinal bacteria in the metabolism of salicylazo-sulfapyridine. Journal of Pharmacology and Experimental Therapeutics. 181: 555-562 (1972).

Peppercorn, M.A. and Goldman, P.: Distribution studies of salicylazosulfapyridine and its metabolites. Gastroenterology 64: 240-245 (1973).

Peppercorn, M.A. and Goldman, P.: Drug-bacteria interactions. Review of Drug Interactions 2: 75-88 (1976).

Rosenkranz, H.S. and Speck, W.T.: Mutagenicity of metronidazole: activation by mammalian liver microsomes. Biochemical and Biophysical Research Communications 66: 520-525 (1975).

Rustia, M. and Shubick, P.: Induction of lung tumors and malignant lymphomas in mice by metronidazole. Journal of the National Cancer Institute 48: 721-729 (1972).

Sandler, M.; Goodwin, B.L.; Ruthven, C.R.J. and Calne, D.B.: Therapeutic implications in Parkinsonism in m-tyramine formation from L-dopa in man. Nature 229: 414-416 (1971).

Scheline, R.R.: Metabolism of foreign compounds by gastrointestinal micro-organisms. Pharmacological Reviews 25: 451-532 (1973).

Searle, A.J.F. and Willson, R.L.: Metronidazole (Flagyl): degradation by the intestinal flora. Xenobiotica 6: 457-464 (1976).

Sharon, P.; Ligumsky, M.; Rachmilewitz, D. and Zor, U.: Role of prostaglandins in ulcerative colitis: Enhanced production during active disease and inhibition by sulfasalazine. Gastroenterology 75: 638-640 (1978).

Svartz, N.: Salazopyrin: a new sulfanilamide preparation. Acta Medica Scandinavica 110: 577-598 (1942).

Tally, F.P.; Sutter, V.L. and Finegold, S.M.: Treatment of anaerobic infections with metronidazole. Antimicrobial Agents and Chemotherapy 7: 672-675 (1975).

Thithapandha, A.: Detection of human intestinal bacterial overgrowth by sulfasalazine. Journal of Clinical Pharmacology 18: 549-555 (1978).

Weisburger, J.H.; Yamamoto, R.S.; Glass, R.M. and Frankel, H.H.: Prevention by arginine glutamate of the carcinogenicity of acetamide in rats. Toxicology and Applied Pharmacology 14: 163-175 (1969).

Wheeler, L.A.; Soderberg, F.B. and Goldman, P.: The relationship between nitro group reduction and the intestinal microflora. Journal of Pharmacology and Experimental Therapeutics 194: 135-144 (1975).

Willis, A.T.; Ferguson, I.R.; Jones, P.H.; Phillips, K.D.; Tearle, P.V.; Fiddian, R.V.; Graham, D.F.; Harland, D.H.C.; Hughes, D.F.R.; Knight, D.; Mee, W.M.; Pashby, N.; Rothwell-Jackson, R.L.; Sachdeva, A.K.; Sutch, I.; Kilbey, C. and Edwards, D.: Metronidazole in prevention and treatment of bacteriodes infections in elective colonic surgery. British Medical Journal 1: 607-610 (1977).

# 10

# Presystemic Hepatic Metabolism: Practical and Pathophysiological Aspects

*D.G. Shand*

Division of Clinical Pharmacology, Duke University Medical Center

There are several factors which can reduce the amount of an orally administered drug that will eventually reach its site of action. Quite apart from its ability to be absorbed across the gastrointestinal tract, the drug may be destroyed or metabolised within the gut lumen or by enzymes in the mucosa. Because of the anatomical arrangement of the hepatic portal circulation, drugs absorbed into the portal vein are also exposed to the liver before they can reach a site of action in the systemic circulation. Drug metabolism prior to the drug entering into the systemic circuit at any of these sites after oral administration is referred to as presystemic or first-pass elimination. The pharmacokinetic consequences of presystemic elimination, however, will vary depending on the anatomical site of the elimination process which may be described as pre- or post-absorptive (Routledge and Shand, 1979a). When metabolism occurs within the gut lumen or at a site in the mucosa accessible only by way of the surface and not to blood-borne drug, the elimination is 'pre-absorptive' because it occurs only during absorption and not during recycling from the systemic circuit. In terms of the parent drug such an effect will be indistinguishable from incomplete absorption. When presystemic elimination occurs in the liver or at a site in the gut that can extract drug from the blood, it is considered to be 'post-absorptive' because elimination also occurs after recycling in the systemic circulation. In the case of post-absorptive elimination it is impossible to distinguish the hepatic and intestinal contributions without invasive catheterisation of the portal vein because they function as a single splanchnic unit. This contribution will focus on the role of the liver as at present this appears the most quantitatively important site of presystemic elimination.

## 1. Detection and Quantification of the Presystemic Effect

The following criteria serve to establish that presystemic elimination is occuring:

1) Systemic availability is incomplete
2) Reduced availability cannot be accounted for by incomplete absorption

3) The kinetic data are consistent with the proposed site and magnitude of the effect.

Systemic availability is defined as the fraction, F, of an oral dose which reaches the systemic circulation where drug concentrations are sampled. It is estimated from the area under the blood or plasma concentration/time curve (AUC) after oral (po) and intravenous (iv) administration as:

$$\frac{AUC_{po}}{AUC_{iv}} = F$$

Clearly, with presystemic elimination, F must be less than $F_a$ where $F_a$ is the fraction of the drug absorbed across the gut and is usually estimated from urinary and faecal recovery of the drug and metabolites after oral administration of an isotope of the parent compound. As mentioned, $F_a$ will include the effects of any preabsorptive metabolism.

Showing quantitative consistency is simple in the case of presystemic hepatic (or splanchnic) elimination because the fraction removed is numerically equal to the hepatic (or splanchnic) extraction ratio, E, and the remainder escapes into the body so that:

$$F = (1 - E)$$

Knowing that hepatic clearances ($Cl_h$) is given by the liver blood flow, Q and E according to:

$$Cl_h = QE$$

allows us to compare the E values derived from F and from the systemic (iv) clearance ($Cl_s$) of the drug. Thus, if only the liver eliminates the drug, then $Cl_h = Cl_s$ and knowing $Q = 1.5$ litres/min then the value of E derived from $Cl_s$ should be compatible with $F = (1 - E)$. This approach is well illustrated by the recent work of Perucca and Richens (1979) who showed that the low systemic availability of lignocaine (38 %) in normal volunteers was entirely consistent with its intravenous clearance and liver blood flow.

Two situations exist when availability and intravenous clearance data may not be consistent with presystemic elimination alone. Systemic clearance may be predicted from F and Q as:

$$\text{'Cl'} = Q (1 - F)$$

If 'Cl' is greater than the determined $Cl_s$, then either absorption is incomplete or pre-absorptive metabolism is occurring. When 'Cl' is less than $Cl_s$, then extrahepatic elimination must be occurring.

Most of the reported studies have involved estimation of intravenous and oral kinetics on separate occasions. This assumes that the drug is cleared identically under the two conditions, an assumption that does not always apply. For example, the kinetics of propranolol differ according to the route, dose and duration of therapy (Routledge and Shand, 1979b), so that availability cannot be accurately assessed with separate studies. This problem can be overcome by giving different isotopes by the two routes and estimating them separately (Kornhauser et. al., 1978), thereby allowing simultaneous determination of intravenous and oral kinetics. In this way it has been shown that the steady-state systemic clearance of propranolol was reduced compared to single doses and that the systemic availability increased as a result of reduced hepatic presystemic extraction (Wood, et. al., 1978a). This is an extraordinarily powerful technique which, in the case of a drug like propranolol that is completely absorbed and eliminated only in the liver (Pessayre et. al., 1978), can also be used to estimate hepatic blood flow (Wilkinson and Shand, 1975: Kornhauser et. al., 1978).

## 2. Factors Affecting Presystemic Elimination

Presystemic hepatic elimination is clearly determined by the magnitude of the hepatic extraction ratio. Thus little or no first-pass metabolism occurs with very poorly extracted compounds such as antipyrine, tolbutamide and warfarin (Andreasen and Vesell, 1974). As extraction increases, so does presystemic elimination until it becomes particularly marked with highly extracted drugs, such as lignocaine and propranolol. A full listing of the drugs involved may be found in the review by Routledge and Shand (1979a).

In contrast to poorly extracted drugs, whose hepatic elimination depends largely on drug metabolising activity (intrinsic clearance), the hepatic clearance of highly extracted compounds is dependent on blood flow and is less sensitive to changes in intrinsic clearance. Even with such compounds, however, the apparent clearance of an oral dose is largely dependent on intrinsic clearance. This apparent paradox is a result of presystemic extraction and can be seen from the determinants of oral clearance ($Cl_o$) and systemic (or hepatic) clearance ($Cl_s$) that are described by the following series of relationships (Wilkinson and Shand, 1975):

$$Cl_o = \frac{D}{AUC_{po}} = \frac{Cl_s}{(1-E)} = \frac{QE}{(1-E)}$$

Let us now suppose that a large change in intrinsic clearance results in only a small (5 %) increase in E from 90 to 95 %. As a result $Cl_s$ will only increase by 5 %. However, $(1-E)$ decreases quite obviously from 10 to 5 % and oral clearance more than doubles because the term $E/(1-E)$ increases from 9 to 19. Conversely, an increase in Q will produce an almost proportional change in $Cl_s$ and intravenous clearance. However, increased Q does reduce E to a small extent. Again, however, $(1-E)$ increases more obviously and the increase in availability offsets the increased $Cl_s$ so that $AUC_o$ changes little. It is this line of reasoning that has led to the conclusion that with highly extracted drugs changes in intrinsic clearance largely affect orally administered drugs, while changes in flow affect their kinetics much more after intravenous administration (Rowland, 1972; Wilkinson and Shand, 1975). Although no data are available on the effects of altered flow, there is ample evidence to support this statement concerning altered enzyme activity. Thus the administration of enzyme inducers reduced the concentrations of orally administered metyrapone (Meikle et. al., 1969), alprenolol (Alvan et. al., 1977) and lidocaine (Perucca and Richens, 1979), but had little or no effect on the kinetics after intravenous administration. In the same way inhibition of propranolol metabolism by chlorpromazine only increased circulating concentrations after oral drug (Vestal et. al., 1979). The obvious changes in oral clearance after enzyme inhibition and induction can therefore be rationalised in terms of the reciprocal relationship between E and F due to the presystemic effect. However, this does little to help us quantify the activity of the drug metabolising enzymes (intrinsic clearance), nor to quantify its role in determining systemic and oral clearance. The central, and unresolved, problem is that we cannot measure intrinsic clearance directly *in vivo*, but must use a model in order to calculate it from estimates of Q and $Cl_s$ or E. We can define intrinsic clearance ($Cl_i^1$) as the volume of liver water cleared of drug in unit time. It can be simply shown (Routledge and Shand, 1979a) that the hepatic clearance of total (bound and free) drug cleared from the blood at steady-state is given by:

$$Cl_h = \frac{Cl_i^1 \; fB \; C_L}{C_{in}}$$

where fB is the free (unbound) fraction of drug in blood, $C_{in}$ the inflow drug concentration and $C_L$ an estimate of free drug concentration in the liver. Two models are available which make different assumptions about the value of $C_L$ which cannot be directly determined. According to the venous equilibration model (Rowland et. al., 1973), $C_L$ is given by the concentration of free drug in the hepatic venous effluent. It is a simple matter to show that $AUC_{po}$ is the same as the AUC in the hepatic veins when the same dose is given intravenously (Wilkinson and Shand, 1975). It is this that allows the estimation of Q from the oral and intravenous kinetics. Furthermore, making the relevant substitutions in the previous equation it follows that:

$$\frac{D}{AUC_{po}} = Cl_i^1 \; fB$$

Thus the venous equilibration model predicts that oral drug clearance is numerically equal to the intrinsic clearance of total drug and would suggest that altered drug metabolism is quantitatively translated into changes in apparent oral clearance.

An alternative (sinusoidal) model was originally proposed by Brauer (1963) and expanded by Winkler et al. (1973). This model suggests that drug concentrations decline as a first-order (exponential) function across the liver so that $C_L$ becomes the logarithmic average of inflow and outflow concentrations. An extensive theoretical comparison of the two models has been made by Pang and Rowland (1977) and many of the differences are practically speaking beyond the ability of experimental differentiation, with the exception of the determinants of oral clearance. In particular the venous equilibration model predicts that $Cl_o$ depends only on intrinsic clearance and drug binding in blood, while the sinusoidal model predicts that altered blood flow will also influence $Cl_o$. Even then, however, the effects of altered intrinsic clearance will still have a greater effect after oral than after intravenous administration of highly extracted drugs. While the weight of evidence based on the animal experiments favours venous equilibration, not all the data are consistent and the question remains unresolved.

So far we have made only a cursory reference to the effects of drug binding in blood on the kinetics of highly extracted drugs. There are two good reasons for this: firstly, the methods are inconvenient so that drug binding is seldom investigated, and secondly, the effects of altered drug binding are the most complex we have to deal with because they involve not only drug elimination, but also drug distribution. Nonetheless, consideration of drug binding is of paramount importance because drug bound to blood or non-specific sites cannot be bound to its site of action, so that drug efficacy and toxicity may safely be assumed to be a function of its free (unbound) concentration. Of all the highly extracted drugs, only propranolol has been investigated thoroughly enough to make any firm conclusions. After intravenous administration, the hepatic extraction is so avid compared to plasma binding, that the drug is functionally stripped from its binding sites in blood during a single pass through the liver. In this situation, altered binding has no effect on the hepatic clearance of *total* drug (Evans et al., 1973). Because the intravenous clearance was unaltered by plasma binding, elimination was termed 'non-restrictive' to contrast the situation with that of poorly extracted drugs, like warfarin, whose elimination was so inefficient that it was reduced by plasma drug binding (Levy and Yacobi, 1974), a situation in which elimination was classified as 'restrictive' (Wilkinson and Shand, 1975). Thus after intravenous administration, altered plasma binding will not affect steady-state total plasma concentration, but *will* proportionately change free (active) drug concentrations. For example, reduced binding will increase steady-state free drug concentration. At the same time, however, more drug is available for tissue distribution, so that the increased volume of distribution will prolong drug half-life. These combined effects will raise trough levels of free drug to a greater extent than peak concentrations during intermittent intravenous therapy. Again after oral administration the effect is different. As mentioned, total drug concentrations after oral administration are dependent largely on intrinsic clearance and the free drug fraction in blood. Thus reduction in binding when fB increases, will cause a reduction in steady-state total concentration and free drug will change little or not at all. With the change in half-life however, peak free concentration will be lower and trough levels higher during intermittent therapy. In this sense the effects of altered binding on the kinetics of highly extracted drugs after oral administration resembles the 'restrictive' situation. In terms of testing these predictions, there are no data in which a change in fB occurs without altered intrinsic clearance. It has, however, been shown that the systemic clearance of propranolol is not affected by individual variation in plasma binding (Evans et al., 1973; Kornhauser et al., 1978). Unfortunately, after oral administration in normals intrinsic clearance varies much more than fB, so that no statement can be made about the effects of fB alone (Kornhauser et al., 1978).

## 3. The Effects of Cirrhosis

The known pathophysiological alterations that occur in cirrhotic patients offers an interesting opportunity to apply the simple principles previously outlined. Thus we know that the number of viable hepatocytes is reduced as a result of the precipitating injury. In addition, regenerating nodules and fibrosis destroy the normal micro-architecture and cause islands of poorly perfused tissue and the development of intrahepatic shunts. We would therefore confidently predict that the intrinsic clearance of the whole organ would be reduced. Although it is often stated that total liver blood flow is reduced, this effect is variable and in general the fall of flow is modest and much less than the reduction in hepatic extraction which is due primarily to a fall in intrinsic clearance (Branch and Shand, 1976; Pessayre et al., 1978). Thus we could with some confidence predict that systemic drug clearance would be impaired. This in general holds true, though some notable exceptions involving primary glucuronidation exist (Wilkinson and Schenker, 1976). As a result of the reduced hepatic extraction, we would also predict that presystemic elimination would be reduced. As a result of increased availability and the subsequent poor clearance of drug that enters the systemic circulation, oral drug levels should be even more elevated than those after intravenous administration. This tendency will be further magnified by the presence of any mesenteric portacaval anastomosis which would bypass any presystemic elimination. These predictions have been amply borne out by studies of the high clearance drugs, lignocaine (lidocaine) [Tschanz et al., 1979], propranolol (Wood et al., 1978b) and pethidine and pentazocine (Neal et al., 1979).

In summary, we have learned a considerable amount about the biological factors that influence the presystemic elimination of highly extracted drugs. This should form a better basis for understanding the disposition of these compounds in both health and disease.

# References

Alvan, G.; Piafsky, K.; Lind, M. and Von Bahr, C.: Effect of pentobarbital on the disposition of alprenolol. Clinical Pharmacology and Therapeutics 22: 316-321 (1977).

Andreasen, P.B. and Vesell, E.S.: Comparison of plasma levels of antipyrine, tolbutamide and warfarin after oral and intravenous administration. Clinical Pharmacology and Therapeutics 16: 1059-1065 (1974).

Branch, R.A. and Shand, D.G.: Propranolol disposition in chronic liver disease: A physiological approach. Clinical Pharmocokinetics 1: 264-279 (1976).

Brauer, R.W.: Liver circulation and function. Physiological Reviews 43: 115-213 (1963).

Evans, G.H.; Nies, A.S. and Shand, D.G.: The disposition of propranolol III, Decreased half-life and volume of distribution as a result of plasma binding in man, monkey, dog and rat. Journal of Pharmacology and Experimental Therapeutics 186: 114-122 (1973).

Kornhauser, D.M.; Wood, A.J.J.; Vestal, R.E.; Wilkinson, G.R.; Branch, R.A. and Shand, D.G.: Biological determinants of propranolol disposition in man. Clinical Pharmacology and Therapeutics 23: 165-174 (1978).

Levy, G. and Yacobi, A.: Effect of plasma protein binding on elimination of warfarin. Journal of Pharmaceutical Sciences 63: 805-806 (1974).

Meikle, A.W.; Jubiz, W.; Matsukura, S.; West, C.D. and Tyler, F.H.: Effect of diphenylhydantoin on the metabolism of metyrapone and release of ACTH in man. The Journal of Clinical Endocrinology 29: 1553-1558 (1969).

Neal, E.A.; Meffin, P.J.; Gregory, P.B. and Blaschke, T.F.: Enhanced bioavailability and decreased clearance of analgesics in patients with cirrhosis. Gastroenterology 77: 96-102 (1979).

Pang, K.S. and Rowland, M.: Hepatic clearance of drugs. 1, Theoretical considerations of a 'well-stirred' and a 'parallel tube' model. Influence of hepatic blood flow, plasma and blood cell binding and the hepatocellular enzyme activity on hepatic drug clearance. Journal of Pharmacokinetics and Biopharmaceutics 5: 625-653 (1977).

Perucca, E. and Richens, A.: Reduction of oral bioavailability of lignocaine by induction of first pass metabolism in epileptic patients. British Journal of Clinical Pharmacology 8: 21-31 (1979).

Pessayre, D.; Lebrec, D.; Descatoine, D.; Peignouxe, M. and Benhamou, J.P.: The mechanism for reduced drug clearance in patients with cirrhosis. Gastroenterology 74: 566-571 (1978).

Routledge, P.A. and Shand, D.G.: Presystemic drug elimination. Annual Reviews of Pharmacology 19: 477-468 (1979a).

Routledge, P.A. and Shand, D.G.: Clinical pharmacokinetics of propranolol. Clinical Pharmacokinetics 4: 73-90 (1979b).

Rowland, M.: Influence of route of administration on drug availability. Journal of Pharmaceutical Sciences 61: 70-74 (1972).

Rowland, M.; Benet, L.Z. and Graham, G.: Clearance concepts in pharmacokinetics. Journal of Pharmacokinetics and Biopharmacetuics 1: 123-136 (1973).

Tschanz, C.; Hignite, C.H.; Huffman, D.H. and Azarnoff, D.L.: Predicting the first pass effect of lidocaine in patients with liver disease in: Preisig and Bircher (Eds) The Liver: Quantitative aspects of structure and function. (Editio Cantor, Aulendorf 1979).

Vestal, R.E.; Kornhauser, D.M.; Hollifield, J.W. and Shand, D.G.: Inhibition of propranolol metabolism
    by chlorpromazine. Clinical Pharmacology and Therapeutics 25: 19-24 (1979).
Wilkinson, G.R. and Shand, D.G.: A physiological approach to hepatic drug clearance. Clinical Phar-
    macology and Therapeutics 18: 377-390 (1975).
Wilkinson, G.R. and Schenker, S.: Effects of liver disease on drug disposition in man. Biochemical Phar-
    macology 25: 2675-2681 (1976).
Winkler, K.; Keiding, S. and Tygstrup, N.: Clearance as a quantitative measure of liver blood flow; in
    Paumgartner and Preisig (Eds) The Liver: Quantitative Aspects of Structure and Function p.
    144-155. (S. Karger, New York, 1973).
Wood, A.J.J.; Carr, K.; Vestal, R.E.; Belcher, S.; Wilkinson, G.R. and Shand, D.G.: Direct measurement
    of propranolol bioavailability during accumulation to steady state. British Journal of Clinical Phar-
    macology 6: 345-350 (1978a).
Wood, A.J.J.; Kornhauser, D.M.; Wilkinson, G.R.; Shand, D.G. and Branch, R.A.: The influence of cir-
    rhosis on steady state blood concentrations of bound and unbound propranolol after oral ad-
    ministration. Clinical Pharmacokinetics 3: 478-487 (1978b).

## Discussion

*C.T. Dollery* (Chairman): What are the limitations of the simultaneous administration of stable isotopes and non-labelled compounds by different routes?

*D.G. Shand*: You are assuming that there is instantaneous and complete mixing
of the isotope, be it radioactive or stable. You are also assuming that there is no tri-
tium exchange. In our experience, once the drug is injected intravenously the terminal
half-life appears identical for the 2 isotopes. There is also the possibility that the
isotopes might be handled differently in the body.

*C.T. Dollery*: I think this mixing problem is a real one and I wondered about
your decision to use a single intravenous dose with chronic oral dosing. I would have
thought it more sensible to use single doses by both routes.

*D.G. Shand:* The kinetics are different with the 2 single doses and the most relevant clinical situation with propranolol is chronic administration.

*B.G. Woodcock* (Frankfurt): I wonder about the use of a highly extracted drug
such as propranolol for estimating blood flow as an alternative to indocyanine green
clearance. Propranolol has an extraction ratio of approximately 0.6 and there are
drugs for which it is higher. With propranolol the intrinsic clearance depends to some
extent upon enzyme activity. If the extraction ratio were higher you would get a better
correlation between systemic clearance and blood flow. Do you think that a drug with
an extraction ratio of 0.9 for example could be used clinically to determine blood flow
simply by measuring the systemic clearance?

*D.G. Shand*: Absolutely not. That was a holy grail sought by clinical
hepatologists and physiologists 20 years ago. The problem is that in liver disease,
there are changes not only in flow but also in extraction so that the clearance then is
not determined entirely by the flow. It will never be possible to measure liver blood
flow this way in patients with liver disease, although it could be done in normal
people.

*C.T. Dollery*: But you cannot show that either, unless some assumptions are
made about your model. You seem to be producing an intact sinusoid hypothesis.

*D.G. Shand*: No, the blood flow estimate is model independent. It depends only
on the marker being fully absorbed and eliminated only by the liver. However, intrinsic clearance estimates are very model dependent.

*R. Schneider* (Birmingham): We were not able to confirm the higher plasma
propranolol concentrations reported by others in the elderly. In our studies the
plasma propranolol curves were marginally below those in normal younger controls

and were practically superimposable. The reason may be that our elderly subjects represented a different group of people and they were not hospital patients. They were 65 to 81 years of age and were active, reasonably healthy retired members (including myself) of Birmingham University staff.

*D.G. Shand*: Our data were obtained in the community and not in a geriatric ward. We were very fortunate. The p value came out less than 0.05 so we threw up our hands in joy and said that some journal will accept this. However, the values for r and especially $r^2$ were not very good at all and we have by no means accounted for all the variables. There are so many factors including diet and age and in small populations, one may get very different answers.

*C.T. Dollery*: This important point applies to much clinical research and not just to pharmacological research. The extremely naive sampling techniques are sometimes forced on us through lack of suitable subjects.

*J.A. Blair* (Birmingham): You spoke of the elderly as lacking certain enzymes which are responsible for the metabolism of propranolol. Which enzymes?

*D.G. Shand*: They are best described as mixed function oxidases but the precise enzymes are not known. At the last count 17 metabolites of propranolol had been identified. I do not know which enzyme limits the rate of propranolol metabolism.

# 11

# Presystemic Hepatic Metabolism — Interaction with Ethanol

*T. Zyssett and J. Bircher*

Department of Clinical Pharmacology, University of Berne

The effect of a single dose of ethanol on drug disposition has been studied repeatedly. In every instance an inhibition of drug elimination — albeit of variable degree — has been noted resulting in persistence of the drug within the organism (Rubin et al., 1970; Audetat et al., 1977; Sellers and Holloway, 1978).

In recent years, factors determining the rate of hepatic drug disposition — intrinsic clearance, protein binding, and blood flow — have become better understood (Rowland et al., 1973; Wilkinson and Shand, 1975). In addition, the concept of first-pass elimination has been emphasised (Rowland, 1972; Gillette and Pang, 1977). On this basis it appeared likely that the effect of ethanol on hepatic elimination of orally administered drugs should be particularly prominent for those compounds which normally undergo extensive first-pass elimination. In such cases an acute interaction with ethanol might result not only in persistence of the drug but also in decreased first-pass elimination. Plasma concentrations would therefore be increased and toxicity could result.

In view of the potential practical importance of this hypothesis experiments were carried out in dogs to test the effect of single doses of ethanol on the fate of mephenytoin. In addition preliminary studies were carried out with chlormethiazole in rabbits.

## 1. Material and Methods

### 1.1 Studies in Dogs

Four trained female dogs were given intravenously either physiological saline or ethanol in saline according to a cross-over design. After a loading dose of 18.5mmol/kg administered within 30 minutes an infusion of 2.2mmol/kg per hour was continued for 8 hours. This procedure resulted in a mean ethanol blood concentration of 22.4mmol/litre (1.03g/L) which remained virtually constant throughout the 8-hour period of study. At least 4 weeks were allowed between experiments.

Mephenytoin was given by mouth together with about 20g of minced meat in doses of 12.5, 25 and 100µmol/kg either immediately after the loading dose of ethanol or after the start of the saline infusion. In dogs not receiving ethanol doses of 25µmol/kg were also injected intravenously.

Heparinised blood samples (5 ml) were obtained at intervals for 8 hours and urine was collected using a catheter. Two dogs had previously been cholecystectomised and a Thomas-duodenal cannula was inserted. In these animals a catheter was also placed in the common duct and bile obtained by gravity drainage during the whole 8-hour period. To correct for the loss of bile acids sodium taurocholate was infused intravenously (approximately 20µmol/min). Plasma, bile, and urine samples were stored at − 20°.

Mephenytoin and its metabolites were measured as described previously (Kupfer and Bircher, 1979).

## 1.2 Studies in Rabbits

For these preliminary studies rabbits were nephrectomised on the left side and catheters inserted into the left renal artery and vein, and the inferior mesenteric vein. This gave access to the portal vein without the need for anaesthesia.

Experiments were carried out at weekly intervals with intravenous ethanol in physiological saline or saline alone according to a cross-over design. The loading dose of ethanol (39mmol/kg) was given within 20 minutes and then followed by a continuous infusion of 22mmol/kg per hour resulting in ethanol blood concentrations of 33 to 43mmol/litre (1.5-2g/L).

Chlormethiazole was infused intravenously or intraportally at 117µmol/kg per hour. Heparinised arterial blood samples were obtained at intervals and plasma was stored at − 20°.

Plasma concentrations of chlormethiazole were determined with a gas-liquid chromatographic method using 2-methylquinoline as internal standard. Plasma containing internal standard was alkalinised with sodium hydroxide and extracted with ether. The ether phase was evaporated after addition of 20µl of a hexanol/ether mixture (0.8/10). The residue was dissolved in acetone and aliquots injected into a 6' glass column containing 3% OV 17 at 120°. A nitrogen-selective detector was used. Standard curves were linear between 0.2 and 20nmol/ml.

## 1.3 Calculations

Areas under the plasma concentration-time curves (AUC) were calculated with the trapezoidal rule and, if necessary, extrapolated to infinity by the ratio of the last plasma concentration to the disappearance rate constant. Standard statistical methods were applied (Sachs, 1974).

## 2. Results

### 2.1 Mephenytoin

Without ethanol the AUC 0-8h was compared after oral and intravenous administration and the mean systemic availability was 38.1 ± SEM 3.1%. Thus, an

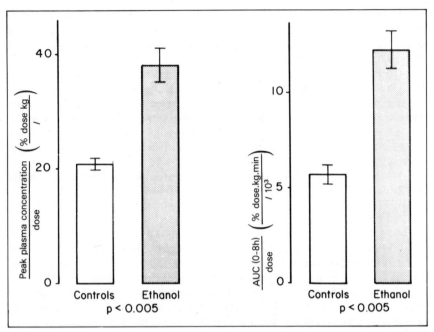

*Fig. 1.* Relative peak plasma concentrations and AUC 0-8h of mephenytoin after oral administration in dogs with and without ethanol infusion. Values are means ± SE (n = 12).

average of 61.9% had been eliminated in the first passage through the intestine and the liver.

With ethanol peak plasma concentrations of mephenytoin were twice as high as during control experiments. Similarly the AUC values were much larger than in studies without ethanol. Thus, the systemic availability of mephenytoin was significantly increased by ethanol (fig. 1).

In order to evaluate the effects of ethanol more completely an attempt was made to assess the recovery of mephenytoin and its metabolites (nirvanol and p-hydroxy-mephenytoin). The amount of mephenytoin and of nirvanol in the rabbits was estimated by multiplying the respective plasma concentrations at 8 hours with the corresponding volumes of distribution previously determined from studies with intravenous mephenytoin or nirvanol (Kupfer et al., 1977). To these amounts the quantities of metabolites found in urine were added.

Total recovery of mephenytoin and its metabolites was about 70% when the drug was given by mouth and 77% when it was injected intravenously (fig. 2). Thus absorption of oral mephenytoin had been virtually complete and unaffected by ethanol. As expected, ethanol produced significant reduction of mephenytoin metabolites in blood, urine and bile ($p < 0.05$).

## 2.2 Chlormethiazole

Infusions of about 2 µmol/kg per min of chlormethiazole resulted in a condition close to steady-state within 60 to 90 minutes. After termination of the infusion,

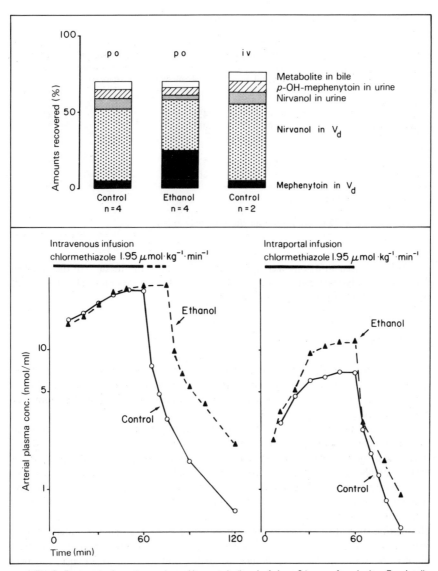

*Fig. 2.* Recovery of mephenytoin and its metabolites in 4 dogs 8 hours after dosing. For details see text.

*Fig. 3.* Plasma concentrations of chlormethiazole in nonanaesthetised rabbits receiving intraportal or intravenous infusion of the drug with and without ethanol.

plasma concentrations fell rapidly to the limit of detection (fig. 3). The total clearance after intravenous administration was calculated as the ratio of the infusion rate to the plasma concentration at steady-state and as the ratio of the dose to the AUC extrapolated to infinity. The latter method gave values about 10 % higher, but both methods agreed in showing that during ethanol infusion the clearance was reduced by about 10 % (table I).

*Table I.* Kinetics of chlormethiazole in a rabbit

|  | Plasma concentration (at steady-state) nmol/ml | AUC 0-∞ nmol/ml/min | Infusion rate[1]/plasma concentration ml/min/kg | Dose[2]/ AUC 0-∞ ml/min/kg |
|---|---|---|---|---|
| Intravenous infusion[1] |  |  |  |  |
| without ethanol | 26.8 | 1450 | 73 | 81 |
| with ethanol | 29.6 | 1964[3] | 66 | 74[3] |
| Intraportal infusion[1] |  |  |  |  |
| without ethanol | 7.0 | 375 | 278 | 312 |
| with ethanol | 11.9 | 566 | 163 | 207 |

1   1.95µmol/kg per min.
2   117µmol/kg.
3   Infusion for 75 minutes to a total dose of 146µmol/kg.

When similar infusions were given into the portal vein, the ratio of the infusion rate to the steady-state concentration and the ratio of the dose to the AUC (0-∞) fell by 41 and 34% respectively after ethanol.

## 3. Discussion

The systemic availability of orally administered mephenytoin is clearly increased in dogs acutely intoxicated by moderate doses of ethanol. The observed plasma ethanol concentrations of approximately 22mmol/litre ( = 1g/L) are often found or even exceeded in man.

Different mechanisms could be responsible for the ethanol-induced increase in the plasma concentrations of mephenytoin. The volumes of distribution — assessed when the drug was given intravenously — were not modified by ethanol and the extent of mephenytoin absorption also was not substantially changed. In contrast, biotransformation by demethylation to nirvanol or by hydroxylation to *p*-hydroxy-mephenytoin was decreased by ethanol. Theoretically, an increase in the AUC (0-∞) could be due to reduced elimination of mephenytoin, to a decrease in first-pass elimination or both. In order to distinguish between these possibilities mephenytoin was also given intravenously to 2 dogs receiving an ethanol infusion. First-pass elimination was 43% in the presence of ethanol and 57% in its absence. Furthermore, the disappearance of mephenytoin from plasma was slowed by ethanol. Thus both first-pass elimination and subsequent drug metabolism were inhibited by ethanol. This interpretation is consistent with the decreased recovery of mephenytoin metabolites in experiments with ethanol.

The preliminary experiments with chlormethiazole in rabbits demonstrate the important effect of ethanol on hepatic first-pass elimination of a drug used frequently in alcoholics. However, the disposition of chlormethiazole in rabbits is quite complex. For instance, the total clearance of 70 to 80 ml/kg per minute is larger than the expected hepatic blood flow, suggesting that organs other than the liver participate in the rapid elimination of the drug from the circulation.

After portal administration of chlormethiazole, the ratio of the infusion rate to the steady-state plasma concentration represents the total clearance (Cl) divided by the systemic availability (f). Similarly the ratio of the dose to the AUC $(0-\infty)$ corresponds to Cl/f. Thus f was calculated to be 0.36 to 0.40 in the presence of ethanol and 0.26 in its absence. This represents a 50 % increase in systemic availability. In contrast, ethanol reduced the systemic clearance of chlormethiazole only by about 10 %.

Our studies have shown that in two species and with two different model compounds, ethanol reduces their first-pass elimination. This effect may be particularly relevant for drugs with extensive first-pass elimination. However the effects of ethanol on drug disposition seem to vary from drug to drug and may be different in man.

## Acknowledgement

The authors wish to acknowledge the support of the Swiss National Science Foundation. The mephenytoin and chlormethiazole were kindly supplied by Sandoz, Basle and Astra, Lakemedel, Sweden respectively.

## References

Audetat, V.; Preisig, R. and Bircher, J.: Der Aminopyrin-Atemtest unter akuter Aethanoleinwirkung. Schweizerische Medizinische Wochenschrift 107: 231-235 (1977).

Gillette, J.R. and Pang, K.S.: Theoretic aspects of pharmacokinetic drug interactions. Clinical Pharmacology and Therapeutics 22: 623-639 (1977).

Kupfer, A. and Bircher, J.: Stereoselectivity of differential routes of drug metabolism: The fate of the enantiomers of 14C-mephenytoin in the dog. Journal of Pharmacology and Experimental Therapeutics 209: 190-195 (1979).

Kupfer, A.; Bircher, J. and Preisig, R.: Stereoselective metabolism, pharmacokinetics and biliary elimination of phenyl-ethylhydantoin (nirvanol) in the dog. Journal of Pharmacology and Experimental Therapeutics 203: 493-499 (1977).

Rowland, M: Influence of route of administration on drug availability. Journal of Pharmaceutical Sciences 61: 70-74 (1972).

Rowland, M.; Benet, L.Z. and Graham, G.: Clearance concepts in pharmacokinetics. Journal of Pharmacokinetics and Biopharmaceutics. 1: 123-136 (1973).

Rubin, E.; Gang, H.; Misra, P.S. and Lieber, C.S.: Inhibition of drug metabolism by actue ethanol intoxication. American Journal of Medicine 49: 801-806 (1970).

Sachs, L.: Angewandte Statistik, 4th ed. (Springer, Berlin 1974).

Sellers, E.M. and Holloway, M.R.: Drug kinetics and alcohol ingestion. Clinical Pharmacokinetics. 3: 440-452 (1978).

Wilkinson, G.R. and Shand, D.G.: A physiological approach to hepatic drug clearance. Clinical Pharmacology and Therapeutics. 18: 377-389 (1975).

## Discussion

*J.A.J.H. Critchley* (Edinburgh): How far can you extrapolate these single-dose studies in rabbits who have never had an alcoholic drink before, to the situation in humans chronically taking alcohol and in whom blood ethanol concentrations are often much higher than 100mg/dl?

*J. Bircher*: In man, we must distinguish between chronic alcohol ingestion and acute alcohol intoxication. We have studied only the latter. However, chronic alcohol intake leads to an increase in mixed function oxidase activity with stimulation of drug metabolism. We carefully avoided chronic administration in these animals and always allowed time between experiments.

*D.P. Vaughan* (Sunderland): After propranolol with ethanol, the plasma concentration curve is very flat compared to the control study with propranolol alone.
The whole curve is different so that the kinetics of transport and perhaps the volume
of distribution have changed. You have been looking at the area but not at the shape
of the curve.

*J. Bircher*: I agree that the shape of the curve is different.

*C.P. Dollery* (Chairman): I have met one or two drunk dogs but never a drunk
rabbit! I do not know what happens to the cardiac output in drunk humans but you
find flushing and tachycardia. I imagine that the cardiac output and the liver blood
flow would change. Have you calculated the liver blood flow from your data to see if
there is a change?

*J. Bircher*: Mephenytoin and chlormethiazole do not fulfil the necessary criteria
to calculate liver blood flow. Mephenytoin is probably subject to some intestinal
metabolism and there must be extra-hepatic elimination of chlormethiazole too,
because its total clearance is much greater than liver blood flow. In the dog, liver
blood flow does not change during acute ethanol intoxication.

# 12

# First-pass Effects in Health and Disease: Pharmacokinetic Studies on Dextropropoxyphene

*Gerhard Levy and Kathleen M. Giacomini*

Department of Pharmaceutics, School of Pharmacy, State University of New York

There have been numerous investigations into the effect of disease on the absorption and elimination of drugs (Benet, 1976; Kato, 1977) but little is known about the effect of disease on presystemic (first-pass) biotransformation of orally administered medicinal agents. Pharmacokinetic theory permits some reasonable predictions of the magnitude of the first-pass effect on drugs that are eliminated entirely by apparent first-order hepatic biotransformation (Perrier and Gibaldi, 1972; Perrier et al., 1973) but many drugs are partly metabolised during absorption in both intestinal and hepatic tissues. Moreover, oral administration usually exposes the intestine and the liver to much higher concentrations of the drug during absorption than does intravenous injection, so that presystemic biotransformation may be non-linear (capacity-limited) in the gut wall, in the liver, or in both.

Another frequent complication encountered in clinical studies is that practical and/or ethical considerations may prevent intravenous administration of certain first-pass drugs to ill patients. Without intravenous data, it is impossible to determine the absolute systemic availability. In animal studies we use whenever possible the optimum methodology: concomitant administration of an intravenous and an oral dose, one suitably labelled and the other 'cold' (Crow et al., 1979). With greater availability of drugs labelled with stable isotopes, this methodology can be expected to be more commonly used in clinical investigations.

It is to be expected, and it has in fact been demonstrated (Neal et al., 1979) that the first-pass effect on certain drugs is reduced in patients with hepatic dysfunction. The likelihood that diseases other than hepatic disease may affect the presystemic biotransformation of drugs came to our attention as a result of reports, by two groups of investigators (Lowenthal et al., 1974; Bianchetti et al., 1976), that oral doses of propranolol produced much higher drug concentrations in the blood of anephric patients than in normal subjects. To explore the possibility that this may also occur with other drugs, we selected the analgesic agent dextropropoxyphene for investigation.

Dextropropoxyphene is the most widely prescribed oral analgesic in the United States. It is often given to patients with renal or hepatic dysfunction, and there have been no reports of serious adverse effects of this drug in the type of patient who was to participate in our studies. During our investigations there appeared several reports and public statements, well summarised recently by the Food and Drug Administration (1979), indicating that dextropropoxyphene is frequently associated with suicide and accidental deaths. Significantly, it appears that some of the latter occurred apparently as a result of the consumption of amounts of dextropropoxyphene only slightly in excess of therapeutic doses. These accidental deaths have usually involved the concomitant use of one or more central nervous system depressants (Food and Drug Administration, 1979), but in doses that would not be toxic had these CNS drugs been taken alone. This information indicated to us that dextropropoxyphene is not only a useful model drug for the study of factors affecting presystemic biotransformation, but that it required investigation in its own right. Considering that most individuals appear to absorb only one-third or less of the drug intact (Perrier and Gibaldi, 1972), one must consider the possibility that some persons, for one reason or another, absorb a much larger fraction of the dose in unmetabolised form and that these individuals may be especially at risk when they take dextropropoxyphene together with other CNS depressants.

Dextropropoxyphene is eliminated practically entirely by biotransformation; a major biotransformation pathway is N-demethylation to norpropoxyphene. This metabolite, which is cleared by the body much more slowly than its precursor, is also pharmacologically active. It may contribute to the cardiotoxicity associated with dextropropoxyphene poisoning (Nickander et al., 1977; Lund-Jacobsen, 1978; Holland and Steinberg, 1979). Most of the metabolite is eliminated by renal excretion and some by conjugation (Verebely and Inturrisi, 1974). We considered it important therefore to monitor the plasma concentrations not only of dextropropoxyphene but also of norpropoxyphene, particularly in anephric patients.

The research summarised here consists of initial studies in dogs and rats to obtain some information not readily determinable in man, followed by clinical investigations involving normal subjects, anephric patients and patients with hepatic cirrhosis. The detailed data, methodology and appropriate references are available in the reports by Giacomini et al., (1980), Gibson et al., (1980), and Roberts and Levy (1980).

## 1. Methods

### 1.1 Animal Studies

The studies on dogs were performed before and after construction of a side-to-side portacaval shunt which included tying off the portal vein just proximal to the liver. Dextropropoxyphene hydrochloride was administered intravenously (2mg/kg) and orally (7.5mg/kg in solution by gastric tube) on separate occasions, both before and after construction of the shunt. Blood samples were obtained serially and plasma was assayed for dextropropoxyphene and norpropoxyphene.

Adult male rats received a single intravenous dose of either uranyl nitrate or saline solution. 5 days later, when serum creatinine concentrations in the treated animals had increased to about 150mg/100 ml (about 15mg/100 ml in the control animals), all rats received an intravenous injection of tritium-labelled dextropropoxy-phene, about 8µg/kg. Blood samples were obtained over 6 to 8 hours, serum was separated and extracted, the extract was subjected to thin layer chromatography and the isolated dextropropoxyphene was determined by scintillation spectrometry.

### 1.2 Clinical Studies

Clinical studies were performed by administering a single oral dose of dex-tropropoxyphene hydrochloride to healthy adults, anephric patients (both surgical and physiological), and patients with hepatic cirrhosis. The concentrations of dex-tropropoxyphene and norpropoxyphene in plasma were determined over 12 to 24 hours.

Dextropropoxyphene and norpropoxyphene in plasma of dogs and humans was determined by gas chromatography. Standard methods were used for phar-macokinetic analyses.

## 2. Results

### 2.1 Animal Studies

The systemic availability of dextropropoxyphene in dogs was only about 25%, and increased to an average of 54% after construction of a portacaval shunt (table I). The increase of AUC values (area under plasma concentration-time curve) was even more pronounced since some of the dogs exhibited a significant decrease in the systemic clearance of dextropropoxyphene after shunt surgery.

The ratio of AUC values, norpropoxyphene:dextropropoxyphene, following in-travenous injection of dextropropoxyphene, was similar before and after shunt surg-ery. On the other hand, the AUC ratio following oral administration of dextropro-poxyphene to the dogs was substantially reduced after shunt surgery (table II).

The systemic clearance and apparent volume of distribution of intravenous dex-tropropoxyphene were 61.4 ± 11.7ml/kg/min and 10.3 ± 3.2L/kg, respectively, in control rats, and 59.1 ± 13.2ml/kg/min and 8.31 ± 2.13L/kg, respectively, in uraemic rats (mean ± SD, n = 6). The differences are not statistically significant.

### 2.2 Clinical Studies

The AUC values of dextropropoxyphene were significantly larger and the max-imum plasma concentrations of the drug were significantly higher in 7 anephric patients than in 7 normal subjects (table III). The biological half-life of the drug ap-pears to be similar in the patients and normal subjects (fig. 1). Norpropoxyphene con-centrations tended to be higher (table III) and declined more slowly (fig. 2) in the anephric patients.

Patients with hepatic cirrhosis had considerably higher dextropropoxyphene and much lower norpropoxyphene plasma concentrations than normal subjects (table IV). Most strikingly, the AUC ratio, norpropoxyphene:dextropropoxyphene, decreased from a normal value of about 4 to less than 1 (table IV).

*Table I.* Systemic availability and total clearance of dextropropoxyphene in dogs before and after portacaval shunt

| Dog | Before shunt | | After shunt | |
|---|---|---|---|---|
| | availability[1] (%) | clearance[2] (ml/kg/min) | availability[1] % | clearance (ml/kg/min) |
| 1 | 24.9 | 14.4 | 72.6 | 15.8 |
| 2 | 16.2 | 25.8 | 25.1 | 11.0 |
| 3 | 20.3 | 31.8 | 59.1 | 12.3 |
| 4 | 39.7 | 17.9 | 60.1 | 15.7 |
| Mean | 25.3 | 22.5 | 54.2[3] | 13.7 |
| SEM | 5.1 | 3.9 | 10.2 | 1.2 |

1   Systemic availability of an oral dose of 6.79mg (base)/kg.
2   Total plasma clearance of a 1.81mg (base)/kg intravenous dose.
3   Significantly different from availability before shunt ($p < 0.05$ by paired $t$-test).

*Table II.* Concentrations of norpropoxyphene in plasma of dogs following intravenous and oral administration of dextropropoxyphene before and after portacaval shunt

| | Intravenous[1] | | Oral[2] | |
|---|---|---|---|---|
| | before shunt | after shunt | before shunt | after shunt |
| Max. concentration (ng/ml) | 459 ± 152[3] | 462 ± 67 | 2310 ± 1040 | 1820 ± 775 |
| Time of max. concentration (h) | 0.8 ± 0.2 | 3.6 ± 1.0 | 1.8 ± 0.8 | 3.5 ± 1.0 |
| Area under 0 to 8h curve (ng/ml/h) | 2440 ± 855 | 3380 ± 795 | 12600 ± 5700 | 11000 ± 5300 |
| Ratio of areas[4], norpropoxyphene:dextropropoxyphene | 1.87 ± 0.46 | 1.90 ± 0.47 | 10.4 ± 3.1 | 3.34 ± 1.14[5] |

1   1.81mg (base)/kg.
2   6.79mg (base)/kg.
3   Mean ± SEM, n = 4.
4   Areas under 0 to 8h plasma concentration curve.
5   Significantly different from ratio value before shunt ($p < 0.05$ by paired $t$-test).

## 3. Discussion

There is evidence that dextropropoxyphene is completely absorbed, partly in metabolised form, after oral administration and that the systemic clearance of the drug in humans is at least as high as the hepatic blood flow rate (Gram et al., 1979). Our studies in dogs demonstrated a pronounced first-pass effect upon oral administration of the drug. Systemic availability was increased substantially when the dogs had a portacaval shunt, but was still much less than total. It appears therefore that dextropropoxyphene is subject to both hepatic and prehepatic biotransformation during absorption. The existence of a portacaval shunt was associated with a pro-

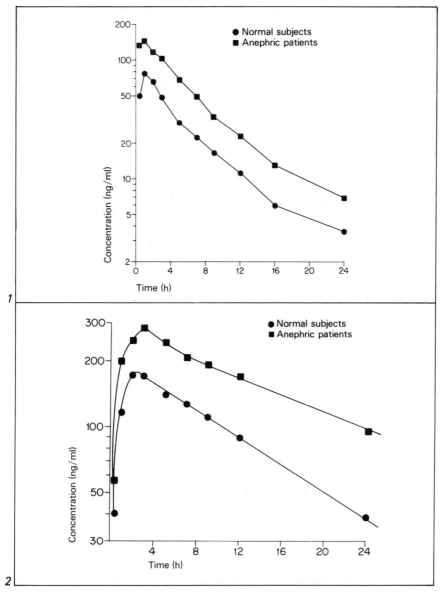

Fig. 1. Mean dextropropoxyphene concentrations in the plasma of 7 normal subjects and 7 anephric patients after oral administration of 130mg dextropropoxyphene hydrochloride in solution.

Fig. 2. Mean norpropoxyphene concentrations in the plasma of 7 normal subjects and 7 anephric patients after oral administration of 130mg dextropropoxyphene hydrochloride in solution.

nounced decrease of the norpropoxyphene:dextropropoxyphene plasma concentration ratio following oral, but not intravenous administration of dextropropoxyphene.

Rats, like man, clear dextropropoxyphene at a high rate and exhibit a large apparent volume of distribution for the drug. Experimental renal dysfunction had no apparent effect on these pharmacokinetic characteristics.

*Table III*. Summary of plasma dextropropoxyphene and norpropoxyphene concentrations in 7 normal subjects and 7 anephric patients following oral administration of 130mg dextropropoxyphene hydrochloride

| Concentration | Normal subjects | | Anephric patients | |
|---|---|---|---|---|
| | actual | normalised[1] | actual | normalised[1] |
| AUC[2] (0-12) dextropropoxyphene, ng/ml/h | $383 \pm 191$[3] | $434 \pm 184$ | $808 \pm 321$ (p < 0.02) | $762 \pm 314$ (p < 0.05) |
| Maximum concentration, dextropropoxyphene, ng/ml | $80.8 \pm 34.6$ | $92.4 \pm 32.8$ | $177 \pm 16$ (p < 0.001) | $174 \pm 71$ (p < 0.02) |
| AUC (0-24) norpropoxyphene, ng/ml/h | $2250 \pm 1050$ | $2620 \pm 1230$ | $4310 \pm 1520$ (p < 0.05) | $4100 \pm 1640$ (NS) |
| Maximum concentration, norpropoxyphene, ng/ml | $201 \pm 94$ | $229 \pm 92$ | $305 \pm 88$ (NS) | $288 \pm 87$ (NS) |

1   Normalised to a body weight of 70kg.
2   AUC is the area under drug concentration-time curve over the period of time (h) indicated in parentheses.
3   Mean $\pm$ SD. Statistical significance of difference between corresponding values for normal subjects and anephric patients is shown in parentheses below the mean values for the patients.

*Table IV*. Summary of plasma dextropropoxyphene and norpropoxyphene concentrations in cirrhotic patients following oral administration of 130mg dextropropoxyphene hydrochloride

| Concentration | Mean[1] | SEM |
|---|---|---|
| AUC (0-12) dextropropoxyphene, ng/ml/h | 967 | 310 |
| Maximum concentration, dextropropoxyphene, ng/ml | 269[2] | 100 |
| AUC (0-12) norpropoxyphene, ng/ml/h | 432[3] | 120 |
| Maximum concentration, norpropoxyphene, ng/ml | 53.4[4] | 12 |
| AUC ratio, norpropoxyphene:dextropropoxyphene | 0.672[5] | 0.344 |
| Plasma free fraction of dextropropoxyphene | 0.263 | 0.031 |

1   Concentration and AUC values were normalised to a body weight of 70kg; (n = 4).
2   Significantly different (p < 0.05) from normal subjects ($92.4 \pm 32.8$ng/ml, mean $\pm$ SD, n = 7).
3   Significantly different (p < 0.025) from normal subjects ($1740 \pm 920$ng/ml/h).
4   Significantly different (p < 0.01) from normal subjects ($229 \pm 92$ng/ml).
5   Significantly different (p < 0.001) from normal subjects ($3.94 \pm 0.83$).

Comparable oral doses of dextropropoxyphene produced much higher plasma concentrations in anephric patients than in normal subjects. Since the drug is very rapidly absorbed by both types of individual and in view of published evidence of complete absorption in normal volunteers, increased systemic availability or decreased systemic clearance appear to be the most likely reasons for the higher plasma concentrations in the patients. We favour increased systemic availability for the following reasons:

1) The biological half-life of dextropropoxyphene is similar in normal subjects and anephric patients
2) Plasma protein binding of the drug in these 2 groups is not significantly different (Giacomini et al., 1978)
3) Neither the systemic clearance nor the apparent volume of distribution of the drug is affected by renal dysfunction in the rat
4) The systemic clearance of dextropropoxyphene in man is so high as to be blood flow rate-limited and should therefore be quite insensitive to possible changes in the activity of drug-metabolising enzyme systems.

As expected, the cirrhotic patients had considerably higher plasma concentrations of dextropropoxyphene than the concentrations produced by comparable doses in normal subjects. We interpret the pronounced reduction of the norpropoxyphene:dextropropoxyphene plasma concentration ratio in the patients as suggestive of the formation of endogenous shunts, based upon our observation of a similar decrease in dogs with a surgically constructed portacaval shunt.

There are indications that patients with liver disease may be particularly sensitive to certain narcotic and sedative drugs (Laidlaw et al., 1961; Neal et al., 1979). We observed pronounced CNS depression in the cirrhotic patients following dextropropoxyphene administration; no such effects were observed in the anephric patients or normal subjects.

In conclusion, oral doses of dextropropoxyphene produce much higher plasma concentrations in anephric and cirrhotic patients than in normal subjects, on the average. There are strong indications that this is due largely to decreased presystemic biotransformation of dextropropoxyphene in the patients.

## Acknowledgements

This research was supported in part by grant GM 20852 from the National Institute of General Medical Sciences, National Institutes of Health.

## References

Bianchetti, G.; Graziani, G.; Brancaccio, D.; Morganti, A.; Leonetti, G.; Manfrin, M.; Sega, R.; Gomeni, R.; Ponticelli, C. and Morselli, P.L.: Pharmacokinetics and effects of propranolol in terminal uraemic patients and in patients undergoing regular dialysis treatment. Clinical Pharmacokinetics 1: 373-384 (1976).
Benet, L.Z. (Ed): The Effect of Disease States on Drug Pharmacokinetics (American Pharmaceutical Association, Washington 1976).
Crow, J.W.; Gibaldi, M. and Levy, G.: Comparative pharmacokinetics of courmarin anticoagulants XLI: Effect of phenobarbital on systemic availability of orally administered dicumarol in rats. Journal of Pharmaceutical Sciences 68: 958:962 (1979).
Food and Drug Administration, Department of Health, Education, and Welfare: Propoxyphene. Federal Register 44: 11837-11849 (1979).
Giacomini, K.M.; Gibson, T.P. and Levy, G.: Plasma protein binding of d-propoxyphene in normal subjects and anephric patients. Journal of Clinical Pharmacology 18: 106-109 (1978).
Giacomini, K.M.; Nakeeb, S.M. and Levy, G.: Pharmacokinetic studies of propoxyphene I: Effect of portacaval shunt on systemic availability in dogs. Journal of Pharmaceutical Sciences (in press).
Gibson, T.P.; Giacomini, K.M.; Briggs, W.A.; Whitman, W. and Levy, G.: Propoxyphene and norpropoxyphene plasma concentrations in anephrics. Clinical Pharmacology and Therapeutics 27: 665-670 (1980).

Gram, L.F.; Schou, J.; Way, W.L.; Heltberg, J. and Bodin, N.O.: d-Propoxyphene kinetics after single oral and intravenous doses in man. Clinical Pharmacology and Therapeutics 26: 473-482 (1979).

Holland, D.R. and Steinberg M.I.: Electrophysiologic properties of propoxyphene and norpropoxyphene in canine cardiac conducting tissues *in vitro* and *in vivo*. Toxicology and Applied Pharmacology 47: 123-13 (1979).

Kato, R.: Drug metabolism under pathological and abnormal physiological states in animals and man. Xenobiotica 7: 25-92 (1977).

Laidlaw, J.; Read, A.E. and Sherlock, S.: Morphine tolerance in hepatic cirrhosis. Gastroenterology 40: 389-396 (1961).

Lowenthal, D.T.; Briggs, W.A.; Gibson, T.P.; Nelson, H. and Cirksena, W.J.: Pharmacokinetics of oral propranolol in chronic renal disease. Clinical Pharmacology and Therapeutics 16: 761-769 (1974).

Lund-Jacobsen, H.: Cardio-respiratory toxicity of propoxyphene and norpropoxyphene in conscious rabbits. Acta Pharmacology and Toxicology 42: 171-178 (1978).

Neal, E.A.; Meffin, P.J.; Gregory, P.B. and Blaschke, T.F.: Enhanced bioavailability and decreased clearance of analgesics in patients with cirrhosis. Gastroenterology 77: 96-102 (1979).

Nickander, R.; Smits, S.E. and Steinberg, M.I.: Propoxyphene and norpropoxyphene: Pharmacologic and toxic effects in animals. Journal of Pharmacology and Experimental Therapeutics 200: 245-253 (1977).

Perrier, D. and Gibaldi, M.: Influence of first-pass effect on the systemic availability of propoxyphene. Journal of Clinical Pharmacology 12: 449-452 (1972).

Perrier, D.; Gibaldi, M. and Boyes, R.N.: Prediction of systemic availability from plasma-level data after oral drug administration. Journal of Pharmacy and Pharmacology 25: 256-257 (1973).

Roberts, S.M. and Levy, G.: Pharmacokinetic studies of propoxyphene IV: Effect of renal failure on systemic clearance in rats. Journal of Pharmaceutical Sciences 69: 263-264 (1980).

Verebely, K. and Inturrisi, C.E.: Disposition of propoxyphene and norpropoxyphene in man after a single oral dose. Clinical Pharmacology and Therapeutics 15: 302-309 (1974).

## Discussion

*C.T. Dollery* (Chairman): The findings in patients with cirrhosis and portacaval shunts are not really surprising are they? The interesting changes are in the anephric patients. Do you have any explanation?

*G. Levy*: I think we are looking mainly at pre-hepatic biotransformation, probably in the intestine.

*R.E. Rangno* (Montreal): Did propoxyphene have an increased effect in the anephric individuals?

*G. Levy*: There was no obvious evidence of this. However, the patients with cirrhosis were knocked out and not necessarily in relation to the plasma concentrations. Our findings are consistent with the clinical impression of increased end-organ sensitivity to opiates in patients with cirrhosis.

# 13

# Drug Absorption and Toxicity

*Hartmut Uehleke*

Department of Toxicology, Federal German Health Office, Berlin

Various physiological factors can influence the absorption of drugs from the gut, for example pH, intestinal motility, blood perfusion of the intestine, secretion into the stomach and intestine, biliary and pancreatic secretion, intestinal microflora, entero-hepatic circulation and intestinal drug metabolism.

The diet may interfere with the extent and rate of absorption. Chemical interactions occur frequently between nutritional constituents and drugs, or between drugs and other chemicals. Occasionally, drug absorption changes during continuous administration.

In toxicology we are rarely confronted with agreement between the kinetics and body levels of toxic agents and their effects (Uehleke, 1974, 1980). Mutagenic and carcinogenic properties of chemicals cannot usually be correlated with blood or organ concentrations and the effects may appear months or even years after exposure. Persisting actions of chemicals such as liver damage, or pulmonary hypertension produced by phospholipidosis of the lung are examples in which kinetic analysis seems to be of little direct value.

## 1. Kinetics, Effects and Toxicity in Fed and Starved Animals and Man

During a series of investigations in dogs on the pharmacokinetics of trimebutin, one dog showed very delayed absorption. Retrospective investigation showed that the animal had escaped from its individual cage and had joined other dogs for feeding. It was a Monday morning, and this was not reported. However this accidental happening produced a beautiful example of greatly delayed but otherwise identical absorption (fig. 1). In addition, the cumulative urinary excretion curve was shifted correspondingly by about 6 hours (fig. 2) [Glasson et al. 1975].

A marked influence of gastric emptying rate on tissue concentrations of imipramine in the rat was reported by Beaubien and Mathieu (1976) and similar effects have been described with other drugs.

Sometimes drugs retard stomach emptying and delay absorption (Franklin, 1977; Nimmo et al., 1971; Prescott, 1974a,b).

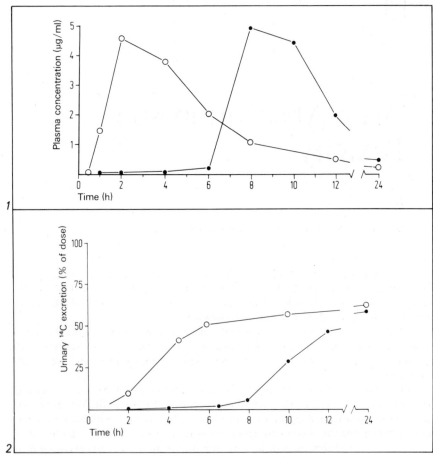

*Fig. 1.* Plasma concentrations of $^{14}C$-labelled trimebutine after oral administration of 100mg to a female beagle dog (11.5kg), starved ○ and fed ● (Glasson et al., 1975).

*Fig. 2.* Cumulative urinary excretion of $^{14}C$ in the same dog as figure 1; ○ starved, ● fed.

## 2. Influence of Diet, Solvents and Vehicles

Toxicologists are becoming aware that nutritional status can have a profound effect on the response to a given dose of a poisonous substance. The influence of food and diet on gastrointestinal drug absorption has been reviewed by Welling (1977) and Melander (1978). Diseases can also change drug absorption and the response to drugs (Gugler, 1979). There is increasing evidence that diet, solvents and vehicles can influence the effects and toxicity of drugs administered orally.

Some organotin compounds added as stabilisers to plastic material used in food packaging are rather toxic and small amounts may contaminate food and beverages. Organotin compounds can influence the reticulo-endothelial system and loss of thymus weight in young rats is the most sensitive index (Seinen and Willems, 1976). In a series of toxicity tests the compounds were given to weanling rats for 10 days. Several laboratories reported reduced sensitivity of their rats compared with the study of Seinen and Willems (1976), in which the tin compound was given by gavage in an aqueous suspension with 2% carboxymethyl cellulose. We reinvestigated the problem and found that only from a solution in oil were the di-n-octyltin dichloride and similar derivatives absorbed at a rate comparable to that observed with a rat diet containing 5 to 6% fat.

Differences in the metabolism of lindane were observed in rats following administration by gavage (aqueous suspension) or by incorporation in the diet. The rats receiving lindane in the diet excreted significantly more conjugated 2,4,6-trichlorophenol and 2,3,4,6-tetrachlorophenol, as well as total urinary metabolites, than rats receiving lindane by gavage who excreted more unchanged lindane. Stimulation of drug metabolism *in vitro* was achieved only by lindane in the diet (Copeland and Chadwick, 1979).

β-HCH is absorbed less well from the gastrointestinal tract than the γ-isomer (lindane) and its acute oral toxicity is less than that of lindane. However, during continuous dosing for weeks β-HCH turns out to be considerably more toxic than lindane. Slower metabolism and excretion of the β-isomer results in tissue levels 5 to 10 times higher. β-HCH is said to be more toxic than lindane but a proper comparison of toxicities at comparable tissue concentrations has never been carried out.

In another example, Koss and Koransky (1975) demonstrated that 80% of $^{14}$C-labelled hexachlorobenzene was absorbed when the substance was given to rats orally as a solution in oil. When given as an aqueous solution (with 6% gum arabic) only 6% was absorbed, and the toxicity was considerably lower.

The oral toxicity of chemicals is influenced by the method of administration (Worden and Harper, 1964). In many toxicity studies chemicals are given orally dissolved in various solvents such as water, oil, alcohols and glycols. Sometimes, emulsifiers or surfactants are used. A recent survey of solvent effects on drug absorption from the rat gut *in situ* demonstrated considerable differences (Stavchansky et al., 1979). These differences may contribute to the wide variation of $LD_{50}$ values produced in different laboratories in identical species and even in the same strains. Many of the tabulated $LD_{50}$ values (e.g. Spector, 1956) and their cited sources do not indicate solvents pH or volumes etc.

Drugs may influence food intake by their inherent pharmacological actions and by the same mechanisms the absorption of essential dietary constituents may also be limited during continuous administration (Vaupel et al., 1979; Brands et al., 1979; Ho and Aranda 1979).

Occasionally drugs may influence both absorption and metabolism. The compound SKF 525A (2-diethylaminoethyl-2,2-diphenyl valerate) is a widely used experimental inhibitor of microsomal drug metabolism. It inhibits the hepatotoxicity of carbon tetrachloride, and this is consistent with the role of cytochrome P-450 in the production of liver damage by carbon tetrachloride (Reiner and Uehleke, 1971; Reiner et al., 1972; Uehleke and Werner, 1975). However, SKF 525A also slows the absorption of carbon tetrachloride from the intestinal tract and lowers blood and tissue concentrations (Marchand et al., 1970). Another interesting relationship between intestinal absorption and hepatic drug metabolism was reported by Tuma et al. (1978) who found impaired hepatic drug metabolism in rats after jejuno-ileal bypass.

## 3. Test Compounds in the Diet

Problems may arise when laboratory animals are fed diets containing a high percentage of nontoxic test compounds such as sugars, polysaccharides, cellulose, hydrocolloids, and alginates etc. Frequently, sugars in concentrations of 5 % or more in the diet produce diarrhoea, and weight retardation (or loss) in rodents. In one chronic feeding study with a modified cellulose, the animals showed weight retardation and a scrawny appearance after 4 to 6 months. The pathologists could not define any damage and it was eventually found that trace elements in the diet and drinking water had been chelated by the modified cellulose.

Deficiencies of certain minerals and vitamins as well as high intake of dietary fat can alter the toxicity of metals. Recent reviews on lead (Levander, 1979) and on cadmium (Fox, 1979) toxicity emphasise the importance of intestinal mechanisms and nutritional factors.

10 % alginate in the standard rat diet increased the absorption of $^{203}$Pb by a factor of about 2.5 but with a milk diet there was an approximately 2.5 fold reduction (Carr et al., 1969). However the absorption of lead was practically unchanged in adults by alginate supplementation of food (Harrison et al., 1969). The effect of gel fibres on gastric emptying and absorption of drugs and sugars was investigated by Holt et al., (1979), and the influence of hydrocolloids on drug absorption was reviewed by Forster and Hoos (1976).

Dietary plant fibres protect experimental animals from the toxicity of various chemicals including amaranth, cyclamate, tartrazine and Sunset Yellow (FD & C Yellow, No. 6) when fed with a purified diet (Ershoff, 1977). As cellulose affords poor protection this effect may be due to the physicochemical properties of the fibres rather than to their chemical content.

Occasionally, high concentrations of test compounds can be used as nutrients by experimental animals. Thus methyl cellulose in a purified standard diet enhanced weight gain in guinea pigs and rats. Herbivorous animals and ruminants can of course utilise cellulose and modified cellulose.

Much of the starch in tinned food may be modified to form substances such as hydroxypropyl distarch phosphate. Diets containing 10 to 20 % hydroxy-propyl starches caused diarrhoea and enlargement of the caecum in rats (Leegwater et al., 1974). The changes were benign and reversible, but the clinical implications are unknown.

## 4. Intestinal Microflora

The gut micro-organisms contribute to drug metabolism, and occasionally to drug toxicity. The reduction of nitro groups, and the splitting of azo bonds frequently produce more toxic metabolites (Uehleke, 1964, 1971). However, in isolated perfused livers these reactions are hardly detectable (Werner et al., 1976). Gastrointestinal bacteria play a major role in nitro reduction and azo splitting (Zachariah and Juchau, 1974). For example, the conversion of cyclamate to cyclohexylamine is performed almost exclusively by gut bacteria and there is great variation between species and individuals (Scheline, 1973; Renwick, 1977). Diets which alter intestinal microflora and consequently influence bacterial metabolism in the intestine, can also change intestinal motility and absorption (Tennant et al., 1971).

## 5. Drug Metabolism by the Intestinal Mucosa

The mammalian intestine can metabolise and conjugate drugs and diet can affect small intestine enzyme activity (e.g. β-glucuronidase, β-galactosidase, N-acetyl-β-

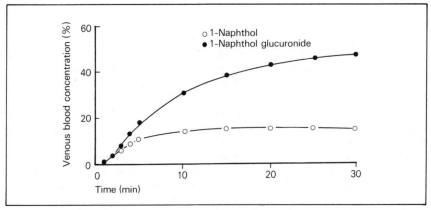

*Fig. 3.* Appearance of 1-naphthol glucuronide and free naphthol in intestinal venous blood after instillation of 100nmol (0.6µCi) $^{14}$C-1-naphthol into the rat closed jejunal loop. Means of 6 experiments (Bock and Winne, 1975).

glucosamidase, α-galactosidase) in man and animals (Rosenzweig et al., 1971; Koldovsky et al., 1972).

Some early *in vitro* investigation of the microsomal fraction of intestinal mucosa revealed rather low concentrations of cytochrome P-450, and limited dealkylation of N-methyl aniline (Uehleke, 1969). Ullrich and co-workers improved sensitivity by incubation of intact pieces of the intestinal wall and employing the very sensitive fluorescence of umbelliferone produced by the 0-dealkylation of 7-ethoxycoumarin. In mice dealkylation activity was highest in the jejunum and was greatly increased by pretreatment with phenobarbitone (Lehrmann et al., 1973). Pre-incubation of the isolated pieces of mouse intestine in the presence of phenobarbitone for 2 hours increased 7-ethoxycoumarin dealkylation by a factor of 2 to 3 (Scharf and Ullrich, 1974).

Furthermore, the determination of metabolites and conjugates gave additional information on the metabolic capacity of the gut. Substrates such as oestrogens, thyroxine, salicylic acid, retinol, nitrophenols, phenols and bilirubin are readily conjugated with glucuronic acid (Hartiala, 1973). Sulphate conjugation, acetylation and amino acid conjugation (glycine and 0-methylation) is also well documented.

The capacity of the intestine to metabolise and conjugate chemicals can have effects on bioavailability and response. Extensive glucuronidation of morphine and 1-naphthol occurs during absorption from the lumen of the rat intestinal loop (fig. 3). In contrast, there is little glucuronidation of paracetamol (Josting et al., 1976). *In vitro* experiments with intestinal mucosal cells confirmed the capacity for 1-naphthyl glucuronidation (Shirkey et al., 1979). In contrast to sulphate, glucuronic acid and acetyl conjugation, the ability of the rat intestinal mucosal cells to conjugate aryl acids with glycine is very low.

Small doses of some chemicals may be almost completely conjugated during absorption and this may account for certain threshold phenomena. On the other hand, splitting of the conjugates by mucosa and gut bacteria liberates the free compounds again.

Endogenous sulphate can be depleted by chronic administration of substrates which are metabolised and excreted via sulphate conjugates. The availability of sulphate from well balanced animal diets can be quite sufficient in acute experiments, but insufficient during chronic administration of large doses. Consequent changes of metabolic pattern can be normalised by feeding additional sulphate.

Even more important is the availability of glutathione (GSH) since this can be consumed rapidly by chemicals such as paracetamol, bromobenzene, polycyclic hydrocarbons, substituted benzenes, halothane, chloroform, halogenated ethylenes, and epoxides or their metabolites. If the availability of cysteine, methionine and other sources of SH-groups is limited by diet or malabsorption, the sensitivity of experimental animals to halogenated aliphatic solvents and compounds such as paracetamol may be dramatically altered (McLean and McLean, 1969).

The influence of nutritional status on chloroform toxicity was recognised more than 60 years ago (Davis and Whipple, 1919) and protein depleted dogs are extremely susceptible to chloroform liver injury. The protective action of methionine and cystine was well described by Miller et al. (1940) and by Miller and Whipple (1942) but it took another 35 years to elucidate the molecular mechanisms of metabolic activation of chloroform, the reactions with cysteine and the effects of GSH-depletion (Docks and Krishna, 1976; Pohl et al., 1977).

Occasionally, changes in gut function during long term drug administration produce considerable changes in the kinetics, metabolism and toxicity of foreign compounds. After single doses of 2-acetylaminofluorene (AAF), rats excreted only small amounts of the conjugated and ultimately carcinogenic metabolite N-hydroxy-2-acetylaminofluorene (N-OH-AAF). However, after continuous administration of AAF in the diet the urinary excretion of the N-OH-AAF conjugate increased to nearly 20% of the dose ingested (Miller and Miller, 1960). Subsequent investigation showed that the increased excretion of N-OH-AAF was mainly due to modification

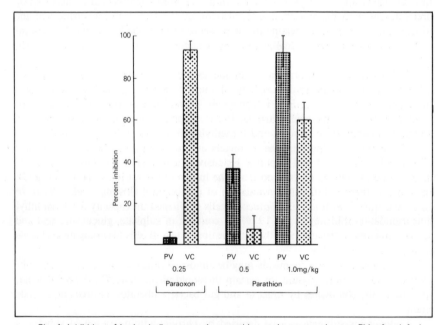

*Fig. 4.* Inhibition of brain cholinesterase by parathion and paraoxon in rats. PV: after infusion into the portal vein; VC: infusion into vena cava (Westermann, 1962).

of the intestinal flora which normally splits the glucuronide conjugate of N-OH-AAF excreted in the bile and reduces it back to AAF.

Intestinal metabolism also contributes to the activation of parathion. Only paraoxon, the oxidation product of parathion, is a potent inhibitor of acetylcholinesterase. The infusion of parathion and paraoxon into the rat portal vein or vena cava showed that paraoxon is hydrolysed much faster than parathion in the liver (fig. 4) [Westermann, 1962]. Although the toxicity of oral parathion was expected to be greater in rats pretreated with phenobarbitone, it was in fact reduced (Kato, 1961). The basis of this apparent paradox is that the hepatic oxidative desulphuration of parathion is increased in the phenobarbitone-treated rats, together with enhanced oxidation of parathion and hydrolysis to nitrophenol and alkyl phosphate in the intestinal mucosa. Consequently, only small amounts of intact parathion reached the liver. When parathion was infused into the portal vein of induced rats, the acute toxicity of parathion increased as expected (Westermann, 1962; DuBois and Kinoshita, 1968).

The well known 'cheese reaction' with monoamine oxidase inhibitors is a further example of a pharmacological interaction at the intestinal level. Monoamine oxidase inhibitors block the deamination of dietary biogenic amines in the intestinal wall (Lembeck et al., 1964). Consequently, tyramine (in cheese and wine), and other sympathomimetic amines reach the portal circulation in much higher concentrations.

## 6. Intestinal Metabolism and Carcinogenesis

The liver carcinogenic action of 2-acetylaminofluorene is reduced by chloramphenicol (Weisburger et al., 1967). This was thought to be due to competitive inhibition of AAF-metabolite binding by chloramphenicol at the nucleic acid templates. However, the carcinogenic N-hydroxy metabolite of AAF was increased in the urine of rats fed AAF and concurrent chloramphenicol which greatly depresses the gut microflora (Grantham et al., 1968). With this knowledge it was understandable that considerably more extrahepatic tumours were induced when AAF was administered with chloramphenicol.

Bock and Lilienblum (1979) have studied the glucuronidation of N-hydroxy metabolites of carcinogenic amines by hepatic and intestinal glucuronyltransferases and Clayson (1975) has reviewed the influence of nutrition on experimental carcinogenesis. Azoxymethane or methylnitrosourea produced a higher incidence of colorectal tumours in rats when they were fed a semipurified diet containing 15% undegraded carrageenan (Watanabe et al., 1978).

## 7. Conclusions

Twenty-five years ago Barnes and Denz (1954) stated: 'A chronic toxicity test is always a makeshift affair to be replaced as soon as possible by a more permanent structure of knowledge built on a foundation of physiology, biochemistry and other fundamental medical science'. Consequently, foresight requires some knowledge of the kinetic and metabolic behaviour of a given chemical in the test organism. Differences in sensitivity to a given chemical between experimental animals and man many be encountered but in many cases these differences become smaller if actions are compared at similar drug concentrations in the body, especially in target organs. Drug absorption plays a prominent part in acute and long term toxicity studies.

# References

Barnes, J.M. and Denz, F.A.: Experimental methods used in determining chronic toxicity. A critical review. Pharmacological Reviews 6: 191-242 (1954).

Beaubien, A.R. and Mathieu, L.F.: Influence of stomach emptying rate on tissue radioactivity after ($^{14}$C) imipramine in the rat. Journal of Pharmacy and Pharmacology 28: 451-452 (1976).

Bock, K.W. and Lilienblum, W.: Activation and induction of rat liver microsomal UDP-glucuronyltransferase with 3-hydroxybenzo(a)pyrene and N-hydroxy-2-naphthylamine as substrates. Biochemical Pharmacology 28: 695-700 (1979).

Bock, K.W. and Winne, D.: Glucuronidation of 1-naphthol in the rat intestinal loop. Biochemical Pharmacology 24: 859-862 (1975).

Brands, B.; Thornhill, J.A.; Hirst, M. and Gowdey, C.W.: Suppression of food intake and body weight gain by naloxone in rats. Life Sciences 24: 1773-1778 (1979).

Carr, T.E.F.; Nolan, J. and Durakovic, A.: Effect of alginate on the absorption and excretion of $^{203}$Pb in rats fed milk and normal diets. Nature 224: 1115 (1969).

Clayson, D.B.: Nutrition and experimental carcinogenesis: A review. Cancer Research 35: 3292-3300 (1975).

Copeland, M.F. and Chawick, R.W.: Comparative metabolism of lindane in rats following administration by two oral routes. Toxicology and Applied Pharmacology 48: A8 (1979).

Davis, N.C. and Whipple, G.H.: The influence of fasting and various diets on the liver injury effected by chloroform anesthesia. Archives of Internal Medicine 23: 612-635 (1919).

Docks, E.L. and Krishna, G.: The role of glutathione in chloroform induced hepatotoxicity. Experimental and Molecular Pathology 24: 13-22 (1976).

DuBois, K.P. and Kinoshita, F.K.: Influence of induction of hepatic microsomal enzymes by phenobarbital on toxicity of organic phosphate insecticides. Proceedings of the Society for Experimental Biology and Medicine 129: 699-702 (1968).

Ershoff, B.H.: Effects of diet on growth and survival of rats fed toxic levels of tartrazine (FD & C Yellow No. 6). Journal of Nutrition 107: 822-828 (1977).

Forster, H. and Hoos, I.: in Pflanzliche Hydrokolloide. Wirkung auf die intestinale Resorption. Heft 85 Schriftr. Bund fur Lebensmittelrecht und Lebensmittelkunde, ISV Informations-Seminar-und Verlagsgesellschaft mbH, D-8901 Konigsbrunn, 1976.

Fox, M.R.S.: Nutritional influences on metal toxicity: Cadmium as a model toxic element. Environmental Health Perspectives 29: 95-104 (1979).

Franklin, R.A.: The influence of gastric emptying on plasma concentrations of the analgesic meptazinol. British Journal of Pharmacology 59: 565-569 (1977).

Glasson, B.; Benakis, A.; Boillat, E.; Vitus, J.; Uehleke, H. and Poplawski, M.: Localisation, distribution, metabolism and excretion of 3,4,5-trimethoxybenzoic acid, 2-phenyl-2-dimethylamino-n-butyl ester in rats and in dog. VI. International Congress of Pharmacology, Helsinki, p. 579, 1975.

Grantham, P.H.; Mohan, L.; Horton, R.E.; Weisburger, E.K. and Weisburger, J.H.: Metabolism of N-hydroxy-N-2-fluorenyl-acetamide (N-OH-Faa) in germ free rats. Proceedings of the American Association for Cancer Research 9: 26 (1968).

Gugler, R.: The effect of disease on the response to drugs, in Advances in Pharmacology and Therapeutics, vol. 6, p.67-76 (Pergamon, Oxford 1979).

Harrison, G.E.; Carr, T.E.F.; Sutton, A. and Humphreys, E.R.: Effect of alginate on the absorption of lead in man. Nature 224: 1115-1116 (1969).

Hartiala, K.: Metabolism of hormones, drugs and other substances by the gut. Physiological Reveiws 53: 496-534 (1973).

Ho, R.S. and Aranda, C.G.: The influence of 2,2-dimethyl-1-(4-methylphenyl)-1-propanone (SaH 50-283) on food efficiency in rats. Archives Internationales de Pharmacodynamie et de Therapie 237: 98-109 (1979).

Holt, S.; Heading, R.C.; Carter, D.C.; Prescott, L.F. and Tothill, P.: Effect of gel fibre on gastric emptying and absorption of glucose and paracetamol. The Lancet 1: 636-639 (1979).

Josting, D.; Winne, D. and Bock, K.W.: Glucuronidation of paracetamol, morphine and 1-naphthol in the rat intestinal loop. Biochemical Pharmacology 25: 613-616 (1976).

Kato, R.: Modification of the toxicity of strychnine and octomethylpyrophosphoramide (OMPA) induced by pretreatment with phenaglycodol and thiopental. Arzneimittel-Forschung 11: 797-801 (1961).

Koldovsky, O.; Palmieri, M. and Jumawan, J.: Comparison of activities of acid β-galactosidase, β-glucuronidase, N-acetyl-β-glucosaminidase and α-galactosidase in jejunum and ileum of adult and suckling rats. Comparative Biochemistry and Physiology 43B: 1-8 (1972).

Koss, G. and Koransky, W.: Studies on the toxicity of hexachlorobenzene I. Pharmacokinetics. Archives of Toxicology 34: 203-212 (1975).

Leegwater, D.C.; de Groot, A.B. and Kalmthout-Kuyper, M.: The aetiology of caecal enlargement in the rat. Food and Cosmetics Toxicology 12: 687-697 (1974).

Lehrmann, C.; Ullrich, V. and Rummel, W.: Phenobarbital inducible drug monooxygenase activity in the small intestine of mice. Naunyn-Schmiedebergs Archives of Pharmacology 276: 89-98 (1973).

Lembeck, F.; Winne, D. and Sewing K.-Fr.: The cheese reaction. The Lancet 1: 933 (1964).

Levander, O.A.: Lead toxicity and nutritional deficiencies. Environmental Health Perspectives 29: 115-125 (1979).

Marchand, C.; McLean, S. and Plaa, G.: The effect of SKF 525A on the distribution of carbon tetrachloride in rats. Journal of Pharmacology and Experimental Therapeutics 174: 232-238 (1970).

McLean, A.E.M. and McLean, E.K.: Diet and toxicity. British Medical Bulletin 25: 278-281 (1969).

Melander, A.: Influence of food on the bioavailability of drugs. Clinical Pharmacokinetics 3: 337-351 (1978).

Miller, J.A. and Miller, E.C.: The N- and ring-hydroxylation of 2-acetylaminofluorene during carcinogenesis in the rat. Cancer Research 20: 950-962 (1960).

Miller, L.L.; Ross, J.F. and Whipple, G.H.: Methionine and cystine, specific protein factors preventing chloroform liver injury in protein-depleted dogs. American Journal of the Medical Sciences 200: 739-756 (1940).

Miller, L.L. and Whipple, G.H.: Liver injury, liver protection and sulfur metabolism. Journal of Experimental Medicine 76: 421-435 (1942).

Nimmo, J.; Heading, R.C. and Prescott, L.F.: The relationship between gastric emptying rate and drug absorption. Scottish Medical Journal 16: 337 (1971).

Pohl, L.R.; Bhoshan, B.; Whittaker, N.F. and Krishna, G.: Phosgene: A metabolite of chloroform. Biochemical and Biophysical Research Communications 79: 684-691 (1977).

Prescott, L.F.: Gastric emptying and drug absorption. British Journal of Clinical Pharmacology 1: 189-190 (1974a).

Prescott, L.F.: Gastrointestinal absorption of drugs. Medical Clinics of North America 58: 907-916 (1974b).

Reiner, O.; Athanassopoulos, S.; Hellmer, K.H.; Murray, R.E. and Uehleke, H.: Bildung von Chloroform aus Tetrachlorkohlenstoff in Lebermikrosomen, Lipidperoxidation und Zerstorung von Cytochrom P-450. Archives of Toxicology 29: 219-233 (1972).

Reiner, O. and Uehleke, H.: Bindung von Tetrachlorkohlenstoff an reduziertes mikrosomales Cytochrom P-450 und an Ham. Hoppe-Seyler's Zeitschrift fur Physiologische Chemie 352: 1048-1052 (1971).

Renwick, A.G.: Microbial metabolism of drugs; in Parke and Smith (Eds.) Drug Metabolism from Microbe to Man, p.169-189 (Taylor and Francis, London 1977).

Rosenzweig, N.S.; Herman, R.H. and Stifel, F.B.: Dietary regulation of small intestinal enzyme activity in man. American Journal of Clinical Nutrition 24: 65-69 (1971).

Scharf, R. and Ullrich, V.: In vitro induction by phenobarbital of drug monooxygenase activity in mouse isolated small intestine. Biochemical Pharmacology 23: 2127-2137 (1974).

Scheline, R.R.: Metabolism of foreign compounds by gastrointestinal microorganism. Pharmacological Reviews 25: 451-523 (1973).

Seinen, W. and Willems, M.I.: Toxicity of organotin compounds. I Atrophy of thymus and thymus-dependent lymphoid tissue in rats fed di-n-octyltincichloride. Toxicology and Applied Pharmacology 35: 63-75 (1976).

Shirkey, R.J.; Kao, J.; Fry, J.R. and Bridges, J.W.: A comparison of xenobiotic metabolism in cells isolated from rat liver and small intestinal mucosa. Biochemical Pharmacology 28: 1461-1466 (1979).

Spector, W.S.: Handbook of Toxicology, vol. 1: Acute Toxicities (Saunders, Philadelphia 1956).

Stavchansky, S.; Martin, A. and Loper, A.: Solvent system effects on drug absorption. Research Communications in Chemical Pathology and Pharmacology 24: 77-85 (1979).

Tennant, B.; Reina-Guerra, M. and Harrold, D.: Influence of microorganisms on intestinal absorption. Annals of the New York Academy of Science 176: 262-272 (1971).

Tuma, D.J.; Vanderhoof, J.A. and Sorrell, M.F.: Impaired hepatic drug metabolism after jejunoileal bypass in rats. Journal of Pharmacology and Experimental Therapeutics 206: 167-171 (1978).

Uehleke, H.: Biologische Oxydation und Reduktion am Stickstoff aromatischer Amino- und Nitroderivate und ihre Folgen fur die Therapie. Progress in Drug Research. 8: 195-260 (1964).

Uehleke, H.: Extrahepatic microsomal drug metabolism; in DeBaker and Tripod (Eds) Sensitization to Drugs. Proceedings of the European Society for the Study of Drug Toxicity, vol. X, p.94-100 (Excerpta Medica, Amsterdam 1969).

Uehleke, H.: Stoffwechsel von Arzneimitteln als Ursache von Wirkungen, Nebenwirkungen und Toxizitat. Progress in Drug Reasearch 15: 147-203 (1971).

Uehleke, H.: The formation and kinetics of reactive drug metabolites in mammals. Mutation Research 25: 159-167 (1974).

Uehelke, H.: Kinetics in toxicology in Gladke and Heiman (Eds) Pharmacokinetics, 25 years in Retrospect (Fischer-Verlag, Heidelberg 1980).

Uehleke, H. and Werner, Th.: A comparative study on the irreversible binding of labelled halothane, trichlorofluoromethane, chloroform, and carbon tetrachloride to hepatic protein and lipids *in vitro* and *in vivo*. Archives of Toxicology 34: 289-308 (1975).

Vaupel, D.B.; Nozaki, M.; Martin, W.R.; Bright, L.D. and Morton, C.: The inhibition of food intake in the dog by LSD, mescaline, psilocin, d-amphetamine and phenylisopropylamine derivatives. Life Sciences 24: 2427-2432 (1979).

Watanabe, K.; Reddy, B.S.; Wong, Ch.Q. and Weisburger, J.H.: Effect of dietary undegraded carrageenan on colon carcinogenesis in F 344 rats treated with azoxymethane or methylnitrosourea. Cancer Research 38: 4427-4430 (1978).

Weisburger, J.H.; Shirasu, Y.; Grantham, P.H. and Weisburger, E.K.: Chloramphenicol, protein synthesis, and the metabolism of the carcinogen N-2-fluorenylacetamide in rats. Inhibition by chloramphenicol of carcinogen binding. Journal of Biological Chemistry 242: 372-378 (1967).

Welling, P.G.: Influence of food and diet on gastrointestinal drug absorption. A review. Journal of Pharmacokinetics and Biopharmaceutics 5: 291-334 (1977).

Werner, R.; Uehleke, H. and Wohrlin, R.: Reduction of azobenzene to hydrazobenzene by liver fractions. Naunyn-Schmiedeberg's Archives of Pharmacology (Suppl.) 293: R 54 (1976).

Westermann, E.O.: Discussion; in Brodie and Erdos (Eds) Metabolic Factors Controlling Duration of Drug Action, Proceedings of the First International Pharmacological Meeting, Stockholm, 1961, p.205-211 (Pergamon, London 1962).

Worden, A.N. and Harper, K.H.: Oral toxicity as influenced by method of administration; in Davey (Ed) Some Factors Affecting Drug Toxicity. Proceedings of the European Society for the Study of Drug Toxicity, Vol. IV, p.107-110 (Excerpta Medica, Amsterdam 1964).

Zachariah, P.K. and Juchau, M.R.: The role of gut flora in the reduction of aromatic nitro-groups. Drug Metabolism and Disposition 2: 74-78 (1974).

# 14

# Important Formulation Factors Influencing Drug Absorption

*Arnold H. Beckett*

Department of Pharmacy, Chelsea College, University of London

The properties of a drug are a direct result of its molecular structure and as such cannot be altered except by chemical change. However, the concentration and rate of change of concentration at different sites following absorption, metabolism and elimination can be influenced by the presence of other molecules.

The absorption of drugs through membranes in general depends upon the drug molecules being in aqueous solution at the surface of the membrane. The rate of delivery, the concentration and the location of these aqueous solutions of the drug at membranes are amenable to control by formulation, i.e. by compounding into pharmaceutical products and by the administration of such products by various routes.

Until relatively recently, the formulation of drugs into such pharmaceutical products as tablets, capsules, suppositories etc. has been used to provide a convenient and practical means of administering the drug to the patient in a stable or at least relatively stable form. Now increasing emphasis is being placed on formulation to overcome the different disadvantages of certain drug molecules.

One of the main therapeutic problems at present is lack of patient compliance (table I) [Howells, 1977]. Obviously it is useless to have superb drugs and correct formulations and expert physicians if patients fail to take the products or take them irregularly.

If a patient has to take a number of drug products, some twice a day, others 4 times a day, some before meals, some after meals, any attempt to keep to a defined regimen is doomed to failure. If some of these products cause side effects then even the desire to keep to the regimen is decreased. Other speakers in this Conference have stressed that compliance decreases with increasing frequency of product administration and with the number to be taken.

Even in good hospitals, the proportion of patients who have serum concentrations of their drugs within the accepted 'therapeutic range' is remarkably small (table II) [Merkus, 1976]. Those drugs which are metabolised extensively by first-pass metabolism can give very big differences in plasma concentrations with the same dose and the same regimen in different patients (fig. 1) [Merkus, 1976].

*Table I.* Data from various countries on patient compliance with drug taking (Boncey, 1977; Howells, 1977)

| | |
|---|---|
| United Kingdom | 30.7% hospital outpatients were non-compliant |
| Sweden | 13% inpatients received incorrect medication |
| Czechoslovakia | 25% of all patients do not follow instructions given with their medication |
| | 40% of all medication is ineffective |

*Table II.* Numbers of hospital patients with drug serum levels outside the therapeutic range (after Merkus, 1976)

| Drug | Therapeutic range | Number of patients | Patients with serum concentrations | |
|---|---|---|---|---|
| | | | above therapeutic range (%) | below therapeutic range (%) |
| Phenobarbitone | 1-3mg/100ml | 337 | 47.8 | 10.4 |
| Phenytoin | 0.3-1.7mg/100ml | 221 | 7.7 | 41.6 |
| Carbamazepine | 0.5-1.5mg/100ml | 116 | 5.2 | 33.6 |
| Salicylates | 20-30mg/100ml | 73 | 17.8 | 30.1 |
| Digitoxin | 15-30ng/ml | 2141 | 36.5 | 14.3 |
| Digoxin | 0.9-2.4ng/ml | 562 | 23.3 | 19.9 |
| Primidone | 0.5-1.5mg/100ml | 75 | 0 | 56.0 |
| Quinidine | 0.3-0.6mg/100ml | 71 | 22.5 | 18.3 |

Important aims of formulation of drugs to influence absorption are therefore to improve patient compliance, to reduce side effects and to reduce inter-subject variations in plasma concentrations without the need to substantially alter the amount of drug administered. These aims can be partially met if product administration is required not more than every 12 hours, and preferably only every 24 hours, even for drugs with inherently short biological half-lives.

# 1. Application of Formulation Factors to Influence Drug Absorption

The important factors involve control of the rate of delivery of drug to absorption sites, location and distribution of the drug delivery systems and the association of the drug with other molecules to alter water/lipid partitioning.

It is essential to consider these factors in relation to the anatomical and physiological conditions at the chosen absorption sites. For instance, if the oral or rectal route is being considered, the pH and fluidity of the medium, the transit times past different absorption sites and the surface area of the different absorbing regions must

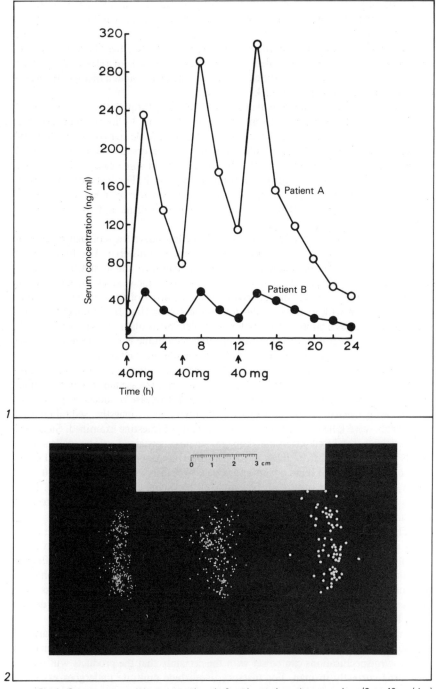

Fig. 1. Serum propranolol concentrations in 2 patients given the same dose (3 × 40mg/day) [after Merkus, 1976].

Fig. 2. Sustained release pellets with diffusion rate-controlling membranes.

be considered in conjunction with the route of removal of drug after absorption and the type of drug presentation if we are to evaluate 'biological windows of drug absorption' (table III).

Because many drugs have different biological half-lives, the above therapeutic objectives can only be met provided there is a controlled rate of release of the drug from a delivery system, i.e. controlled (sustained) release becomes a therapeutic necessity and not a commercial gimmick.

The transit time of a tablet which keeps its integrity through the gastrointestinal tract varies in different subjects from a few hours to 20 to 30 hours; thus sustained release products such as those based on the non-degradable matrix or the 'OROS' principle cannot fully achieve the objective of a dose every 24 hours (or even 12 hours) without leading to inter-subject differences and in some cases failure to give complete release of the drug during gastrointestinal transit. For instance, movement of the product from stomach to duodenum depends greatly on what a person has eaten or drunk, the timing of the dose relative to food or drink and also upon mood and activity.

Drugs in the form of suspension or small pellets, leave the stomach by a zero-order or first-order process depending on the amount administered. Also they become widely scattered as they pass down the gastrointestinal tract and do not move downward in the same way as a tablet. Their average transit time is much longer. Thus, it is desirable that a sustained release product should consist of drug incorporated into small pellets each with their own rate-controlling system (fig. 2) to reduce inter-subject variation in absorption and yet obtain complete bioavailability over a 12- or 24-hour period. In general, a diffusion rate-limiting membrane is to be preferred to one from which the release of drug depends upon membrane rupture or unit erosion.

If high drug concentrations cause local mucosal irritation, then sustained release pellets which scatter widely are preferable to a sustained release tablet which confines drug delivery to a restricted site. Different sustained release products of potassium chloride were injected into the upper gastrointestinal tract of anaesthetised rabbits and the animals were killed after 4 hours and segments of intestine examined. Sustained release tablets produced extensive damage whereas sustained release pellets gave results indistinguisable from those of the controls (Block and Thomas, 1978). Differences in the irritancy of these tablets and pellets were also shown in monkeys and the pellets gave the correct release profiles and full bioavailability in man (fig. 3). Even pellets designed to give twice the rate of release of potassium did not cause intestinal irritation in rabbits (Beckett et al., 1978).

Theophylline is known to have local gastrointestinal irritant effects when given orally as well as adverse central effects if the plasma concentrations are too high. Thus it is an excellent candidate for the application of formulation factors to influence absorption. Although the mean plasma concentrations in subjects given theophylline in solution and as sustained release pellets were not very high (fig. 4), there was a big difference in the incidence of side effects which still remained after 5 days of dosing (table IV) [Wesley-Hadzija et al., unpublished data].

Sustained release pellets can be designed to give different release rates in standard dissolution studies and the results correlated with bioavailability studies in man so that in vitro specifications can be set with the certainty that the products will release their drug correctly in man. For instance, isosorbide dinitrate undergoes extensive first-pass metabolism and has a short biological half-life. However, sustained release products can be designed which maintain plasma concentrations for a 12-hour period (fig. 5). Pellets designed to have a different rate of release gave different plasma con-

*Table III*. Biological windows for drug absorption

| Gastrointestinal tract absorption sites | Prevailing conditions | Route of drug removal | Drug presentation | Methods of monitoring absorption |
|---|---|---|---|---|
| Mouth | pH 6.8-7.0<br>Much fluid | Non-portal | Solution<br><br>Suspension | |
| Stomach | pH 1.0-5.0<br>Fluidity varies<br>with ingestion<br>of food and drink | Portal | SR pellets<br>Tablet,<br>disintegrating | Directly<br><br>Indirectly, by<br>measuring drugs<br>and metabolites in: |
| Upper gastrointestinal tract | pH increases<br>towards 7.5.<br>Fluidity decreases<br>Transit rate<br>decreases | Portal | Tablet, keeps<br>integrity<br>(i.e. OROS)<br>SR tablet<br>(i.e. matrix)<br>Enteric-coated<br>tablet | blood<br>plasma<br>saliva<br>urine<br>faeces |
| Lower gastrointestinal tract | pH about 7.5<br>Fluidity nil<br>Transit rate<br>very slow | Portal | Hard capsule<br>(disintegrates<br>quickly)<br>Soft capsule<br>(disintegrates<br>quickly)<br>Enteric capsule | |
| Rectum | pH 6.8-7.0<br>Fluidity, mucus<br>at membrane<br>Transit depends<br>on defaecation | Portal,<br>upper<br>Non-portal,<br>lower | Solution<br>Suspension<br>Suppository<br>SR pellets | |

*Table IV*. Side effects noted in volunteers after aminophylline ( ≡ 300 theophylline) taken as a solution or sustained release pellets. After 5 days dosing ( ≡ 600mg theophylline/24h) adverse reaction scores were 135 when given as a solution and 18 when given as pellets (Wesley-Hadzija, unpublished data)

| Side effect | Number of volunteers experiencing side effects | |
|---|---|---|
| | solution | SR pellets |
| Nausea | 10 | 0 |
| Headache | 4 | 0 |
| Diarrhoea | 3 | 0 |
| 'Gastritis' | 2 | 0 |
| Vertigo | 5 | 0 |
| Nervousness | 3 | 1 |

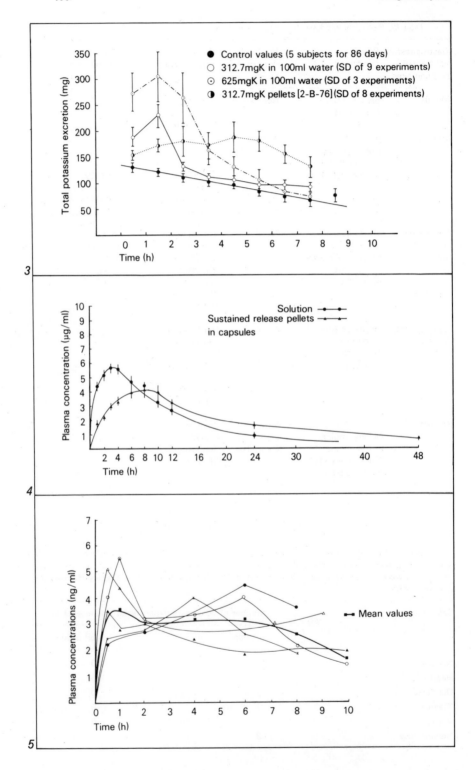

3

4

5

centrations (fig. 6). One of the products gave an appropriate biological response in man (fig. 7) [Goldman, personal communication].

Some of the pellets pass through the gastrointestinal tract faster than others and rapidly reach a region of higher pH and much lower fluidity (table III). These pellets must be so designed that they release their drug more quickly at thise site if they are not to carry some of their drug into the faeces resulting in reduced bioavailability. This aspect becomes especially important if the sustained release product is designed to give adequate plasma concentrations of a drug over a 24-hour period.

Many acidic anti-inflammatory drugs have relatively short biological half-lives and do not protect against morning stiffness because the effects of a dose taken at night have worn off by morning. Sustained release pellets designed to give plateau plasma concentrations between 5 to 8 hours after administration, with release over a 24-hour period, can help to overcome the inherent deficiency of the drug molecule (figs. 8 and 9) [Beckett and Hassanzadeh, unpublished data].

It is said by some that there is no scientific or therapeutic reason for producing sustained release products for drugs with a long biological half-life. This ignores the fact that side effects associated with high concentrations reached during the absorption phase can be reduced, without loss of efficacy or duration of effect, using the same dose, by flattening the peak. For instance, we have found that L-hyoscyamine administered as sustained release pellets is an effective anti-emetic without side effects such as dry mouth and impaired vision which limit its dosage in non-sustained dosage forms; yet L-hyoscyamine has a long biological half-life in man. Such sustained release products are effective for about 20 to 24 hours in the control of vomiting in cancer chemotherapy.

## 2. Application of Formulation Factors to Influence Rectal Drug Absorption

Absorption of many drugs from the rectum is good if they are administered in aqueous solution. However, in many types of suppository, absorption is less effective than from oral preparations of the drug (fig. 10) [Merkus, 1976]. Thus the formulation of many suppository bases impairs drug absorption.

The layer of mucus on the rectal walls may slow the absorption of some drugs but the presence of other molecules such as surface active agents and ions which can form 'ion-pairs' may facilitate absorption.

Sustained release may be used to prolong the rectal absorption of drugs. We have administered sustained release pellets of a variety of drugs and obtained not only

---

*Fig. 3.* Mean urinary potassium excretion in man after administration of potassium chloride in solution and as sustained release pellets.

*Fig. 4.* Plasma theophylline concentrations in 12 volunteers after single doses (300mg) as a solution and sustained release pellets.

*Fig. 5.* Plasma concentrations in 5 subjects after 40mg of isosorbide dinitrate formulated as sustained release pellets in capsules.

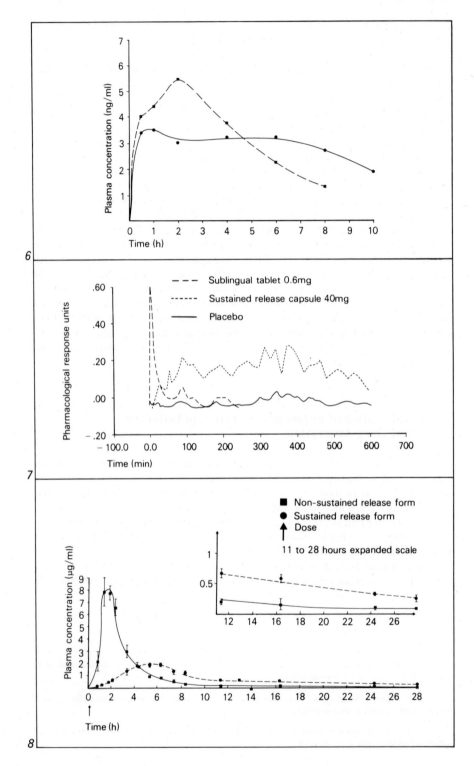

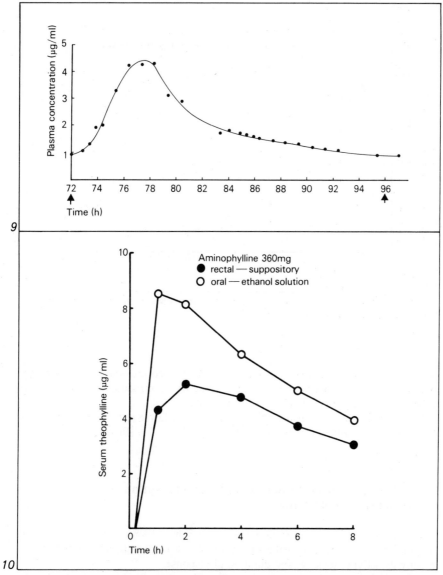

Fig. 6. Isosorbide dinitrate plasma concentrations after 2 sustained release pellet dosage forms designed to give different *in vitro* release rates. Results are the average values for 5 subjects.

Fig. 7. Mean diastolic amplitude in 12 volunteers showing a smoother biological response with sustained release capsules than with sublingual tablets.

Fig. 8. Mean plasma concentrations in 6 subjects given 100mg of an anti-inflammatory drug in a sustained release and a non-sustained release form.

Fig. 9. Projected plasma concentrations for the fourth dose of 200mg of an anti-inflammatory drug formulated as sustained release pellets to be given at 24-hour intervals.

Fig. 10. Theophylline serum concentrations after the oral and rectal administration of 360mg aminophylline (after Merkus, 1976).

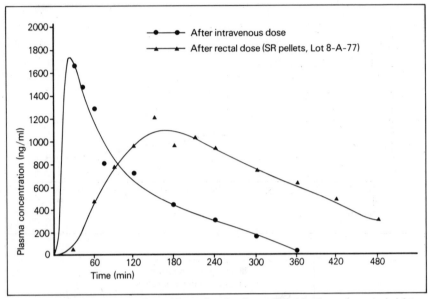

*Fig. 11.* Plasma concentrations of lignocaine after intravenous injection and rectal administration as slow-release pellets.

prolonged release but complete absorption. If the products are designed to release the drug by zero-order kinetics, then it is only necessary to introduce another dose after defaecation to keep a constant rate of drug delivery.

If steps are taken to ensure absorption from the lower part of the rectum then first-pass metabolism can be substantially avoided (fig. 11) [Johnston, unpublished data].

## 3. Influence of Formulation on Drug Absorption — General Considerations

Although only oral and rectal administration have been considered so far, formulation may be used to alter the absorption of a drug given by any route and thus modify its activity, toxicity, and duration of response.

It is unfortunate that in some countries, adverse reactions are reported for the drug rather than the drug product. Regulatory bodies and purchasing authorities in many countries do not consider sufficiently that a knowledge of the drug content of a product does not necessarily define the quality and performance.

Today the technology is available to control the rate of absorption by formulation and thus reduce the frequency of administration to maintain plasma concentrations and perhaps also reduce side effects. When patients have experienced the advantages of the newer delivery systems they will not return to the classical methods of non-controlled drug release. These improved methods of drug administration, although more expensive per item are in general no more expensive in daily treatment than the old fashioned methods.

# References

Beckett, A.H.; Samaan, A.C. and Ellis, A.C.: Sustained release potassium chloride products. Journal of Pharmacy and Pharmacology 30: 69 (1978).

Block, B.P. and Thomas, M.B.: A method for testing intestinal irritancy of sustained release potassium chloride preparations in animals. Journal of Pharmacy and Pharmacology 30: 70 (1978).

Boncey, J.: quoted in: Lower contamination level of medicaments in small pots. Pharmaceutical Journal 219: 348 (1977).

Howells, R.: Pharmacy in Czechoslovakia. Pharmaceutical Journal 219: 420 (1977).

Merkus, F.W.H.M.: The integration of biopharmaceutics and pharmacokinetics and professional activities. Pharmaceutisch Weekblad III: 1136-1146 (1976).

# 15

# Absorption Screening and New Drug Development

*S.A. Kaplan*

Department of Pharmacokinetics and Biopharmaceutics, Hoffman-LaRoche, Inc., New Jersey

Drug absorption variables influence the interpretation of data during every phase of drug development including:

1) Choice of analogue or salt of a compound
2) Surface property requirements of the solid substance
3) Design of drug delivery systems for acute and chronic pharmacological and toxicological screening and evaluation programmes
4) Nature and intensity of the observed response
5) Choice of excipients and manufacturing techniques for optimising drug bioavailability from dosage forms to overcome potential physicochemical and physiologically impaired bioavailability characteristics
6) Pharmacokinetic profile of a drug
7) Predictability and reproducibility of the desired clinical response.

In the early stages of drug development, when many compounds are being screened, it is not always practicable or economical to perform the appropriate bioavailability studies on every compound. However, it would be equally imprudent to discard a potentially useful and novel compound, or inadvertently accept a potentially toxic compound for further testing because the drug was incompletely or erratically absorbed from its delivery system. Such factors must be defined with a modicum of precision.

An orally administered solid drug must first dissolve in the gastrointestinal tract prior to absorption across the gastrointestinal mucosa into the systemic circulation. Therefore, this process can be evaluated, *in vitro,* early in drug development to determine whether dissolution as a function of pH or permeability may be a rate-limiting step in the oral absorption of a drug.

Biopharmaceutical studies require the development of analytical methods. Most *in vitro* studies can be performed using relatively simple analytical procedures since drug concentrations are usually high. However, *in vivo* studies require sensitive and specific assay procedures to quantitate drugs and metabolites in biological fluids, using either chemical techniques or radioactive drug.

A case history of a drug recently developed will be presented to exemplify an absorption screening programme conducted at appropriate times throughout the

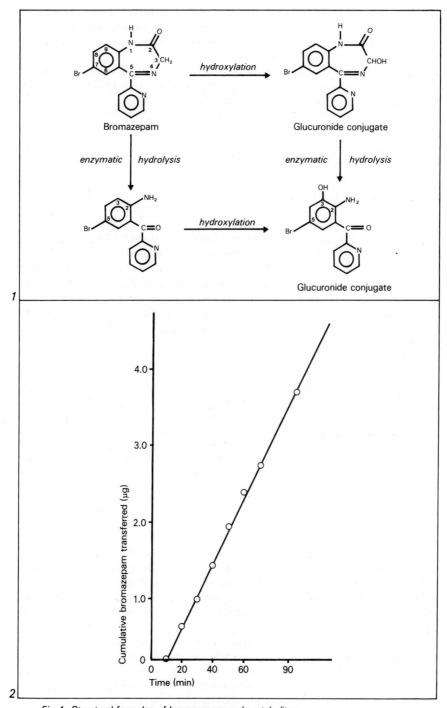

*Fig. 1.* Structural formulae of bromazepam and metabolites.

*Fig. 2.* Everted sac profile for bromazepam.

preclinical and clinical phases of a drug's development. Data reported for other drugs will be included to contrast biopharmaceutical properties not otherwise discussed.

The drug to be discussed is the 1,4-benzodiazepine compound, bromazepam (fig. 1) [Kaplan et al., 1976].

Blood specimens were assayed by an EC-GLC procedure and urine specimens were assayed by differential pulse polarography (de Silva et al, 1974). The *in vitro* measurements were made using a spectrophotometric procedure.

## 1. Biopharmaceutically Relevant Physicochemical Properties

### 1.1 Solubility and Dissolution

The aqueous solubility of bromazepam at 37°C was determined and found to decrease with an increase of pH, i.e., 18.4mg/ml at pH 1.0 and 0.17mg/ml at pH 5.3 or above. The intrinsic dissolution rate of bromazepam was determined at 37°C at a rotation speed of 50rpm at pH 1 and 5.3, and found to be 0.55 and 0.015mg/min/cm$^2$ respectively. The results suggested that the aqueous solubility at pH 1 is sufficiently high for good absorbability; however, the moderate dissolution rate, which decreases as the pH increases, may affect the absorption rate of bromazepam.

### 1.2 Permeability

The everted intestinal sac has been used to determine whether the permeability of drugs is a potential rate-limiting factor in drug absorption (Kaplan and Cotler, 1972). This *in vitro* parameter was assessed by its lag time and the cumulative amount of drug transferred. The short lag time for bromazepam, as shown in figure 2, is consistent with good absorption. A series of everted sac curves for several compounds is presented in figure 3. The curves for compounds 3, 6, and 10 would be consistent with oral absorption rate-limited by permeability.

## 2. *In Vivo* Screen

Preclinical bioavailability is assessed as a function of blood concentration and/or urinary excretion following intravenous and oral administration of the drug, usually to the dog. A typical study consists of fasting the dog for a period of 24 hours prior to intravenous and oral administration of the drug, and taking appropriate blood and urine samples. A typical blood level profile for bromazepam in the dog is shown in figure 4.

Comparison of the blood level curves following administration of the intravenous standard and experimental oral formulations, i.e. a gelatin capsule containing drug without excipients and a formulated tablet, indicated that the overall extent of absorption of bromazepam was essentially the same from both formulations as determined by the equivalence of areas under the blood level curves. The higher blood level peak and earlier peak times for the tablet indicated that the drug is absorbed more rapidly from the well formulated tablet than from the hand-packed capsule containing

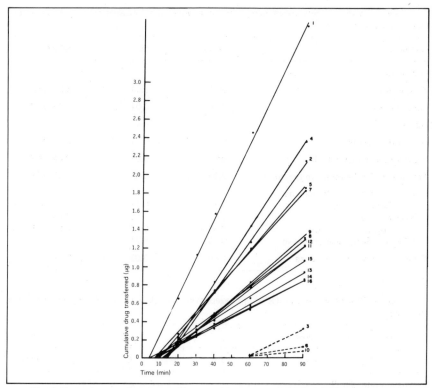

*Fig. 3.* Everted sac profiles for poorly permeable compounds (3, 6 and 10) and adequately permeable ones (others).

no excipients. The data suggested, however, that the simple gelatin capsule could be used for the chronic animal toxicology studies.

## 2.1 Comparison with Clonazepam

The bromazepam data are contrasted with data obtained for clonazepam, in which unformulated drug in gelatin capsule was negligibly absorbed. The biopharmaceutical screen with clonazepam had indicated the aqueous solubility of the drug at pH 1 to be very low and to decrease with an increase in pH. The dissolution was found to be extremely slow. The permeability characteristics were shown to be consistent with good absorption. The blood level curves obtained following single dose administration to the dog of intravenous and oral solutions, a formulated tablet with micronised drug and non-micronised drug hand-packed in a gelatin capsule are shown in figure 5. The negligible absorption from the capsule probably reflects poor 'wetability'. However, the projected low therapeutic doses of clonazepam, coupled with its good permeability characteristics, suggested proper formulation might overcome the potential problem in a clinical setting. Clonazepam was formulated with excipients that enhanced its wetability and dissolution so that the drug was completely absorbed, as shown in figure 6.

*Table I.* Pharmacokinetic parameters of bromazepam in man following single oral administration to 10 subjects

| Parameter | Mean | SD | Range |
|---|---|---|---|
| Dose (mg) | 12 | — | |
| Weight (kg) | 84.2 | 5.54 | 68.1-122.6 |
| Dose (mg/kg) | 0.15 | 0.01 | 0.09-0.17 |
| Peak time (h) | 1.5 | — | — |
| Peak height (µg/ml) | 0.13 | 0.01 | 0.10-0.17 |
| $\beta$, overall elimination rate/h | 0.06 | 0.01 | 0.04-0.09 |
| Area under blood level curve (µg/ml/h) | 2.99 | 0.33 | 1.92-4.25 |
| Percent of dose in 0-72h urine as: | | | |
| intact bromazepam | 2.3 | 0.25 | 1.7-4.1 |
| 3-OH bromazepam | 27.1 | 1.85 | 16.4-34.8 |
| benzoylpyridine derivative | 0.66 | 0.19 | 0.22-0.75 |
| 3-OH benzoylpyridine derivative | 39.5 | 6.21 | 9.1-70.7 |
| Total percent recovery of dose | 69.6 | 6.03 | 33.9-102.0 |

*Table II.* Pharmacokinetic profile of bromazepam in man following chronic oral administration to 6 subjects

| Parameter | Subject | | | | | | |
|---|---|---|---|---|---|---|---|
| | 1 | 2 | 3 | 5 | 6 | 7 | mean |
| Elimination rate, $\beta(h^{-1})$ | | | | | | | |
| first day | 0.063 | 0.049 | 0.051 | 0.065 | 0.036 | 0.088 | 0.058 |
| last day | 0.071 | 0.046 | 0.042 | 0.059 | 0.016 | 0.070 | 0.056 |
| Blood concentration (µg/ml) | | | | | | | |
| max. experimental | 0.081 | 0.106 | 0.144 | 0.154 | 0.131 | 0.103 | 0.120 |
| max. theoretical | 0.083 | 0.125 | 0.147 | 0.140 | 0.166 | 0.118 | 0.130 |
| min. experimental | 0.063 | 0.076 | 0.105 | 0.101 | 0.113 | 0.050 | 0.085 |
| min. theoretical | 0.051 | 0.086 | 0.101 | 0.086 | 0.128 | 0.060 | 0.085 |

*Table III.* Comparison of the absolute bioavailability of bromazepam in man, administered as a tablet (t) and an oral solution (os) using intravenous (iv) administration as a standard

| Subject | Tablet | | | Oral solution | | | AUC ratio t:os |
|---|---|---|---|---|---|---|---|
| | AUC ratio t:iv | $t_{max}$ (h) | $C_{max}$, ng/ml | AUC ratio os:iv | $t_{max}$, (h) | $C_{max}$, (ng/ml) | |
| C.P. | 0.59 | 1.5 | 78 | 0.55 | 0.33 | 109 | 110 |
| M.A. | 0.68 | 2.0 | 86 | 0.70 | 0.50 | 102 | 98 |
| U.S. | 0.87 | 0.33 | 73 | 0.58 | 0.75 | 49 | 152 |
| U.H. | 0.71 | 0.50 | 81 | 0.41 | 2.0 | 54 | 174 |
| R.S. | 0.76 | 0.33 | 120 | 0.64 | 2.0 | 63 | 123 |
| P.M. | 0.96 | 0.33 | 116 | 0.72 | 0.17 | 123 | 135 |
| Mean | 0.76 | 0.83 | 92.3 | 0.60 | 0.96 | 83.3 | 132 |
| SE | ±0.13 | ±0.73 | ±20.4 | ±0.11 | ±0.83 | ±31.7 | ±11.3 |

## 3. Clinical Screen

The first (phase I) clinical studies are conducted under well controlled conditions in a small number of subjects. The primary objective of this type of study is to determine a safe and tolerated human dose. These studies will be conducted using a dosage form whose bioavailability has been assessed in animal studies. The ability to conduct clinical trials unhindered by variable drug absorption can be critical for the success of the compound. Phase I studies should include an evaluation of a drug's absorption and physiological disposition; pharmacokinetic protocols can be included in single and multiple dose phase I studies as summarised below.

### 3.1 Single Dose Pharmacokinetic Study

10 male volunteers each received a single 12mg oral dose of bromazepam in its tablet formulation previously screened in the dog. 5ml oxalated blood specimens were

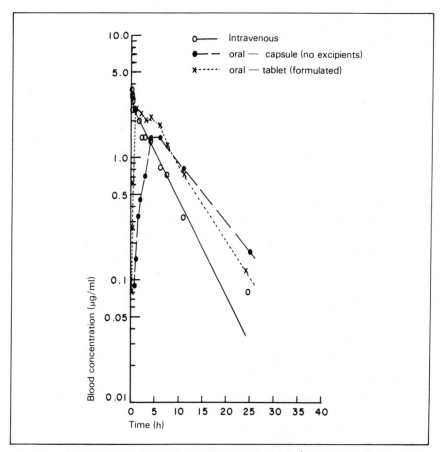

*Fig. 4.* Bromazepam blood levels in a dog receiving single 5mg/kg doses by different routes in different forms.

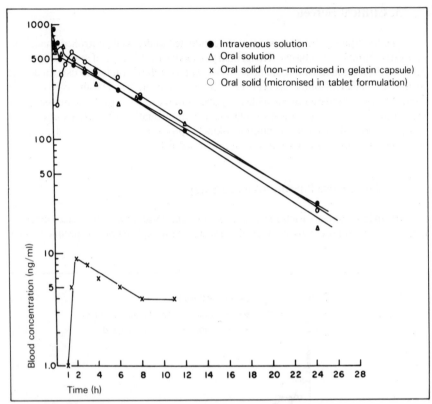

*Fig. 5.* Clonazepam blood levels in a dog following intravenous and oral administration of 2.3mg/kg doses.

drawn just prior to the dose at 0 hour and at 0.5, 1, 2, 4, 6, 8, 12, 24, 30, 48 and 72 hours following administration. Urine collections were made at 24-hour intervals from − 24 hours to 72 hours following administration. A typical blood level curve is presented in figure 7, and the single dose pharmacokinetic parameters are summarised in table I.

## 3.2 Multidose Pharmacokinetic Study

A typical multidose study is outlined below.

Two weeks after the single dose study, 6 of the subjects each received bromazepam over a 30-day period as follows:

3mg for 4 days (6am)
6mg for 5 days (3mg at 6am and 9pm)
9mg for 19 days (3mg at 6am, noon and 9pm)
6mg for 1 day (3mg at 6am and 9pm)
3mg on the last day (6am).

5ml oxalated blood specimens were drawn just prior to dosing and at 1, 2, and 6 hours after administration on days 1, 4, 9, 10, 12, 15, 17, 19, 22, 24, and 26 of the

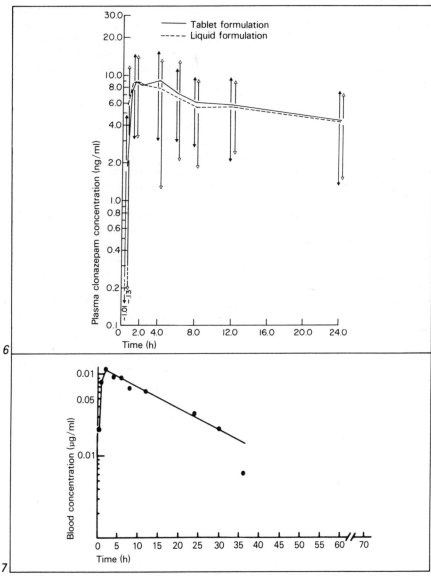

Fig. 6. Mean plasma levels of clonazepam in man after 2mg doses in tablet and liquid formulations.

Fig. 7. Bromazepam blood levels in man following the administration of a single oral 12mg dose.

study. On day 30, blood samples were drawn prior to the last dose in the morning, and at 1, 2, 4, 6, 12, 24, 36, 48, 60, 72, 84 and 96 hours following administration.

A typical multiple dose blood level profile is presented in figure 8 which includes the simulated multiple dose curve calculated using the pharmacokinetic parameters obtained following the single dose administration. The experimental and calculated steady-state blood concentrations are presented in table II.

The steady-state profile confirms that the extent of absorption of bromazepam is constant and reproducible in the 3 to 12mg dose range and indicates that unpredicted drug accumulation or enzyme induction will not occur. It should also be noted that although the drug exhibited a potential for dissolution-rate-limited absorption, overall variability is not evident on multiple dosing since steady-state levels can be accurately predicted.

## 4. Comparison with Intravenous Data

Although such data confirm constant and reproducible absorption, the actual extent of absorption cannot be assessed without comparison with data obtained following intravenous administration. If the drug is not intended for intravenous use, the preclinical safety studies required to dose man intravenously will generally not be conducted. It should be emphasised however, the reproducible absorption is the most critical factor for drug development. The inability to assess the absolute bioavailability of the drug in man does not detract from the drug development programme. It is important to realise however, that other sources of data can help assure the investigator that he has a drug formulation which results in satisfactory bioavailability. The most important is the intravenous and oral comparison in the dog which assesses absolute bioavailability and confirms complete absorption. With bromazepam a second parameter is that 70% of the dose is excreted in the urine as known metabolites which confirms that at least 70% of the dose is absorbed.

Pressure from regulatory agencies to obtain additional bioavailability data in man prompted a study to compare the tablet formulation of bromazepam to an orally

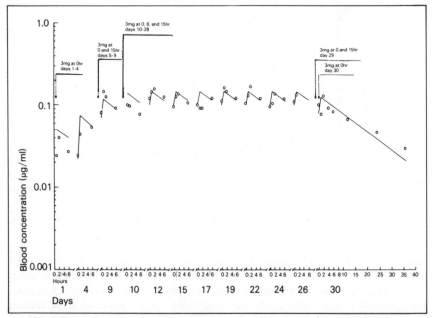

*Fig. 8.* Bromazepam multiple dose blood level profile in man (data points) with pharmacokinetically calculated curve (solid line). See text for dose schedule.

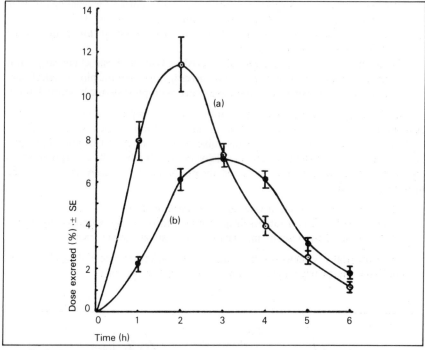

Fig. 9. Excretion rate after oral ingestion of nitrofurantoin suspended in (a) water and (b) methylcellulose solution (from Seager, 1969, reproduced with kind permission of the author and publisher).

administered solution and to the intravenously administered drug. The findings are presented in table III. The mean absolute bioavailability of the tablet was 76%, when compared with the intravenous data. The corresponding absolute bioavailability of the oral solution was lower, at 60%. The relative mean ratio of areas under the blood level curve of tablet to oral solution was 132%. Such data, which indicate a lesser absorption of bromazepam from an oral solution than from the tablet formulation, preclude the use of an oral solution as a reference standard in this case.

## 5. Solutions or Suspensions as Reference Standards

Unfortunately, unless a drug is intended for intravenous use in man, appropriate intravenous safety data in animals to assess absolute bioavailability in man are unlikely to be obtained. In such cases, it has been advocated that a solution or suspension of the drug be used as a standard for bioavailability assessment.

The administration of an oral solution as a reference standard may result in an erroneous conclusion about its bioavailability, because of:

1) The drug exhibiting a pH-dependent molecular rearrangement
2) Stability problems in the gastrointestinal tract, as has been observed with erythromycin (Boggiano and Gleeson, 1976) and clorazepate (Abruzzo et al., 1976)

3) Gastrointestinal first-pass metabolism as was reported for levodopa (Cotler and Kaplan, 1976) and morphine (Iwamoto and Klaassen, 1977)
4) Liver first-pass metabolism which has been reported for many drugs (Routledge and Shand, 1979)
5) Adsorption, binding and viscosity variables (which physicochemical phenomena are less widely appreciated by investigators than the physiological phenomena listed above, which are associated with presystemic biodegradation).

In choosing a suspending agent the influence of adsorption or interaction of the drug with the suspending agent must be considered (as well as the resulting viscosity of the suspension) on absorption of insoluble drugs from the gastrointestinal tract. Suspension of a drug usually results in a delivery system where the absorption rate is limited by the dissolution rate. Decreased absorption due to increased viscosity of the medium may reflect:

1) A decreased dissolution rate due to adsorption effects
2) Decreased diffusion rate of drug molecule through the boundary layer, or
3) Agitation of the viscous materials in the gastrointestinal tract.

Mechanistically, viscous solutions may further affect the rate of drug absorption by modifying the gastric emptying time or intestinal transit rate.

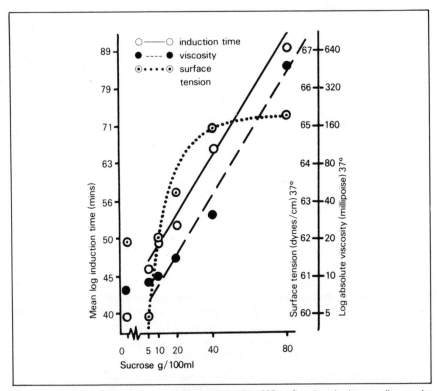

*Fig. 10.* Relationship of narcosis induction time after 200mg/kg phenobaritone sodium to the viscosity and surface tension of various sucrose syrup vehicles (from Malone et al. 1960, with kind permission of the publisher).

An example of retarded absorption from a viscous solution was reported for nitrofurantoin, a relatively insoluble urinary anti-infective (Seager, 1969) when administered as 0.5 % w/v suspensions in water and in 5 % w/v methylcellulose (fig. 9). In another study, the induction time for narcosis with phenobarbitone sodium was found to increase with increasing concentrations of sucrose in aqueous solutions (Malone et al., 1960). The increased induction time was shown to be a function of the increased viscosity in the more concentrated sucrose solution as shown in figure 10. The absorption of both salicylic acid and ethanol from the rat stomach was shown to be inversely proportional to the viscosity of the methylcellulose solution used (Levy and Jusko, 1965).

Such potential variables in drug absorption from solution and suspension suggest that a well formulated solid dosage form with a rapid dissolution rate may be the best controlled reproducible delivery system for many drugs for use as a bioavailability reference standard. Single or multiple dose pharmacokinetic parameters, as reported here for bromazepam tablets, may be sufficient to confirm the constancy and reproducibility of absorption of a drug.

# 6. Conclusion

It is important to emphasise that these absorption evaluations are based on the pharmacokinetic treatment of data. The degree of mathematical sophistication used in a pharmacokinetic analysis may vary with the expertise of the investigator and the quality of the available data; the more sophisticated the pharmacokinetic treatment, the more useful the information gained is likely to be in design and interpretation of subsequent clinical studies. The intended therapeutic use of the drug must also be considered in evaluating absorption data. A drug which must exhibit a rapid onset of activity, such as a hypnotic or cardiovascular agent, must be absorbed rapidly and it is thus more important to choose a compound and formulation with this in mind than it would be were the drug to be used for chronic administration. Since the purpose of drug development is to identify efficacious compounds with reproducible onset and duration of activity, drug absorption studies, coupled with a knowledge of the pharmacokinetic profile, provide a basis for the further investigation of the new drug by those from the other scientific disciplines involved.

# References

Abruzzo, C.W.; Brooks, M.A.; Cotler, S and Kaplan, S.A.: Differential pulse polarographic assay procedure and *in vitro* biopharmaceutical properties of dipotassium clorazepate. Journal of Pharmacokinetics and Biopharmaceutics 4: 29-41 (1976).

Boggiano, B. and Gleeson, M: Gastric acid inactivation of erythromycin stearate in solid dosage forms. Journal of the Pharmaceutical Sciences 65: 497-502 (1976).

Cotler, S. and Kaplan, S.A.: Influence of route of administration on physiological availability of levodopa in dogs. Journal of the Pharmaceutical Sciences 65: 822-827 (1976).

de Silva, J.A.F.; Bekersky, I.; Brooks, M.A.; Weinfeld, R.E.; Glover, W. and Puglisi, C.: Determination of bromazepam in blood by electron-capture GLC and its major urinary metabolites by DPP. Journal of the Pharmaceutical Sciences 63: 1440-1445 (1974).

Iwamoto, K. and Klaassen, C.: First-pass effect of morphine in rats. Journal of Pharmacology and Experimental Therapeutics 200: 236-244 (1977).

Kaplan, S.A. and Cotler, C.: Use of cannulated everted intestinal sac for serial sampling as a drug absorbability (permeability) screen. Journal of the Pharmaceutical Sciences 61: 1361-1365 (1972).

Kaplan, S.A.; Jack, M.L.; Weinfeld, R.E.; Glover, W.; Weissman, L. and Cotler, S.: Biopharmaceutical and clinical pharmacokinetic profile of bromazepam. Journal of Pharmacokinetics and Biopharmaceutics 4: 1-16 (1976).

Levy, G. and Jusko, W.: Effect of viscosity on drug absorption. Journal of the Pharmaceutical Sciences 54: 219-225 (1965).

Malone, M.; Gibson, R. and Miya, T.S.: A pharmacologic study of the effects of various pharmaceutical vehicles on the action of orally administered phenobarbital. Journal of the American Pharmaceutical Association 49: 529-536 (1960).

Routledge, P. and Shand, D.: Presystemic drug elimination. Annual Review of Pharmacology and Toxicology 19: 447-468 (1979).

Seager, H.: The effect of methylcellulose on the absorption of nitrofurantoin from the gastrointestinal tract. Journal of Pharmacy and Pharmacology 20: 968-974 (1969).

## Discussion

*R.N. Boyes* (Chairman): I agree with your general philosophy. You seem to be suggesting that an assay must be available now at a very early stage in the development of a drug.

*S.A. Kaplan*: It is becoming a fact of life. We are going to be required to monitor drug levels during toxicity programmes, at least in the United States.

# 16

# Novel Drug Delivery Systems

*F. Theeuwes*

Alza Research, Palo Alto, California

Pharmacological studies defining the optimal time course of drug concentrations required to elicit the desired therapeutic response — and to minimise unwanted effects — indicate the need for novel dosage form design to achieve and maintain those concentrations. Pharmacokinetic analysis specifies drug input rates to the body necessary to maintain the time-concentration profiles so identified. In pharmaceutics, dosage form design is directed to developing systems that can deliver drugs as a function of time to match any of the higher, rationally defined input functions. From the medical area, the input required is the experience defining the regimens that optimise therapeutic outcome.

Thus, devising rational and acceptable dosage forms requires insight from 4 areas of expertise: pharmacology, pharmacokinetics, pharmaceutics, and medicine. Performance criteria are definable from the perspective of each of those areas.

This paper discusses the design of a class of osmotic pump drug delivery systems for systemic treatment within the framework discussed above. Zero-order drug delivery has been given special attention for the well documented class of drugs with defined therapeutic indices.

## 1. Criteria for Selection of Drugs and Dosing Schedules in Chronic Treatment

There is a growing list of drugs (Koch-Weser, 1972; Urquhart, 1979) that need to be taken chronically and for which a correlation between plasma concentration and effect is established. The preferred therapeutic range for these drugs is defined as the range above which a substantial number of side effects are encountered and below which the drugs are virtually ineffective. This concentration range can then be considered as safe and effective. If this zone is narrow or the ratio of the maximum safe to minimum effective plasma concentration — defined as therapeutic index — is low, a high degree of control over the plasma concentration must be exerted to maintain the concentration within this range.

When a drug half-life is long compared to its administration interval, convenient twice daily dose scheduling with conventional dosage forms e.g., tablets and liquids, can maintain the plasma concentration within the safe and effective range. When the half-life is short, however, controlled metering of drug into the circulation is necessary to compensate for its rapid elimination. Thus, for chronic therapy the desired input function into the body is constant drug delivery, also referred to as zero-order delivery. The magnitude of the zero-order delivery rate, Z, needed to maintain the plasma concentration, $C_p$, is given in equation:

$$Z = C_p \cdot \dot{V}_{cl} \qquad\qquad \text{Eq. 1}$$

where $V_{cl}$ is the total clearance of drug from the body.

In conventional oral or rectal therapy, the optimal dosing interval can be estimated (Theeuwes and Bayne, 1977) from the equation:

$$\tau \leqslant t_{1/2} \frac{\ln TI}{\ln 2} \qquad\qquad \text{Eq. 2}$$

This expression indicates the dosing interval, $\tau$, needed to maintain plasma concentration within the therapeutic range for repetitive injections. This expression was derived by requiring that the fluctuations in plasma concentrations, expressed as the dosage form index (DI), should not be larger than its therapeutic index. A one-compartment pharmacokinetic model was assumed. The dosage form index (Theeuwes and Bayne, 1977) was defined as the ratio of the maximum to minimum plasma concentration achieved on repetitive dosing at quasi-steady-state. For example when the therapeutic index $TI = 2$ [a frequent occurrence (Koch-Weser, 1972)] equation 2 indicates that the dosing interval for conventional dosage forms should be shorter than the half-life.

In addition to the pharmacological and pharmacokinetic rationale, patient compliance is an important factor, since it relates the therapy the clinician prescribes to the therapy that the patient actually receives. Quantitative analysis of this problem in the work of Sackett and Haynes provides an idea of the effect of compliance on therapeutic outcome.

Haynes (1976) reviewed 44 clinical studies of a range of clinical conditions, and found that an increase in compliance of 88 % of these cases resulted in a direct increase in therapeutic success for 75 % of the cases. Designing a therapeutically effective dosage form and schedule thus requires understanding of the correlation between compliance and frequency of administration. Gatley (1968) carried out a survey of 86 patients who were on mixed treatments for 1 to 4 weeks. His results indicate that the percentage of patients taking 95 to 105 % of the full number of tablets was 67, 50, 44 and 22, respectively, for once, twice, thrice, and 4 times daily treatment, demonstrating the validity of the widely held view that once daily treatment is preferred. It should also be noted that the overall extent of drug absorption on any prescribed drug regimen is not the drug dosage prescribed times the fraction absorbed; more realistically it is the drug dosage prescribed times the fraction absorbed *times the probability that dosing will occur*. Hence, the actual bioavailability is not equal to the theoretical bioavailability when measured in clinical trials under controlled conditions.

Equation 2 indicates that when the elimination half-life of a drug is short and its therapeutic index is low, zero-order controlled delivery is desirable. In contrast, with conventional dosage forms, the dosing intervals providing optimum therapy would be inconveniently frequent, with a predictably very low compliance for other than acute symptom-related treatments.

## 2. Constraints Posed by the Gastrointestinal Tract

In addition to considering drug selection from the pharmacological, pharmacokinetic, and patient compliance points of view, the constraints imposed by the route of administration must be considered. For oral dosage forms these factors are:

i) First-pass effect
ii) Gut wall metabolism
iii) Drug stability in the gastrointestinal tract
iv) Transport of drug to the gut wall
v) Useful lifetime of the drug delivery system

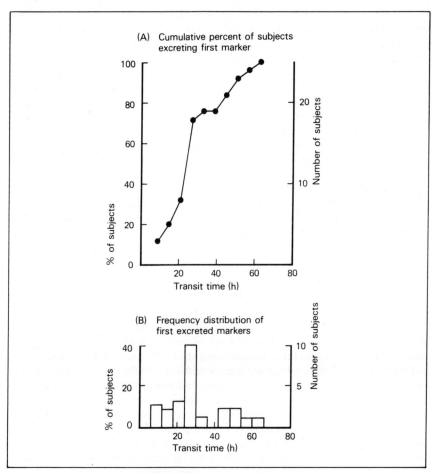

*Fig. 1.* Transit time (mouth-to-anus) of inert objects in the gastrointestinal tract of man. (Reproduced with the permission of Gut.)

vi)  Boundary conditions on the delivery mechanism (pH, temperature, relative
     humidity, mechanical agitation, pressure fluctuations)
vii) Magnitude and time-course of desired delivery rate.

Drug specific tissues (i-iii and vii) require consideration on a drug-by-drug basis.

For a systems design point of view, iv-vii can be addressed most readily. The
magnitude of the delivery rate (constraint vii) which the potency of the drug dictates is
addressed by selecting the appropriate delivery mechanism and structure for the
dosage form. This selection also gives rise to certain expectations as to what effect the
boundary conditions (constraint vi) in the gastrointestinal tract will exert on the
system's delivery rate. These issues are addressed in section 3 for a class of novel
osmotic systems.

The useful lifetime of an oral dosage form (constraint v) is that time interval over
which significant drug absorption can take place from the gastrointestinal tract; it is
equal to the length of absorptive intestinal tract divided by the average speed of travel
of the dosage form. This time is a certain fraction of mouth-to-anus transit time, depending on where absorption occurs for a particular drug. Many data on gastrointestinal transit times have been published; those of Hinton et al. (1969), based on using
orally ingested inert markers, are especially applicable. A conservative view of useful
transit time is obtained by considering the time of first appearance in the stool after
simultaneous ingestion of several markers (fig. 1).

On average, the shortest transit time observed in a normal male population was
about 24 hours, and only 20% of this population had a transit time less than 20
hours. Although systems design may allow zero-order drug delivery for 24 hours,
such a design may not be desirable since absorption may not occur over this full duration of time. In spite of this assertion, once-a-day therapy may be achievable by
systems that deliver at zero-order for a substantial fraction of 24 hours. If, for such
drugs, the therapeutic index and biological half-life are sufficiently large, the plasma
concentration achieved at the end of the absorption period could maintain therapy for
the optimum duration of 24 hours.

For rectal dosage forms, constraints i-vii listed above are equally valid. Measurement of the defaecation interval provides an estimate of the useful absorption time
available for this route of administration.


## 3. Pharmaceutics: Dosage Form Design and
## System Functionality *In Vitro*

The pharmacological and pharmacokinetic considerations reviewed above
demonstrate that controlled zero-order drug delivery is preferred in certain cases and
should be achieved within the constraints imposed by the gastrointestinal tract. From
a therapeutic perspective, patient compliance problems clearly show the need for once
or twice daily administration. These considerations make the class of system based on
delivery of drug by osmosis an interesting category to consider.

1) Osmotic systems can be designed to deliver a substantial fraction of their contents at zero-order rate. A consequence of such a delivery profile is that it allows the
maximum bioavailability (extent of absorption) within a limited absorption time in
the gastrointestinal tract, for the lowest (safest) plasma concentration at all times.
This characteristic will tend to maximise the bioavailability and control over plasma
concentrations at the same time.

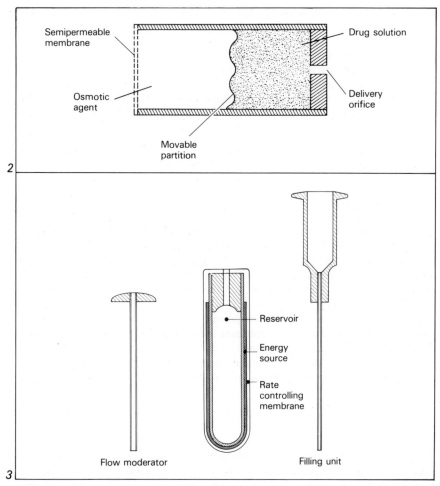

*Fig. 2.* Representation of a generic osmotic pump. (Reproduced with permission of the Annals of Biomedical Engineering.)

*Fig. 3.* Osmotic pump and components. (Reproduced with permission of the Annals of Biomedical Engineering.)

2) Drug delivery can occur at rates up to 50 to 80mg/h from a dosage form that can be taken orally. These high rates are meaningful for systemic treatment with practically all drugs at hand.

3) Delivery rate can be substantially independent of fluctuations in pH, agitation, and pressure that occur in the gastrointestinal tract, allowing systems to deliver *in vitro* and *in vivo* as designed.

Dosage form characteristics (1) and (3), further illustrated below, have also been recognised as important attributes (Cabana, 1979) in guidelines for evaluating the bioavailability of controlled release dosage forms.

Osmotic delivery systems currently under development consist basically of 3 types:

i) The generic osmotic pump (Theeuwes and Yum, 1976). Several systems of
this type are marketed for use in reasearch animals as the ALZET[1] osmotic
minipumps. These systems deliver their contents independently of the properties of the drug formulation

ii) The elementary osmotic pump (Theeuwes, 1975). Various embodiments of
this system are under development as solid oral and rectal dosage forms

iii) The push-pull osmotic pump (Theeuwes, 1978). The aim of developing this
system as a solid dosage form is to provide controlled delivery of drugs that
are extremely soluble or insoluble in water.

The characteristics of these 3 dosage forms and some areas of application for
them as oral and rectal dosage forms are discussed below.

### 3.1 The Generic Osmotic Pump

A cross-section of the generic system, and its embodiment as the osmotic
minipump are shown in figures 2 and 3. The researcher fills the minipump with liquid or semisolid formulation by using the filling unit — a syringe attached to a
needle that is inserted through an orifice on top of the system (fig. 3). Applications requiring low flow rates on the order of $1\mu l/h$ necessitate insertion of the flow modera-
tor before use (fig. 4).

In operation, water from the environment is imbibed across the semipermeable
membrane into the compartment containing the osmotic agent at a flow rate $dV/dt$ to
displace an equal amount of drug solution flowing from the reservoir through the
orifice. Appropriate selection of osmotic driving agent, membrane, and its dimen-
sions permit preprogramming of the volume flow rate $dV/dt$ from the minipump:

$$\frac{dV}{dt} = k \cdot \frac{A}{h} \; (\pi_o - \pi_e) \qquad\qquad \text{Eq. 3}$$

Here A is the membrane area, h the thickness, k the membrane permeability to
water, $\pi_o$ the osmotic pressure of the osmotic driving agent, and $\pi_e$ the osmotic
pressure of the environment (7.7atm for isotonic saline at 37°C). Delivery of practically all the drug at zero-order rate is ensured by including a sufficient amount of
osmotic agent to keep the osmotic driving solution saturated throughout the functional lifetime of the system. The user can choose the mass delivery rate from the
system by selecting the desired drug concentration, $C_d$, in the formulation (eq. 4).

$$\frac{dm}{dt} = \frac{dV}{dt} \cdot C_d \qquad\qquad \text{Eq. 4}$$

The ALZET® systems, programmed at a constant flow rate of $dV/dt = 1\mu l/h$
for 1 week, or $0.5\mu l/h$ for 2 weeks, have been useful in steady-state, or zero-order
pharmacology (Wei and Loh, 1976; Aguilera and Catt, 1978; Sikic et al., 1978;
Frankel et al., 1979; Kasamatsu et al., 1979; Lorkovic, 1979; Smits and Struyker-
Boudier, 1979) for establishing concentration-effect relationships, since it can maintain drug concentration at target sites at a constant value.

1   'Alzet®' osmotic minipumps, ALZA Corp., Palo Alto, CA.

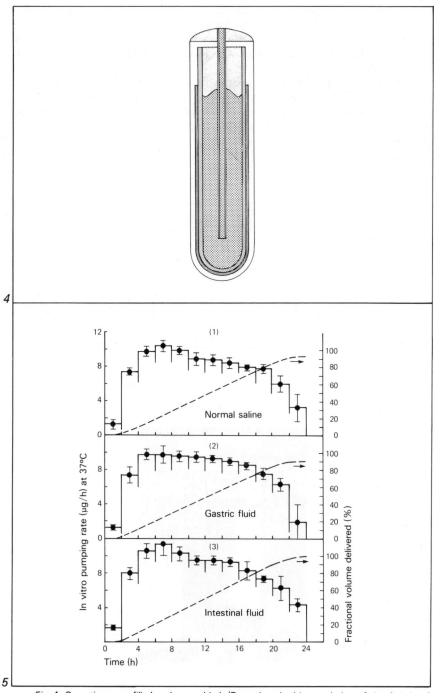

*Fig. 4.* Osmotic pump filled and assembled. (Reproduced with permission of the Annals of Biomedical Engineering.)

*Fig. 5.* Delivery rate from 24-hour generic pump.

The generic osmotic pump can also be designed with flow rates such that the total content is delivered over 1 day, or a fraction thereof, by adjusting the membrane permeability k, osmotic pressure $\pi_o$, and to some extent A and h, as seen in equation 3. Systems of this type have been made (Theeuwes and Eckenhoff, in press) with the delivery profile shown in figure 5.

Like the ALZET® minipumps, the generic pumps with delivery duration of 6, 12, or 24 hours are playing a growing role as research tools for studying the optimum delivery times for oral and rectal dosage forms. In some cases, the systems can be used to determine effective and optimum drug input rates into the body. In many cases they can serve to identify the time period over which drugs can be absorbed from the gastrointestinal tract.

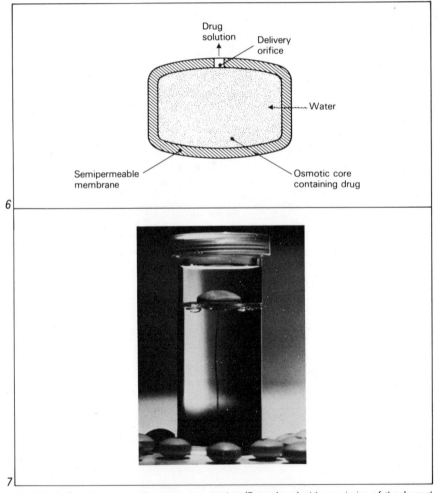

*Fig. 6.* Elementary osmotic pump cross-section. (Reproduced with permission of the Journal of Pharmaceutical Sciences.)

*Fig. 7.* Delivery from the elementary osmotic pump in which a blue dye simulates the drug.

## 3.2 The Elementary Osmotic Pump (EOP)

When both the osmotic driving agent and drug component are one and the same, or when the osmotic agent and drug are combined in the same compartment, the osmotic pump can be reduced to its most elementary form (fig. 6). In operation, the system continuously imbibes water from its environment to create a saturated solution of agent within the compartment, which it delivers at a constant rate through the orifice (fig. 7).

Again, the zero-order mass delivery rate from the system is given in equation 4, where the volume flux has the same form as given in equation 3. Thus, the mass delivery rate can be written as:

$$\left(\frac{dm}{dt}\right)_z = \frac{A}{h} \cdot k\,(\pi_f - \pi_e) \cdot S_d \qquad\qquad \text{Eq. 5}$$

$S_d$ is the concentration of drug in the compartment, $\pi_f$ the osmotic pressure of the drug formulation, and the other symbols are as expressed above. In many systems the osmotic pressure of the drug formulation is large enough compared to the osmotic pressure of the environment to permit expressing the zero-order delivery rate thus:

$$Z = \left(\frac{dm}{dt}\right)_z = \frac{A}{h} \cdot k \cdot \pi_f \cdot S_d \qquad\qquad \text{Eq. 6}$$

For the special case where drug is the sole driving agent, systems will pump at a constant rate as long as excess solid drug remains inside the system. This excess assures that both the influx of water and the concentration of the outgoing solution are constant. When all solid drug has been delivered, the release rate will fall parabolically, due to decreases in influx of water and outflux of diluted solution. The non-zero-order declining rate is given in equation:

$$\frac{dm}{dt} = \frac{Z}{\left[1 + \dfrac{Z}{SV}(t - t_z)\right]^2} \qquad\qquad \text{Eq. 7}$$

where Z and S are as defined above and V is the internal volume of the system. A typical release rate profile is shown in figure 8 for an elementary osmotic pump with a potassium chloride content of 500mg and delivery rate of 22mg/h.

The zero-order portion of the delivery rate profile lasts a time period $t_z$:

$$t_z = \frac{m_z}{Z} \qquad\qquad \text{Eq. 8}$$

where $m_z$ is the mass of drug delivered at zero-order rate. When the drug is highly soluble, the fraction not delivered at zero-order will be large, since this is the amount of drug dissolved within the inside membrane shell at saturated concentration. The fraction of total system drug content $m_t$ delivered at zero-order is indicated by equation 9 and represented graphically in figure 9.

$$\frac{m_z}{m_t} = 1 - \frac{S}{\rho} \qquad\qquad\text{Eq. 9}$$

Here, $\rho$ is the density of the solid drug core of the system.

### 3.3 The Push-pull Osmotic Pump

The push-pull system is designed for delivering solutions of drugs that are excessively soluble, and for delivering insoluble drugs as suspensions. The system (fig.10) consists of 2 compartments separated by a flexible partition. The top compartment contains solid drug and has a delivery orifice communicating with the outside, while the bottom compartment contains a solid osmotic driving agent formulation. A semi-permeable membrane surrounds both compartments and separately regulates the influx of water into each. In operation, the drug compartment formulates solid drug into solution by pulling water from its environment at a rate F. Simultaneously, the osmotic driving compartment imbibes water at a different rate Q and, in expanding, exerts pressure against the top compartment to push the drug formulation through the orifice.

In the treatment that follows, it is assumed that the flexible partition is impermeable. The system is programmed to deliver drug at the rate described in equation 10, wherein both volume flows, F and Q, work in tandem — not unlike the action of the push-pull amplifier known in electronics — to dispense drug formulation of concentration $C_d$:

$$\frac{dm}{dt} = (F + Q)\,C_d \qquad\qquad\text{Eq. 10}$$

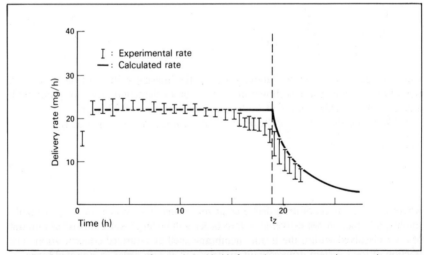

Fig. 8. *In vitro* release rate of potassium chloride from elementary osmotic pumps in water at 37°C. (Reproduced with permission of the Journal of Pharmaceutical Sciences).

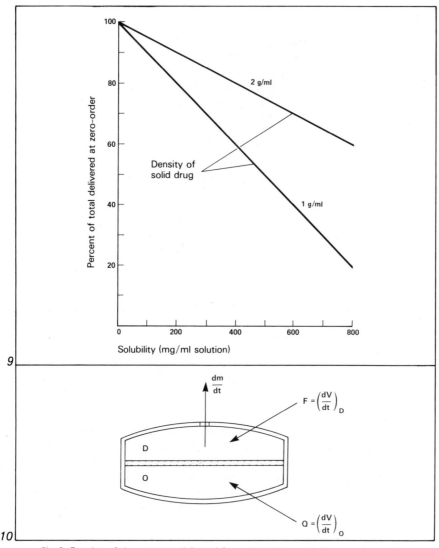

*Fig. 9.* Fraction of drug content delivered from elementary osmotic pump at constant rate. (Reproduced with permission of the Journal of Pharmaceutical Sciences.)

*Fig. 10.* Cross-section of the push-pull osmotic pump.

When enough osmotic driving agent is present in the push compartment to maintain $Q$ constant throughout the functional lifetime of the system, the value of $Q$ can be programmed at any constant rate between 0 and $Q_m$. The value $Q_m$ is the maximum volume imbibition rate into the push compartment. That value corresponds to the volume dissolution rate of drug from the drug compartment effected by $F_s$:

$$F_s = k_d \cdot \pi_{ds} \cdot \frac{A_d}{h_d} \qquad\qquad \text{Eq. 11}$$

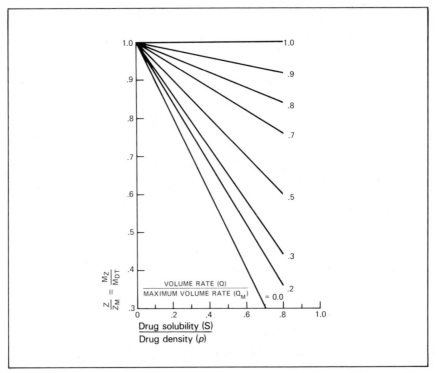

*Fig. 11.* Fraction of drug delivery at zero-order rate from the push-pull osmotic pump.

At fluxes above $Q_m$ the system will distort and lose the control desired.

All symbols have the meaning described above; subscripts d and s respectively represent drug compartment and the saturated state of drug. $Q$ and $Q_m$ are programmed as expressed by an equation of the form of equation 11, with subscript o relating to the osmotic push compartment. The values of $F_s$ and $Q_m$ are then related by equation 12 wherein S and $\rho$ are the drug solubility and density:

$$Q_m = F_s \; \frac{1}{\rho} \; \frac{S}{1 - S/\rho} \qquad\qquad \text{Eq. 12}$$

When the push compartment operates at its maximum value, $Q_m$, all drug is delivered at its maximum zero-order rate, $Z_m$. At values of $Q$ less than $Q_m$, the zero-order rate, $Z$, is a fraction of $Z_m$, as given by equation 13:

$$\frac{Z}{Z_m} = 1 - \frac{S}{\rho} \left( 1 - \frac{Q}{Q_m} \right) \qquad\qquad \text{Eq. 13}$$

It was demonstrated that the normalised zero-order rate, equation 14, is equal to the fraction of drug that this system delivers at zero order.

$$\frac{Z}{Z_m} = \frac{m_z}{m_{dt}}$$

Eq. 14

If equation 13 is plotted as a function of $S/\rho$ in figure 11, the lines have a slope of $(1 - Q/Q_m)$. Equation 13 is analogous to equation 9; this becomes apparent by comparing figures 9 and 11. In figure 11, the line $Q = 0.0$ represents figure 9. The push-pull system delivers higher fractions of drug at zero-order as the value of $Q$ more closely approximates $Q_m$. For values of the driving rate, $Q$, smaller than its maximum value, the system pumps at zero-order rate less than $Z_m$ and consequently also delivers the remaining fraction at non-zero-order rate.

It is interesting to note that, for values of $Q$ from 0 to $Q_m$, the magnitude of the zero-order rate is different but the zero-order time period is the same for a system identical in $F_s$. This becomes intuitively clear in considering that $t_z$ is the time period needed to dissolve all the drug formulation in the drug compartment; drug dissolves at a rate that is solely a function of $F_s$ for that drug formulation. For that same reason equation 14 follows. The zero-order time period is given by:

$$t_z = \frac{m_{dt}}{\rho \cdot Q_m}$$

Eq. 15

The non-zero-order rate has been described analytically as indicated by equation 16, in which all symbols are as defined above:

$$\frac{1}{Z_m}\frac{dm}{dt} = \frac{\dfrac{F_s}{Q_m} \cdot \dfrac{S}{\rho}}{\left[1 - \dfrac{F_s}{Q}\ln\dfrac{1 - \dfrac{t}{t_z} \cdot \dfrac{Q}{Q_m}}{1 - \dfrac{Q}{Q_m}}\right]^2} + \frac{\dfrac{Q}{Q_m} \cdot \dfrac{S}{\rho}}{\left[1 - \dfrac{F_s}{Q}\ln\dfrac{1 - \dfrac{t}{t_z} \cdot \dfrac{Q}{Q_m}}{1 - \dfrac{Q}{Q_m}}\right]}$$

Eq 16

As indicated in figure 11, by selecting the appropriate $Q/Q_m$ design parameters one can develop systems defined by different $S/\rho$ values that deliver equal fractions at zero order. Figure 12 provides an illustration; for both examples a and b, the value of $m_z/m_{dt} = 0.85$ was achieved. However, as is evident from this figure, the shapes of the non-zero-order portion differ for these different cases. Because of the added driving compartment, the delivery rate profile can be designed to terminate at a specific time $t_f$ (fig. 12), which can be selected to be shorter than the average absorption time, thereby maximising the bioavailability. $t_f$ is the time at which the partition membrane meets the membrane with delivery orifice and all the drug has been delivered.

The push-pull osmotic pump is complementary in design to the elementary osmotic pump; the latter is desirable for its simplicity. For certain applications, however, the push-pull system is desirable, as for the delivery of very water soluble drugs or those with high $S/\rho$ values. For example, the elementary osmotic pump would deliver only 20% of procainamide hydrochloride, a drug with $S = 860mg/ml$, at zero-order. Push-pull systems containing this drug delivered about 80% at constant rate (fig. 13).

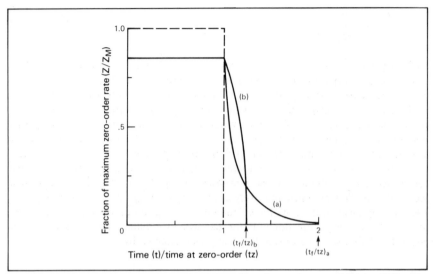

*Fig. 12.* Theoretical release rate profile of the push-pull osmotic pump delivering 85% of its drug content at zero-order a: $[Q/Q_m = 0.5; S/\rho = 0.3]$; b: $[Q/Q_m = 0.8; S/\rho = 0.75]$.

## 4. Pharmacokinetics: System Functionality *In Vivo* and Plasma Concentrations

The purpose of dosage form design, as described here, is to arrive at systems that deliver their contents predictably at the site of application.

The test for achievement of this goal is to measure the release rate of the system *in vivo* and to compare it with its functionality *in vitro* under bioanalogous conditions. Such conditions can be defined as those that simulate the biological environment sufficiently well that the dosage form delivers its contents at a rate approximating the rate *in vivo,* reproducibly and within narrow limits. These bioanalogous conditions are the boundary conditions on the physical chemical mechanism, by which the dosage form operates, and therefore, such conditions are not necessarily the same for different dosage forms operating on different principles. For the osmotic systems, 3 fluid media selected are: isotonic saline, artificial gastric fluid, and artificial intestinal fluid without enzymes, at 37°C. Two types of measurement are performed:

1. The rate $dm/dt$ is obtained by transferring a system to successive receptor vessels, where it resides for time intervals that are short compared to its total lifetime. Each vessel then contains the amount of drug, m, delivered per unit time, $\Delta t$.

2. The cumulative amount is measured from the initial and final drug content of a particular system ($m_i$ and $m_f$, respectively) after recovering it from the test medium where it resided for a known time period, t. Plotting for several systems ($m_i - m_f$) versus time for each system then provides the cumulative amount of drug released as a function of time.

Data provided by the first method, from which cumulative amounts delivered were calculated (figs. 5 and 13), have been plotted in figures 5, 8 and 13. Method (1) lends itself well to *in vitro* experimentation. Method (2) has served to measure performance *in vivo;* in these cases *in vitro* data are obtained in the same way to serve as a standard of comparison. Data of this type are plotted in figures 14 and 15.

Data on functionality of the minipump (fig. 14) show an *in vitro* release rate about 10% above the *in vivo* rate. Figure 15 shows an example of elementary osmotic pump systems delivering acetazolamide *in vitro* and in the gastrointestinal tract of dogs. Again, *in vitro-in vivo* data agree within ± 10%.

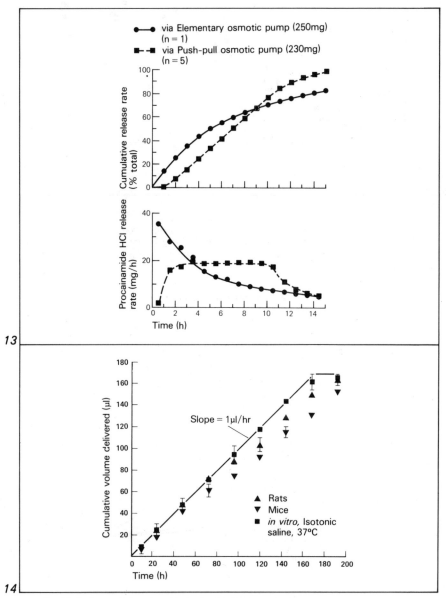

*Fig. 13.* Delivery of procainamide hydrochloride by osmosis.

*Fig. 14.* Comparison of *in vitro* and *in vivo* cumulative amounts delivered from the ALZET® osmotic minipump (each unit represents five minipumps). Reproduced with permission of the Annals of Biomedical Engineering.)

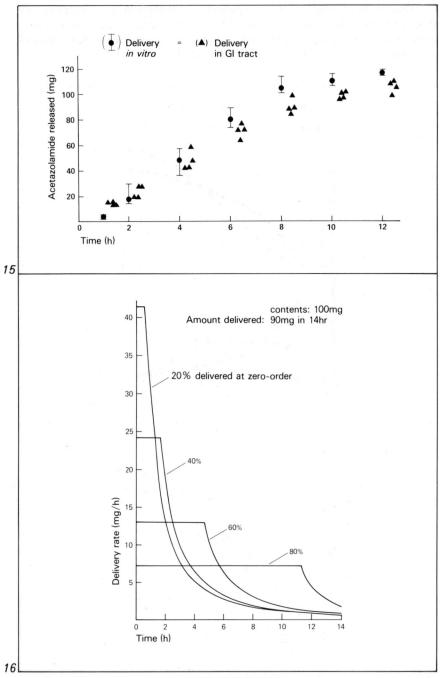

Fig. 15. Cumulative amount of acetazolamide delivered from the elementary osmotic pump *in vitro* (saline 37°C) and *in vivo* (into gastrointestinal tract of 4 dogs).

Fig. 16. Release rate profile of elementary osmotic pump systems characterised by percentage of drug delivered at zero-order.

Since these osmotic systems function *in vivo* as predicted by the theory, calculations that simulate drug input into the body according to the systems' well defined delivery rates permit defining ideal system-dosing schedules and indicate what system is appropriate for achieving them. The analysis will indicate use of the push-pull osmotic pump or the elementary osmotic pump according to defined selection criteria. Simulations (Bayne et al., in preparation) from which data have been summarised here, provide only approximations, because:

1) The body is treated as a linear, single-compartment model; and
2) Absorption half-life is assumed to be zero.

The application addressed is chronic treatment, and the measure of the flatness of the plasma concentration curve achieved is expressed by the dosage form index. The regimen selected is dosing every 12 hours for a system characterised by the fraction of drug it delivers at zero-order. The system content is selected as 100mg, of which 90% is delivered in $t_{90}$ = 14h (the time assumed for drug absorption). Thus, systems having different delivery rates may be considered equal with respect to extent of drug absorption. For the simulation, the fraction delivered at zero-order was allowed to vary from 20% to 90% with $t_{1/2}$ varying from 0.5 to 8 hours.

The input function of the elementary osmotic pump described by Z, $t_z$, and dm/dt can be expressed in terms of $t_{90}$ and y, the fraction not delivered at zero-order, by equations 17, 18, and 19:

$$Z = \frac{m_t}{t_{90}} (10y^2 - 2y + 1) \qquad \text{Eq. 17}$$

$$t_z = \frac{t_{90} (1 - y)}{10y^2 - 2y + 1} \qquad \text{Eq. 18}$$

$$\frac{dm}{dt} = \frac{Z}{\left[ 1 + \dfrac{Z}{m_t \cdot y} (t - t_z) \right]^2} \qquad \text{Eq. 19}$$

System release rate profiles thus calculated indicate (fig. 16) that repetitive dosing of systems with low fractions delivered at zero-order will result in large plasma fluctuations. These fluctuations, expressed as dosage form index, will be damped when the elimination half-life is large and will closely resemble actual fluctuations in the gut when the half-life is short. A summary of the results (fig. 17) shows a dosage form index for each simulation plotted as a function of the fraction of drug delivered at zero-order at constant elimination half-lives. The minima shown for the curves at 80% are an artifact of the simulations, since it was assumed that $t_{90}$ = 14h. For 90% of drug delivered at zero-order with dosing every 12h, the successive doses overlap by 2 hours, resulting in a spike in the input function that is actually artificial, since for such cases $t_z$ can be selected to be shorter.

Figure 17 shows, as expected, that drugs with long half-lives do not require a delivery system of high quality. When the therapeutic index is low and the drug half-

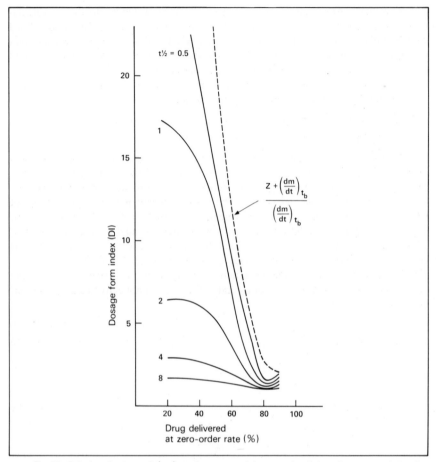

*Fig. 17.* Calculated values of: (---) maximum-to-minimum ratio of the release rate of the elementary osmotic pump in the gastrointestinal tract: (——) maximum-to-minimum ratio of the plasma concentration following dosing with the elementary osmotic pump.

life is short, however, a large fraction should be delivered at zero-order; substantial gains result when this fraction exceeds 60 %. The amplitude of the oscillating plasma concentration (dosage form index) for such drugs with short half-life approximates the amplitude of the oscillating delivery rate pattern (dashed line figure 17) in the gut. For drugs with a therapeutic index of 2 and short half-life, systems delivering up to 80 to 90 % at zero-order are indicated.

## 5. Conclusions

Dosage form design is aimed at the administration of a drug compound in the most beneficial way to ensure optimum safety and therapeutic efficacy. This optimum treatment requires prescription of the dosage form according to a convenient schedule. The pharmacological effect produced and the absence of side effects provide measures of the value of the treatment and dosage form.

When a correlation is found between pharmacological response and drug concentration at a certain site in the body e.g., the central compartment, it may be possible to describe a concentration or zone of concentrations as a function of time within which optimum treatment is achieved for this drug. A dosage form and schedule can then be rated in pharmacokinetic terms by the difference between the concentration actually achieved and the concentration desired.

The quality of treatment can further be judged, in the area of pharmaceutics, by comparing the release rate of the dosage form achieved *in vitro* with the desired rate, if the *in vitro* rate equals the *in vivo* rate. In this manner, the *in vitro* specifications of a dosage form also constitute the safeguard for the quality and reproducibility of therapy.

The osmotic class of delivery systems is a category of dosage forms that, within the framework described above, have the following desirable properties:

1) Their *in vivo* delivery rates are equal to their *in vitro* rates in a bioanalogous medium to within 10%
2) Depending on the selection of drug salts, osmotic agents, and membrane components, the systems can be designed to deliver at a variety of release rates
3) Systems can be designed to deliver, at substantially zero-order rates, drugs of widely varying physical chemical properties
4) Systems of defined rate, such as the osmotic generic pump, can be used as tools for studying the pharmacokinetics, and in some cases the pharmacology, of suitable drug candidates before engaging in full-scale dosage form development
5) Zero-order delivery rates can be maintained by these osmotic systems, which may allow optimum once-a-day treatment.

## Acknowledgments

I thank Dr W. Bayne and Mr G. Rogers for the pharmacokinetic analyses, Dr J. Urquhart for his helpful suggestions and discussion, and Mrs Constance Mitchell for her editorial assistance.

## References

Augilera, G. and Catt, K.J.: Regulation of aldosterone secretion by the renin-angiotensin system during sodium restriction in rats. Proceedings of the National Academy of Science USA 75: 4057-4061 (1978).

Bayne, W.; Rogers, G. and Theeuwes, F.: Pharmacokinetics of elementary osmotic pump systems (unpublished).

Cabana, B.E.: Guidelines for evaluating the bioavailability of controlled release dosage forms; presented at the American Pharmaceutical Association, Academy of Pharmaceutical Sciences, Midwest Regional Meeting, May 21, 1979, Chicago.

Frankel, B.J.; Schmid, F.G. and Grodsky, G.M.: Effect of continuous insulin infusion with an implantable 7-day 'minipump' in the diabetic Chinese hamster. Endocrinology 105: 1532-1539 (1979).

Gatley, M.S.: To be taken as directed. Journal of the Royal College of General Practitioners. 16: 39-44 (1968).

Haynes, R.B.: Strategies for improving compliance: A methodologic analysis and review; in Sackett and
    Haynes (Eds) Compliance with Therapeutic Regimens, p. 69-82 (Johns Hopkins University Press,
    Baltimore 1976).
Hinton, J.M.; Lennard-Jones, J.E. and Young, A.C.: A new method for studying gut transit times using
    radioopaque markers. Gut 10: 842-847 (1969).
Kasamatsu, T.; Pettigrew, J.D. and Ary, M.: Restoration of visual cortical plasticity by local microperfu-
    sion of norepinephrine. Journal of Comparative Neurology 185: 163-181 (1979).
Koch-Weser, J.: Drug therapy. Serum drug concentrations as therapeutic guides. New England Journal of
    Medicine 287: 227-231 (1972).
Lorkovic, H.: Effects of motor nerve anesthesia and tenotomy on muscle membrane properties. Pflugers
    Archiv European Journal of Physiology 379: 89-93 (1979).
Sikic, B.I.; Colins, J.M.; Mimnaugh, E.G. and Gram, T.E.: Improved therapeutic index of bleomycin
    when administered by continuous infusion in mice. Cancer Treatment Report 62: 2011-217 (1978).
Smits, J.F.M. and Struyker-Boudier, H.A.J.: Steady-state disposition of propranolol and its total metabol-
    ites in the spontaenously hypertensive rat: chronic subcutaneous versus intracerebroventricular infu-
    sion with osmotic minipump. Journal of Pharmacology and Experimental Therapeutics 209:
    317-322 (1979).
Theeuwes, F.: Elementary osmotic pump. Journal of Pharmaceutical Sciences 64: 1987-1991 (1975).
Theeuwes, F.: U.S. Patent 4,111,202 (1978).
Theeuwes, F. and Bayne, W.: Dosage form index: an objective criterion for evaluation of controlled
    release drug delivery systems. Journal of Pharmaceutical Sciences 66: 1388-1392 (1977).
Theeuwes, F. and Eckenhoff, B.: Applications of osmotic drug delivery; in Proceedings of the 6th Interna-
    tional Symposium on Controlled Release of Bioactive Materials, August 6-8, 1979, New Orleans (in
    press).
Theeuwes, F. and Yum, S.I.: Principles of the design and operation of generic osmotic pumps for the
    delivery of semisolid or liquid drug formulations. Annals of Biomedical Engineering 4: 343-353
    (1976).
Urquhart, J.: Opportunities for research: methods of drug administration; in Simon (Ed) Proceedings of
    the National Academy of Sciences, Institute of Medicine, Conference on Pharmaceuticals for
    Developing Countries, January 29-31, 1979, p.320-339 (1979).
Wei, E. and Loh, H.: Physical dependence on opiate-like peptides. Science 193: 1262-1263 (1976).

## Discussion

*A.H. Beckett* (London): The key point is transit time. You have given some information, but were subdivided or tablet units used? What information have you on the
transit time of your oral preparation in man? Can you deliver a drug for 24 hours
without loss of bioavailability?

*F. Theeuwes*: The data were obtained with radio-opaque markers (225mm) and
the rate of emptying from the stomach was the same as that of a solution. The
systems were given 20 at a time and with a meal. Had there been retention in the
stomach, the differences would have been obvious. Tablets of larger size are retained
by the stomach for longer periods. A number of clinical trials have shown that we
can maintain plasma concentrations for long periods of time, depending on the size of
the system, the drug substance and food intake etc.

# 17

# Prodrugs: Principles and Practice

*Takeru Higuchi*

Department of Pharmaceutical Chemistry, University of Kansas

New drugs are usually identified by screening techniques carried out in circumstances different from those of their ultimate use. Presumed antibiotics, for example, are usually evaluated initially on cultures of micro-organisms rather than in animals and the relative activity of anticholinergics may be measured first on isolated strips of guinea pig ileum. These tests are usually designed so that the diffusional path from the point of application to the site of action is relatively open and efficient. Most drugs are, as a result, initially chosen on the basis of their activity directly on their receptors. Their molecular structures, consequently, are selected so as to maximise these interactions. At this stage physicochemical requirements for delivery to sites of action under therapeutic conditions are not of concern.

Active drugs identified in this manner would not necessarily have those attributes required for their effective transport from points of administration to receptor sites when incorporated into dosage forms such as tablets, capsules or parenteral solutions. Those chemical and physicochemical properties which would permit, for example, efficient delivery into the circulation from an oral preparation or into the skin from a topical preparation have no direct relationship with requirements which must be met at the target site. The prodrug approach may help to solve the problem of design of drug molecules with the optimal configuration for these two requirements (Stella, 1975).

In optimising the therapeutic activity of any drug by structural modification it is usually necessary to balance the effect of structural changes on the activity of the agent at its point of action against the effects of these same changes, among others, on the pharmaceutics of the system. By the prodrug approach, these independent structural requirements may be separated by, first identifying the otherwise optimal structure for activity and, secondly, cloaking it temporarily during delivery in another form with optimal transport properties. Thus near optimal activity and delivery can be achieved.

Many of the drugs now in use are actually prodrugs in the sense that new chemicals generated from them after administration are actually responsible for their presumed activity (table I). In most instances the drugs listed were identified by trial and error and scant thought was given to their probable prodrug nature. It is nevertheless evident that, at least with hindsight, the prodrug concept represents a

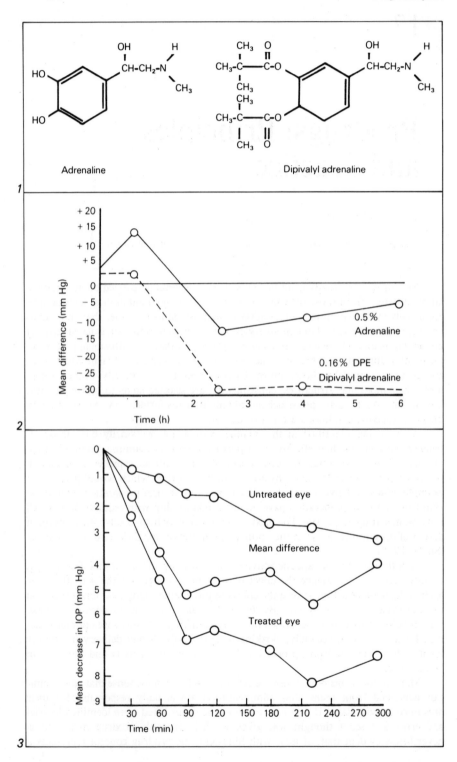

*Table I.* Examples of various prodrugs

| Prodrug examples | | | |
| --- | --- | --- | --- |
| vitamins | antibiotics | steroids | others |
| Vitamin A acetates, palmitates, etc. | Oxytetracycline magnesium chelate | Steroid acetonides, esters, etc. | Ara-C derivatives |
| | Pivampicillin, etc. | Conjugated oestrogens, oestrogens of different degrees of saturation | Aspirin |
| Thiamine | | | Derivatives of cardiac glycosides |
| Nicotinamide | Hetacillin | | |
| Riboflavin species | Chloramphenicol palmitate (taste masking) | | Clofibrate |
| Vitamin D species | | Mestranol | Chloral hydrate |
| Pro-thiamines | Chloramphenicol succinate, etc. | Depot progestagens | Codeine |
| $B_{12}$ | Clindamycin esters | | Cyclophosphamide |
| | Erythromycin esters (taste masking) | | Dipivalyl adrenaline |
| | Triacetyloleandomycin | | Dyphylline |
| | | | Fluorouracil |
| | Steroid phosphates (for solubility) | | Levodopa |
| | | | Phenacetin |
| | | | Phenylbutazone |
| | | | Sulphanilamide |

highly effective route to new and improved drugs. We will examine the physicochemical characteristics for optimal pharmaceutics and the chemistry involved.

## 1. Pharmaceutics

Let us start by examining a typical prodrug candidate and how its physical properties were manipulated to improve delivery. Some years ago we were involved in the synthesis and development of an antiglaucoma drug, a prodrug of adrenaline (epinephrine). This is an old story (McClure, 1975) but it illustrates the basic principles of this approach.

Adrenaline eye drops have been used for many years to reduce ocular hypertension but have numerous drawbacks in terms of side effects and instability. The dipivalyl ester (DPE) of the active drug (fig. 1) has been shown to improve delivery

*Fig. 1.* Structural formulae of adrenaline and dipivalyl adrenaline (dipivalyl epinephrine, DPE).

*Fig. 2.* Comparison of the effects of adrenaline and its dipivalyl ester on the intraocular pressure of rabbits.

*Fig. 3.* The effect of 1 drop of 0.025 % dipivalyl adrenaline on intraocular pressure (IOP); mean findings in 9 glaucomatous subjects.

and efficacy over the parent agent. Thus it is more effective in reducing the intraocular pressure (IOP) in rabbits (fig. 2), and also is effective in reducing IOP of glaucomatous patients in concentrations at which adrenaline itself is essentially inactive (fig. 3). Analysis of ocular tissues following administration of DPE and adrenaline has shown conclusively that the active compound, adrenaline, was delivered much more effectively when applied in the prodrug form rather than in its free state.

This was made possible by designing into the pro-adrenaline compound physical chemical characteristics which facilitate its transport across the corneal barrier. Adrenaline itself is a relatively polar molecule and interacts strongly with water. The free energy requirement for dehydration prior to its uptake by the lipoidal corneal tissue is sufficiently high to make this partitioning process relatively unfavourable. The esterified derivative, on the other hand, would be expected to require much less energy to move across the interface and moves through the barrier much more rapidly than the catechol. Adrenaline is regenerated in the anterior chamber through action of endogenous enzymes. Derivatisation of the active drug appears at the same time to have dramatically reduced the unwanted cardiovascular effect of the agent. The significant suppression of the hypertensive effect (fig. 4) is probably due to slowed release of the active form and changed distribution. Improved performance of prodrugs in general is largely based on such alteration of related thermodynamic properties.

In most instances thermodynamic quantities of major interest are:

1) The binding energies responsible for the condensed state of the pure agents
2) The hydration energies of the same in aqueous solution.

In designing prodrugs, therefore, we must understand the effects of molecular modification on these energetic quantities.

Solubility of a pure solid in water, for example, is directly determined by the above 2 quantities. If, therefore, we wish to increase or decrease solubility to solve a formulation or a drug delivery problem, we can manipulate either or both of these energetic quantities by appropriate structural changes. An excellent example of how solubility can be increased by reducing only the crystalline binding energy is the effect of esterification of adenosine arabinoside (ARA-A) at its 5' position (Repta, 1975; Repta et al., 1975). The 5' formate ester has approximately 100 times greater water solubility than the parent drug thus permitting ready formulation of a parenteral form of the drug, the prodrug being rapidly cleaved in the blood. Since the hydration free energies of the 2 compounds would not be expected to be significantly different, the increased aqueous solubility must be due primarily to reduction in the free energy of crystal formation. On the other hand, the observed increase in water solubility, for example, of conjugated oestrogens over their parent forms, most certainly must arise from increase in hydration free energy.

In the example of pro-adrenaline discussed above we were not directly concerned with the solubility of the pure drug. In this situation it is evident that the energetics of the solid play no immediate role. The observed increased permeability of the prodrug, however, resulted directly from structural changes designed to reduce its interaction with water molecules. The substitution of the 2 pivalyl groups for the hydroxyl functions materially reduced the hydration free energy of the parent drug.

Manipulation of these energies can confer wide-ranging means of solving problems in pharmaceutics and drug delivery. Taste (chloramphenicol palmitate), stability (erythromycin stearate), gut absorption (thiamine derivatives) and dermal delivery (various steroids) provide other examples.

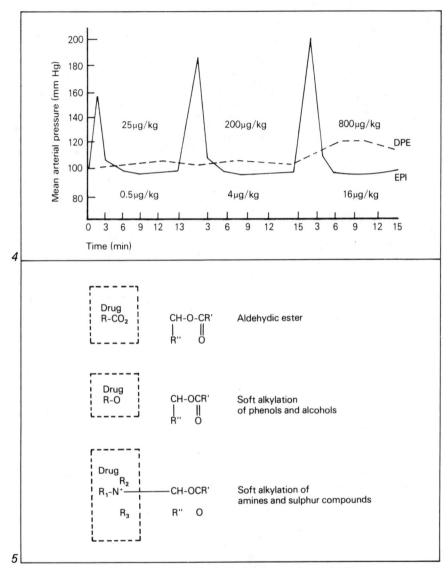

*Fig. 4.* Effect of intravenous adrenaline (EPI) and its dipivalyl ester (DPE) on blood pressure in dogs.

*Fig. 5.* Examples of prodrugs of hydroxyl-and carboxyl-containing drugs designed around aldehydes.

Bioavailability and the overall efficiency of drug delivery can, of course, be affected by factors other than those under thermodynamic control. Among the major mechanisms responsible for losses during transport, drug metabolism must be considered. The prodrug approach can play a useful part in minimising the effects of such metabolic reactions by protecting sensitive portions of a drug. A case in point is the oral bioavailability of mestranol as compared to the corresponding phenolic steroids

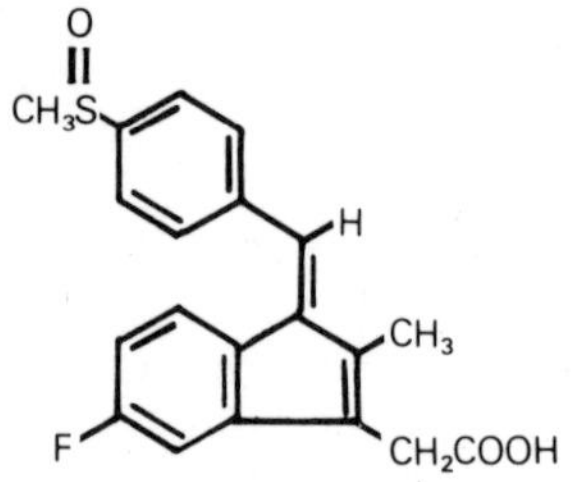

Sulindac

2-PAM                    Pro 2-PAM

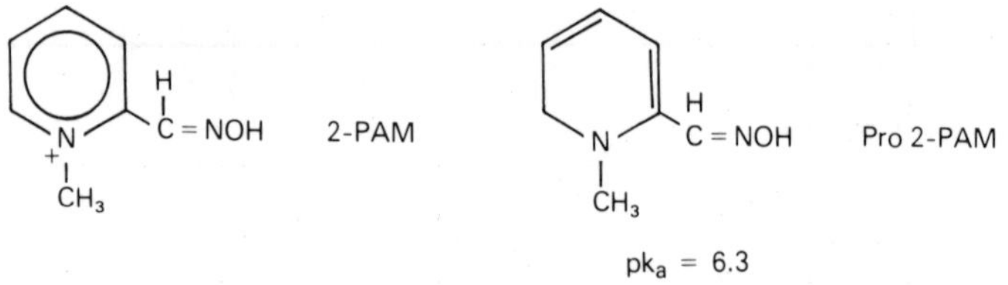

$pk_a = 6.3$

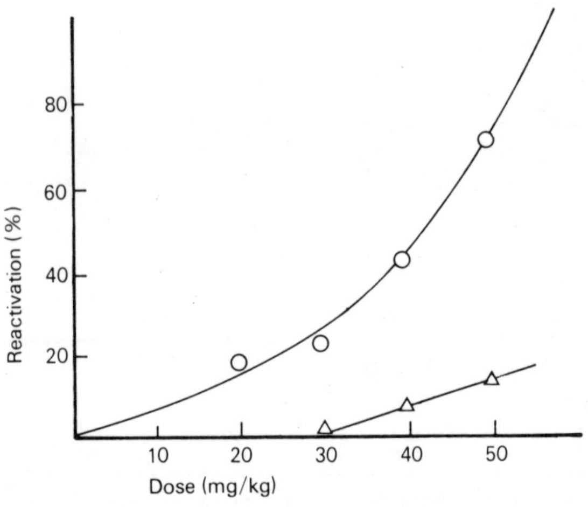

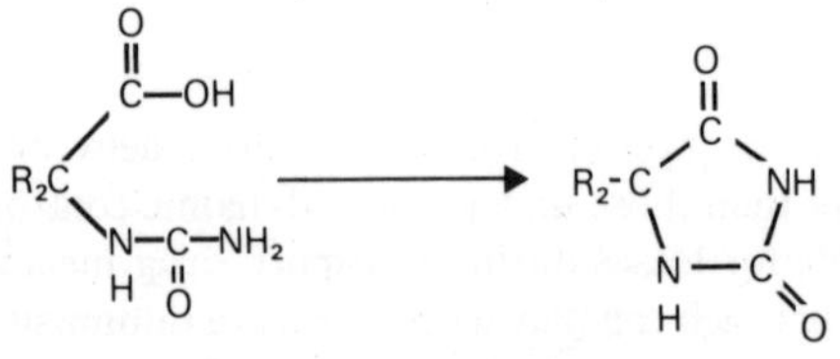

(Longcope and Williams, 1975; Williams et al., 1975). The latter are largely conjugated during passage through the gut mucosal layer whereas the methoxy compound becomes phenolic and active only after dealkylation in the liver.

## 2. Chemical Aspects

The administered prodrug should be converted rather quickly to its parent form shortly after it becomes a part of the biological system. A certain degree of lability, therefore, needs to be built into its structure. On the other hand if it has a significant tendency to revert spontaneously, there may be a real stability problem. In designing prodrugs, therefore, a great deal of ingenuity is required to obtain a structure which meets the requirements from the standpoint of pharmaceutics, yet is capable of rapidly synthesising the active drug *in situ*. In many instances we are able to do so, for example, by using the body's own biochemical mechanism to carry out the necessary chemistry. In others, significant changes in pH conditions have been used to trigger the reactions.

The simplest and probably the most common prodrugs are those based on hydrolytic activation. Thus active drug species containing acylable hydroxyl groups or carboxyl groups which can be esterified are frequently found as esters. The active forms are readily regenerated by enzymatic cleavage within the body. Dipivalyl adrenaline, for example, reverts to the catechol form by the action of hydrolytic enzymes present in the ocular fluid. Drugs such as clofibrate, chloramphenicol palmitate, triacetyloleandomycin, vitamin E acetate, vitamin A acetate, also fall into this group. Drugs containing hydroxyl groups can be rendered less soluble, as in chloramphenicol palmitate, by acylation with a hydrophobic acyloxy group, or made more water soluble by conversion to the salt form (e.g. chloramphenicol succinate, steroid phosphate and oestrogen monosulphate). The chemistry of hydrolysis of these species, whether enzyme-mediated or purely chemical, has been extensively studied.

Recently a number of prodrug candidates of hydroxyl- and carboxyl-containing drugs have been designed around aldehydes (fig. 5). All of these species revert to their parent drug form *in vivo* through esterase-mediated release of the derivatising group. Talampicillin, for example, basically follows this chemistry although the acyl and the aldehydic functions are on the same molecule.

Active drugs can often be regenerated through biochemically-mediated reductive or.oxidative processes. Amine oxides, sulphoxides and disulfides have all been suggested as prodrugs. These are reduced to their active tertiary amine, thioether and reduced sulphur forms. Sulindac, for example (fig. 6), apparently is active only when reduced to its thioether form (Kwan, personal communication). Fursultiamine, a disulphide, converts to thiamine on reduction.

---

*Fig. 6.* Sulindac structural formula.

*Fig. 7.* The pyridinium quaternary compound 2-PAM and its prodrug form pro-2-PAM.

*Fig. 8.* Reactivation of acetylcholinesterase in the brain tissue of mice poisoned with organophosphate by pro-2-PAM (upper curve) and 2-PAM (lower curve).

*Fig. 9.* Diphenylhydantoin generated by ring closure from a prodrug.

*Table II.* Total radioactivity in the brains of mice calculated as 2-PAM iodide and pro-2-PAM, 15 min after intravenous administration of 50mg/kg of the corresponding radiolabelled materials

| 2-PAM iodide | | | Pro-2-PAM | | |
|---|---|---|---|---|---|
| brain weight (wet) mg | total amount µg | concen- tration mg% | brain weight (wet) mg | total amount µg | concen- tration mg% |
| 469.7 | 1.23 | 0.262 | 407.9 | 45.15 | 11.070 |
| 453.7 | 0.97 | 0.214 | 472.7 | 11.92 | 2.522 |
| 444.0 | 1.12 | 0.252 | 479.5 | 46.64 | 9.727 |
| 439.6 | 1.44 | 0.328 | 427.1 | 6.74 | 1.578 |
| 442.8 | 1.64 | 0.370 | 451.1 | 24.60 | 5.452 |
| 449.8 | 2.11 | 0.469 | 428.6 | 12.08 | 2.818 |
| 437.6 | 3.90 | 0.891 | 465.0 | 9.32 | 2.011 |
| | Mean: | 0.398mg% | | | 5.025mg% |
| | SE: ± | 0.098mg% | | | ± 1.60mg% |

Prodrugs based on oxidative mechanisms provide exceptionally interesting delivery advantages. Active oestrogens, for example, when taken orally are essentially totally conjugated during absorption. If the phenolic function is temporarily protected by methylation as in mestranol the active species is regenerated only by oxidative demethylation in the liver and thus is protected during initial passage through the intestinal wall. Mestranol is therefore orally active whereas phenolic oestrogens are not. Another example involves a pyridinium quaternary compound (fig. 7). The drug was developed as an antidote for anticholinesterase poisoning, being relatively effective in reactivating choline esterases which have been inhibited with organophosphates. Being a quaternary cation, however, it does not readily pass across the lipoidal blood-brain barrier. To overcome this deficiency the dihydro compound has been proposed (Bodor et al., 1975, 1976). In mice pro-2-PAM was much more effective in delivering 2-PAM to the brain than the drug itself. A 10-fold greater concentration of the active form was achieved in the brain with the reduced agent (table II) and this was reflected in reactivation of the cholinesterase (fig. 8).

Recently a number of prodrugs have been proposed based on generation of active drug by ring closure reactions under biological conditions. We studied the feasibility of generating diphenylhydantoin *in vivo* by such a reaction (Davis et al., 1974). Although the reaction takes place under acidic conditions the rate is too slow for the free acid to serve as a prodrug (fig. 9). Its esters, however, cyclise quite rapidly with a half-life of about 10 minutes at pH 7.4 *in vitro* or *in vivo*. Open forms of spironolactone and a cephalosporin have recently been proposed as soluble prodrugs.

## 3. Conclusions

It is possible to cloak many drugs with a mantle of new physical chemical and thermodynamic properties which substantially improves delivery.

The pharmaceutics and the chemistry of the prodrug approach offer intriguing challenges to clever pharmaceutical scientists trying to solve drug delivery problems. Yet mere solution of these problems does not guarantee that the system will perform according to expectations under clinical conditions. We have not considered the differences in the distribution of the prodrug and the active drug. What new compartments are entered? What changes in metabolism take place? The answers to these questions are less important when the half-life of the prodrug is short but this cannot always be achieved.

All successful prodrugs are, of course, drugs; many drugs are prodrugs. In the future the concepts and approaches discussed above will probably be increasingly applied during drug development. The prodrug approach will not be considered as an after-the-fact, separate programme but will be more and more integrated into the initial stages of drug design. In this sense the identity of the approach may eventually be lost.

## References

Bodor, N; Shek, E. and Higuchi, T.: Delivery of a quaternary pyridinium salt across the blood barrier by its dihydropyridine derivative. Science 190: 155-156 (1975).

Bodor, N.; Shek, E. and Higuchi, T.: Improved delivery through biological membranes. 1. Synthesis and properties of 1-methyl-1, 6-dihydropyridine-2-carbaldoxime, a prodrug of N-methylpyridinium-2-carbaldoxime chloride. Journal of Medicinal Chemistry 19: 102-107 (1976).

Davis, S.S.; Higuchi, T. and Rytting, J.H.: Determination of thermodynamics of functional groups in solutions of drug molecules. Advances in Pharmaceutical Sciences 4: 73-261 (1974).

Longcope, C. and Williams, K.I.H.: The metabolism of synthetic estrogens in non-users and users of oral contraceptives. Steroids 25: 121-129 (1975).

McClure, D.A.: The effects of a pro-drug of epinephrine (dipivalyl epinephrine) in glaucoma — general pharmacology, toxicology, and clinical experience; in Higuchi and Stella (Eds) Pro-drugs as a Novel Drug Delivery System, p.224-235 (American Cancer Society, Washington, D.C., 1975).

Repta, A.J.: Case histories of the development of pro-drugs for use in the formulation of cytotoxic agents in parenteral solutions: in Higuchi and Stella (Eds) Pro-drugs as a Novel Drug Delivery Systems, p.196-223 (American Cancer Society, Washington, D.C., 1975).

Repta, A.J.; Rawson, B.J.; Shaffer, R.D.; Sloan, K.B.; Bodor, N. and Higuchi, T.: Rational development of a soluble prodrug of a cytotoxic nucleoside: preparation and properties of arabinosyladenine 5'-formate. Journal of Pharmaceutical Sciences 64: 392-396 (1975).

Stella, V.: Pro-drugs: an overview and definition; in Higuchi and Stella (Eds) Pro-drugs as a Novel drug Delivery System, p.1-115 (American Cancer Society, Washington, D.C., 1975).

Williams, J.G.; Longcope, C. and Williams, K.I.H.: Metabolism of 4-$^3$H- and 4-$^{14}$HC-17$\alpha$-ethynylestradiol 3-methyl ether (mestranol) by women. Steroids 25: 343-354 (1975).

## Discussion

*B.W. Barry* (Bradford): The thermodynamic activities of pure compounds in hydrocarbon solvents which you showed are very important because they can be used to predict the maximum permeation rate of a drug through any biological membrane. Were these values experimentally determined and if so, how?

*T. Higuchi*: The escaping tendencies of these agents were related directly to their solubility in the particular hydrocarbon. The convention used was to set the activity coefficient equal to zero and the concentration of the solvent approached zero. It turns out that for most drugs of low solubility, the activity would be equal to their solubility so it is a relatively easy thing to determine.

# 18

# Transdermal Therapeutic Systems

*J.E. Shaw and S.K. Chandrasekaran*

Alza Corporation, Palo Alto, California

Transdermal delivery for systemic therapy is now widely recognised as feasible, on the basis of performance of ointment preparations of nitroglycerin, anti-inflammatory agents, and hormones. Techniques are now available to make this route of drug administration reproducible and reliable. Although skin is one of the most impermeable body tissues, functioning as an effective barrier against water loss and the invasion of micro-organisms and viruses, some drugs can be delivered through intact skin to elicit a systemic therapeutic effect.

During the topical application of ointments or creams the area and thickness of applied formulation can vary from treatment to treatment; as a result, the amount of drug applied and the duration of the therapeutic response may vary. Furthermore, the inherent permeability of skin to a particular drug formulation varies at different sites of each individual (Feldmann and Maibach, 1967) and at the same site of different individuals. The permeability of normal skin also varies between sexes and among different age and ethnic groups (Montagna et al., 1972; Zbinden, 1976). Moreover, changes in environmental conditions and physiological variations in skin blood flow and sweat gland function can change skin permeability. All of these factors contribute to variable, unpredictable rates of systemic absorption from ointments or creams.

Scheuplein (1965, 1967a, b, 1973) has established that molecular permeability of skin is a passive rather than a biologically active property. Using excised human skin, it was demonstrated that stratum corneum is the principal barrier to drug permeation. These results prompted Scheuplein and Blank (1971) to model the skin as a 3 layer laminate of stratum corneum, epidermis, and dermis, with permeation occurring by Fickian diffusion of the penetrating species through the 3 layers in series array.

We have developed a mathematical model of stratum corneum as a 2-phase protein-lipid heterogeneous membrane that correlates the permeability of the membrane with a specific penetrant, and its water solubility and lipid-protein partition coefficient (Michaels et al., 1975). The interstitial lipid phase of the stratum corneum appears to account for the exceedingly low diffusivity of solutes and serves as the principal permeation barrier. Regional differences in skin permeability may be related to regional differences in specific lipid content of the epidermis (Elias et al., in press).

We are interested in understanding the extent and nature of variation in skin permeability so that we can provide continuous systemic input of drugs at predetermined, controlled rates. To this purpose, we have developed a class of dosage forms called transdermal therapeutic systems (TTS), which control delivery of drug to the surface of intact skin, from whence it permeates the skin and enters the systemic circulation (Chandrasekaran and Shaw, 1977). To ensure that the system, and not the skin, controls the administration of drug to the systemic circulation, the system must deliver less drug per unit area than the skin is capable of absorbing; therefore, to facilitate design of a transdermal system, one must define the extent of variability in skin permeation to the drug in question.

## 1. Methods and Materials

### 1.1 *In Vitro* Study of Skin Permeability in Different Regions

Skin was excised from different regions of cadavers; samples were preserved in heat-sealed plastic bags and stored at 4°C prior to use. The epidermis was separated from the remaining layers of tissue by stirring the skin for 45 to 60 seconds in water at 60°C. The stratum corneum was subsequently isolated by digesting the epidermis with 0.10% trypsin in 0.005M Tris-HCl pH 7.9 for 45 minutes, followed by rinsing with water. The isolated stratum corneum, which floated on the water, was lifted on a stiff plastic film, the excess water blotted off, and the thickness measured with a Dial indicator (Michaels et al., 1975).

Permeation measurements were conducted in glass permeation cells (fig. 1) kept at a constant temperature, with concentrated radiolabelled drug in contact with the stratum corneum surface, and drug-free solution in contact with the underlying surface of the skin. Periodic sampling of the downstream solution and assay of drug content by liquid scintillation counting or liquid chromatography permitted determination of the amount and rate of drug permeation.

Drug content of the tissue at the end of the permeation experiment was determined by digestion in a proteolytic solvent and subsequent scintillation counting.

### 1.2 *In Vivo* Measurement of Skin Temperature, Drug Release Rate, and Urinary Excretion

Transdermal therapeutic systems incorporate a rate-controlling membrane between the drug reservoir and the skin surface (fig. 2). The membrane limits the amount of drug delivered per unit area of skin surface, to an amount that *in vitro* experiments have indicated to be less than the least permeable skin can absorb at 30°C. The required therapeutic rate of drug input is then attained by fabricating a system of appropriate area. Thus, the system, and not the skin, dominates in controlling the rate of drug input to the skin surface and hence to the systemic circulation.

The Transdermal Therapeutic System (scopolamine) [TTS (scopolamine)] (fig. 3) is a multilayer laminate, 2.5cm² in area and approximately 200μ thick. The system comprises a drug reservoir containing scopolamine in a polymeric gel, sandwiched between an impermeable backing membrane and a rate-controlling, microporous membrane. The scopolamine-containing adhesive layer serves both as an adhesive to secure the system to the skin and as a reservoir for a priming dose of drug. The priming dose was chosen on the basis of the pharmacokinetic properties of scopolamine administered transdermally. The protective removable film is removed just prior to

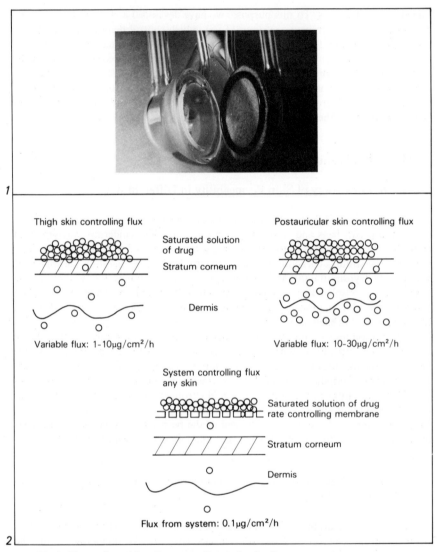

Fig. 1. Glass cell used for skin permeation studies *in vitro*.

Fig. 2. Schematic representation of drug flux through the skin, when applied in an ointment or delivered from a transdermal therapeutic system.

application of the system to the skin surface. The membrane permits release of scopolamine from the system at the steady rate of 4µg/cm²/h, a rate 5-fold less than the average permeation of scopolamine through postauricular skin *in vitro* at 30°C.

Two groups of 7 and one group of 6 subjects wore a TTS (scopolamine), programmed to deliver 0.5mg scopolamine *in vivo* over 3 days, on the skin overlying the mastoid process. Urine was collected at 12-hour intervals during use and after removal, and assayed for unchanged scopolamine (Bayne et al., 1975). For comparison, urine was similarly collected and analysed while scopolamine was administered intravenously at a precise rate in the range of 4 to 6µg/h by means of an AR/MED® infusor[1] to 6 subjects.

To determine the effect of occlusion on skin temperature, subjects were acclimatised in first a cold (6°C) and then a hot (28°C) environment. Skin temperatures in different parts of the body were measured using a small thermistor after allowing time for equilibration. To determine the scopolamine content of stratum corneum after removal of the transdermal system, the skin was subjected to 25 consecutive strippings with Scotch tape and the drug content of each stripping analysed separately.

## 2. Results and Discussion

### 2.1 Regional Differences in Skin Permeation

Regional variation in skin permeability *in vivo* in animals and man is well documented (Feldmann and Maibach, 1967; Maibach et al., 1971; Bartek et al., 1972). For example, monitoring radioactivity in the urine after topical application of $^{14}$C-hydrocortisone has established that the respective permeabilities of skin on the scrotum and jaw angle are 12- and 13-fold greater than the permeability of skin on the forearm which in turn is 7 times more permeable than skin on the plantar surface of the foot arch (Feldmann and Maibach, 1967). Studies using topically applied organic phosphates have confirmed that skin on the scrotum is 12 times more permeable than that on the forearm (Maibach et al., 1971).

Skin from the postauricular area is the most permeable to scopolamine, while skin from the thigh offers the most resistance to diffusion (fig. 4) with an approximately 10-fold variation between these 2 sites.

Scopolamine permeation through skin from the same region of different cadavers varies by as much as 5- to 10-fold. These marked individual differences cannot be correlated simply with age, sex, or ethnic group. When comparing skin from different regions of the same donor, or from the same region of different donors, we found differences not only in drug permeation, but also in drug content upon completion of the experiment. Skins that permitted the greatest permeation of drug tended to have the least drug content.

### 2.2 Effect of Temperature on Skin Permeability *In Vitro*

With skin from the postauricular or thigh area the transdermal flux of drug *in vitro,* increased 2- to 3-fold when the temperature was increased (from 30°C to 36°C) [fig. 5]. In contrast, the skin content of scopolamine did not increase when the temperature was raised, indicating that an increase in temperature may increase the rate of drug diffusion through the tissue without affecting the drug content of the skin.

### 2.3 Urinary Excretion of Scopolamine

Three groups of subjects wore a TTS (scopolamine) programmed to deliver 0.5mg drug *in vivo* over 3 days. Analyses of the urine for free scopolamine verified

---

[1] ALZA Corporation, Palo Alto, CA.

constant delivery from the TTS into the systemic circulation (fig. 6). In each group of subjects, the rate of excretion of unchanged drug attained a maximum value within 12 to 24 hours, decreased slightly, and then remained constant during the remainder of the time the systems were worn. For up to 12 hours following removal of the systems, excretion remained at this level, evidently as a result of continued drug input from the skin. During the steady-state phase of drug administration (24-72 hours),

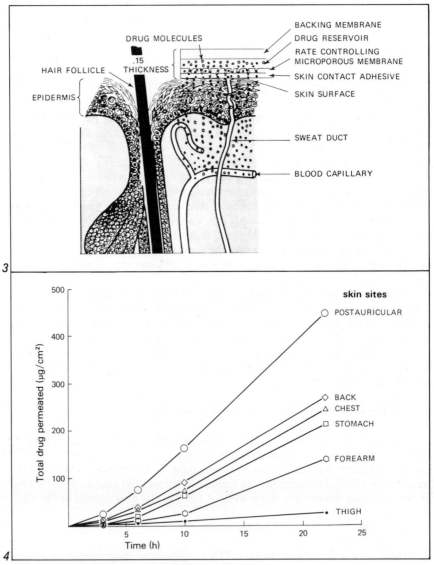

*Fig. 3.* Representation of the transdermal therapeutic system in place on the skin (after Ariens, 1979 with permission of the publisher).

*Fig. 4.* Permeation of scopolamine *in vitro* at 30°C through human skin from various body areas (donor solution: scopolamine free base in mineral oil, 4.7mg/g).

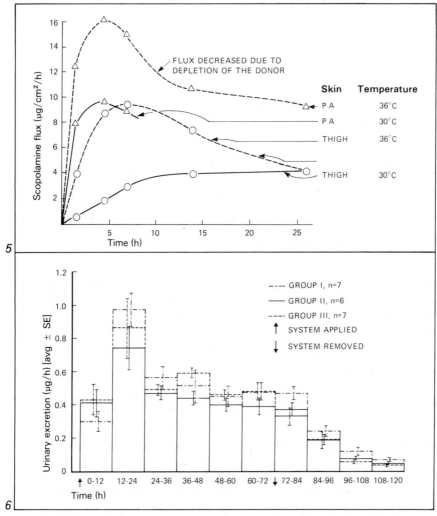

*Fig. 5.* Effect of temperature on the *in vitro* permeation of scopolamine through human postauricular (PA) and thigh skin at 30°C and 36°C (donor: gelled scopolamine).

*Fig. 6.* Urinary excretion of scopolamine during and after the wearing of a TTS (scopolamine).

the coefficients of variation within and between subjects were 20% and 20% for Group II and 16% and 18% for Group III. During intravenous infusion of scopolamine at steady-state, 6.03 to 11.27% of the administered drug was excreted unmetabolised; the coefficients of variation between and within subjects were 26.7 and 23.2%, respectively. The coefficients of variation associated with transdermal and intravenous drug administration were thus similar. Two conclusions can be drawn:

1) The system functions consistently in different individuals; and

2) Administration of scopolamine from a TTS placed in the postauricular area is the functional equivalent of infusing the drug intravenously.

*Table I.* Surface temperature (°C) of human skin in various regions (under occlusion)

|        | Thigh | Forearm | Back  | Chest | Post-auricular |
|--------|-------|---------|-------|-------|----------------|
| Mean   | 32.27 | 32.90   | 33.38 | 34.30 | 34.92          |
| SD     | 1.26  | 1.20    | 1.08  | 0.90  | 1.26           |
| $t^1$  | 8.89  | 7.84    | 5.28  | 2.72  |                |
| p <    | 0.001 | 0.001   | 0.001 | 0.01  |                |

1    Comparisons with postauricular temperature (Student's paired *t* test, n = 20 in all groups).

## 2.4 Effect of Temperature on Skin Permeability and Release of Drug from the Transdermal System *In Vivo*

Under occlusion, the surface temperature of the skin of 20 subjects ranged from 30°C to 37°C in different regions of the body; the order of average temperatures was thigh < forearm < back < chest < postauricular area (table I). The temperature of postauricular skin was, on average, 2.5°C higher than that of thigh skin. This finding may correlate with the higher permeability of the postauricular area observed *in vivo*, but cannot account for the relative increase *in vitro* when all skins were kept at 30°C (fig. 4). The temperature of occluded postauricular and forearm skin varied by no more than 5°C when subjects were acclimatised.

Changes in skin temperature might be expected to modify the rate of drug released from the system. Since the activation energy is 10Kcal/mol, a 5% change in the drug release from the system is expected for every 1°C rise in temperature within the physiological range. Therefore, drug release from the TTS (scopolamine) would not vary by more than 20 to 25% for every 5°C change in temperature, in contrast to the permeability of the skin, which can vary as much as 300% during similar temperature changes (fig. 5). When the transdermal system and skin are brought together, the transdermal system dominates, and so the variability in drug permeability due to a 5°C temperature change is limited to 20 to 25%.

If skin is the controlling factor, a combination of regional differences in skin temperature and inter- and intra-individual differences in skin permeability, are responsible for the marked variations in systemic absorption of a drug following topical administration. For drugs with a narrow therapeutic index — for which there must only be a small variation in systemic absorption, not only within but also between individuals — control of drug input must not reside within the skin, but within the dosage form.

## 3. Conclusion

By utilising an appropriate dosage form design, and placing the transdermal system on the optimal area of the skin for solute permeation, we have minimised inter-individual differences in skin permeability to the drug and minimised the effects of environmental temperature changes.

# References

Ariens, E. (Ed): Drug design, vol. 8, p.149 (Academic Press, New York, 1979).

Bartek, M.J.; LaBudde, J.A. and Maibach, H.I.: Skin permeability *in vivo*: comparison in rat, rabbit, pig and man. Journal of Investigative Dermatology 58: 115-123 (1972).

Bayne, W.F.; Tao, F.T. and Crisologo, N.: Submicrogram assay for scopolamine in plasma and urine. Journal of Pharmaceutical Sciences 64: 288-291 (1975).

Changdrasekaran, S.K. and Shaw, J.E.: Design of transdermal therapeutic systems; in Pearce and Schaefgen (Eds) Contemporary Topics in Polymer Science, vol. 2, p.291-308 (Plenum, New York 1977).

Elias, P.M.; Cooper, E.; Korc, A. and Brown, B.E.: Importance of stratum corneum structural parameters vs lipid composition for percutaneous absorption. Clinical Research (in press).

Feldmann, R.J. and Maibach, H.I.: Regional variation in percutaneous penetration of $^{14}$C cortisol in man. Journal of Investigative Dermatology 48: 181-183 (1967).

Maibach, H.I.; Feldmann R.J.; Milby, T.H. and Serat, W.F.: Regional variation in percutaneous penetration in man. Pesticides. Archives of Environmental Health 23: 208-211 (1971).

Michaels, A.S.; Chandrasekaran, S.K. and Shaw, J.E.: Drug permeation through human skin: theory and *in vitro* experimental measurement. American Institute of Chemical Engineers Journal 21: 985-996 (1975).

Montagna, W.; Van Scott, E.J. and Stoughton, R.B. (Eds): Pharmacology and the Skin. 20th Symposium on the Biology of the Skin. Advances in Biology of the Skin Series, vol. 12, p.540-546 (Appleton-Century-Croft, New York 1972).

Scheuplein, R.J.: Mechanism of percutaneous absorption. I. Routes of penetration and the influence of solubility. Journal of Investigative Dermatology 45: 334-346 (1965).

Scheuplein, R.J.: Mechanism of percutaneous absorption. II. Transient diffusion and the relative importance of various routes of skin penetration. Journal of Investigative Dermatology 48: 79-88 (1967a).

Scheuplein, R.J.: Molecular Structure and Diffusional Processes across Intact Epidermis. Edgewood Laboratory, Contract Report 18 (1967b).

Scheuplein, R.J.: Mechanism of percutaneous absorption. IV. Penetration of non-electrolytes (alcohols) from aqueous solutions and from pure liquids. Journal of Investigative Dermatology 60: 286-296 (1973).

Scheuplein, R.J. and Blank, I.H.: Permeability of the skin. Physiological Reviews 51: 702-747 (1971).

Zbinden, G. (Ed): Percutaneous drug permeation; in Progress in Toxicology, vol. 2, p.50-59 (Springer-Verlag, New York 1976).

# Discussion

*B.W. Barry* (Bradford): Have you tried to incorporate penetration enhancers such as dimethylsulphoxide and dimethylformamide into the transdermal therapeutic system?

*J.E. Shaw*: Yes. There are a number of ways that you can enhance penetration of drug through skin. For example, by the control of pH and the use of agents such as you described. We developed a transdermal system which delivered concomitantly a permeation enhancer and the drug. You have to choose a rate-controlling membrane that will deliver both the drug and the permeation enhancer at the same time in a vehicle which is compatible with both. There is no universal permeation enhancer. Dimethylsulphoxide is not very useful because it has to be delivered continuously in high concentrations.

# 19

# Advances in Controlled Gastrointestinal Absorption

*Gilbert S. Banker and Vinay E. Sharma*

Industrial and Physical Pharmacy Department, Purdue University, Indiana

The absorption rate of orally administered drugs is determined by one of two factors, depending on which is rate-limited (slower): the inherent absorption ability of the gastrointestinal tract of that subject for that drug, or the dissolution release rate of the drug from the dosage form.

The ideal objectives of an optimised oral drug delivery system are given in table I. Few drug products that are marketed today achieve all these objectives. For drugs that are well absorbed along the small intestine, are chemically stable, have a wide therapeutic index and have a near ideal duration of action following a single dose, the practical significance of not meeting all these objectives may not be great. However, for other drugs, optimisation of delivery may be of considerable importance depending on the relevance of the various objectives in table I.

The ideal design attributes and principles of oral controlled drug release systems are listed in table II. If a product is not highly sensitive to environmental factors, variation in these factors will have less influence on its performance. Likewise a system with a release mechanism not keyed to a single physiological variable such as pH, gastric emptying, or enzyme activity, will be more reliable and predictable. Obviously too, a product the design and mechanism of release control of which is based on physicochemical principles, rather than pharmaceutical art, will be more reliable.

Some physiological and other factors affecting drug absorption are given in table III (Bates and Gibaldi, 1970; Davenport, 1971; Wagner, 1971). Gastric motility and emptying is the primary uncontrolled variable influencing drug absorption and the gastric emptying half-life may vary from a few minutes to 20 hours (Hunt and Mac-Donald, 1954; Davenport, 1971). Gastric emptying is important because the duodenum and the proximal jejunum are the major areas of absorption for most orally administered drugs.

Factors influencing gastric emptying and the disintegration/de-aggregation/dissolution of solid oral dosage forms are numerous and not necessarily similar in their effect on drug absorption. Factors which slow gastric emptying include hot meals, increased viscosity or osmotic pressure, fats or fatty acids, increased acidity, lying on the left side, physical exertion and aggression or excitement as well as disease (Wagner, 1961; Hunt and Knox, 1963; Gibaldi, 1970; Lagerlof, 1973; Costhill and Saltin, 1974; Hancock et al., 1974).

*Table I.* Objectives of an optimised oral drug delivery system

| | |
|---|---|
| 1. | Prolong and control duration of drug action |
| 2. | Control of rate and site of release in the gastrointestinal tract |
| 3. | Complete and reliable absorption |
| 4. | Minimal irritant or unwanted local effects |
| 5. | Minimal effects of physiological variables on drug absorption |
| 6. | Maximal chemical and physical stability |
| 7. | Minimal systemic side effects through precise control of tissue concentrations |

*Table II.* Ideal design attributes and principles of oral controlled drug delivery systems

| | |
|---|---|
| 1. | Lack of sensitivity to physiological variables |
| 2. | Drug release determined by physicochemical principles |
| 3. | Drug release not keyed to a single physiological variable |
| 4. | A high order of drug dispersion (molecular scale optimum) |
| 5. | A flexible system capable of incorporating a wide variety of drugs, doses, and release rates |
| 6. | Physical and chemical stability |

*Table III.* Factors affecting gastrointestinal drug absorption

| | |
|---|---|
| 1. | Gastric motility and emptying |
| 2. | pH of the gut contents |
| 3. | Enzyme activity |
| 4. | Food |
| 5. | Fluid volume, composition and viscosity |
| 6. | Posture and activity |
| 7. | Mental state |
| 8. | Individual variability |
| 9. | Disease |

Several methods of circumventing variable gastric emptying have been suggested (table IV). Most have involved retention of the drug in the stomach without simultaneous control of drug release. For example, administration in viscous media or the generation of high viscosity in the gastric contents has been used to reduce the gastric emptying rates of drugs (Levy and Rao, 1972; Ashley and Levy, 1973). This method has limited usefulness with systemically-acting drugs but it is the basis of several antacid products marketed with claims for prolonged activity. Creation of a bulky mass of hydrated polymer or a low density floating mass has also been attempted to prolong the residence time of antacids in the stomach.

Drugs such as anticholinergics and metoclopramide influence gastric emptying and can therefore alter the rate of absorption of other drugs taken at the same time (table IV). In a few cases bioavailability may be changed (Levy et al., 1972). Neither the co-administration of such drugs nor high fat meals (table IV), are practical ways

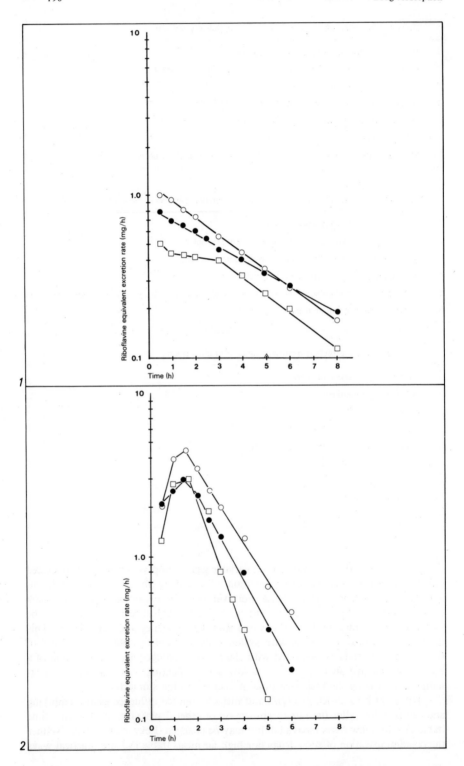

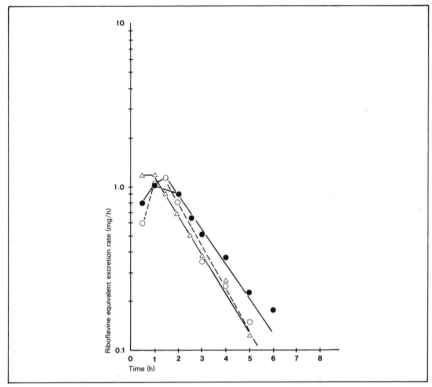

*Fig. 3.* Riboflavine equivalent urinary excretion rates for 3 fasting subjects after oral administration of uncoated tablets each containing 28mg of riboflavine phosphate sodium (uncoated tablet, formulation 2, table V).

of reducing the rate of gastric emptying for the purpose of enhancing drug absorption efficiency or reliability.

Several investigators have demonstrated that spheres larger than 15 to 20mm diameter do not freely pass the pylorus (Nielsen and Christiansen, 1932; Edwards, 1961). Hard spheres empty more slowly than compliant spheres of the same diameter (Schlegel et al., 1966). Radio-opaque uncoated tablets, disintegrating and forming a 2 to 3cm mass are retained in the human stomach until the mass disperses into smaller particles (Levy, 1963).

Cross-linked polymeric tablet coatings may have the ability to swell greatly in gastric contents, forming a fluid-filled balloon-like system. The expanded hydrated film provides a controlled release membrane which can give a constant drug release rate while the expanded system remains in the stomach (Banker, 1973, 1974). The extent of swelling of the hydrated film is related to the degree of cross-linking of the

*Fig. 1.* Riboflavine equivalent urinary excretion rates for 3 fasting subjects after oral administration of 28mg of riboflavine phosphate sodium in aqueous solution.

*Fig. 2.* Riboflavine equivalent urinary excretion rates for 3 subjects after oral administration of 28mg of riboflavine phosphate sodium in aqueous solution (non-fasting).

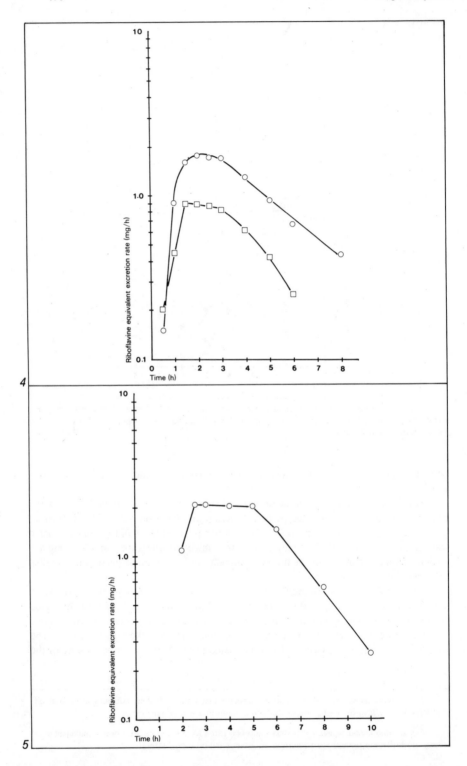

polymeric film, the plasticisation of the film, and the osmotic pressure produced by the tablet contents as they dissolve in the gastric fluid drawn into the coated dosage form as the film hydrates. After the soluble components within the tablet have substantially diffused through the hydrated film membrane, the hydrostatic pressure drops, the inflated membrane collapses and empties from the stomach. Plasticisers

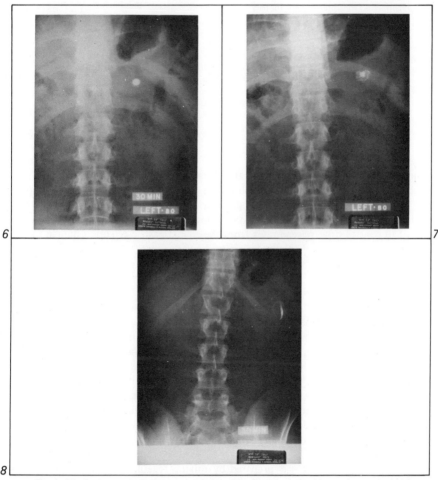

*Fig. 4.* Riboflavine equivalent urinary excretion rate for 2 fasted subjects after oral administration of 7/16″ coated (8:0.56:4) tablets containing 28mg of riboflavine phosphate sodium.

*Fig. 5.* Riboflavine equivalent urinary excretion rate for a non-fasted subject after oral administration of a 7/16″ coated (8:0.56:4) tablets containing 28mg of riboflavine phosphate sodium.

*Fig. 6.* X-ray taken 30 minutes after administration of the riboflavine coated tablet in the subject reported in figure 5. The dosage form has not yet expanded appreciably.

*Fig. 7.* X-ray taken 90 minutes after administration (same subject as fig. 6). The dosage form has expanded but is not fully hydrated.

*Fig. 8.* X-ray taken 30 minutes after administration of a coated soluble tablet illustrating rapid swelling and retention in the stomach.

*Table IV.* Methods of circumventing variable gastric emptying

---

A.   Mechanical approaches without controlled release
     1.  High viscosity[1]
     2.  Creation of a bulky or intact mass
     3.  Flotation

B.   Other drugs[2]
     Pharmacological alteration of motility

C.   Food[3]

D.   Mechanical approaches with controlled release
     1.  A rapidly expanding permeable membrane (the controlled gastric retention ball)
     2.  Bioadhesive particulate drug loaded systems

---

1   Levy and Rao, 1972; Ashley and Levy, 1973.
2   Gothoni et al., 1972; Levy et al., 1972; Nimmo, 1973; Nimmo et al., 1973; Pearson, 1973.
3   Kraml et al., 1962; Levy and Jusko, 1966.

---

which are soluble in gastric fluid may also be incorporated in the film membrane and leach out of the film to produce controlled film rupture and subsequent gastric emptying. Film thickness and cross-linking, drug solubility in gastric fluid or in the medium within the membrane sac, and osmotic pressure within the sac may be altered to control drug release rates from the coated gastric retention dosage form.

# 1. Methods

The effect of controlled gastric retention on the absorption of several classes of drug with incomplete bioavailability has been studied. Riboflavine was selected as a model drug reportedly absorbed in the duodenum with saturable absorption characteristics (Levy and Jusko, 1966). It has enhanced bioavailability when given with food (Levy and Jusko, 1966) or drugs which retard gastric emptying (Levy et al., 1972). As a model drug it is safe for human testing and its bioavailability can be readily and accurately quantified by non-invasive means (urinary elimination).

The tablets to be coated were prepared by mixing drug and excipient and forming a granulation by standard wet granulation techniques if direct compression was not feasible. The tablets were compressed on a rotary tablet machine or a motorised Carver press.

The coating solution was prepared by mixing together 3 previously prepared stock solutions of the anhydride copolymer, the cross-linking agent and the plasticiser. An anhydride copolymer such as styrene maleic anhydride, ethylene maleic anhydride or an alkyl vinyl ether/maleic anhydride may be used. A high molecular weight poly (methyl vinyl ether/maleic anhydride)[1] may be the agent of choice based on existing Food and Drug Applications. An 8 to 10% solution of the polymer was prepared in an anhydrous solvent such as a 65:35 mixture of anhydrous ethyl acetate and acetone. A separate 10% stock solution of the cross-linking agent, polyoxyethylene sorbitan monolaurate[2] and of the plasticiser, glyceryl triacetate

---

1   Gantrez AN-169, GAF Corporation, New York, N.Y.
2   Tween 20, Atlas Chemical Industries, Inc., Wilmington, Del.

Table V. Composition of the riboflavine phosphate sodium tablet formulations

| Formulation | Tablet size | Formulation components (mg) | |
|---|---|---|---|
| 1 | 9/16″ | TRIS (ball milled) | 400.0 |
| | | Sodium bicarbonate | 150.0 |
| | | Riboflavine phosphate sodium | 28.0 |
| | | Barium sulphate | 272.0 |
| 2 | 7/16″ | TRIS (ball milled) | 150.0 |
| | | Sodium bicarbonate | 150.0 |
| | | Riboflavine phosphate sodium | 28.0 |
| | | Barium sulphate | 272.0 |
| 3 | 9/16″ | TRIS (ball-milled) | 450.0 |
| | | Sodium bicarbonate | 450.0 |
| | | Riboflavine phosphate sodium | 28.0 |
| | | Barium sulphate | 272.0 |

(Triacetin)[3] as a 40 or 50% solution, was made in the same solvent mixture. The solutions were combined in the proper ratio of polymer to cross-linker to plasticiser immediately prior to the coating process. The coating process is best conducted in a conventional air suspension tower or by an immersion process (Banker, 1975). The coated dosage forms were then exposed to elevated humidity and temperature, (such as 50% relative humidity at 40°C for 12 hours), or alternatively were packaged in a sealed container with a moistened pledget containing sufficient water to catalyse the transesterification cross-linking reaction between the cross-linking agent and the polymer.

Riboflavine was used as the model drug but the solubility of riboflavine-5'-phosphate sodium in gastric fluid was too low for it to permeate the hydrated film membrane at an adequate rate. To increase the pH within the membrane sac and thereby increase the riboflavine salt solubility, tris (hydroxymethyl) amino methane[4] (TRIS) was used.

The composition of some of the riboflavine tablet formulations is given in table V. The barium sulphate was included to facilitate x-ray visualisation. A flow-through cell was used to determine the release characteristics of the dosage forms in Simulated Gastric Fluid TS at 37°C. The samples were analysed fluorometrically for riboflavine content, after making suitable dilutions.

Subjects who had been asked to avoid vitamins, drugs and certain foods (yeast, liver) known to contain appreciable amounts of riboflavine for at least 48 hours were given the coated dosage forms in the morning with 100ml of water. Thereafter, the subjects drank 100ml of water every hour for 2 hours but no food or beverages were permitted for 3 hours. Studies were carried out in fasted and non-fasted subjects and comparisons were also made using uncoated tablets and riboflavine solution. Urine samples were collected at intervals up to 24 hours.

The urine samples were analysed by the procedure of Levy and Jusko (1966) but the samples were read at a $\gamma_{max}$ excitation of 465nm and $\gamma_{max}$ emission of 528nm.

---

3   Mallinckrodt Chemical Co., St. Louis, Mo.
4   Schwarz/Mann, New York, N.Y.

Sodium hydrosulphite was excluded and fluorescence of the blank urine was deducted from the sample fluorescence value.

The location of the coated tablet dosage form in the gastrointestinal tract was followed by x-ray examination at 30 and 90 minutes and 3 hours.


## 2. Results

The tablet formulations of table V, when coated with polymer: cross-linker: plasticiser weight ratios of 8:0.15:4 to 8:.55:4, using the preferred materials and conditions named in the methods section, swelled in simulated gastric fluid within 30 to 60 minutes, and thereafter released the drug linearly over at least 3 hours.

Figures 1 and 2 present the data for subjects given 28mg of riboflavine phosphate sodium in aqueous solution. In the fasted subjects, (fig. 1), the peak urinary excretion rates were already reached at the first sampling point (30 min), and the maximum excretion rates were 1mg per hour or less. In the same subjects given the same solution, but not fasted, the peak elimination rates occurred later (between 1 and 2h) and the maximum excretion rates were 3 to 5mg per hour (fig. 2). Following administration of the uncoated tablet to the same fasted subjects the maximum elimination rate was about 1mg per hour, the same as observed for the solution, but the peak was shifted to 1 hour, probably reflecting the gradual disintegration of the tablet and delayed dissolution of the drug (fig. 3).

In 2 of the fasting subjects administered the specially coated tablet, complete film swelling was apparently delayed for 1 hour as judged by the lag time to achieve the peak excretion rate (fig. 4). The high plateau of maximum excretion for 3 to 4 hours after administration suggested gastric retention with a constant rate of drug release. Whether the coated tablets emptied from the stomach at this time or the TRIS buffer could no longer maintain the pH within the sac to solubilise the drug cannot be determined from this data. However, the subjects in figure 4 were also x-rayed. The hydrated sacs were not well formed at 30 minutes, but were well formed at 90 minutes and still visible in the stomach at 3 hours, which suggests that these coated tablets first fail through loss of buffer capacity.

Figure 5 presents data on a non-fasting subject who received the coated dosage form. The 30-minute x-ray (fig. 6) confirmed that the tablet was in the stomach but the hydrated sac had not yet formed, which explains the absence of riboflavine in the urine at this time. At 90 minutes the x-ray (fig. 7) clearly shows an incompletely 'ballooned' sac. The sac was fully expanded at 3 hours and apparently remained intact releasing drug at a constant rate until at least the fifth hour. The gastric pH may have been higher in this subject and the TRIS buffer was probably not as quickly exhausted as in the fasted subjects.


## 3. Discussion

The study suggests that it is feasible to deliver a drug at a controlled rate from a dosage form having a prolonged residence time in the stomach. This may enhance the bioavailability of a drug such as riboflavine which is absorbed by a saturable process in the intestine. It is easier to produce coated products that balloon fully within 15 to 30 minutes in the stomach (fig. 8) if buffering of the sac contents is not required, dissolution is rapid or rapidly dissolving excipients which increase osmotic pressure can be added.

Physical size is perhaps the major factor accounting for the gastric retention of this dosage form, together with its spherical shape and resistance to deformation when fluid-filled under pressure. Another suspected factor is buoyancy, which may be promoted initially as the coating hydrates and swells, by incorporation of carbon dioxide-generating material such as sodium bicarbonate. Other factors may include charge effects. The gastric mucosa tends to have an overall positive charge due to the secretion of hydrogen ions and the hydrated film contains unesterified carboxyl groups which are potential negative ionogenic sites. Surface effects very likely also play a role. Finholt and Solvang (1968) determined the surface tension of human gastric secretions to be 36 to 44 dynes/cm. Dilution with an equal volume of water increased the surface tension by only 1 to 3 dynes/cm. This low surface tension would help wet and hydrate the cross-linked coating and promote fluid penetration. It may also explain why the hydrated swollen sacs were always seen to be in contact with the gastric mucosa in studies with dogs.

The prolonged gastric residence dosage form may have other clinical applications. The duration of action of drugs such as antacids and anthelminthics could be prolonged and, since only drug in solution passes through the hydrated membrane film, the local toxicity of irritant drugs such as potassium chloride might be reduced.

# References

Ashley, J. and Levy, G.: Effect of vehicle viscosity and an anticholinergic agent on bioavailability of a poorly absorbed drug (phenosulfonphthalein) in man. Journal of Pharmaceutical Sciences 62: 688-190 (1973).

Banker, G.S.: Netherlands Patient No. 7,307,737; Assigned to Purdue Research Foundation, December 11, 1973: Oral pharmaceuticals-with hydrophylic polyer coating and predetermined stomach residence time.

Banker, G.S.: West German Patent No. 2,328,580; Assigned to Purdue Research Foundation, January 10 1974: Coated Medicament formulations with controlled gastric retention.

Banker, G.S.: U.S. Patent 3,896,792; Assigned to Purdue Research Foundation, July 1975: Coating apparatus.

Bates, T.R. and Gibaldi, M.: Gastrointestinal absorption of drugs; in Swarbrick (Ed) Current Concepts in the Pharmaceutical Sciences: Biopharmaceutics, p.58-78 (Lea and Febiger, Philadelphia 1970).

Costill, D.L. and Saltin, B.: Factors limiting gastric emptying during rest and exercise. Journal of Applied Physiology 37: 679-683 (1974).

Davenport, H.W.: Physiology of the Digestive Tract (3rd ed) 49, 171 (Year Book Medical Publishers, Chicago 1971).

Edwards, D.A.W.: Physiological concepts of the pylorus. Proceedings of the Royal Society of Medicine 54: 930-933 (1961).

Finholt, P. and Solvang, S.: Dissolution kinetics of drugs in human gastric juice — the role of surface tension. Journal of Pharmaceutical Sciences 57: 1322-1326 (1968).

Gibaldi, M.: Biopharmaceutics; in Lachman, Lieberman and Kanig (Eds) The Theory and Practice of Industrial Pharmacy, p.237-242 (Lea and Febiger, Philadelphia 1970).

Gothoni, G.; Pentikainen, P.; Vapaatalo, H.I.; Hackman, R. and Bjorksten, K. Af.: Absorption of antibiotics: Influence of metoclopramide and atropine on serum levels of pivampicillin and tetracycline. Annals of Clinical Research 4: 228 (1972).

Hancock, B.D.; Bowen-Jones, E.; Dixon, R.; Testa, T.; Dymock, I.W. and Cowley, D.J.: The effect of posture on the gastric emptying of solid meals in normal subjects and patients after vagotomy. British Journal of Surgery 61: 945 (1974).

Hunt, J.N. and MacDonald, I.: The influence of volume on gastric emptying. Journal of Physiology 126: 459 (1954).

Hunt, J.N. and Knox, M.T.: Regulation of gastric emptying; in Code (Ed) Alimentary Canal, Vol. 11: p.1918-1935 (American Physiological Society, Washington 1963).

Kraml, J.; Dubuc, J. and Beall, D.: Gastrointestinal absorption of griseofulvin I: addition of surfactants and corn oil on level of griseofulvin in serum of rats. Canadian Journal of Biochemical Physiology 40: 1449 (1962).

Lagerlof, H.O.; Johansson, C. and Edelund, K.: Studies of gastrointestinal reactions. Gastric secretion and duodenal reflux in man after a composite meal. The influence of glucose on gastric secretion. Scandinavian Journal of Gastroenterology 8: 735-742 (1973).

Levy, G.: Effect of certain tablet formulation factors on dissolution rate of the active ingredient I. Importance of using appropriate agitation intensities for *in vitro* dissolution rate measurements to reflect *in vivo* conditions. Journal of Pharmaceutical Sciences 52: 1039 (1963).

Levy, G. and Jusko, W.J.: Factors affecting the absorption of riboflavin in man. Journal of Pharmaceutical Sciences 55: 285 (1966).

Levy, G.; Gibaldi, M. and Procknal, J.A.: Effect of an anticholinergic agent on riboflavin absorption in man. Journal of Pharmaceutical Sciences 61: 798-799 (1972).

Levy, G. and Rao, B.I.: Enhanced intestinal absorption of riboflavin from sodium alginate solution in man. Journal of Pharmaceutical Sciences 61: 279 (1972).

Nielsen, N.A. and Christiansen, H.: Acta Radiologica 13: 678 (1932).

Nimmo, J.: The influence of metoclopramide on drug absorption. Postgraduate Medical Journal 49 (Suppl. 4): 25-27 (1973).

Nimmo, J.; Heading, R.C.; Tothill, P. and Prescott, L.F.: Pharmacological modification of gastric emptying: Effects of propantheline and metoclopramide on paracetamol absorption. British Medical Journal 1: 587-589 (1973).

Pearson, M.C.; Edwards, D.; Tate, A.; Gilkes, R.; Saxon, H.M. and Howland, C.: Comparison of the effects of oral and intravenous metoclopramide on the small bowel. Postgraduate Medical Journal 49 (Suppl. 4): 47-49 (1973).

Schlegel, J.F.; Coburn, W.M. Jr. and Code, C.F.: Gastric emptying of solid and compliant spheres in dogs. Physiologist 9 (3): 283 (1966).

Wagner, J.G.: Biopharmaceutics: absorption aspects: Journal of Pharmaceutical Sciences 50: 359 (1961).

Wagner, J.G.; Biopharmaceutics and Relevant Pharmacokinetics; p.3-5 (Drug Intelligence Publications, Washington 1971).

# 20

# Drug Formulation to Minimise Gastrointestinal Toxicity

*John Sjogren*

Department of Pharmaceutics, AB Hassle, Sweden

Gastrointestinal side effects are very common in association with drug therapy and 20 to 40 % of all reported side effects affect the gastrointestinal tract (Zentler-Munro and Northfield, 1979). Most drugs can induce symptoms from the alimentary canal and the degree of seriousness can vary from fairly innocent discomfort to life threatening. Even the less serious effects may be clinically important because they may deter the patient from following the prescribed dosage regimen.

Although gastrointestinal symptoms are an important clinical problem and formulation factors obviously can affect such symptoms, surprisingly little has been published in this field. One probable explanation is that it is considerably more difficult to perform well controlled studies on side effects than to measure bioavailability on a reasonably sized group of subjects. Generally large groups are needed to demonstrate differences in side effects between formulations. Studies on volunteers are useful only to a certain extent and animal studies are often of limited value because of anatomical and physiological differences in the gastrointestinal tracts of man and animals. Consequently most of our knowledge in this field is based on retrospective clinical studies or on pilot studies on small groups of healthy volunteers.

Drug-induced gastrointestinal symptoms may appear in any region from the mouth to the rectum. They include local effects such as pain, ulceration and tissue damage and also systemic effects such as anorexia, nausea and vomiting. In general, it is easier to modify local than systemic side effects by changing the dosage form or route of administration.

Gastrointestinal side effects may be reduced by:

1) Preventing contact between the drug and sensitive regions of the gastrointestinal tract
2) Reducing the drug concentration at the gastrointestinal mucosa
3) Reducing the mucosal cell uptake by buffering or complexation
4) Adding substances which have the opposite effect on the gastrointestinal tract.

*Table I.* Frequency of swallowed capsules or tablets becoming stuck in the oesophagus in 45 patients (after Carlborg et al., 1978)

|            | Without water | With 40ml water |
|------------|---------------|-----------------|
| Capsules   | 66%           | 7%              |
| Tablets    | 23%           | 0%              |

## 1. Reducing Contact with Vulnerable Regions of the Gastrointestinal Tract

If a specific part of the gastrointestinal tract is more vulnerable than others it may be possible to design products with acceptable bioavailability which do not release the drug in these regions.

Oral symptoms, such as discoloration of the teeth or stomatitis can generally be avoided by administration of the drug as capsules or tablets. Such solid dosage forms of irritating drugs may, on the other hand, produce side effects in the oesophagus if they are held up. This problem may be much more common than we believe because very often the patient does not notice that the tablet has stuck and does not associate the symptoms with the drug. In an x-ray study Carlborg et al. (1978) demonstrated that tablets became stuck as frequently in patients unaware of any problems in swallowing tablets as in patients having such problems. When taken without water tablets and especially capsules very frequently became stuck (table I). Administration with 40ml of water reduced the problems considerably. Many common drugs are irritating or even ulcerogenic to the oesophageal mucosa and several reports have been published of damage by potassium chloride, doxycycline, alprenolol, and emepronium bromide. Most problems occur when the products are taken without water immediately before going to bed (Hughes, 1979). All solid dosage forms, especially of irritating drugs, should be swallowed with water. Tablets may be safer than capsules in this respect (table I) and are preferred for ulcerogenic drugs. Little is known, however, of the importance of other formulation factors such as size, shape or coatings. Patients with known lower oesophageal disease should not be given irritating drugs in solid dosage forms at all.

Enteric coating has long been used to reduce gastric side effects from irritating substances such as potassium chloride and acetylsalicylic acid. A good enteric coated product should not release any drug in the stomach but should allow complete absorption when released in the intestine. Furthermore the drug must not irritate the intestinal mucosa which may be exposed to high concentrations of drug when the coating disintegrates. It is doubtful whether drugs which are gastric irritants are innocuous to the intestine and in many cases the advantage of enteric coated tablets is questionable. The well known problems with potassium chloride illustrate this.

Acetylsalicylic acid (aspirin) is one drug which is particularly harmful to the gastric mucosa. When it is absorbed into the mucosal cells it breaks the mucosal protective barrier and allows back diffusion of $H^+$, which results in erosions and haemorrhage. Enteric coated tablets have been reported to cause less bleeding (Howe et al., 1977) although in some studies improvement over plain tablets has not been demonstrated (Pierson et al., 1961; Scott et al., 1961). The reason for this discrepancy is obscure.

No enteric coated aspirin product tested so far has completely abolished gastrointestinal bleeding, however. This may be due to release of aspirin in the stomach, regurgitation of dissolved drug from the intestine back into the stomach or bleeding from the small intestine. Another problem with enteric coated tablets is great variation in absorption, especially when given after a meal (fig. 1) [Bogentoft et al., 1978]. The differences are probably due to variable gastric emptying because the amount eventually absorbed is about the same as from plain tablets.

A capsule product containing enteric coated aspirin beads gave more reproducible absorption with reduced gastrointestinal bleeding (fig. 2) [Arvidsson et al., 1977]. Bleeding still occurred, however in spite of the minute amounts of aspirin released *in*

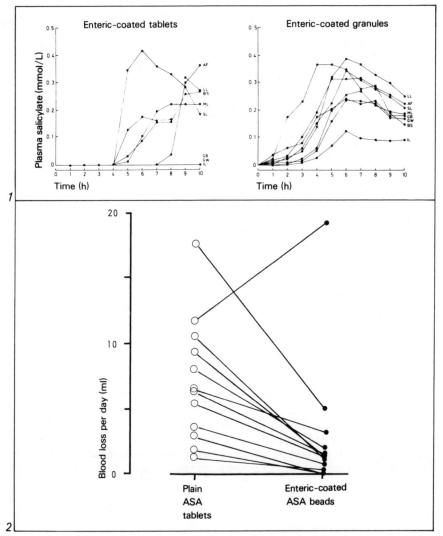

*Fig. 1.* Individual plasma salicylate levels in 8 subjects after administration of 1.0g acetylsalicylic acid with meal. (Bogentoft et al. 1978; reproduced with the authors permission.)

*Fig. 2.* Daily blood loss ($^{51}$Cr in faeces) during acetylsalicylic acid (ASA) treatment 1.0g 3 times a day. (Arvidsson et al., 1977; reproduced with permission.)

*Table II.* Number of subjects reporting gastric pain during 3 days of potassium chloride administration, 1g 3 times a day (n = 30) [after Graffner and Sjogren, 1971]

|                                      | Ordinary tablets | Controlled release tablets |
|--------------------------------------|:----------------:|:--------------------------:|
| Total number                         | 19               | 6                          |
| Ranked as more severe than the others | 16              | 2                          |

*vitro* at gastric pH. A dosage form which spreads out the dose in the intestine as thousands of small beads can be expected to reduce the risk of erosive side effects. Enteric coated beads might therefore offer substantial advantages over the traditional enteric coated tablets with regard to both absorption reproducibility and side effects. This type of enteric coated formulation may prove successful for some other drugs.

With rectal administration of drugs only the terminal gastrointestinal part of the tract is exposed but this route is not often used as a means of reducing side effects. Most drugs that are irritating to the upper gastrointestinal tract also give problems in the rectum where the area for absorption is limited and the amount of available fluid is small.

## 2. Reducing Drug Concentration at the Mucosa

When possible drugs should be given with a meal to reduce local concentrations. It makes it easier for the patient to remember his medicine and in general reduces the incidence of gastrointestinal side effects. Both factors can be expected to improve patient compliance. Some drugs however, interact with food and are therefore poorly absorbed.

Administration of ulcerogenic drugs as dilute solutions, syrups etc. is generally considered to be safe and is used to some extent. The taste may be difficult to mask, however, and this may preclude the use of such dosage forms. Liquid products are also inconvenient to handle. Effervescent tablets or powder mixtures, which are dissolved in a glass of water immediately prior to administration, are sometimes used and are considered more convenient than liquid products. Also it is often easier to obtain an agreeable taste in carbonated drug solutions.

The use of poorly soluble salts or complexes of drugs should provide another means of reducing local concentrations, but there is the risk of erratic or incomplete absorption. Aloxiprin appears to be one of the few examples where this approach is used clinically. It is an aluminium oxide complex with aspirin which has limited solubility at low pH but is more soluble in the intestinal environment. This complex has been shown to provoke less gastrointestinal bleeding than plain aspirin (Wood et al., 1962).

Controlled release dosage forms are designed to give reliable absorption in spite of slow drug release. They give lower drug concentrations in the gastrointestinal tract than ordinary tablets and reduction of side effects is one important reason for using controlled release dosage forms. Potassium chloride products are perhaps the best known in this respect.

Potassium chloride in plain tablets or capsules produces prohibitive gastrointestinal toxicity. Enteric coating appeared to solve most of the problems but instead produced small bowel ulcerations and strictures as became apparent when potassium supplementation came into widespread use 15 to 20 years ago.

Controlled release potassium chloride tablets give less pain and nausea than plain tablets in healthy volunteers, (table II) and less intestinal damage in animals than enteric coated tablets. The frequency of intestinal stenosis or ulceration has decreased dramatically since enteric coated potassium products were replaced by controlled release tablets. Bystedt and Raaf (1970) investigated the number of cases of potassium chloride-induced intestinal ulceration in the Stockholm area from 1966 to 1969 and found 10 cases, of whom 3 died. All 10 had taken enteric coated potassium chloride. During this period the consumption of controlled release potassium tablets was about 3 times higher than that of enteric coated tablets but there were no reports of similar damage. The incidence of small bowel lesions after enteric coated tablets was reported to be less than 1 in 1000 patient years which agrees well with the incidence reported from the USA of 440 per million patient years (Hutcheon, 1976). The incidence after controlled release tablets was stated to be 1.7 per million patient years.

As potassium controlled release tablets are very widely used it is not surprising that several cases of oesophageal and intestinal ulcers or strictures have been reported. The risks do not appear to be negligible in patients with obstruction or impaired motility of the gastrointestinal tract. Little information is available regarding differences between potassium controlled release products. Most side effects have been reported with a wax matrix controlled release tablet but this may be attributable to its widespread use. Animal studies indicate that different potassium controlled release products may have different ulcerogenic potential (Renker et al., 1977; Block and Thomas, 1978) and that dosage forms containing a large number of individually coated beads may be safer than matrix tablets. It remains to be shown whether this also holds true in clinical practice, however. As such products are more expensive, it is unlikely that they will supersede the matrix type of potassium tablets except perhaps for high risk patients.

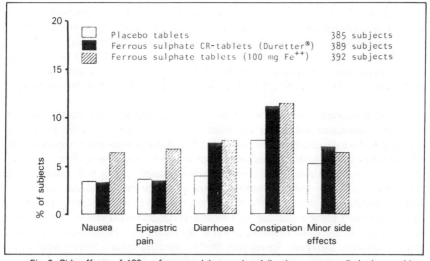

*Fig. 3.* Side effects of 100mg ferrous sulphate twice daily given as controlled release tablets or as ordinary tablets. (Rybo and Solvell, 1971; reproduced with permission.)

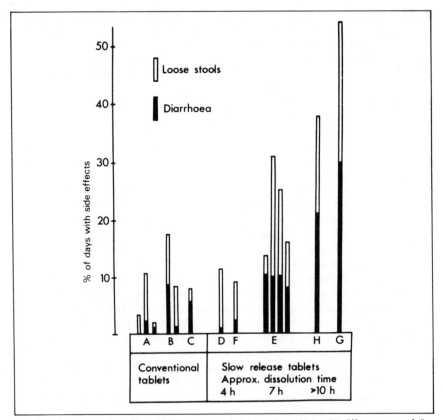

*Fig. 4.* Laxative side effects of lithium salts administered as tablets with different rates of dissolution in a dose of 24mmol twice daily.

Ferrous sulphate is another gastrointestinal irritant. Generally less than 10 % of the dose is absorbed and thus the substance should be less suitable for controlled release dosage forms. It is possible, however, to formulate such products which are absorbed at least as well as plain tablets (Boye-Nielsen et al., 1976). The controlled release tablets gave less nausea and epigastric pain than rapidly releasing tablets but the incidence of diarrhoea and constipation was not affected (fig. 3) [Rybo and Solvell, 1971].

Another example is lithium which may cause troublesome side effects, some of which are gastrointestinal. Many controlled release products of lithium have been marketed and we developed tablets with different release profiles and compared them with ordinary tablets in a series of cross-over studies on volunteers. Plain tablets of lithium carbonate, sulphate or citrate frequently caused nausea and anorexia and these symptoms were reduced slightly by retarding the rate of release. Diarrhoea which is another side effect of lithium was not reduced by slow release but was instead much more pronounced (fig. 4). Our interpretation is that lithium ions stimulate peristalsis in the distal intestine and if a significant part of the dose is released there it provokes diarrhoea. In another study controlled release tablets were given fasting and with a meal. There was a striking difference in the incidence of diarrhoea (table III). Administration with a meal probably retards gastric emptying and intes-

*Table III.* Number of subjects reporting loose stools or diarrhoea after a single dose of 24mmol lithium sulphate controlled release tablets (n = 30) [after Jeppsson and Sjogren, 1975]

|  | Fasting | Non-fasting |
|---|---|---|
| Loose stools | 6 | 1 |
| Diarrhoea | 8 | 0 |

tinal transit and most of the salt will consequently be released before the tablets reach the lower part of the intestine. The diluting effect of the meal may also be of importance (Borg et al., 1975b).

## 3. Reducing Uptake by Complexation or Buffering

The penetration of drug into the mucosal cells can be reduced by decreasing the absorbable form of the drug in solution. Complexation is used to some extent in iron therapy. Sodium iron edetate can for instance be administered as solution without staining the teeth, but the absorption is, however, poor (Brise and Hallberg, 1962).

Buffering has been used successfully as a means of reducing gastric bleeding from aspirin tablets. As the bleeding is associated with the amount of aspirin taken up by the gastric mucosal cells, it is reasonable to assume that it is advantageous to maintain a high pH and thereby reduce the concentration of unionised aspirin. It is not sufficient to use the sodium salt alone because the acidic gastric juice will transform the salt into the unionised form. The product must have sufficient buffer capacity to maintain the pH above 6 as long as aspirin remains in the stomach. A buffer capacity is necessary to minimise bleeding (fig. 5) [Leonards and Levy, 1969]. In this study the buffered products were given as solutions and this undoubtedly contributed to the reduced bleeding.

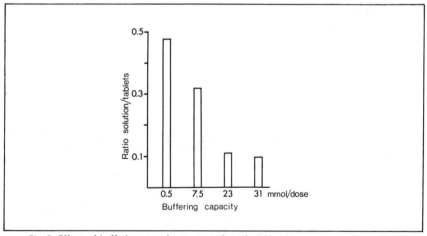

*Fig. 5.* Effect of buffering capacity on gastrointestinal blood loss expressed as ratio of loss after buffered acetylsalicylic acid solutions over loss after unbuffered tablets. (Leonards and Levy, 1969; reproduced with permission.)

Buffered aspirin products are often formulated as effervescent tablets which dissolve rapidly and give a dilute, buffered solution. Buffered aspirin solutions appear to be emptied more rapidly from the stomach than a plain solution, as illustrated in figure 6. All these factors (dilution, buffering and gastric emptying) should have a beneficial effect on gastric side effects and less bleeding has been demonstrated both in controlled studies using [51]Cr labelled blood cells and visually by gastrocamera observation of the gastric mucosa (table IV) [Edmar, 1975].

The dissolution properties are also of importance for buffered products because they influence the length of time that the drug is kept in the stomach and thus in con-

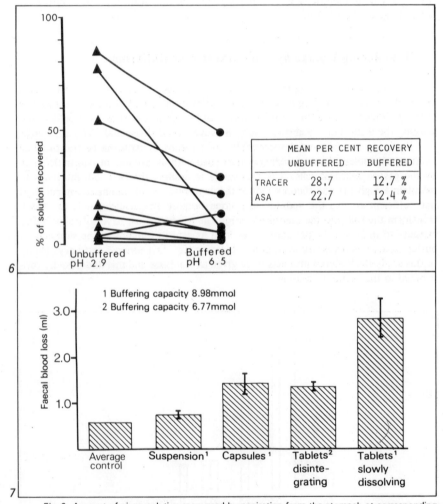

Fig. 6. Amount of given solution recovered by aspiration from the stomach at corresponding times (mean 19 min) after administration of unbuffered or buffered acetylsalicylic acid (ASA) solutions. (Doterall and Ekenved, 1976; reproduced with permission.)

Fig. 7. Daily average faecal blood loss in 12 dogs after 650mg acetylsalicylic acid as the sodium salt plus buffer in various dosage forms. (Phillips and Palermo, 1977; reproduced with permission of the copyright owner.)

*Table IV.* Presence of erosions in the gastric mucosa after aspirin according to gastrocamera observations (after Edmar, 1975)

| Erosions | Aspirin tablets | | Aspirin buffered solution | |
|---|---|---|---|---|
| | before | after | before | after |
| None visible | 7 | — | 8[1] | 4[1] |
| Few, localised | — | — | — | 3 |
| Multiple and prominent | — | 7 | — | 1 |

1   Including 1 subject not tested with the aspirin tablets.

tact with the mucosa. Phillips and Palermo (1977) demonstrated in dogs that a slowly dissolving sodium aspirin tablet caused significantly more bleeding than a rapidly disintegrating product or a suspension although all products were buffered with calcium and magnesium carbonates (fig. 7).

Buffering obviously improves the tolerability of aspirin. It has also been tried for other irritants such as anti-inflammatory drugs, but little improvement has been demonstrated and buffering is certainly not a remedy for all gastrointestinal side effects.

Administration of aspirin as suppositories very frequently causes rectal pain, reflex defaecation or rectal bleeding (Borg et al., 1975). Formulations based on the calcium salt of aspirin are considerably better tolerated (fig. 8) in spite of the higher

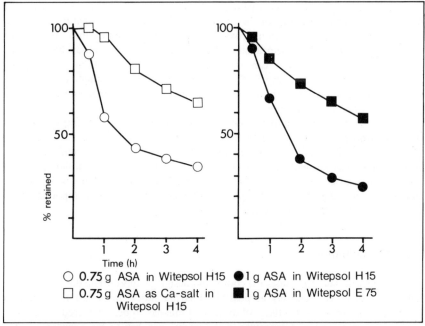

O  0.75 g  ASA  in  Witepsol H15    ● 1 g  ASA  in  Witepsol H15
□  0.75 g  ASA  as  Ca-salt  in     ■ 1 g  ASA  in  Witepsol E 75
        Witepsol H15

*Fig. 8.* Amount of administered acetylsalicylic acid (ASA) suppositories retained at different times after administration.

*Table V.* Constipating/laxative effect of antacid tablets: 5 tablets 4 times a day for 5 days in 10 subjects

| Daily dose (g) | | | Number of bowel evacuations as | | | |
|---|---|---|---|---|---|---|
| MgO | $Al_2O_3$ | ratio | hard lumps | normal semi-solid | loose stools | diarr-hoea |
| 0.53 | 2.80 | 0.2 | 25 | 21 | 1 | — |
| 1.02 | 3.18 | 0.3 | 3 | 41 | 16 | 5 |
| 2.20 | 1.70 | 1.3 | — | 20 | 43 | 19 |
| 3.40 | 1.14 | 3.0 | — | 16 | 9 | 90 |

water solubility of the salt. The ionised form is absorbed more slowly (fig. 9) and this probably explains the reduction in side effects. A modification of the suppository base, which results in a slower absorption of aspirin, gave about the same reduction in side effects as the use of the salt.

## 4. Addition of Counteracting Substances

Many drugs affect the bowel habit and substances with the opposite effect are sometimes added. For example several iron products contain laxatives to reduce constipation. The combination is probably useful for patients who suffer from constipation but is far from ideal for those patients who suffer from diarrhoea even after plain iron tablets. Diarrhoea is one of the common side effects of iron therapy (fig. 3).

Antacids generally contain hydroxides or carbonates of aluminium, magnesium or calcium. Besides their neutralising effect magnesium compounds have a pronounced laxative effect and can therefore seldom be used alone in antacids. Aluminium and calcium compounds are constipating, on the other hand, and are often used in combination with magnesium compounds. The proportions of the compounds are of course important.

It was recently reported that about 30 % of patients on antacid therapy developed diarrhoea (Ippoliti et al., 1978) indicating a serious problem with some products. We have investigated the influence of the ratio between aluminium and magnesium compounds in antacid suspensions and tablets and it is possible to formulate products with a widely differing influence on bowel function (table V). Not only is the ratio of importance, however, but also the physicochemical nature of the compounds. Sorbitol can also be used to reduce the constipating effect.

## 5. Conclusion

Drug formulation includes the choice and design of appropriate dosage forms to deliver the drug as effectively as possible. Pharmaceutical formulation can have a great influence on the side effects of drugs and this has to be considered in biopharmaceutical optimisation. Gastrointestinal toxicity also has to be considered when comparing different bioequivalent products.

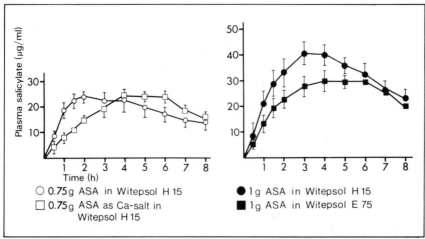

*Fig. 9.* Plasma concentration of salicylate after rectal administration of acetylsalicylic acid (ASA). Mean and SEM from 5 subjects.

Side effect studies require many patients or subjects and the evaluation of several different formulations is therefore difficult. Better methods should be developed because only by systematic studies with different formulations is it possible to achieve a deeper biopharmaceutical knowledge regarding the effect of formulation on gastrointestinal toxicity.

## References

Arvidsson, B.; Magnusson, A.; Magnusson, B. and Solvell, L.: Acetylsalicylic acid and gastrointestinal bleeding. Lakartidningen 74: 4101-4102 (1977).

Block, B.P. and Thomas, M.B.: A method for testing intestinal irritancy of sustained release potassium chloride preparations in animals. Journal of Pharmacy and Pharmacology 30 (Suppl.): 70P (1978).

Bogentoft, C.; Carlsson, I.; Ekenved, G. and Magnusson, A.: Influence of food on the absorption of acetylsalicylic acid from enteric coated dosage forms. European Journal of Clinical Pharmacology 14: 351-355 (1978).

Borg, K.O.; Ekenved, G.; Elofsson, R.; Sjogren, J. and Solvell, L.: Bioavailability and tolerance studies on acetylsalicylic acid suppositories. Acta Pharmaceutica Suecica 12: 491-498 (1975a).

Borg, K.O.; Jeppsson, J. and Sjogren, J.: The influence of food on side effects and absorption of lithium. Acta Psychiatrica Scandinavica 51: 285-288 (1975b).

Boye-Nielsen, J.; Ikkala, E.; Solvell, L.; Bjorn-Rasmussen, E. and Ekenved, G.: Absorption of iron from slow-release and rapidly disintegrating tablets — a comparative study in normal subjects, blood donors and subjects with iron deficiency anemia. Scandinavian Journal of Haematology (Suppl. 28): 89-97 (1976).

Brise, H. and Hallberg, L.: Absorbability of different iron compounds. Acta Medica Scandinavica 171 (Suppl. 376): 23-37 (1962).

Bystedt, T. and Raf, L.: Stenoserande tunntarmssar vid kaliumterapi. Lakartidningen 67: 3754-3759 (1970).

Carlborg, B.; Kumlien, A. and Olsson, H.: Medikamentella esofagusstrikturer. Lakartidningen 75: 4609-4611 (1978).

Dotevall, G. and Ekenved, G.: Absorption of acetylsalicylic acid from the stomach in relation to introgastric pH. Scandinavian Journal of Gastroenterology 11: 801-805 (1976).

Edmar, D.: The effects of acetylsalicylic acid on the human gastric mucosa as revealed by gastrocamera. Scandinavian Journal of Gastroenterology 10: 495-499 (1975).

Graffner, C. and Sjogren, J.: Side-effects of potassium chloride in products with different dissolution
    rates. Acta Pharmaceutica Suecica 8: 19-26 (1971).
Howe, G.B.; Champion, G.D.; Corrigan, A.B.; Hewson, J.; Haski, A.; Day, R.O.; Paull, P.D. and
    Graham, G.G.: The effects of enteric coating of aspirin tablets on occult gastrointestinal blood loss.
    Australian and New Zealand Journal of Medicine 7: 600-604 (1977).
Hughes, R.: Drug-induced oesophageal injury. British Medical Journal 2: 132 (1979).
Hutcheon, D.E.: Benefit-risk factors associated with supplemental potassium therapy. Journal of Clinical
    Pharmacology 16: 85-87 (1976).
Ippoliti, A.F.; Sturdevant, R.A.L.; Isenberg, J.I.; Binder, M.; Camacho, R.; Cano, R.; Cooney, C.; Kline,
    M.M.; Koretz, R.L.; Meyer, J.H.; Samloff, I.M.; Schwabe, A.D.; Strom, E.A.; Valenzuela, J.E. and
    Wintroub, R.H.: Cimetidine versus intensive antacid therapy for duodenal ulcer. Gastroenterology
    74: 393-395 (1978).
Jeppsson, J. and Sjogren, J.: The influence of food on side-effects and absorption of lithium. Acta Psy-
    chiatrica Scandinavica 51: 285-288 (1975).
Leonards, J.R. and Levy, G.: Reduction or prevention of aspirin-induced occult gastrointestinal blood loss
    in man. Clinical Pharmacology and Therapeutics 10: 571-575 (1969).
Phillips, B.M. and Palermo, B.T.: Physical form as a determinant of effect of buffered acetylsalicylate for-
    mulations on GI microbleeding. Journal of Pharmaceutical Sciences 66: 124-127 (1977).
Pierson, R.N.; Holt, P.R.; Watson, R.M. and Keating, R.P.: Aspirin and gastrointestinal bleeding.
    American Journal of Medicine 31: 259-265 (1961).
Renker, H.; Schaub, E.; Burgin, M.; Zanoletti, A.; Chovan, K. and Muller, A.: Vertraglichkeitstudie mit
    verschiedenen oralen Kaliumpraparaten an Ratten. Arzneimittel-Forschung 27: 845-851 (1977).
Rybo, G. and Solvell, L.: Side effect studies on a new sustained release iron preparation. Scandinavian
    Journal of Haematology 8: 257-264 (1971).
Scott, J.T.; Porter, I.H.; Lewis, S.M. and Dixon, A.S.J.: Studies of gastrointestinal bleeding caused by
    steroids, salicylates and other analgesics. Quarterly Journal of Medicine 30: 167-188 (1961).
Wood, P.H.N.; Harvey-Smith, E.A. and Dixon, A. St. J.: Salicylates and gastrointestinal bleeding.
    Acetylsalicylic acid and aspirin derivatives. British Medical Journal 1: 669-675 (1962).
Zentler-Munro, P.L. and Northfield, T.C.: Drug-induced gastrointestinal disease. British Medical Journal
    1: 1263-1265 (1979).

## Discussion

*J.B. Fregnan* (Milan): When a tablet or a capsule sticks in the oesophagus, how
long does it take to reach the stomach?

*J. Sjogren*: If you take the drug and go to bed, it can take the whole night and
that is probably the most common reason for oesophageal ulceration. If you take a
glass of water afterwards, you can generally flush down the product but even so, capsules may still stick.

*G.S. Banker* (Lafayette, Indiana): One way to minimise gastrointestinal toxicity
is to prevent contact of crystalline drug with the gastrointestinal mucosa. This can be
achieved by giving solutions but it can also be done with solid dosage forms. One
method is to prepare a molecular dispersion system such as a solid solution or a col-
loidal polymeric dispersion. Another way is to coat the tablet with a permeable
membrane so that the drug only leaves the dosage form in solution.

*J. Sjogren*: I am not sure that you can avoid side effects just by preventing contact between crystals and the mucosa because most side effects occur when the
molecules penetrate the mucosa. If you have rapid absorption from a solution, you
can still have side effects as, for instance, with aspirin. As long as you maintain slow
dissolution or slow absorption, then you can reduce side effects.

*G.S. Banker*: Where you need rapid release, it is very difficult or impossible to
avoid irritation.

# 21

# Slow-release Preparations in Clinical Perspective

*J. Koch-Weser and P.J. Schechter*

Centre de Recherche Merrell International, Strasbourg

From the clinician's point of view the best way to administer a drug is the simplest and cheapest method that reliably achieves and maintains therapeutically effective and safe drug action. The desirable intensity of pharmacological activity falls into the range between the weakest drug action sufficient to cause a satisfactory therapeutic effect and the highest degree of beneficial drug action not associated with unacceptable side effects (fig. 1). This range varies enormously with different drugs, patients and diseases. Sometimes, as in the treatment of highly susceptible bacterial infections with bactericidal antibiotics, it is so wide that almost any dose and a great variety of dosage intervals and routes of administration are therapeutically acceptable. In other situations, such as during maintenance of controlled intra-operative hypotension with nitroprusside, the range of desirable intensity of action is so narrow that an intravenous infusion whose rate is continuously titrated against the arterial pressure is the only feasible method of administration. Almost all other pharmacotherapeutic situations fall somewhere between these two extremes.

The design of satisfactory administration schedules for a given drug, patient and therapeutic goal is constrained by the range of desirable intensity of drug action and by the time course of action of the drug. These two factors inevitably determine the possible dosage sizes and intervals. The first factor is essentially immutable, but the time course of drug action is often highly manipulatable. This is eminently the case when the time course of action of the drug is closely determined by its pharmacokinetic fate.

The intensity of action of many drugs is predictably and constantly related to their concentration at the site of action and even in the serum (Koch-Weser, 1972). There are, of course, important exceptions. The onset of action of some drugs, for example digitoxin or guanethidine, lags considerably behind their appearance in the serum. The pharmacological effects of other drugs, such as irreversible enzyme inhibitors, greatly outlasts the presence of the active compound in the body. Many drugs are biotransformed to active metabolites and these must be taken into account in the concentration-effect relation. Finally, there are drugs such as the coumarin anticoagulants whose serum concentration is proportional to the intensity of their pharmacological action (inhibition of hepatic synthesis of vitamin K-sensitive clotting factors) but not to that of their clinically decisive effect (concentration of the pro-

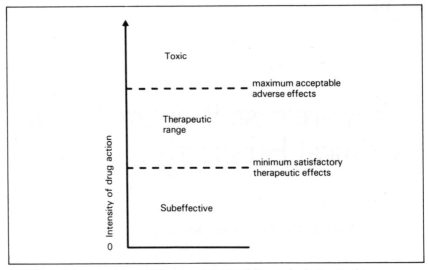

*Fig. 1.* Schematic representation of the intensity of drug action in therapeutics.

thrombin complex in plasma). Nevertheless, drugs whose serum concentration bears a continuous relationship to the intensity of their therapeutically important action appear to be in the majority (Koch-Weser, 1977). Since they most clearly illustrate the interrelation of therapeutically desirable concentration ranges, pharmacokinetics and effective dosage schedules, we shall briefly focus on such drugs. However, the same considerations apply to all drugs if intensity of action is considered instead of serum concentration and time course of action instead of pharmacokinetic fate.

## 1. Concentration Ratios

In discussing the therapeutically acceptable range of drug concentrations in the body or the serum, it is useful to consider the *therapeutic concentration ratio* (TCR). The TCR is defined as the ratio of the highest therapeutic concentration free of unacceptable side effects to the lowest concentration producing the desired therapeutic effect (fig. 2). The TCR is not just an attribute of a given drug but also a function of the specific patient and his disease. Nevertheless, because of individual differences in pharmacokinetics, the TCR is almost invariably less variable and smaller than the corresponding *therapeutic dosage ratio*. The usual TCR has been fairly well defined for many therapeutically important drugs and is generally at least 2 (table I). Drugs whose TCR is much smaller are unlikely to be clinically useful except in malignancy and other life-threatening diseases. Clearly the TCR is a useful index only for those drugs whose serum concentration is constantly related to the intensity of their pharmacological actions. It cannot be applied to irreversible enzyme inhibitors, cytotoxic agents and drugs such as reserpine. It is also not meaningful for compounds such as the β-adrenoceptor antagonists and many antihypertensive drugs whose pharmacodynamic half-life considerably exceeds the plasma half-life.

To design dosage schedules that achieve and maintain serum concentration of a drug in the therapeutically desirable range one must consider its pharmacokinetic

*Table I.* Usual therapeutic serum concentration range of some important drugs

| Drug | Concentration |
|---|---|
| Digitoxin | 12–25µg/L |
| Digoxin | 1.0–2.0µg/L |
| Ethosuximide | 40–80mg/L |
| Lignocaine | 1.5–4.5mg/L |
| Lithium | 0.5–1.3mEq/L |
| Phenytoin | 10–20mg/L |
| Procainamide | 4.0–8.0mg/L |
| Quinidine | 2.0–4.0mg/L |
| Salicylate | 0.15–0.30g/L |
| Theophylline | 10–20mg/L |

fate. The *dosage interval concentration ratio* (DICR) is the ratio of the maximum concentration during one dosage interval to the minimum concentration (fig. 2). The DICR reflects both the frequency of dosing with a drug and the entry of the drug into and removal from the body. The DICR for any drug increases with the rates of systemic absorption and of elimination and with the dosage interval. The rate of absorption depends both on the drug and on its formulation, while the rate of elimination is a property of the drug alone.

It is obvious that a satisfactory therapeutic regimen with most drugs requires that the DICR be kept smaller than the TCR. Important exceptions are drugs like diuretics, certain antibiotics, and analgesics and hypnotics for some clinical settings in which a sustained pharmacological effect is not required. It is no problem to keep the DICR below the TCR in the case of drugs whose TCR is very large or whose elimination half-life is very long. The latter is true of many important drugs, so that

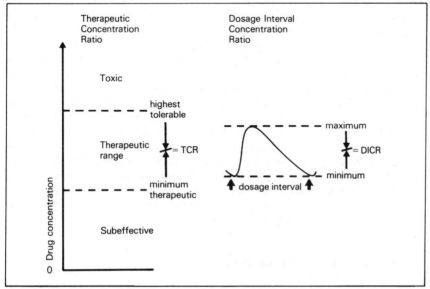

*Fig. 2.* Schematic representation of the therapeutic concentration ratio (TCR) and the dosage interval concentration ratio (DICR).

even a single dose per day will keep their serum concentration acceptably stable. When a drug is possessed neither of a large TCR nor of a long chemical and, more importantly, pharmacodynamic half-life, the clinical therapist must focus closely on maintaining DICR smaller than TCR.

It is occasionally possible to increase the TCR, for example by correcting hypokalaemia during digitalis therapy or acidosis during the use of vasopressors. Generally, however, one aims at decreasing the DICR. This may be achieved by one or all of 3 manipulations: shortening the dosage interval, slowing the elimination of the drug, or prolonging its absorption.

## 2. The Dosage Interval

Shortening of the dosage interval while lowering each dose is the most predictably effective way to decrease the DICR. The ultimate example of this is the constant rate intravenous infusion which enables therapy with drugs whose duration of action is only a few minutes. For drugs whose pharmacodynamic half-life exceeds an hour, and which have a reasonably high TCR, intermittent oral administration becomes possible. The smaller the TCR and the shorter the half-life, the shorter must be the dosage interval. Obviously, there are practical limitations to the frequency of dosing.

Except in semi-acute situations it is unreasonable to expect patients to waken during the night in order to take their medication. It is also unlikely that a daytime regimen requiring very frequent drug intake would long be followed by any but the most conscientious patients. This does not apply of course to drug intake stimulated by acute symptoms and resulting in their prompt relief: many patients with angina pectoris take 10 or more nitroglycerin tablets each day and consumption of cough drops can reach heroic frequencies.

There is no comprehensive information about the relationship between the dosage interval and patient compliance in drug taking. This is not surprising since compliance is also influenced by a host of other factors relating to the patient, his physician, his environment, his disease and the specific drug (Stewart and Cluff, 1972; Blackwell, 1973). The general statement that compliance decreases with the dosage interval is widely accepted and seems reasonable up to a point. It is by no means clear, however, that this applies to all patients, drugs and diseases. It is even less clear whether it applies to longer dosage intervals. Is compliance less when a drug is to be taken twice a day than when a single dosage is prescribed? Most of us manage to get out of and into bed, to brush our teeth and to eat at least twice daily. One factor frequently disregarded in statements about compliance and frequency of dosing is that the consequences of omission of one dose per day are more serious when 1 or 2 doses are prescribed than when 3 or 4 doses are to be taken. Even non-compliance involving a given fraction of all doses is more likely to lead to important therapeutic losses the longer the dosage interval. For the time being it remains doubtful that prolonging the dosage interval beyond 8 hours is important for patient compliance, but shorter intervals seem generally undesirable.

## 3. Retardation of Elimination

It is feasible to slow the elimination of some drugs by changing their distribution in the body, inhibiting their biotransformation, inhibiting their renal tubular secre-

*Table II.* Types of slow-release preparation (after Ballard and Nelson, 1975)

Coated slow-release beads
Tablets with slow-release cores
Repeat-action tablets
Tableted mixed-release granules
Multiple-layer tablets
Porous inert carriers
Ion-exchange resins
Slightly soluble salts
Slightly soluble complexes
Liquid preparations

tion or promoting their tubular reabsorption. Unfortunately, these approaches almost always involve the concomitant administration of other drugs and are seldom routinely applicable. Chemical modification of drugs to increase their binding to plasma proteins or other inactive reservoirs or to slow their elimination has been commonly successful but involves the creation of new drugs.

## 4. Prolongation of Absorption

Prolongation of the absorption of each dose of a drug is a conceptually appealing approach to reduction of the DICR without shortening the dosage interval or to prolonging the dosage interval without increasing the DICR. By slowing the initial high rate of absorption of each dose and by spreading its absorption over a longer period of time one will reduce the peak concentration and raise the lowest concentration of the drug during a given dosage interval. Theoretically, prolonged absorption of a drug dose can be achieved by administering it in a formulation which releases the drug slowly. From the clinical perspective such preparations are attractive, since they enable the physician to prescribe fewer doses without running foul of the need to keep the DICR smaller than the TCR. Some undesirable drug effects, such as flushing after nicotinic acid or disturbances in intellectual function after administration of benzodiazepines appear to be largely related to the rate at which the drug enters the body. Slowing the intestinal absorption of such drugs may attenuate or eliminate adverse effects, even if the same peak drug concentration in the body is ultimately attained (Greenblatt et al., 1977). A final advantage of preparations that release a drug slowly in the gastrointestinal tract lies in the possible reduction of adverse effects on the gastrointestinal mucosa that result from high concentrations of some drugs at the site of rapid disintegration and dissolution of their ordinary solid dosage formulations.

## 5. Slow-release Preparations

The terminology used to describe drug formulations designed to slow the rate at which active drug becomes available for intestinal absorption is chaotic. The adjectives 'gradual', 'long', 'prolonged', 'slow', 'sustained' or 'timed' and the nouns 'release', 'absorption' or 'action' have all been used more or less interchangeably.

'Release' would seem to be the only appropriate noun, since it refers to a property of the formulation, while long duration of absorption or action is secondary to slow release in this context and may be due entirely to non-formulation factors. Several of the adjectives are appropriate, but 'slow' recommends itself as a general term which stresses the differences between these formulations and the usual ones for which fast disintegration and dissolution are considered virtues.

Many different types of slow-release formulations have been devised and tested (table II). Compared to the usual ready-release preparations, all have in common that the rate of dissolution of some of the drug from the dosage form into the surrounding intestinal fluid is slowed by chemical or physical techniques. Most contain in addition a rapidly dissolving portion of drug similar to the usual therapeutic dose. However, the various types differ greatly in performance characteristics and reliability. Very few if any slow-release preparations result in a constant rate of absorption of the contained drug. The pharmaceutical aspects of slow-release preparations have been extensively reviewed (Lazarus and Cooper, 1961; Ballard and Nelson, 1975) and will not be discussed here further.


## 5.1 Intestinal Function and Slow-release Preparations

Most drugs are predominantly absorbed from the small intestine. Weakly acidic drugs exist in the stomach in the undissociated form and can be significantly absorbed from this site. However, the relatively small absorptive surface area of the stomach and the usual rate of gastric emptying cause even such drugs to be mainly absorbed from the large intestine. The absorption of most drugs from the large intestine has not been carefully studied but appears to be very incomplete and erratic in the case of many (Schanker, 1959).

The human small intestine is 3 to 7 metres long and possesses an absorptive area of the order of 7 square metres (Davenport, 1966; Spiro, 1977). The post-duodenal part is arbitrarily divided into an upper 40% (jejunum) and a lower 60% (ileum). Absorption is much more active in the jejunum and so is motility (Spiro, 1977). The factors governing the rate of aborption of drugs in the small intestine are at least partially understood (Schanker, 1961, 1971; Jollow and Brodie, 1972; Prescott, 1974) but cannot be discussed here. It is well established that some drugs can be absorbed along the entire length of the small intestine, though probably none with uniform avidity. It is equally certain that other drugs are effectively absorbed only from a limited area of the small intestine, usually in the jejunum. The extent of the absorptive site for most drugs remains entirely unknown.

It is perfectly obvious that slow release of a drug from any formulation, no matter how perfectly sustained and reliable, is of no value if it occurs after the formulation has moved past the absorptive site for the drug. Strangely, this limitation has often been ignored by pharmaceutically orientated researchers or they have optimistically assumed that 12 hours are available for delivery of the drug to absorbing surfaces.

Reliable information about transit time through the human small intestine and even more through individual segments is very limited. Most commonly foodstuffs are said to spend 'several hours' in the small intestine. The transit time to the caecum for barium in saline usually varies between 1 and 4 hours. Little is known about the sojourn of pharmaceutical preparations of various types in the small intestine. However, it was shown many years ago that very wide dispersion of encapsulated slow-

Table III. Usual elimination half-lives $(t_{1/2\beta})$ of some drugs marketed in slow-release preparations

| Drug | Half-life (h) |
|------|---------------|
| Atropine | 12-36 |
| Chlorphentermine | 36-48 |
| Chlorpheniramine | 12-18 |
| Chlorpromazine | 16-32 |
| Fenfluramine | 12-36 |
| Lithium | 14-24 |
| Phenobarbitone | 48-96 |
| Phenytoin | 14-36 |
| Salicylate | 12-18[1] |

1 At anti-inflammatory serum concentrations.

release granules throughout this part of the bowel occurs within 2 hours of ingestion and that many enter the colon within 4 hours and most within 6 hours (Green, 1954; Feinblatt and Ferguson, 1956). Hinton et al. (1969) found intestinal transit times $(t_{50\%})$ between 2.3 and 8.0 hours (mean 4.8) in 10 patients with ileostomies, and Bechgaard and Ladefoged (1978) obtained similar results with pellets of usual density. However, ileostomy patients may have atypically long small intestinal transit times, since some functional 'colonisation' of the terminal ileum may occur after colectomy.

It is quite certain that there are very large differences in small intestinal transit time among individuals and at different times in the same person. Indeed, few physiological parameters appear to be as variable. Intestinal motility is altered by a host of psychological and physiological factors (Jollow and Brodie, 1972). According to Spiro (1977) propulsive activity of the small intestine is greatly increased by eating and even by the anticipation of such. On the other hand, Davenport (1966) states that the rate of transport of intestinal contents is reduced by food intake. Certainly, quality and quantity of what is in the intestine affects the speed of its passage, and this applies not only to food but also to pharmaceutical preparations (Bechgaard and Ladefoged, 1978). Intestinal motility is profoundly altered in many disease states. A large number of drugs increase or decrease intestinal motility and transit time (Koch-Weser, 1974; Parsons, 1979).

Incomplete absorption is an inevitable consequence of all formulations which release drug so slowly that some portion of the dose becomes available for absorption only distal to effective absorptive sites. If the usual transit time through the small intestine is 4 to 6 hours and the drug is not reliably absorbed from the colon, it is of questionable value to swallow preparations or devices that release drug over 8 to 12 hours. As an inescapable corollary it is unlikely that any slow-release formulation can reliably convert the required dosage interval of any drug from 12 to 24 hours.

An additional major difficulty lies in the spectrum of absorptive efficiency for drugs. On one extreme are drugs that are well absorbed over the entire length of the small intestine, so that their absorption can remain complete even if intestinal transit time becomes very short. The opposite extreme is formed by drugs that are absorbed slowly and only in a limited area of the intestine with the result that their absorption is incomplete even when they enter the duodenum already dissolved and intestinal transit is slow. Inevitably, some drugs that are completely absorbed when given in rapidly releasing formulations must become incompletely absorbed when some of the dose is released only in the lower small intestine. From the clinical point of view this is a serious shortcoming because incomplete absorption always implies variable and unpredictable absorption (Levy, 1972).

It is quite predictable that any slow-release preparation of some drugs in some patients will give less reliable and less complete absorption than the usual formulations which make the entire dose rapidly available to the intestinal mucosa. We do not know which drugs when given in slow-release formulations become incompletely absorbed or more incompletely absorbed, how often and in how many patients, but the problem is probably sizable.

Drugs that undergo extensive but saturable first-pass metabolism in the liver present special problems for slow-release formulation. In the case of such drugs the percentage of a dose that reaches the systemic circulation unchanged may decrease as the rate of intestinal absorption is slowed. In extreme cases a drug can thus almost totally lose its bioavailability by the oral route.

Another conceivable problem with slow-release preparations is the possibility of precipitate release of the drug under some circumstances. Since the drug dose in a slow-release formulation needs to be greater than in the usual dosage form, such an accident could lead to toxic effects. It has, therefore, been recommended that drugs with a small therapeutic index should not be administered in slow-release preparations. However, a mishap of this kind has never been convincingly demonstrated and should be preventable by appropriate production controls.

## 5.2 Clinical Performance of Slow-release Preparations

A very large number of drugs have been marketed in slow-release preparations. This even includes some drugs whose elimination half-life is long enough to render such formulation quite superfluous (table III). The time course of absorption of active drug in the human gastrointestinal tract from many, though by no means all, slow-release preparations has been studied (Campbell and Morrison, 1962; Nelson, 1963; Lazarus et al., 1964; Ballard, 1978). Unfortunately, most of these investigations suffer from such major deficiencies that they do not tell us what we need to know.

Many studies on slow-release preparations have been totally uncontrolled and have not included comparisons with more frequent administration of proportionately smaller doses in fast-release preparations or in solution. This problem is compounded when, as has often been the case, the criteria for effectiveness and time course of absorption have been subjective responses rather than measurable pharmacodynamic parameters or chemical determinations of absorbed drug in blood or urine. The few adequately controlled objective studies, on the other hand, have usually employed normal, young, fasting volunteers. It still needs emphasis that satisfactory absorption from a drug product by such an individual does not guarantee the same in a sick patient with multiple nervous, circulatory and intrinsic mechanisms for disturbed bowel function who is concomitantly receiving other drugs and unpredictably ingesting various foods (Koch-Weser, 1974; Prescott, 1974; Parsons, 1977; Welling, 1977). From the clinical perspective adequate definition of the time course and completeness of absorption of a drug from any dosage form requires study under clinical conditions.

With these important reservations one may judge from the published studies that some slow-release formulations of certain drugs give satisfactory clinical results when administered less frequently than usual preparations of these drugs. Such formulations enable longer dosage intervals for drugs like procainamide (Graffner et al.,

1975) and theophylline (Bell and Bigley, 1978) which, because of their short half-lives (Koch-Weser and Klein, 1971; Ellis et al., 1976), must be given with inconvenient frequency in ready-release tablets. Other slow-release preparations, however, quite clearly make the contained drug partly and unpredictably bio-unavailable as judged by objective pharmacodynamic or pharmacokinetic criteria. Two examples from many must suffice. In a well-controlled clinical trial absorption of iron from a slow-release formulation of ferrous sulphate was up to 10 times less complete and far more variable than from a standard tablet (Crosland-Taylor and Keeling, 1965). As compared to a ready-release gelatin capsule, a slow-release formulation of papaverine decreased the degree of peripheral vasodilation obtained in patients with arteriosclerosis obliterans (Lee et al., 1978). Wide individual variation in response to slow-release formulations is very common. Clinicians are thus well advised to doubt equivalent and reliable bioavailability of a drug from a slow-release preparation unless it has been demonstrated by appropriate measurements in controlled studies on the specific formulation.

## 6. Overall Clinical Perspective

Slow-release preparations are clearly unnecessary for drugs that do not need to exert a sustained action. They are equally redundant in the case of drugs whose therapeutic concentration range is so wide or whose elimination is so slow that the dosage interval can be conveniently long even when fast-release preparations are used. Finally, they are superfluous when the pharmacodynamic action of a drug is long even though the elimination half-life is not.

Slow-release preparations are impractical for drugs that must be administered in large amounts. They should not be employed for drugs that are incompletely absorbed even when administered in fast-release preparations. They can further complicate and render ineffective therapy with drugs that undergo extensive first-pass metabolism.

Slow-release preparations are capable of and useful for increasing the required dosage interval for some drugs from a few hours to 6 to 8 hours. To decrease the necessary frequency of dosing from 4 times a day or more to 2 or 3 times daily is unquestionably convenient for patients and probably increases compliance of some patients. On the other hand, a twice daily dosage schedule is perfectly acceptable to almost all patients and there is no good evidence that it is less well complied with than a once-a-day regimen. Furthermore, in many patients and on many occasions intestinal transit time is such that drug absorption from a slow-release formulation becomes unreliable beyond 6 hours after ingestion. Thus, slow-release formulations cannot predictably prolong the action of a drug by more than this interval.

No slow-release preparation should be marketed unless its ability to prolong absorption predictably without sacrificing bioavailability has been demonstrated in suitable patient populations. Clinicians should not risk sacrificing effectiveness of drug therapy in order to achieve a minor patient convenience. They should also remember that the cost of slow-release preparations is almost always twice or more and occasionally 10 to 20 times that of ordinary formulations containing the same amount of drug. Unnecessary drug costs are socially unacceptable and, when borne by the patient, unquestionably decrease compliance.

It is difficult to avoid the conclusion that many slow-release preparations have been created for commercial reasons and not to answer any valid pharmacotherapeutic need. From the clinical perspective, even a reliably performing slow-release preparation is justified only when it increases the effectiveness and safety of the incorporated drug.

## References

Ballard, B.E.: An overview of prolonged action drug dosage forms; in Sustained and Controlled Release Drug Delivery Systems, p.1-69 (Marcel Dekker, New York 1978).

Ballard, B.E. and Nelson, E.: Prolonged-action pharmaceuticals; in Remington's Pharmaceutical Sciences, 15th ed., p.1618-1643 (Mack, Eaton 1975).

Bechgaard, H. and Ladefoged, K.: Distribution of pellets in the gastrointestinal tract. The influence on transit time exerted by the density and diameter of pellets. Journal fo Pharmacy and Pharmacology 30: 690-692 (1978).

Bell, T. and Bigley, J.: Sustained-release theophylline therapy for chronic childhood asthma. Pediatrics 62: 352-358 (1978).

Blackwell, B.: Patient compliance. New England Journal of Medicine 289: 249-252 (1973).

Campbell, J.A. and Morrison, A.B.: Oral prolonged-action medication. Journal of the American Medical Association 181: 102-105 (1962).

Crosland-Taylor, P. and Keeling, D.H.: A trial of slow-release tablets of ferrous sulphate. Current Therapeutic Research 7: 244-248 (1965).

Davenport, H.W.: Physiology of the Digestive Tract, 2nd ed. (Year Book Medical Publishers, Chicago 1966).

Ellis, E.F.: Koysooko, R. and Levy, G.: Pharmacokinetics of theophylline in children with asthma. Pediatrics 58: 542-547 (1976).

Feinblatt, T.M. and Ferguson, E.A. Jr.: Timed-disintegration capsules; an in vivo roentgenographic study. New England Journal of Medicine 254: 940-943 (1956).

Graffner, C.; Johnsson, G. and Sjogren, J.: Pharmacokinetics of procainamide intravenously and orally as conventional and slow-release tablets. Clinical Pharmacology and Therapeutics 17: 414-423 (1975).

Green, M.A.: One year's experience with sustained release antihistamine medication; experimental and clinical study. Annals of Allergy 12: 273-283 (1954).

Greenblatt, D.J.; Shader, R.I.; Harmatz, J.S.; Franke, K. and Koch-Weser, J.: Absorption rate, blood concentrations, and early response to oral chlordiazepoxide. American Journal of Psychiatry 134: 559-562 (1977).

Hinton, J.M.; Lennard-Jones, J.E. and Young, A.C.: A new method for studying gut transit times using radiopaque markers. Gut 10: 842-847 (1969).

Jollow, D.J. and Brodie, B.B.: Mechanisms of drug absorption and of drug solution. Pharmacology 8: 21-32 (1972).

Koch-Weser, J.: Serum drug concentrations as therapeutic guides. New England Journal of Medicine 287: 227-231 (1972).

Koch-Weser, J.: Bioavailability of drugs. New England Journal of Medicine 291: 233-237, 503-506 (1974).

Koch-Weser, J.: The value of serum concentration determinations in drug therapy; in Shanks (Ed) Topics in Therapeutics 3, p.61-75 (Pitman Medical, Tunbridge Wells 1977).

Koch-Weser, J. and Klein, S.W.: Procainamide dosage schedules, plasma concentrations and clinical effects. Journal of the American Medical Association 215: 1454-1460 (1971).

Lazarus, J. and Cooper, J.: Absorption, testing, and clinical evaluation of oral prolonged-action drugs. Journal of Pharmaceutical Sciences 50: 715-732 (1961).

Lazarus, J.; Pagliery, M. and Lachman, J.: Factors influencing the release of a drug from a prolonged-action matrix. Journal of Pharmaceutical Sciences 53: 798-802 (1964).

Lee, B.Y.; Sakamoto, H.; Trainor, F.; Brody, G. and Cho, Y.W.: Comparison of soft gelatin capsule versus sustained release formulation of papaverine HCl: vasodilation and plasma levels. International Journal of Clinical Pharmacology 16: 32-39 (1978).

Levy, G.: Bioavailability, clinical effectiveness, and the public interest. Pharmacology 8: 33-43 (1972).

Nelson, E.: Pharmaceuticals for prolonged action. Clinical Pharmacology and Therapeutics 4: 283-292 (1963).

Parsons, M.E.: Gastrointestinal secretion and motility. Pharmacology and Therapeutics 5: 182-190 (1979).

Parsons, R.L.: Drug absorption in gastrointestinal disease with particular reference to malabsorption syndromes. Clinical Pharmacokinetics 2: 45-60 (1977).

Prescott, L.F.: Gastrointestinal absorption of drugs. Medical Clinics of North America 58: 907-916 (1974).

Schanker, L.S.: Absorption of drugs from the rat colon. Journal of Pharmacology and Experimental Therapeutics 126: 283-290 (1959).

Schanker, L.S.: Mechanism of drug absorption and distribution. Annual Review of Pharmacology 1: 29-34 (1961).

Schanker, L.S.: Drug absorption; in LaDu, Mandel and Way (Eds) Fundamentals of Drug Metabolism and Drug Disposition, p.21-43 (Williams and Wilkins, Baltimore 1971).

Spiro, H.M.: Clinical Gastroenterology, 2nd ed., p.394-412 (Macmillan, New York 1977).

Stewart, R.B. and Cluff, L.E.: A review of medication errors and compliance in ambulant patients. Clinical Pharmacology and Therapeutics 13: 463-468 (1972).

Welling, P.G.: Influence of food and diet on gastrointestinal drug absorption; a review. Journal of Pharmacokinetics and Biopharmaceutics 5: 291-334 (1977).

## Discussion

*A.H. Beckett* (London): I completely disagree. Let me take an example. Try to protect against vomiting in cancer chemotherapy using L-hyoscyamine (the active isomer of atropine). Believe me, you cannot do it. But using sustained release L-hyoscyamine in a dose of 2mg, we have 85% success in stopping vomiting for 20 hours. It is quite ridiculous to say that because we have something with a long biological or half-life, we cannot improve it with sustained release. Of course, we can. Fenfluramine is another example. There is less sedation if it is given in a sustained release formulation.

*J. Koch-Weser*: If you can demonstrate in controlled studies that a sustained release preparation offers a definite clinical advantage, either in effectiveness or in reduction of side effects, then a slow release preparation is justified and I would not disagree with its use. What I am saying is that there are very few drugs that have been marketed in sustained release preparations that have been shown to be superior in that form in controlled clinical studies.

*A.H. Beckett*: Today we would never dream of putting out a sustained release preparation without evidence of complete bioavailability. Even the regulatory bodies would surely not accept a sustained release product without proof of bioavailability not only in volunteers but also in patients.

*J. Koch-Weser*: I am not only in agreement with you but also with the regulatory agencies. What I am pointing out is that today, there are still on the market (at least in the USA) a large number of sustained release preparations which have never been examined from this point of view. If you and I agree that these preparations should be examined, so much the better.

*M. Hendeles* (Iowa City): If what Professor Beckett says is true, then why did the USA government recently attempt to place theophylline under the maximum allowable wholesale cost which would encourage pharmacists to dispense a generic equivalent?

*J. Koch-Weser*: Without having determined that they were in fact therapeutically equivalent?

*M. Hendeles*: With actually having sufficient documentation that many formulations vary!

*G.S. Banker*: The Food and Drug Administration is currently assessing the bioavailability of a number of sustained release products. There are some truly terrible products on the market. The best selling papaverine product has about a 20% bioavailability.

# 22

# Drug Absorption Interactions

*Pertti J. Neuvonen*

Department of Clinical Pharmacology, University of Helsinki

Patients are often prescribed several drugs simultaneously and although this polypharmacotherapy usually causes no problems, clinically significant drug interactions may occur. There are several possible mechanisms of interaction; one potentially important level at which interactions occur is during drug absorption.

## 1. Mechanisms of Drug Interaction During Gastrointestinal Absorption

During absorption drugs may, at least theoretically, interact in many different ways. Some possible mechanisms are given in table I.

This list of potential mechanisms of absorption interactions is not complete and, the clinical relevance of certain mechanisms is unclear.

### 1.1 Physical Properties of Gastrointestinal Contents

Drugs may influence physical properties of gastrointestinal secretions such as volume, composition, viscosity and osmotic pressure. As a result the de-aggregation, dissolution and diffusion rates of other drugs may be changed (Levy and Rao, 1972).

An increase in osmotic pressure tends to inhibit drug absorption. Furthermore, the absorption of some drugs is prevented when they are sequestered in a lipoid substance. Thus the absorption of the fat-soluble vitamins A, D and K is reduced by the use of mineral oil. Neomycin may disrupt the intraluminar micellar phase of fat absorption and impair the absorption of fat-soluble vitamins (Barrowman et al., 1973).

In general, however, these types of drug interaction are seldom of clinical significance.

### 1.2 Mucosal Permeability and Active Transport

Neomycin, p-aminosalicylic acid (PAS) and colchicine have toxic effects on the intestinal mucosa and may cause a malabsorption syndrome. As a result, the absorption of drugs such as digoxin, iron, folate and vitamin $B_{12}$ may be reduced. Malab-

*Table I.* Possible mechanisms of drug absorption interactions

Changes in physical properties of gastrointestinal contents
Changes in mucosal permeability and active transport
Changes in gastrointestinal blood flow
Changes in first-pass metabolism
Changes in pH of gastrointestinal fluids
Changes in gastric emptying
Changes in gastrointestinal motility
Physicochemical interactions in the gastrointestinal tract

sorption of vitamin $B_{12}$ has also been detected in patients using biguanides or anticonvulsants.

Drugs, such as methyldopa and levodopa may be absorbed by active transport from the small intestine. Substances of a similar nature might be able to compete for this carrier system. Also, inhibitors of the cell metabolism could, at least theoretically, prevent active transport. Such interactions are of academic rather than practical importance.

## 1.3 Gastrointestinal Blood Flow

Changes in blood flow have been shown to alter the rate of drug absorption in isolated organs of animals and some drugs can greatly modify splanchnic blood flow in humans. It is not known, however, if drug-induced changes in blood flow modify the absorption of other drugs to a clinically significant extent.

## 1.4 First-pass Metabolism

Presystemic drug metabolism may occur not only in the liver and intestinal mucosa but also in gut bacteria. Drugs such as propranolol, alprenolol, verapamil, lignocaine and chlormethiazole, are extensively metabolised during their first-pass and the fraction reaching the systemic circulation unchanged may be only about 10 to 30%. Certain other drugs, which inhibit or induce drug metabolism or alter the intestinal flora, could change the systemic availability of those drugs previously mentioned.

We have studied the effect of alcohol on the bioavailability of chlormethiazole. Relatively high doses of alcohol were ingested with chlormethiazole and blood ethanol concentrations were 1 to 1.5mg/ml during the study. Alcohol seemed to double the bioavailability of oral chlormethiazole (fig. 1; Neuvonen et al., to be published).

The bioavailability of drugs with high first-pass metabolism may be reduced by antiepileptic drugs or other enzyme-inducing agents. However, there are few human studies on these potentially important interactions involving first-pass metabolism.

## 1.5 pH of Gastrointestinal Fluids

Drug-induced changes in the pH of gastrointestinal fluids may have complex and unpredictable effects on the absorption of other drugs.

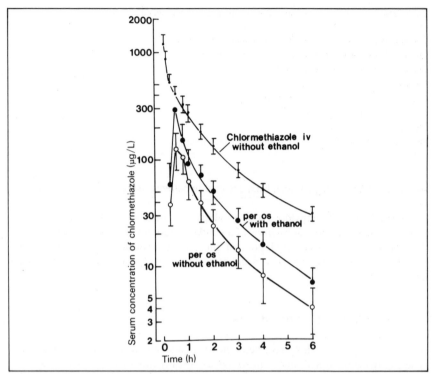

*Fig. 1.* Effect of alcohol ingestion on the bioavailability of chlormethiazole (192mg base) in healthy volunteers.

Most drugs are either weak bases or weak acids. They are usually absorbed better through the lipid membranes when they are in a more lipid-soluble form, i.e., unionised. According to the pH partition theory, raising the pH should decrease the rate of absorption of weakly acidic drugs but increase that of weakly basic drugs. However, the rate of absorption of acidic drugs such as sulphonamides and aspirin is actually increased by the simultaneous ingestion of antacids (Cooke and Hunt, 1970).

A change in pH may have quite opposite effects on lipid-solubility and the dissolution rate of a drug as well as on gastric emptying. For many drugs, the effects of pH on dissolution and gastric emptying seem to be more important than effects on ionisation.

Changes in pH affect the *rate* of absorption and usually not the total *extent* of absorption, provided that the drugs are not acid-labile. Absorption interactions mediated by changes of pH relatively seldom have clinical significance.

## 1.6 Gastric Emptying

Drugs are poorly absorbed from the stomach. Thus the rate of gastric emptying is a limiting factor for their absorption, and a drug which modifies gastric emptying may considerably alter the absorption of other drugs. Accordingly, drugs with anticholinergic properties, narcotic analgesics (fig. 2), aluminium hydroxide, etc. may retard, whereas metoclopramide may accelerate, the absorption of other drugs taken simultaneously (Gothoni et al., 1972b; Nimmo et al., 1973, 1975; Hurwitz, 1977).

Changes in gastric emptying rate usually affect the rate of drug absorption and not the total amount absorbed. However, the therapeutic effect might be totally lost if an adequate drug concentration is not reached, because of slow absorption. Drugs such as levodopa and penicillins are metabolised or inactivated in the stomach and delayed gastric emptying might decrease their bioavailability (Nimmo, 1976; Prescott, 1974).

## 1.7 Gastrointestinal Motility

Changes in gastrointestinal motility caused by a drug may alter both the rate and the extent of absorption of other drugs. Thus, oral propantheline decreases the rate but increases the total extent of absorption of hydrochlorothiazide (Beermann and Groschinsky-Grind, 1978). Anticholinergic agents may increase (fig. 3), and meto-

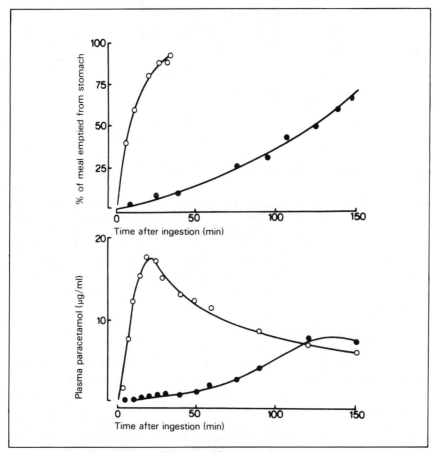

*Fig. 2.* The effect of pethidine (150mg im ●) on gastric emptying and paracetamol absorption compared with saline injection (○) in 1 volunteer (Nimmo et al. 1975, with permission).

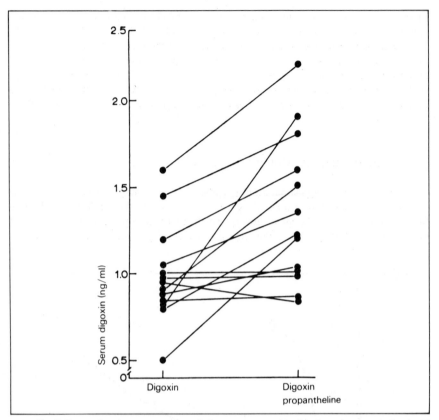

*Fig. 3.* Serum digoxin concentrations during treatment with digoxin and propantheline in 13 patients on digoxin therapy (Manninen et al. 1973, with permission).

clopramide decrease, serum steady-state concentration of digoxin if products with low bioavailability are used (Manninen et al., 1973). If the dissolution rate of a drug is very low, it is more liable to interactions mediated by changes in gastrointestinal motility. Similarly, special formulations such as slow-release or sustained-release tablets are more likely to be affected than conventional products. Sometimes increased absorption caused by an anticholinergic agent is manifest only in patients with a certain pathological condition such as malabsorption or diarrhoea.

## 1.8 Physicochemical Interactions

Certain drugs may form various complexes in the gastrointestinal tract. These complexes may have quite different solubility properties from the individual components. Accordingly, absorption could be greatly decreased or, in some cases even, increased.

Cations such as aluminium, calcium, magnesium, zinc and iron have a high affinity for tetracyclines. *In vitro* they rapidly form tetracycline-metal complexes, many of which are practically insoluble. If antacids containing, for example, aluminium are ingested simultaneously with tetracyclines the absorption of these antibiotics is greatly reduced (Waisbren and Hueckel, 1950; Albert and Rees, 1956; Neuvonen et al., 1970; Penttila et al., 1975).

Basic anion-exchange resins such as cholestyramine bind, in addition to bile acids, acidic drugs such as warfarin, thyroxine, aspirin and digitoxin. Basic and neutral drugs are only slightly bound or not at all (Northcutt et al., 1969).

Kaolin-pectin suspension binds many different drugs including lincomycin, tetracycline and digoxin (Albert et al., 1978). Interestingly, certain PAS granules contain bentonite, a kaolin-like mineral, which prevents the absorption of rifampicin ingested simultaneously with the PAS (Boman et al., 1975).

Magnesium trisilicate decreases both the rate and the extent of nitrofurantoin absorption (Naggar and Khalil, 1979) and activated charcoal usually reduces drug absorption.

The physicochemical interactions mentioned above decrease absorption but, interestingly enough, magnesium hydroxide may increase the absorption of bishydroxycoumarin. Formation of a soluble bishydroxycoumarin-magnesium chelate has been suggested as a cause of this interaction (Ambre and Fischer, 1973).

## 2. Iron-tetracycline Interaction

The interaction between iron and tetracyclines has been studied in more detail than other examples mentioned and can be used as a model physicochemical interaction.

Ferric and ferrous ions have a high affinity for all tetracyclines, forming insoluble chelates with them. When iron tablets are ingested simultaneously with tetracyc-

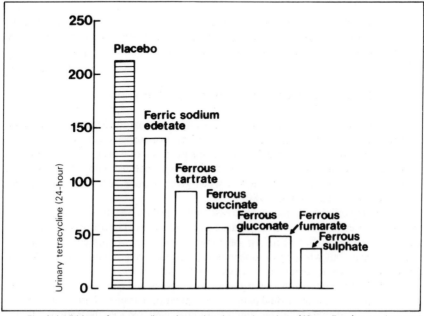

*Fig. 4.* Inhibition of tetracycline absorption by various iron (40mg Fe$^{++}$) salts ingested simultaneously with 500mg of tetracycline (Neuvonen and Turakka, 1974).

lines the absorption of both tetracyclines and iron is reduced (Heinrich et al., 1974; Neuvonen et al., 1975).

The extent of inhibition, however, depends on several factors. When 40mg of iron, in the form of ferrous sulphate tablets, was ingested simultaneously with therapeutic doses of tetracycline or oxytetracycline, the absorption of the antibiotics was reduced to half. The same dose of iron reduced the absorption of methacycline and doxycycline to about 10% of the control values (Neuvonen et al., 1970).

The ability of various iron compounds to liberate ferrous or ferric ions in the upper gastrointestinal tract, before the tetracyclines are absorbed, is essential for this interaction. When the inhibition of tetracycline absorption is measured (fig. 4), [Neuvonen and Turakka, 1974], the order of activity of different iron salts in preventing tetracycline absorption is the same as the order of intestinal absorption of the iron compounds (Brise and Hallberg, 1962).

Pharmaceutical properties are important and the interaction is considerably less if sustained-release or slow-release preparations of iron are used instead of rapidly dissolving ones. Slow release of iron leaves more time for the tetracyclines to be absorbed (Mattila et al., 1972).

The interaction between iron and tetracyclines can be avoided if a time interval of 3 hours is allowed between oral ingestion of these drugs (Gothoni et al., 1972a). Certain tetracyclines, such as doxycycline are secreted to some degree into the gut lumen, with subsequent reabsorption. Thus interaction with the secreted fraction cannot be avoided by the 3-hour interval in dosing but, quantitatively, this interaction is of limited importance (Neuvoven and Penttila, 1974).

# 3. Adsorption by Activated Charcoal

Activated charcoal *in vitro* adsorbs many different drugs and also inhibits the absorption of several drugs *in vivo*. This physicochemical interaction can be used in the treatment of acute intoxication to reduce further absorption of the poison.

## 3.1 Effect of Activated Charcoal on Drug Absorption

Figure 5 demonstrates the ability of activated charcoal to reduce the absorption of some drugs. Activated charcoal (50g) was given as a suspension in water, either 5 minutes or 1 hour after the ingestion of therapeutic doses of 6 drugs. Absorption was usually inhibited more than 95% when charcoal was ingested within 5 minutes but the efficacy of charcoal was much less when given 1 hour later (Neuvonen et al., 1978; Neuvonen and Elonen, 1980).

*In vivo* the efficacy of charcoal increases with the dose despite a constant ratio between the doses of charcoal and the drug to be adsorbed. The absorbed fraction of aspirin is about 80% when 1g of aspirin and 10g of charcoal is ingested simultaneously, but when 5g of aspirin is ingested with 50g of charcoal the fraction absorbed decreases to about 20% (Levy and Tsuchiya, 1972).

Both the time interval between the intake of drugs and charcoal, and the rate of drug absorption in the individual patient are of great importance. With slow drug absorption activated charcoal given after 1 hour effectively reduces absorption, whereas in a subject with rapid absorption the effect of charcoal is small.

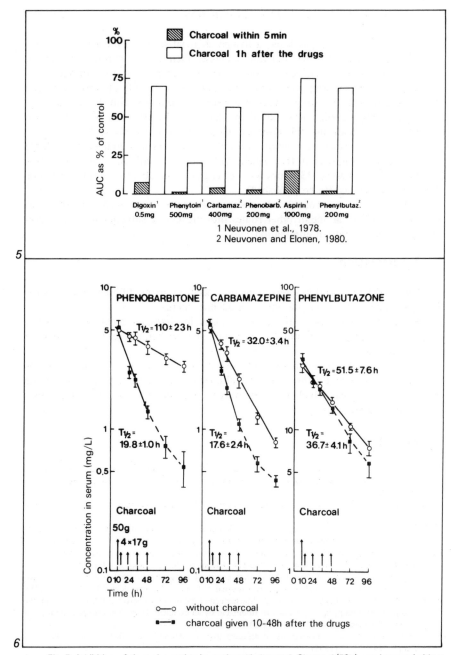

Fig. 5. Inhibition of drug absorption by activated charcoal. Charcoal (50g) was ingested either within 5 minutes or 1 hour of the intake of other drugs, or the drugs were ingested without charcoal (control). AUC = area under the plasma concentration-time curve. (Neuvonen et al., 1978; Neuvonen and Elonen, 1980).

Fig. 6. The effect of multiple oral doses of activated charcoal on the elimination of phenobarbitone, carbamazepine and phenylbutazone in 5 subjects.

## 3.2 Effect of Charcoal on Drug Elimination

When given in multiple doses, activated charcoal seems to prevent the enteral recirculation of several drugs and thus increases their rate of elimination (fig. 6). Charcoal suspension was started 10 hours after single therapeutic doses of phenobarbitone, carbamazepine and phenylbutazone. The mean half-life of phenobarbitone was reduced from 110 hours in the control period to 20 hours with charcoal and the half-life of carbamazepine was halved by charcoal. The effect on phenylbutazone elimination was small but still significant (Neuvonen and Elonen, 1980).

The rate of dapsone elimination in healthy volunteers was doubled by multiple doses of charcoal suspension. In a patient with dapsone overdosage, the serum half-life of dapsone was about 33 hours without charcoal and about 11 hours after four 20g doses of charcoal (to be published).

Activated charcoal probably adsorbs that fraction of drug which is secreted into the intestine either via bile or other routes thus preventing subsequent reabsorption and increasing the rate of elimination.

## 4. Conclusion

During drug absorption interactions may occur by many different mechanisms. Some potential interactions are only of academic interest.

Some drug interactions based on changes in first-pass metabolism, gastric emptying, gastrointestinal motility or on certain physicochemical reactions, may have clinical importance.

Activated charcoal can reduce the absorption of drugs in acute intoxications when given very early. Furthermore, in multiple doses charcoal may increase the rate of elimination of drugs which are extensively secreted into the gut lumen and subsequently reabsorbed.

## References

Albert, K.S.; DeSante, K.A.; Welch, R.D. and DiSanto, A.R.: Pharmacokinetic evaluation of a drug interaction between kaolin-pectin and clindamycin. Journal of Pharmaceutical Sciences 67: 1579-1582 (1978).

Albert, A. and Rees, C.W.: Avidity of the tetracyclines for the cations of metals. Nature 177: 433-434 (1956).

Ambre, J.J. and Fischer, L.J.: Effect of coadministration of aluminium and magnesium hydroxides on absorption of anticoagulants in man. Clinical Pharmacology and Therapeutics 14: 231-237 (1973).

Barrowman, J.A.; D'Mello, A. and Herxheimer, A.: A single dose of neomycin impairs absorption of vitamin A (retinol) in man. European Journal of Clinical Pharmacology 5: 199-202 (1973).

Beermann, B. and Groschinsky-Grind, M.: Enhancement of the gastrointestinal absorption of hydrochlorothiazide by propantheline. European Journal of Clinical Pharmacology 13: 385-387 (1978).·

Boman, G.; Lundgren, P. and Stjernstrom, G.: Mechanism of the inhibitory effect of PAS granules on the absorption of rifampicin: Adsorption of rifampicin by an excipient, bentonite. European Journal of Clinical Pharmacology 8: 293-299 (1975).

Brise, H. and Hallberg, L.: Absorbability of different iron compounds. Acta Medica Scandinavica 171 (Suppl. 376): 23-37 (1962).

Cooke, A.R. and Hunt, J.N.: Absorption of acetylsalicylic acid from unbuffered and buffered gastric contents. American Journal of Digestion Diseases 15: 95-102 (1970).

Gothoni, G.; Neuvonen, P.J.; Mattila, M. and Hackman, R.: Iron-tetracycline interaction: Effect of time interval between the drugs. Acta Medica Scandinavica 191: 409-411 (1972a).

Gothoni, G.; Pentikainen, P.; Vapaatalo, H.J.; Hackman, R. and af Bjorksten, K.A.: Absorption of antibiotics: influence of metoclopramide and atropine on serum levels of pivampicillin and tetracycline. Annals of Clinical Research 4: 228-232 (1972b).

Heinrich, H.C.; Oppitz, K.H. and Gabbe, E.E.: Hemmung der Eisenabsorption beim Menschen durch Tetracyclin. Klinische Wochenschrift 52: 493-498 (1974).

Hurwitz, A.: Antacid therapy and drug kinetics. Clinical Pharmacokinetics 2: 269-280 (1977).

Levy, G. and Rao, B.K.: Enhanced intestinal absorption of riboflavin from sodium alginate solution in man. Journal of Pharmaceutical Sciences 61: 279-280 (1972).

Levy, G. and Tsuchiya, T.: Effect of activated charcoal on aspirin absorption in man. Clinical Pharmacology and Therapeutics 13: 317-322 (1972).

Manninen, V.; Apajalahti, A.; Melin, J. and Karesoja, M.: Altered absorption of digoxin in patients given propantheline and metoclopramide. Lancet 1: 398-401 (1973).

Mattila, M.J.; Neuvonen, P.J.; Gothoni, G. and Hackman, C.R.: Interference of iron preparations and milk with the absorption of tetracyclines; in Excerpta Medica International Congress Series No. 254: Toxicological Problems of Drug Combinations, p.128-133 (1972).

Naggar, V.F. and Khalil, S.A.: Effect of magnesium trisilicate on nitrofurantoin absorption. Clinical Pharmacology and Therapeutics 25: 857-863 (1979).

Neuvonen, P.J.; Elfving, S.M. and Elonen, E.: Reduction of absorption of digoxin, phenytoin and aspirin by activated charcoal in man. European Journal of Clinical Pharmacology 13: 213-218 (1978).

Neuvonen, P.J. and Elonen, E.: Effect of activated charcoal on absorption and elimination of phenobarbitone, carbamazepine and phenylbutazone in man. European Journal of Clinical Pharmacology 17: 51-57 (1980).

Neuvonen, P.J.; Gothoni, G.; Hackman, R. and af Bjorksten, K.: Interference of iron with the absorption of tetracyclines in man. British Medical Journal 4: 532-534 (1970).

Neuvonen, P.J.; Pentikainen, P.J. and Gothoni, G.: Inhibition of iron absorption by tetracycline. British Journal of Clinical Pharmacology 2: 94-96 (1975).

Neuvonen, P.J. and Penttila, O.: Effect of oral ferrous sulphate on the half-life of doxycycline in man. European Journal of Clinical Pharmacology 7: 361-363 (1974).

Neuvonen, P.J. and Turakka, H.: Inhibitory effects of various iron salts on the absorption of tetracycline in man. European Journal of Clinical Pharmacology 7: 357-360 (1974).

Nimmo, J.; Heading, R.C.; Tothill, P. and Prescott, L.F.: Pharmacological modification of gastric emptying: Effects of propantheline and metoclopramide on paracetamol absorption. British Medical Journal 1: 587-589 (1973).

Nimmo, W.S.: Drugs, diseases and altered gastric emptying. Clinical Pharmacokinetics 1: 189-203 (1976).

Nimmo, W.S.; Heading, R.C.; Wilson, J.; Tothill, P. and Prescott, L.F.: Inhibition of gastric emptying and drug absorption by narcotic analgesics. British Journal of Clinical Pharmacology 2: 509-513 (1975).

Northcutt, R.C.; Stiel, J.N.; Hollifield, J.W. and Stant, E.C. Jr.: The influence of cholestyramine on thyroxine absorption. Journal of the American Medical Association 208: 1857-1861 (1969).

Penttila, O.; Hurme, H. and Neuvonen, P.J.: Effect of zinc sulphate on the absorption of tetracycline and doxycycline in man. European Journal of Clinical Pharmacology 9: 131-134 (1975).

Prescott, L.F.: Drug absorption interactions — gastric emptying; in Morselli, Cohen and Garattini (Eds) Drug Interactions, p.11-20 (Raven, New York 1974).

Waisbren, B.A. and Hueckel, J.S.: Reduced absorption of aureomycin caused by aluminium hydroxide gel (Amphojel). Proceedings of the Society for Experimental Biology and Medicine 73: 73-74 (1950).

## Discussion

*J. Urquhart* (Palo Alto): How do you formulate activated charcoal to put 50g in the stomach?

*P.J. Neuvonen*: It is in granulated form suspended in water and is easily swallowed.

*M. Balali* (Edinburgh): Have you ever noticed delayed absorption because of reversible adsorption by the charcoal?

*P.J. Neuvonen*: This may occur with only a single dose of charcoal and the rate of elimination might increase after some days as a result of delayed release of the drugs from the charcoal.

# 23

# Effects of Food and Drink on Drug Absorption in Man

*Bjorn Beermann*

Department of Medicine, Serafimerlasarettet, Stockholm

When a patient is prescribed a drug he often asks whether he should take it with or without food. As a response to that question a large number of studies on the influence of food and drink on drug absorption has been performed and extensive reviews have been published recently (Welling, 1977; Melander, 1978). The aim of those studies should be to obtain knowledge which will enable us to tell our patients how to take their drugs at an optimal time in relation to meals. However, it is not possible to obtain such information from most studies in which one pharmaceutical preparation of a drug is given with and without a more or less standardised meal because the influence of food on the absorption of drugs varies with the composition and the volume of the meal or the drink. For example: the uptake of the lipophilic compounds griseofulvin and sulphamethoxydiazine is increased considerably when given with a high fat meal instead of a high protein or high carbohydrate meal (fig. 1) [Crounse, 1961; Kaumeier, 1979]. Amoxycillin is poorly soluble in water and is absorbed to a greater extent when swallowed with 250ml water than with 25ml (fig. 2) [Welling et al., 1977]. Thus the uptake of the drug should be tested when administered with English, American and continental breakfast. It should also be tested together with various lunch and dinner dishes.

When all this knowledge is collected the situation should be under control. However, it is obvious that many drug-food interactions depend on what pharmaceutical formulation is used. The uptake of nitrofurantoin from tablets is enhanced substantially when given with food although the absorption of the drug from a suspension is unaffected by a meal (fig. 3) [Rosenberg and Bates, 1976].

In contrast the uptake of 2 esters of erythromycin is unaffected when given as a suspension with food (Sylvester and Josselyn, 1953; Griffith et al., 1960; Hirsch et al., 1960) but is decreased when given as tablets or capsules (Hirsch and Finland, 1959; Clapper et al., 1960). The formulation of aspirin determines whether food influences the extent of absorption or delays absorption (fig. 4) [Bogentoft et al., 1978]. Thus, in order to prescribe a drug at an optimal time in relation to a meal it is necessary to know how a particular brand of the drug behaves together with a particular dish.

Possible mechanisms involved in food-drug interactions are presented in table I.

Table I. Factors involved in drug interactions with food and drink

1. Drug dissolution
2. Binding of drug to food constituents
3. Intraluminal decomposition of drug
4. Gastrointestinal transit time
5. Interference with mucosal transport
6. Net water flux
7. First-pass metabolism

# 1. Drug Dissolution

It is most likely that the food-drug interactions mentioned so far depend on factors involved in disintegration and dissolution of the drug preparation, such as residence time in the stomach, fluid volume, intraluminal pH, fat content of the food and bile flow. It should be possible to avoid such interactions by optimal pharmaceutical formulation of preparations such as capsules with suspensions or oil in water emulsions of drugs with dissolution problems.

There are, however, a few known food-drug interactions which are most likely not related to dissolution problems.

# 2. Binding to Food Constituents

A classical example of complex binding is the chelate binding of tetracyclines with polyvalent metal ions such as calcium, magnesium, zinc and ferric ions. Milk products in particular reduce absorption of tetracyclines. This effect can be abolished by EDTA which binds calcium (fig. 5) [Poiger and Schlatter, 1978].

The absorption of isoniazid is reduced when given with a carbohydrate-rich breakfast (Melander et al., 1976) [fig. 6]. The mechanism is not known. However, isoniazid belongs to the hydrazines which readily react with ketones and aldehydes to form hydrazones (fig. 7). It appears likely that such compounds are formed within the gut when isoniazid is given with a carbohydrate-rich breakfast leading to reduced serum levels of isoniazid.

# 3. Drug Degradation or Activation

The absorption of pivampicillin is reduced when given with a meal (Fernandez et al., 1973). This drug is subjected to hydrolysis of the ester bond when incubated with duodenal juice, a process which is not purely pH-dependent (Swahn, 1976). It is likely that the flow of enzymes after a meal induces hydrolysis of pivampicillin to ampicillin which is less well absorbed than the ester.

The anticholinergic effects of propantheline are inhibited when the drug is given with food (fig. 8) [Ekenved et al., 1977]. The reduction in bioavailability can be explained by the postprandial increase in intragastric pH as propantheline is readily hydrolysed in an environment with pH above 5 (fig. 9) [Beermann et al., 1972].

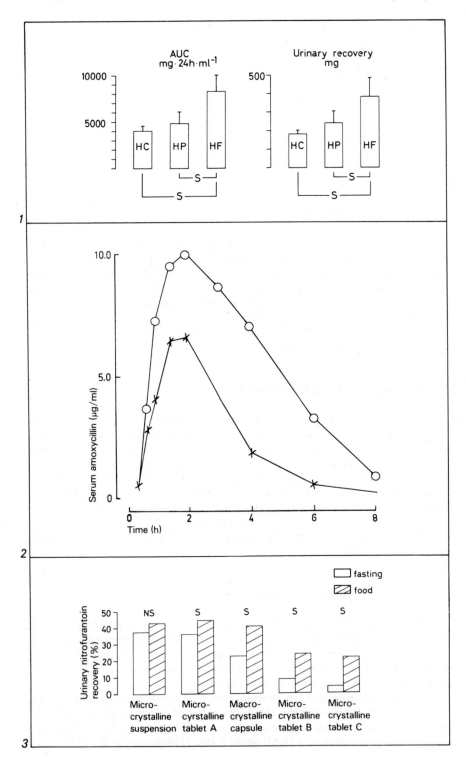

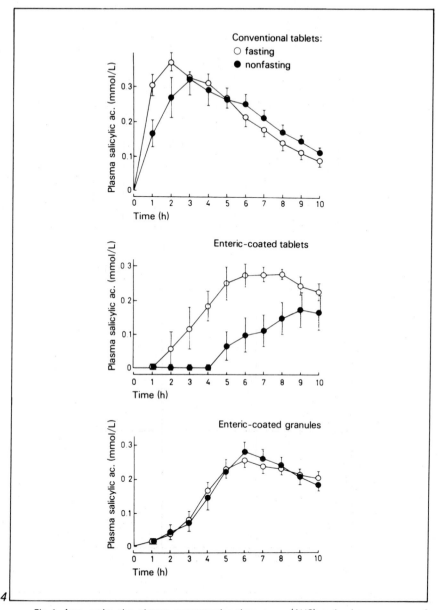

Fig. 1. Area under the plasma concentration-time curve (AUC) and urinary recovery of sulphamethoxydiazine (sulfameter) administered with a high carbohydrate (HC) high protein (HP) and high fat (HF) meal (Kaumeier, 1979 with permission).

Fig. 2. Serum concentrations after 500mg amoxycillin trihydrate given with 25 (x) and 250 (o) ml water (Welling et al., 1977 with permission).

Fig. 3. Urinary recovery of nitrofurantoin after administration as suspension, tablets and capsules with and without a meal (Rosenberg and Bates, 1976 with permission).

Fig. 4. Plasma concentrations of salicylic acid after administration of aspirin (1g) as 3 different pharmaceutical preparations with and without a meal (Bogentoft et al., 1978 with permission).

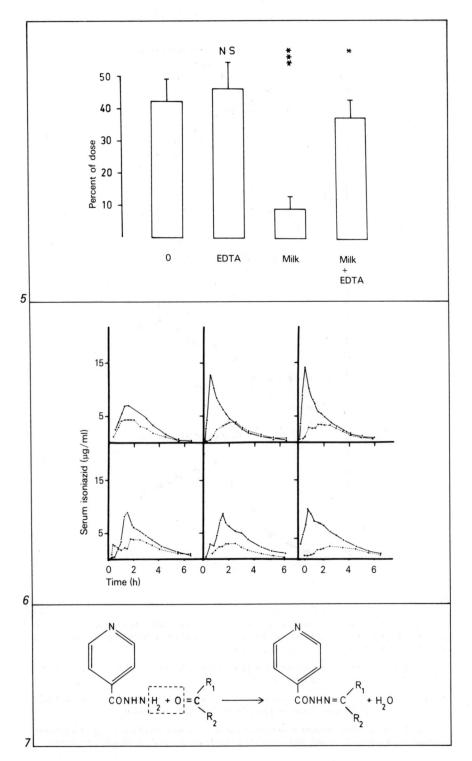

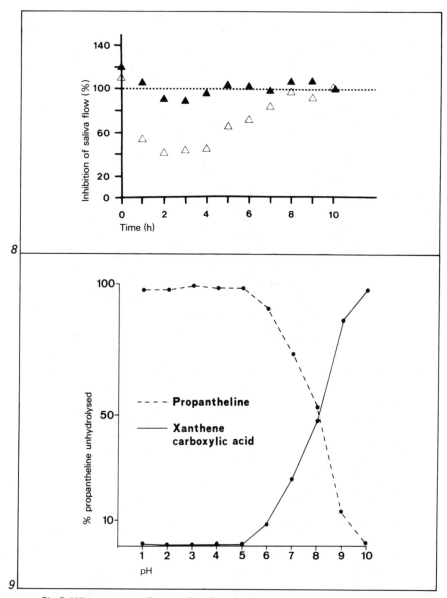

Fig. 5. Urinary recovery of tetracycline after administration with water, EDTA, milk and milk + EDTA (Poiger and Schlatter 1978 with permission).

Fig. 6. Serum concentrations of isoniazid after administration with (---) and without (—) food (Melander et al., 1976 with permission).

Fig. 7. Formation of isoniazid hydrazone.

Fig. 8. Inhibition of stimulated saliva flow by propantheline given with (Δ) and without food (▲) (Ekenved et al., 1977 with permission).

Fig. 9. Hydrolysis of $^{14}$C propantheline incubated for 2 hours in 0.1M buffer solutions of pH 1 to 10 (Beermann et al., 1972 with permission).

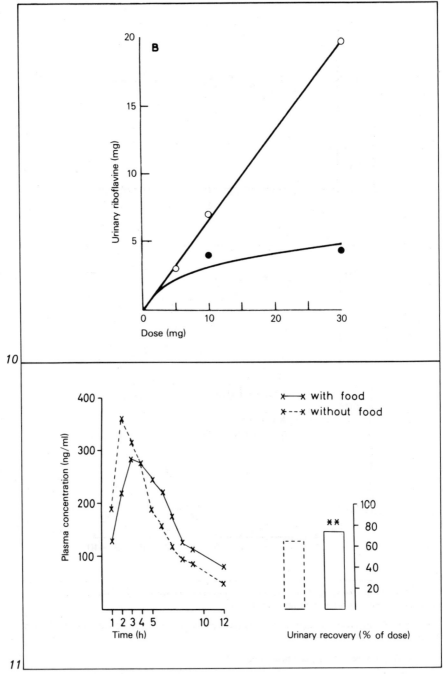

*Fig. 10.* Urinary recovery of riboflavine after administration with (○) and without (●) food (Jusko and Levy 1967 with permission).

*Fig. 11.* Plasma concentrations and urinary recovery of hydrochlorothiazide (75mg) given with and without food (Beermann and Groschinsky-Grind 1978a with permission).

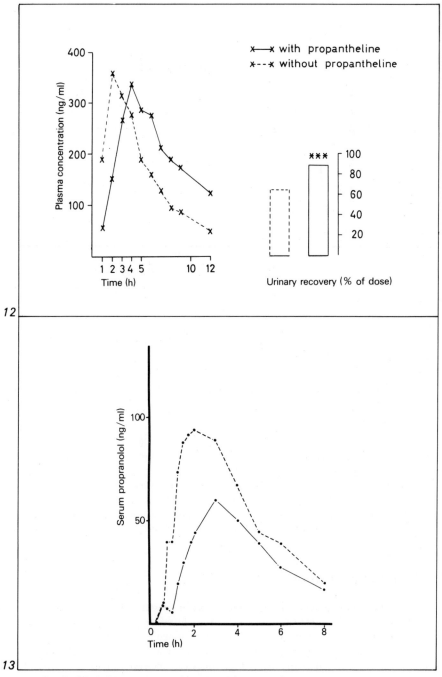

Fig. 12. Serum levels and urinary recovery of hydrochlorothiazide given with and without propantheline (Beermann and Groschinsky-Grind, 1978b with permission).

Fig. 13. Serum concentrations of propranolol after administration (80mg) without (—) and with a meal (---) (Melander et al., 1977 with permission).

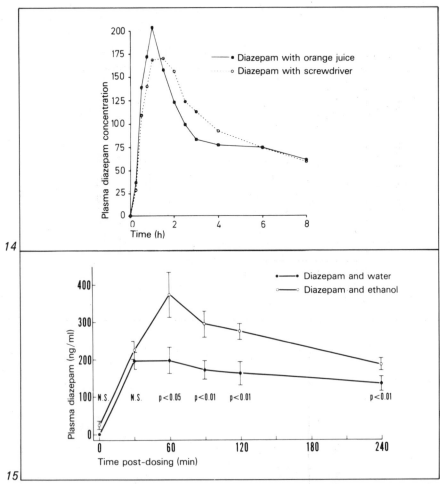

*Fig. 14.* Plasma concentrations of diazepam after administration as a tablet with orange juice and with a 'screwdriver' (Greenblatt et al., 1978 with permission).

*Fig. 15.* Plasma concentrations of diazepam after administration of a crushed tablet (70µg/kg) with water and with a strong drink (Hayes et al., 1977 with permission).

## 4. Intestinal Transit

The absorption process of riboflavin is saturable (fig. 10) [Jusko and Levy, 1967]. The decreased intestinal transit rate in the presence of food increases the up-take as the absorption mechanism will not be saturated.

When hydrochlorothiazide is given as a tablet or a solution to fasting subjects about 65% is recovered in the urine. Food increases the recovery to 75% (fig. 11) and pretreatment with an anticholinergic elevates the recovery to 90% (fig. 12) [Beerman and Groschinsky-Grind, 1978a,b; Jordo et al., 1979]. The uptake of the diuretic is apparently enhanced by a slower gastric emptying rate. As the uptake is the same from a tablet and a solution it is likely that the enhancement of the absorption does

Table II. Effects of food constituents on gastrointestinal absorption of iron

| Increased absorption | Unchanged absorption | Decreased absorption |
|---|---|---|
| Ascorbic acid | Amino acids | Egg yolk |
| Meat | Egg white | Milk |
| Fish | Haemoglobin | Tea |
| Chicken | Coffee | Phytates |
| Thymus | | Bran |

not depend on better dissolution. A dose-dependent absorption process seems to be involved also for this drug.

Changes in the intestinal transit rate also influence the uptake of lithium by a different mechanism. Lithium causes diarrhoea in some patients with subsequently reduced absorption of the drug. A meal prevents the diarrhoea and thereby normalises its absorption (Jeppson and Sjogren, 1975).

## 5. Mucosal Transport

Levodopa is absorbed by a transport system for aminoacids (Granerus et al., 1971). Intake with high-protein food probably diminishes the uptake by competition between the drug and aminoacids (Gillespie et al., 1973).

## 6. Water Flux

Increased net water flux is caused by isotonic and hypotonic solutions. Although such flux enhances the uptake of drugs in rats (Koysooku and Levy, 1974) it does not seem to have been shown in man (Koysooku et al., 1975).

## 7. First-pass Metabolism

Food has been reported to increase bioavailability of metoprolol and propranolol which are absorbed completely in fasting subjects, demonstrating that a meal can decrease first-pass metabolism (fig. 13) [Melander et al., 1977]. It has been demonstrated by means of computer simulations based on a pharmacokinetic perfusion model that transient increases in splanchnic blood flow, typical of those found after a meal, can have significant effects on the availability of high clearance drugs (McLean et al., 1978). Another explanation for the increased availability is competition between the drugs and food constituents for enzyme systems which have probably been developed to metabolise food and not drugs.

For some drugs several mechanisms may operate simultaneously. The uptake of ionised iron is influenced by several food constituents (table II). Factors which increase the absorption have unknown effects on the absorption process per se (Sayers et al., 1973; Bjorn-Rasmussen, 1974; Bjorn-Rasmussen and Hallberg, 1974; Layrisse et al., 1975) while inhibiting factors complex-bind iron (Moore and Dubach,

*Table III*. Effects of ethanol on the gastrointestinal tract

1.    Delayed gastric emptying (Barboriak and Meade, 1970)

2.    Increased gastric secretion of acid and pepsin (Kondo and Magee, 1977)

3.    Increased permeability of the gastric mucosa (Edwards and Silen, 1974)

4.    Decreased biliary and pancreatic secretion (Marin et al., 1973)

1951; Disler et al., 1975). The complexicity of such interactions can be illustrated as follows: let us start with a breakfast composed of coffee, butter, marmalade and white bread. Add a glass of orange juice and the uptake of iron is doubled. Take tea instead of coffee and the effect of the juice is neutralised. If you prefer fibre rich bread the uptake of iron will be reduced. However, if the baker allowed the dough to rise for a long time the content of phytates is reduced with less reduction of iron absorption as a consequence.

Finally I wish to discuss a special type of drink — the common drink. There are several ways in which drinks containing ethanol can alter drug absorption (table III).

Very few studies have been performed but ethanol apparently has no effect on the total absorption of oxazepam (Moosmayer et al., 1976), chlordiazepoxide, thioridazine (Linnoila et al., 1974) and theophylline (Koysooku et al., 1975).

When a diazepam tablet is taken with a cocktail (a 'screwdriver'), the plasma concentrations of diazepam will be the same as when taken with juice (fig. 14) [Greenblatt et al., 1978]. However, if the tablet is crushed and mixed with a strong drink absorption is enhanced considerably (fig. 15) [Hayes et al., 1977].

In conclusion, many food-drink drug interactions appear to depend on dissolution problems which should be avoidable with better pharmaceutical preparations. A small number of interactions seems to be caused by other mechanisms. To detect such mechanisms studies should be performed with drugs in optimal dosage forms.

# References

Barboriak, J.J. and Meade, R.C.: Effect of alcohol on gastric emptying in man. American Journal of Clinical Nutrition 23: 1151-1153 (1970).

Beermann, B. and Groschinsky-Grind, M.: Gastrointestinal absorption of hydrochlorothiazide enhanced by concomitant intake of food. European Journal of Clinical Pharmacology 13: 125-128 (1978a).

Beermann, B. and Groschinsky-Grind, M.: Enhancement of the gastrointestinal absorption of hydrochlorothiazide by propantheline. European Journal of Clinical Pharmacology 13: 385-387 (1978b).

Beerman, B.; Hellstrom, K. and Rosen, A.: On the metabolism of propantheline in man. Clinical Pharmacology and Therapeutics 13: 212-220 (1972).

Bjorn-Rasmussen, E.: Effect of meat on the absorption of food iron in man. An attempt to evaluate the way in which meat acts to promote food iron absorption. Dissertation, Goteborg 1974.

Bjorn-Rasmussen, E. and Hallberg, L.: Iron absorption from maize. Effect of ascorbic acid on iron absorption from maize supplemented with ferrous sulphate. Nutrition and Metabolism 16: 94-100 (1974).

Bogentoft, C.; Carlsson, I.; Ekenved, G. and Magnusson, A.: Influence of food on the absorption of acetylsalicylic acid from enteric-coated dosage forms. European Journal of Clinical Pharmacology 14: 351-355 (1978).

Clapper, W.E.; Mostyn, M. and Meade, G.H.: An evaluation of erythromycin stearate and propionyl erythromycin in normal and hospitalized subjects. Antibiotic Medicine and Clinical Therapy 7: 91 (1960).

Crounse, R.G.: Human pharmacology of griseofulvin: the effect of fat intake on gastrointestinal absorption. Journal of Investigative Dermatology 37: 529-532 (1961).

Disler, P.B.; Lynch, S.R.; Charlton, R.W.; Torrance, J.D.; Bothwell, T.H.; Walker, R.B. and Mayet, F.: The effect of tea on iron absorption. Gut 16: 193-200 (1975).

Edwards, B.G. and Silen, W.: Effect of ethanol, acetylsalicylic acid, acetaminophen and ferrous sulfate on gastric mucosal permeability in man. Surgery 76: 405-412 (1974).

Ekenved, G.; Magnusson, A.; Bodeman, G. and Walan, A.: Influence of food on the effect of pro-pantheline and L-hyoscyamine on salivation. Scandinavian Journal of Gastroenterology 12: 963-966 (1977).

Fernandez, C.A.; Menezes, J.P. and Ximenes, J.: The effect of food on the absorption of pivampicillin and a comparison with the absorption of ampicillin potassium. Journal of International Medical Research 1: 530-533 (1973).

Gillespie, N.G.; Mena, I.; Cotzias, G.S. and Bell, M.A.: Diets affecting treatment of parkinsonism with levodopa. Journal of the American Dietetic Association 62: 525-528 (1973).

Granerus, A.K.; Jagenburg, R.; Rodjer, S. and Svanborg, A.: Phenylalanine absorption and metabolism in parkinsonian patients. British Medical Journal 4: 262-264 (1971).

Greenblatt, D.J.; Shader, R.I.; Weinberger, D.R.; Allen, M.D. and MacLaughlin, D.S.: Effect of a cocktail on diazepam absorption. Psychopharmacology 57: 199-203 (1978).

Griffith, R.S.; Joiner, M. and Kottlowski, H.: Comparison of antibacterial activity in the sera of subjects ingesting propionyl erythromycin lauryl sulfate and erythromycin ethyl carbonate. Antibiotic Medicine and Clinical Therapy 7: 320-326 (1960).

Hayes, S.L.; Pablo, G.; Radomski, T. and Palmer, R.F.: Ethanol and oral diazepam absorption. New England Journal of Medicine 296: 186-189 (1977).

Hirsch, H.A. and Finland, M.: Effect of food on the absorption of erythromycin propionate, erythromycin stearate and triacetyloleandomycin. American Journal of the Medical Sciences 237: 693-708 (1959).

Hirsch, H.A.; Pryles, C.V. and Finland, M.: Effect of food on absorption of a new form of erythromycin propionate. American Journal of the Medical Sciences 239: 198-202 (1960).

Jeppson, J. and Sjogren, J.: The influence of food on side effects and absorption of lithium. Acta Psychiatrica Scandinavica 51: 285-288 (1975).

Jordo, L.; Johnsson, G.; Lundborg, P.; Persson, B.A.; Regardh, C-G. and Ronn, O.: Bioavailability and disposition of metoprolol and hydrochlorothiazide combined in one tablet and of separate doses of hydrochlorothiazide. British Journal of Clinical Pharmacology 7: 563-567 (1979).

Jusko, W.J. and Levy, G.: Absorption, metabolism and excretion of riboflavin 5-phosphate in man. Journal of Pharmaceutical Sciences 56: 58-62 (1967).

Kaumeier, S.: The effect of the composition of food on the absorption of sulfameter. International Journal of Clinical Pharmacology and Biopharmacy 17: 260-263 (1979).

Kondo, T. and Magee, D.F.: The action of intravenous ethanol on gastric secretion. Proceedings of the Society for Experimental Biology and Medicine 156: 299-302 (1977).

Koysooku, R.; Ellis, E.F. and Levy, G.: Effect of ethanol on theophylline absorption in humans. Journal of Pharmaceutical Sciences 64: 299-301 (1975).

Koysooku, R. and Levy, G.: Effect of ethanol on intestinal absorption of theophylline. Journal of Pharmaceutical Sciences 63: 829-834 (1974).

Layrisse, M.; Martinez-Torres, C.; Renzy, M. and Leets, I.: Ferritin iron absorption in man. Blood 45: 689-698 (1975).

Linnoila, M.; Herstrom, O. and Anttila, S.: Serum chlordiazepoxide, diazepam and thioridazine concentrations after the simultaneous ingestion of alcohol or placebo drink. Annals of Clinical Research 6: 4-6 (1974).

Marin, G.A.; Ward, N.L. and Fischer, R.: Effect of ethanol on pancreatic and biliary secretions in humans. American Journal of Digestive Diseases 18: 825-833 (1973).

McLean, A.J.; McNamara, P.J.; du Souich, P.; Gibaldi, M. and Lalka, D.: Food, splanchnic blood flow, and bioavailability of drugs subject to first pass metabolism. Clinical Pharmacology and Therapeutics 24: 5-10 (1978).

Melander, A.: Influence of food on the bioavailability of drugs. Clinical Pharmacokinetics 3: 337-351 (1978).

Melander, A.; Danielson, K.; Hanson, A.; Janson, L.; Rerup, C.; Schersten, B.; Thulin, T. and Wahlin, E.: Reduction of isoniazid bioavailability in normal men by concomitant intake of food. Acta Medica Scandinavica 200: 93-97 (1976).

Melander, A.; Danielson, K.; Schersten, B. and Wahlin, E.: Enhancement of the bioavailability of propranolol and metoprolol by food. Clinical Pharmacology and Therapeutics 22: 108-112 (1977).

Moore, C.V. and Dubach, R.: Observations on the absorption of iron from food tagged with radioiron. Transactions of the Association of American Physicians 64: 245-256 (1951).

Moosmayer, A.; Mallach, H.J. and Staak, M.: Pharmakokinetische Untersuchungen nach oraler Applikation von Oxazepam in Kombination mit Alkohol. Beitrage zur Gerichtlichen Medizin 34: 385-389 (1976).

Poiger, H. and Schlatter, Ch.: Compensation of dietary induced reduction of tetracyclin absorption by simultaneous administration of EDTA. European Journal of Clinical Pharmacology 14: 129-131 (1978).

Rosenberg, H.A. and Bates, T.R.: The influence of food on nitrofurantoin bioavailability. Clinical Pharmacology and Therapeutics 20: 227-232 (1976).

Sayers, M.H.; Lynch, S.R.; Jacobs, P.; Charlton, R.W.; Bothwell, T.H.; Walker, R.B. and Mayet, F.: The effects of ascorbic acid supplementation on the absorption of iron in maize, wheat and soya. British Journal of Haematology 24: 209-218 (1973).

Swahn, A.: Gastrointestinal absorption and metabolism of two $^{35}$S-labelled ampicillin esters. European Journal of Clinical Pharmacology 9: 299-306 (1976).

Sylvester, J.C. and Josselyn, L.E.: Absorption of erythromycin II. Erythromycin stearate. Antibiotics and Chemotherapy 3: 930-932 (1953).

Welling, P.G.: Influence of food and diet on gastrointestinal drug absorption: A review. Journal of Pharmacokinetics and Biopharmaceutics 5: 291-334 (1977).

Welling, P.G.; Huang, H.; Koch, P.A.; Craig, W.A. and Madsen, P.O.: Bioavailability of ampicillin and amoxicillin in fasted and non-fasted subjects. Journal of Pharmaceutical Sciences 66: 549-552 (1977).

## Discussion

*A. Melander* (Malmo): Dr. Beermann has rightly emphasised the complexity of the food and drug issue. I would like to add one simplification and one complication. The simplification relates to the fact that the clinically relevant question is whether food intake influences the *effect* of a drug. Most drugs are 'steady-state drugs' i.e. they are given to reach and maintain a steady-state concentration, the level of which determines the effect. In such cases, food-induced changes in the rate of absorption are irrelevant. What is important is whether the bioavailability, and hence the steady-state level, is altered to such a degree that the effect of the drug is changed. To the best of my knowledge, there has been no report demonstrating such a change, even though our own findings on the influence of food intake on the single dose bioavailability of

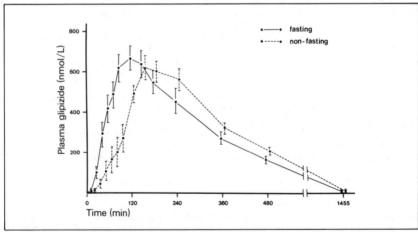

*Fig. 1.* Plasma concentrations of glipizide in 9 healthy volunteers following ingestion of 5mg fasting and non-fasting. There was a significant ($p < 0.05$) delay in the time to peak concentration, but no significant difference in bioavailability.

dicoumarol (85% increase) and hydralazine (200% increase) infer that such changes in effect could occur.

There are, on the other hand, 'hit and run' drugs. Sulphonylureas should be included in this category since they should be employed to normalise insulin release and glucose disposition in response to meals but they should not exert any action between meals. Accordingly, it is important to establish the appropriate relationship between intake of food and administration of sulphonylureas.

Among the available sulphonylureas, glipizide is the most rapid and short acting. We have examined the influence of a standardised breakfast on its kinetics and effects in healthy volunteers and patients with maturity-onset diabetes previously not exposed to sulphonylureas.

Concurrent food intake significantly delayed the absorption of glipizide (5mg) in healthy volunteers (fig. 1). The peak appeared about 30 minutes later in the non-fasting than in the fasting state. Figure 2 shows the absorption of glipizide (5mg) in diabetic patients given the drug 30 minutes before and together with the meal. When glipizide was ingested before the meal, effective plasma concentrations (presumed to be about 100nmol/L or more) had been reached already when the meal was begun. However, when glipizide was ingested with the meal, similar concentrations were not reached until about half an hour after the meal had begun. As shown in figure 3, this difference was clinically relevant: although glipizide promoted insulin release and reduced the blood glucose increase in response to the meal in both instances, insulin release occurred earlier and the blood glucose reduction was more pronounced when the drug was taken 30 minutes before the meal than when meal and drug were ingested concurrently (Wahlin-Boll et al., to be published; Sartor et al., 1978). These findings emphasise the importance of adequate timing between meals and intake of drugs of short-acting, hit and run character.

*J.A.J.H. Critchley* (Edinburgh): Your data with diazepam is interesting. Has anyone investigated the effect of varying the volume of fluid that is taken with hypnotics for example? It is standard practice to take a hypnotic at night with a small sip of water. Would absorption not be faster if it were taken with a larger volume?

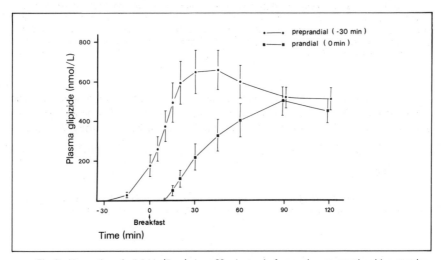

*Fig. 2.* Absorption of glipizide (5mg) given 30 minutes before and concurrently with a standardised breakfast in 14 patients with maturity-onset diabetes.

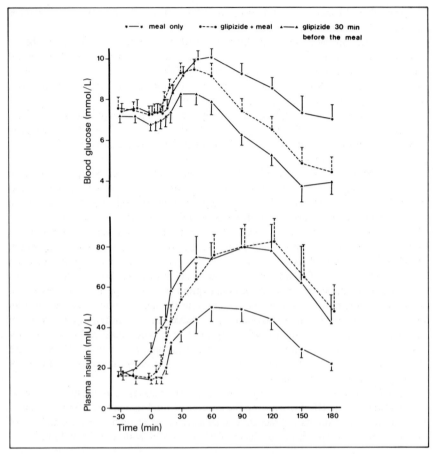

*Fig. 3.* Plasma insulin and blood glucose in 14 patients given glipizide 30 minutes before, and together with, a standardised meal (fig. 2). In addition, the influence of the meal as such is indicated. Glipizide promoted insulin release and blood glucose concentrations were less elevated and displaced and were subsequently reduced more (p < 0.01) when the drug was taken 30 minutes before the meal (Sartor et al., 1978).

*B. Beermann:* I do not think that this has been studied with hypnotics. Gastric emptying might be faster with a very large volume, but on the other hand, if you take a hypnotic with a large volume of water, the bed might be wet during the night!

## Reference

Sartor, G.; Schersten, B. and Melander, A.: Effects of glipizide and food intake on the blood levels of glucose and insulin in diabetic patients. Acta Medica Scandinavica 203: 211 (1978).

# 24

# Age and Drug Absorption

*I.H. Stevenson, S.A.M. Salem, K. O'Malley, B. Cusack and J.G. Kelly*

Department of Pharmacology and Therapeutics, University of Dundee and Department of Clinical Pharmacology, Royal College of Surgeons in Ireland

Gastrointestinal function is abnormal both in the newborn and in the elderly and thus might be expected to alter drug absorption in these age groups. Age-related changes in gastrointestinal physiology have been reviewed for infants and children by Morselli (1976) and Yaffe and Danish (1978) and for the elderly by Bender (1968) and Stevenson et al. (1979) [table I].

The major abnormalities in the newborn are reduced gastric acid secretion and delayed gastric emptying. Gastric pH is normally between 6.5 and 8 at birth and fluctuates considerably thereafter, with acid secretion being closely related to development of the gastric mucosa. Gastric acidity generally reaches adult levels by 3 years of age while gastric emptying time approximates to that in adults some 6 to 8 months after birth. The situation is complicated further, first by the progressive bacterial colonisation of the gastrointestinal tract after birth and secondly, by a continuous decrease from infancy to adulthood in the gastrointestinal tract as a proportion of total bodyweight. In addition biliary function is not fully developed in the newborn and this may influence the enterohepatic circulation of drugs.

At the opposite end of the age spectrum, the changes occurring in gastrointestinal physiology as people age include a reduction in basal and maximal (histamine-stimulated) gastric acid output with consequent increase in gastric pH, a pronounced decrease in splanchnic blood flow and a reduction in small bowel mucosal surface area. Gastric emptying time may be prolonged but, on the other hand, a rise in gastric pH may actually accelerate gastric emptying.

Age-related changes occur in the absorption of several dietary constituents which are absorbed by active or specialised transport mechanisms. For example, the oral absorption of riboflavine is slower in the newborn than in older infants and adults, apparently due both to poorly developed specialised intestinal transport and lower intestinal motility in this age group (Jusko et al., 1970). In a study in newborn rats and mice (Batt and Schachter, 1969) the absorption of calcium, 3-$O$-methylglucose and L-proline was shown to be reduced due to low levels of activity of the active transport mechanism in the neonatal intestinal tract.

In old age the rate or extent of absorption of galactose, 3-$O$-methylglucose, calcium and iron is reduced (Bender, 1968). D-xylose is also actively absorbed but in this case absorption appears not to be impaired in the elderly (Kendal, 1970).

*Table I.* Age-related changes in gastrointestinal physiology

| Process | Abnormality in infancy | Abnormality in elderly |
| --- | --- | --- |
| Gastric acid secretion | Decreased | Decreased |
| Gastric emptying time | Prolonged | Generally prolonged but may also be reduced due to increased pH |
| Intestinal blood flow | Variable | Reduced |
| Mucosal absorbing area | Increased | Reduced |
| Bacterial colonisation | Low but increases progressively | Increased |

These data relating to the influence of age on active transport processes, while of interest, are of little value however in predicting possible age effects on drug absorption since most drugs are absorbed by a simple passive, lipid-diffusion mechanism. Few studies have been undertaken specifically to investigate drug absorption in different age groups and, for the most part, the information available has been obtained from the early phases of drug elimination studies. Furthermore while different plasma drug concentrations may be obtained, following oral drug administration, in subjects of different age, detailed pharmacokinetic analysis is required to identify whether such changes arise, from alterations in absorption, distribution, or elimination. Ideally, studies on drug absorption require comparison of the plasma drug concentration versus time profiles following both oral and intravenous administration. In addition, two aspects of absorption must be considered — rate and extent of absorption. The relative rates of absorption, distribution and elimination determine the time taken to reach the peak plasma drug concentration and the concentrations attained. The extent of absorption is particularly important in chronic dosing since it is a major determinant of drug steady-state plasma concentration. The influence of age on these two parameters has so far not been extensively studied.

## 1. Drug Absorption in Infants and Children

This has been the subject of a number of recent reviews (Rane and Wilson, 1976; Morselli, 1976;.Yaffe and Danish, 1978) [table II]. It is not surprising, in view of the relative gastric achlorhydria of the newborn, that the oral bioavailability of several acid-labile drugs is increased e.g. benzylpenicillin (Huang and High, 1953) and ampicillin (Silverio and Poole, 1973). With the exception of these, however, drug absorption is either impaired or normal in the newborn. Boreus et al. (1975) demonstrated that both the rate and extent of absorption of phenobarbitone is reduced in the newborn up to 2 weeks of age, with rapid and efficient absorption if the drug is given intramuscularly. Delayed absorption in the newborn has also been reported for diphenylhydantoin (Jalling et al., 1970) nalidixic acid (Rohwedder et al., 1970), and paracetamol (Levy et al., 1975). With several sulphonamides, phenylbutazone, co-trimoxazole and diazepam on the other hand absorption in neonates has been found to be comparable with that in older children (Morselli, 1976). In a detailed study with digoxin, Morselli et al. (1975) reported that absorption was efficient by the oral route while slow and erratic by the intramuscular route.

Table II. Drug absorption in infants and children in comparison with adults[1]

| Drug | Oral absorption/bioavailability |
|---|---|
| *Infants* | |
| Acid-labile penicillins | Increased |
| Rifampicin | |
| Gentamicin | |
| Nalidixic acid | |
| Diphenylhydantoin | Decreased |
| Phenobarbitone | |
| Paracetamol | |
| Phenylbutazone | |
| Co-trimoxazole | |
| Sulphonamides | Unaltered |
| Digoxin | |
| Diazepam | |
| *Older subjects and children* | |
| Ethosuximide | |
| Clonazepam | |
| Phenobarbitone | Increased |
| Diazepam | |
| Imipramine | |

1   Data obtained from Morselli (1976) and Yaffe and Danish (1978).

In older children, as opposed to the newborn, the oral absorption of several centrally-acting drugs (ethosuximide, dipropylacetate, clonazepam, phenobarbitone, diazepam and imipramine) appears to be more rapid than in the adult although no data are available on the total extent of absorption (Yaffe and Danish, 1968).

# 2. Drug Absorption in the Elderly

Pharmacokinetics (including absorption) in the elderly has also been the subject of a number of recent reviews (Triggs and Nation, 1975; Crooks et al., 1976; Vestal, 1978; Crooks and Stevenson, 1979). While, in general, there appear to be no striking differences in drug absorption in the elderly, several reviewers have drawn attention to the inadequacy of much of the pharmacokinetic data — in particular to the limited blood sampling over the absorption phase and the failure in almost all cases to carry out comparisons of the intravenous and oral plasma drug concentration *versus* time profiles.

The following section of this paper deals with the absorption in the elderly of aspirin, quinine, digoxin and theophylline including in the case of digoxin and theophylline an intravenous/oral dosing comparison. Details of these studies are published elsewhere (Stevenson et al., 1979; Cusack et al., 1979a,b).

## 2.1 Aspirin and Quinine

Elderly subjects were ambulant volunteers from long-stay wards in geriatric units and had no clinical or biochemical evidence of hepatic or renal disease. Of the 10

*Table III.* Aspirin and quinine absorption in young and elderly subjects[1]

| | Mean age in years (range) | Peak plasma concentration ($\mu$g ml$^{-1}$) | Time to peak plasma concentration (min) | Area under curve ($\mu$g ml$^{-1}$h$^{-1}$) | Absorption rate constant (h$^{-1}$) |
|---|---|---|---|---|---|
| *Acetylsalicylic Acid* | | | | | |
| Young subjects (n = 6) | 27 (24-31) | 35.0 ± 3.0 | 48.0 ± 32.0 | 136.0 ± 36.0 | 13.8 ± 2.5 |
| Elderly subjects (n = 5) | 71 (65-77) | 40.5 ± 11.7 | 69.0 ± 29.9 | 287.0[2] ± 142.0 | 12.5 ± 6.2 |
| *Quinine* | | | | | |
| Young subjects (n = 6) | 29 (24-39) | 1.1 ± 0.4 | 77.2 ± 28.8 | 10.0 ± 3.2 | 2.1 ± 1.6 |
| Elderly subjects (n = 5) | 80 (72-88) | 2.3[3] ± 0.7 | 110 ± 75 | 25.7[2] ± 13.5 | 6.0 ± 4.6 |

1   Results are expressed as means ± SEM and significance values refer to the difference between elderly and young subjects.
2   $p < 0.05$.
3   $p < 0.01$.

subjects studied, 8 were drug free and 2 were receiving diazepam. Young subjects were Medical School staff on no drug therapy. Details of ages are given in table III.

Aspirin or quinine in aqueous solution was given orally in a dose of 4mg/kg and serial blood samples were taken. Subjects were supine and fasted before and during the first 4 hours of the study.

Aspirin was assayed as salicylic acid by a spectrophotometric method and quinine by a specific gas-liquid chromatographic method (Salem, 1977).

Plasma salicylate concentration *versus* time profiles are shown for young and elderly subjects in figure 1 and pharmacokinetic parameters for both drugs are given in table III. With both drugs at all time points, plasma concentrations tended to be higher in the older group. Again with both drugs, the peak plasma concentration tended to be higher and the time to reach peak plasma level longer in the elderly although with only 1 of the 4 values was this significantly so. There were no significant age differences between the absorption rate constants, but the comparison in the case of quinine is unsatisfactory owing to a large scatter of values in the elderly group. The only significant difference occurring with both drugs was a very large increase in the area under the drug concentration *versus* time curve in the older group. However both drugs are eliminated more slowly in the elderly group (Stevenson et al., 1979) thus contributing to a greater area under the curve and, in the case of quinine, a decreased apparent volume of distribution would contribute further to this. Another feature is the greater scatter of values in the elderly group, indicating that drug handling is more variable in the elderly.

## 2.2 Digoxin

Observations were made in 7 elderly and 6 younger patients in whom digoxin was indicated. Details of age are given in table IV and clinical data concerning the

*Table IV*. Digoxin absorption in young and elderly patients[1]

|  | Mean age in years (range) | Peak plasma concentration (nmol L$^{-1}$) | Mean time to peak h (range) | AUC [oral] (nmol ml$^{-1}$h$^{-1}$) | AUC [IV] (nmol ml$^{-1}$h$^{-1}$) | Amount absorb-ed (%) |
|---|---|---|---|---|---|---|
| Younger patients (n = 6) | 47 (34-61) | 4.4 ± 0.8 | 0.95 (0.75-1.25) | 89.7 ± 9.0 | 109.8 ± 15.5 | 84.3 ± 6.5 |
| Elderly patients (n = 7) | 81 (72-91) | 2.6 ± 0.4 | 1.75 (1.0-4.0) | 144.6 ± 39.8 | 171.7 ± 32.8 | 76.0 ± 10.0 |
| p |  | < 0.05 |  |  |  | NS |

1    Data were obtained following oral and intravenous digoxin dosing with 0.5mg (younger patients) and 0.25mg (elderly patients). [Means ± SEM]. Significance values refer to the difference between young and elderly patients.

patients may be referred to elsewhere (Cusack et al., 1979a). 11 of the 13 patients were on maintenance therapy. No drug therapy was given on the morning of testing and, in the case of maintenance digoxin, therapy was stopped for at least 2 weeks prior to the investigation.

Each patient received the same dose of digoxin (elderly 0.25mg, younger subjects 0.5mg)[1] both intravenously and orally in random order, with an interval of at least 2 weeks between doses. Each patient fasted on the morning of the test until 4 hours after receiving digoxin. 15 blood samples were taken over the first 12 hours with a further 3 samples at 12-hourly intervals thereafter. Plasma digoxin concentrations were measured by radioimmunoassay using the Wellcome 'Lanoxitest' kit.

Mean plasma digoxin concentrations following oral and intravenous administration are shown for both age groups in figure 2 and pharmacokinetic data relating to absorption in table IV. In the younger patients a mean peak plasma level of 4.4nmol per litre occurred at 0.95 hours after oral dosage while, after intravenous administration, the highest mean plasma digoxin concentration observed at 15 minutes was 10.5nmol per litre. Mean digoxin concentrations after oral and intravenous administration attained similar levels at 2 hours and followed a similar pattern thereafter.

In the elderly patients the mean peak plasma level of 2.6nmol per litre occurred at 1.75 hours i.e. significantly later (p < 0.05) than in the younger patients. The maximum observed mean concentration at 15 minutes after intravenous administration was 11.9nmol per litre. Concentrations then fell rapidly so that again at 2 hours the mean digoxin concentration was not significantly different from that observed 2 hours after oral administration. Subsequent concentrations followed a similar pattern after both routes of administration.

The mean extent of digoxin absorption, calculated as the ratio of mean areas under the plasma drug concentration *versus* time curves following oral and intravenous administration (table IV) was not significantly different in young and old subjects. Again however, with all the pharmacokinetic parameters reported there was a greater scatter of values in the elderly group.

1    'Lanoxin' (Wellcome).

There was a significantly reduced mean weight-corrected plasma clearance of digoxin in the elderly group, but no significant difference between the 2 age groups in the apparent volume of distribution of digoxin, when corrected for weight (Cusack et al., 1979a).

## 2.3 Theophylline

Five healthy young volunteers and 6 elderly patients from geriatric, convalescent or long-stay beds were studied. Details of age are given in table V. None of the

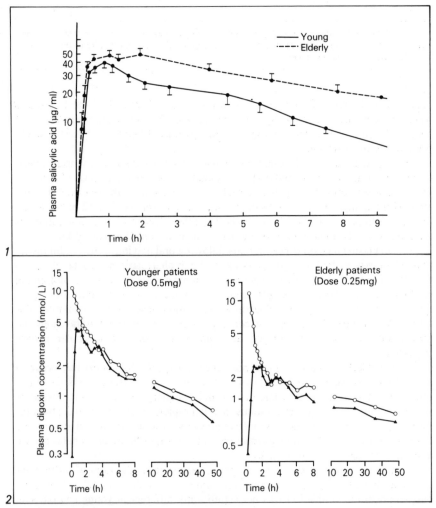

*Fig. 1.* Plasma salicylic acid concentrations in young (n = 6) and elderly (n = 5) subjects following an oral dose of 4mg/kg acetylsalicyclic acid. Values shown are means ± SEM.

*Fig. 2.* Plasma digoxin concentrations following intravenous (○) and oral (▲) digoxin in young and elderly patients.

Table V. Theophylline absorption in young and elderly subjects[1]

|  | Mean age in years (range) | Absorption rate constant $(h^{-1})$ | Amount absorbed (%) |
|---|---|---|---|
| Younger subjects (n = 5) | 26 (21-30) | 1.5 ± 0.35 | 94 ± 7.9 |
| Elderly subjects (n = 6) | 75 (67-81) | 2.1 ± 0.44 | 87 ± 3.7 |
| p |  | NS | NS |

1   Results are presented as means ± SEM. Significance comparisons refer to differences between young and elderly patients.

Table VI. Drugs absorbed normally in the elderly[1]

| | |
|---|---|
| Acetylsalicyclic acid (3 studies) | Morphine |
| Ampicillin | Paracetamol |
| Antipyrine | Pivmecillinam |
| Dextropropoxyphene | Quinine |
| Digoxin (2 studies) | Sulphamethizole |
| Indomethacin | Tetracycline |
| Lithium | |

1   Triggs and Stevenson, 1979.

patients had abnormal liver function tests or conditions, such as cardiac failure, likely to affect theophylline kinetics. All subjects were non-smokers.

Each subject received theophylline 125mg orally and intravenously on separate occasions in random order with at least 1 week between doses. Subjects fasted on the morning of the study until at least 4 hours after drug administration and, in addition, each person abstained from xanthine-containing substances such as tea, coffee, 'Coca Cola' or chocolate for 12 hours before and during the period of blood sampling. Plasma theophylline concentrations were measured by high-pressure liquid chromatography.

After oral administration, mean plasma concentrations of theophylline tended to be higher in the elderly group and the time taken to reach the peak was shorter. There was, however, considerable overlap of values between the 2 groups. The mean values for rate and extent of absorption (calculated from the ratio AUC oral/AUC iv), [table V] show no significant differences between the 2 groups. The mean absorption rate constant was slightly greater and absorption half-time slightly shorter, suggesting somewhat more rapid absorption in the elderly group. Mean values for distribution volume and plasma theophylline clearance were not significantly different in the 2 age groups.

## 3. Discussion

In the studies with aspirin and quinine there was no significant alteration in the rate of absorption. The data do not allow determination of the extent of absorption

*Table VII.* Drugs absorbed abnormally in the elderly[1]

| Drug | Alteration in elderly |
|------|----------------------|
| Acetylsalicyclic acid | $K_{abs}$ reduced |
| Chlordiazepoxide | $CP_{max}$ reduced |
| Chlormethiazole | AUC increased |
| Digoxin (2 studies) | $T_{max}$ delayed |
| Levodopa | AUC increased |
| Metoprolol | $T_{max}$ delayed and $CP_{max}$ |
| Propicillin | $T_{max}$ delayed and $CP_{max}$ increased |
| Propranolol | $CP_{max}$ increased |

1   Triggs and Stevenson 1979.

and the greater area under the plasma drug concentration *versus* time curves probably result from a reduced elimination rate and also, in the case of quinine, a reduced distribution volume. With digóxin and theophylline, the extent of absorption was similar in the 2 age groups and the sole difference was a delay in the absorption of digoxin in the elderly group. This is unlikely to be clinically important since there is a significant delay in the development of inotropism with maximum activity occurring around 4 hours after an oral dose when plasma digoxin concentrations are falling from peak concentrations (Cusack et al., 1979a).

In general, these results are in agreement with other studies in the elderly (Triggs and Stevenson, in press). The effect of age on drug absorption is unpredictable and changes have been observed with some drugs but not with others. In the majority of studies oral drug absorption was not appreciably altered (table VI). Age-related changes in absorption (table VII) are likely to be of greatest significance when there is a reduced first-pass effect in the elderly e.g. with chlormethiazole and propranolol. In the case of levodopa, both reduced first-pass effect and more rapid gastric emptying with reduced gastric degradation are responsible for the greater AUC in the elderly.

In the elderly, plasma drug concentrations and the area under the plasma concentration-time curve are often increased. However, in many cases, these changes are likely to result from impairment of metabolism (e.g. aspirin, chlormethiazole, metoprolol, propranolol and paracetamol), renal excretion (propicillin) or a reduction in distribution volume (quinine) rather than from increased absorption.

# References

Batt, E.R. and Schachter, D.: Developmental pattern of some intestinal transport mechanisms in newborn rats and mice. American Journal of Physiology 216: 1064-1068 (1969).

Bender, A.D.: Effect of age on intestinal absorption: Implications for drug absorption in the elderly. Journal of the American Geriatrics Society 16: 1331-1339 (1968).

Boreus, L.O.; Jalling, B. and Kallberg, N.: Clinical pharmacology of phenobarbital in the neonatal period; in Morselli, Garattini and Sereni (Eds) Basic and Therapeutic Aspects of the Perinatal Pharmacology, p.331-340 (Raven, New York 1975).

Crooks, J.; O'Malley, K. and Stevenson, I.H.: Pharmacokinetics in the elderly. Clinical Pharmacokinetics 1: 280-296 (1976).

Crooks, J. and Stevenson, I.H. (Eds): Drugs and the Elderly: Perspectives in Geriatric Clinical Pharmacology (Macmillan, London 1979).

Cusack, B.: Kelly, J.: Lavan, J.: Noel, J. and O'Malley, K.: The effect of age and smoking on theophylline kinetics. British Journal of Clinical Pharmacology 8: 384P-385P. (1979b).

Cusack, B.; Kelly, J.; O'Malley, K.; Noel, J.; Lavan, J. and Horgan, J.: Digoxin in the elderly; pharmacokinetic consequences of old age. Clinical Pharmacology and Therapeutics (in press, 1979a).

Huang, N.N. and High, R.H.: Comparison of serum levels following the administration of oral and parenteral preparations of penicillin to infants and children of various age groups. Journal of Pediatrics 42: 657-668 (1953).

Jalling, B.; Boreus, L.O.; Rane, A. and Sjoqvist, F.: Plasma concentrations of diphenylhydantoin in young infants. Pharmacologica Clinica 2: 200-202 (1970).

Jusko, W.J.; Khanna, N.; Levy, G.; Stern, L. and Yaffe, S.J.: Riboflavin absorption and excretion in the neonate. Pediatrics 45: 945-951 (1970).

Kendal, M.J.: The influence of age on the xylose absorption test. Gut 2: 498-501 (1970).

Levy, G.; Khanna, N.N.; Soda, D.M.; Tsuzuki, O. and Stern, L.: Pharmacokinetics of acetaminophen in the human neonate: formation of acetaminophen glucuronide and sulfate in relation to plasma bilirubin concentration and D-glucaric acid and excretion. Pediatrics 55: 818-825 (1975).

Morselli, P.L.: Clinical pharmacokinetics in neonates. Clinical Pharmacokinetics 1: 81-98 (1976).

Morselli, P.L.; Assael, B.M.; Gomeni, R.; Mandelli, M.; Marini, A.; Reali, E.; Visconti, U. and Sereni, F.: Digoxin pharmacokinetics during human development; in Morselli, Garattini and Sereni (Eds) Basic and Therapeutic Aspects of the Perinatal Pharmacology p.377-392 (Raven, New York 1975).

Rane, A. and Wilson, J.T.: Clinical pharmacokinetics in infants and children. Clinical Pharmacokinetics 1: 2-24 (1976).

Rohwedder, H.-J.; Simon, C.; Kubler, W. and Hohfnauer, M.: Untersuchungen uber die Pharmakokinetick von Nalidixinsaure bei Kindern Verschiedenen Alters. Zeitschrift fur Kinderheilkunde 109: 124-134 (1970).

Salem, S.A.M.: Some aspects of pharmacokinetics in the elderly: M.Sc. Thesis, University of Dundee (1977).

Silverio, J. and Poole, J.W.: Serum concentrations of ampicillin in newborn infants after oral administration. Pediatrics 51: 578-580 (1973).

Stevenson, I.H.; Salem, S.A.M. and Shepherd, A.M.M.: Studies on drug absorption and metabolism in the elderly; in Crooks and Stevenson (Eds) Drugs and the Elderly, p.51-63 (Macmillan, London 1979).

Triggs, E.J. and Nation, R.L.: Pharmacokinetics in the aged: A review. Journal of Pharmacokinetics and Biopharmaceutics 3: 387-418 (1975).

Triggs, E.J. and Stevenson, I.H.: Pharmacokinetics in the elderly; in Triggs, Swift and Stevenson (Eds) Clinical Pharmacology in the Elderly (Dekker, New York, in press).

Vestal, R.E.: Drug use in the elderly: A review of problems and special considerations. Drugs 16: 358-382 (1978).

Yaffe, S.J. and Danish, M.: Problems of drug administration in the pediatric patient. Drug Metabolism Reviews, 8(2): 303-318 (1978).

# 25

# Gastrointestinal Disease and Drug Absorption

*R.L. Parsons and Jill A. David*

Royal Free Hospital School of Medicine, London

The relative lack of information on oral drug absorption in patients with gastrointestinal disease contrasts with the attention given to research on the changes in absorption of water, electrolytes and nutrients in patients with malabsorption syndromes (Cerda, 1974; Sjoqvist et al., 1976). However, there are many reports about patients with different gastrointestinal diseases and the way in which they absorb drugs given by mouth. The conditions which have been studied are listed in table I. Overall, the results are variable and unpredictable.

Absorption may be increased or decreased depending on the underlying gastrointestinal pathology and the drugs used. It seems that there are no simple explanations nor easy answers to guide the practising doctor who bears the responsibility for treatment. These problems have recently been reviewed (Parsons, 1976, 1977).

## 1. Pathophysiological Changes in Gastrointestinal Disease

Steatorrhoea and malabsorption are not synonymous. Steatorrhoea is an increase in faecal fat excretion and occurs in gastrointestinal disorders such as coeliac and Crohn's disease, small bowel diverticulosis, vagotomy, intestinal resection and after ingestion of neomycin and cholestyramine. It is the outward manifestation of impaired micelle formation and subsequent malabsorption of fat and fat-soluble substances such as vitamins A, D and K. The term malabsorption should be restricted to patients with biochemical changes or clinical evidence of nutrient deficiency such as anaemia, weight loss, oesteomalacia and hypoalbuminaemia.

### 1.1 Small Intestinal Villous Atrophy

Subtotal or total villous atrophy may follow chronic treatment with p-aminosalicylic acid (Heinivaara and Palva, 1964), cytotoxic drugs (Berndt, 1969), colchicine (Race et al., 1970), paramomycin (Keusch et al., 1970), metformin (Tomkin et al., 1971) and slow-release potassium chloride (Palva et al., 1972).

### 1.1.1 Coeliac Disease (Gluten Enteropathy)

Villous atrophy occurs in coeliac disease and dermatitis herpetiformis. Coeliac disease is thought to be caused by sensitivity to cereals and foods containing gluten and it often presents as a malabsorption syndrome. Changes in the rate of gastric emptying have been described in this condition (Moberg and Carlberger, 1974; Holt et al., 1979) and this may contribute to abnormal absorption of propranolol, aspirin, erythromycin ethylsuccinate, sulphamethoxazole, trimethoprim, clindamycin and rifampicin (Parsons et al., 1975, 1976a, 1977a). Another factor influencing drug absorption in coeliac disease might be an increase in the pH of the gut lumen or acid microclimate. This might contribute to more rapid absorption of basic drugs such as propranolol (Cooper et al., 1976; Kitis et al., 1979). On the other hand, the absorption of practolol is delayed in coeliac disease (Parsons et al., 1976a). Practolol is more water soluble than propranolol, is bound less to plasma proteins but has a similar pK value (9.5). The absorption of folic acid is pH-dependent, and might therefore be influenced by changes in acid microclimate in patients with coeliac disease (Kitis et al., 1979). It is possible that the permeability of the intestinal mucosa to drugs might be altered by disease, but little information is available on this point.

Changes in the activity of gastrointestinal mucosal enzymes such as esterases and hydrolases may affect the absorption of ester prodrugs such as erythromycin stearate, pivampicillin, pivmecillinam and talampicillin. However, absorption seems to be impaired with some but not others (Parsons et al., 1975, 1977b). Gastrointestinal first-pass extraction of ethinyloestradiol is also reduced in patients with coeliac disease (Back et al., 1979).

The effect of changes in drug binding to plasma proteins on plasma concentrations after oral absorption is unknown. However, there is a close correlation between the plasma acid $\alpha_1$-glycoprotein concentration and the area under the plasma concentration-time curve (AUC) after oral propranolol (Schneider et al., 1979).

## 1.2 Crohn's Disease

There may be extensive thickening of the gut wall, narrowing of the lumen and secondary changes in motility in this condition. The effects on drug absorption are variable and unexplained. The absorption of rifampicin is unaltered, that of clindamycin and sulphamethoxazole is apparently increased, while the absorption of erythromycin stearate is reduced (figs. 1-4) [Parsons and Paddock, 1975; Parsons et al., 1976b; Parsons, 1977].

## 1.3 Small Bowel Diverticulosis

Perhaps the most important pathophysiological change in this condition is a shift in gut flora to a predominantly anaerobic population which may be responsible for steatorrhoea and malabsorption (O'Grady et al., 1971). Although in such circumstances increased metabolism of drugs by intestinal bacteria might be expected, absorption does not seem to be decreased (table I). Indeed, the absorption of clindamycin and trimethoprim is apparently increased as judged by plasma concentrations although urinary recovery was unaltered (figs. 1 and 2).

Table I. Gastrointestinal diseases in which drug absorption has been studied

| Disease state | Drugs | Absorption pattern | Normal | Increased | Decreased | Reference |
|---|---|---|---|---|---|---|
| **Stomach** Achlorhydria/ hypochlorhydria | Acetylsalicylic acid | After intragastric instillation lower levels in atrophic gastritis and metaplasia | | | + | Siurala et al. (1969) |
| | Phenoxymethyl-penicillin | More rapid absorption | | + | | Pottage et al. (1974) Lupinsky and Berthoud (1973); Davis & Pirola (1968) |
| | | Marginally reduced urinary elimination | | | + | |
| | Salicylamide | Normal | + | | | Hartiala et al. (1963) |
| | Tetracycline | Delayed absorption | | | + | Kramer et al. (1978) |
| **Post-gastrectomy** | Ampicillin | Normal | + | | | Davies (1975) |
| | Cephalexin | More rapid absorption | | + | | Lode et al. (1974) |
| | Digoxin | Normal | + | | | Beerman et al. (1973) |
| | Ethambutol | Absorption reduced and delayed | | | + | Venho et al. (1975) |
| | Ethanol | Peak plasma ethanol higher and earlier | | + | | Cotton & Walker (1973) |
| | Ethionamide | Reduced serum levels (not significantly so) | | | + | Matilla et al. (1969) |
| | Folic acid | Reduced folate absorption | | | + | Elsborg (1974) |
| | Iron | Serum $^{59}$Fe reduced after polyagastrectomy | | | + | Turnberg (1966) |
| | Isoniazid | Normal | + | | | Matilla et al. (1969) |
| | Levodopa | Rapid absorption. High dopa levels | | + | | Rivera-Calimlim et al. (1971); Mearrick et al. (1974) |
| | p-Aminosalicylic acid | Higher serum levels | | + | | Matilla et al. (1969) |
| | Phenoxymethyl-penicillin | More rapid absorption | | + | | Davies (1975) |
| | Quinidine | Peak reduced and delayed. Urinary elimination reduced | | | + | Venho et al. (1975) |
| | Sulphafurazole (Sulphisoxazole) | Peak reduced and delayed. Urinary elimination reduced | | | + | Venho et al. (1975) |
| **Pyloric stenosis** | Enteric coated aspirin | Delayed gastric emptying prevented aspirin tablet disintegration | | | + | Harris (1973) |
| **Pancreas** Pancreatitis | Cyanocobalamin | Reduced urinary excretion | | | + | Toskes et al. (1971) |
| | Phenoxymethyl-penicillin | Normal. Reduced if active | + | | + | Lupinsky & Berthoud (1973) |

| Disease | Drug | Effect | | | Reference |
|---|---|---|---|---|---|
| Cystic fibrosis | Ampicillin | Large individual variation | | | Saggers & Lawson (1968) |
| | Azidocillin | Subtherapeutic serum levels | + | | Raeburn & McCrae (1974) |
| | Cephalexin | Reduced plasma levels | + | | Parsons & Paddock (1975) |
| | Clindamycin | Peak plasma conc. delayed. AUC similar | | + | Raeburn & Devine (1971) |
| | Dicloxacillin | Reduced peak serum levels and AUC | + | | Jusko et al. (1975) |
| | Erythromycin | Variation in blood levels | | | Saggers & Lawson (1968) |
| | Iron | Low plasma Fe | + | | Smith (1964) |
| *Small Bowel* | | | | | |
| Steatorrhoea and malabsorption syndromes | Digoxin | Reduced plasma digoxin in malabsorption. Normal in pancreatitis | + | | Heizer et al. (1971) |
| Intestinal villous atrophy | Chloramphenicol | Normal | | + | Matilla et al. (1973) |
| | Cycloserine | Normal | | + | Matilla et al. (1973) |
| | Isoniazid | Normal | | + | Matilla et al. (1973) |
| | Quinine sulphate | Elevated serum levels | + | | Matilla et al. (1973) |
| | Sodium salicylate | Normal | | + | Matilla et al. (1973) |
| | Sulphafurazole | Retarded serum levels. Reduced urinary excretion | + | | Matilla et al. (1973) |
| Coeliac disease | Amoxycillin | Absorption delayed | + | | Parsons et al. (1974, 1975, 1976c) |
| | Ampicillin | Normal | | + | Parsons et al. (1974a, 1975, 1976c); |
| | Aspirin | Faster absorption | + | | Matilla et al. (1973); Parsons et al. (1977a) |
| | Cephalexin | Higher plasma concentrations and urinary excretion | | + | Parsons et al. (1974a, 1975, 1976c) |
| | Clindamycin | Higher peak plasma concentrations and AUC | | + | Parsons et al. (1974b, 1975) |
| | Co-trimoxazole | Higher peak plasma TMP and SMX conc. | | + | Parsons et al. (1974b, 1975) |
| | Erythromycin ethylsuccinate | Faster absorption | + | | Parsons et al. (1975, 1976c, 1976d) |
| | Ethinyl-oestradiol | Reduced first-pass extraction | | + | Back et al. (1979) |
| | Indomethacin | Normal | | | |
| | Methyldopa | Increased plasma conc. | + | | Parsons et al. (1976d, 1977a) |
| | Paracetamol | Delayed absorption | + | | George et al. (1980); Holt et al. (1979) |
| | Phenoxymethyl-penicillin | Reduced absorption | | + | Davis & Prola (1968) |

| Disease state | Drugs | Absorption pattern | Normal | Incr-eased | Decr-eased | Reference |
|---|---|---|---|---|---|---|
| | Pivampicillin | Slower rate of rise to peak | | | + | Parsons et al. (1974a, 1975, 1976c) |
| | Pivmecillinam | Normal | + | | | Parsons et al. (1977b) |
| | Practolol | Peak plasma concentration delayed | | | + | Parsons & Kaye (1974); Parsons et al. (1976a) |
| | Propranolol | Increased plasma concentrations | | + | | Parsons et al. (1976a); Parsons and Kaye (1974) Schneider et al. (1976) |
| | Rifampicin | Delayed peak plasma conc. | | | + | Parsons et al. (1974b, 1975) |
| | Salicylate | Normal (late sampling after peak salicylate) | + | | | Matilla et al. (1973); |
| | | Faster absorption in coeliacs | | + | | Parsons et al. (1977a) |
| | Sodium fusidate | Increased absorption | | + | | Parsons et al. (1975); Parsons (1977) |
| | Talampicillin | Earlier peak plasma conc. | | + | | Parsons (unpublished) |
| Small bowel diverticulosis | Amoxycillin | Normal | + | | | Parsons et al. (1974c); Parsons & Paddock (1975); Parsons et al. (1976d) |
| | Ampicillin | Normal | + | | | Parson et al. (1974c); Parsons & Paddock (1975); Parsons et al. (1976d) |
| | Cephalexin | Increased peak plasma conc. and AUC | | + | | Parsons & Paddock (1975); Parsons et al. (1976d) |
| | Clindamycin | Increased peak plasma conc. and AUC | | + | | Parsons et al. (1974c); Parsons & Paddock (1975); Parsons et al. (1976d); |
| | Co-trimoxazole | Increased peak plasma TMP and SMX | | + | | Parsons et al. (1974c); Parsons & Paddock (1975); Parsons et al. (1976d) Elsborg (1977) |
| | Lincomycin | Normal | + | | | Parsons et al. (1974c); Parsons & Paddock (1975); Parsons et al. (1976d) |
| | Rifampicin | Normal | + | | | Parsons et al. (1974c); Parsons & Paddock (1975); Parsons et al. (1976d) |

| Condition | Drug | Effect | | | Reference |
|---|---|---|---|---|---|
| Dermatitis herpetiformis | Dapsone | Normal (but late sampling) | | + | Alexander et al. (1970) |
| Selective lactose malabsorption | Acetylsalicylic acid | Normal | | + | Jusilla et al. (1970) |
| Acute | Isoniazid | Reduced serum levels. No difference in urine | + | | Jusilla et al. (1970) |
| | Sulphafurazole | Impaired and delayed absorption | + | | Jusilla et al. (1970) |
| shigellosis | Ampicillin | Decreased plasma levels | + | | Nelson et al. (1972) |
| | Nalidixic acid | Delayed absorption | + | + | Nelson et al. (1972) |
| Crohn's disease | Cephalexin | Reduced peak plasma concentrations | + | | Parsons & Paddock (1975); Parsons et al. (1976b) |
| | Clindamycin | Increased peak plasma conc. and AUC | | + | Parsons et al. (1976b) |
| | Cotrimoxazole | Increased peak plasma TMP and SMX conc. and AUC | | + | Parsons & Paddock (1975); Parsons et al. (1976b); |
| | Erythromycin | Earlier peak plasma conc. | + | + | Parsons et al. (1976b); Mlynaryk & Kirsner (1963) |
| | Hydrocortisone | Normal | + | | George et al. (1980) |
| | Methyldopa | Normal | + | | |
| | Metronidazole | Reduced absorption with greater variability | | + | Melander et al. (1977) |
| | Propranolol | Increased peak plasma propranolol conc. | + | + | Schneider et al. (1976) |
| | Rifampicin | Normal | + | | Parsons et al. (1976b) |
| | Sodium fusidate | Slightly raised plasma concentrations | | + | Parsons et al. (1976b) |
| Small intestinal resections | Digoxin | Normal in majority | + | | Beerman et al. (1973) |
| | 25-Hydroxy-vitamin D | Reduced plasma levels | + | + | Compston & Creamer (1977) |
| *Large bowel* | | | | | |
| Ulcerative colitis | Hydrocortisone | Normal | | + | Mlynaryk & Kirsner (1963) |
| *Other conditions that may affect the gut* | | | | | |
| Pernicious anaemia | Cephalexin | Impaired absorption | | + | Davies et al. (1970) |
| | Penicillin V | Reduced urinary elimination | | + | Lupinsky & Berthoud (1973) |
| | Salicylamide | More rapid absorption | + | | Hartiala et al. (1963) |

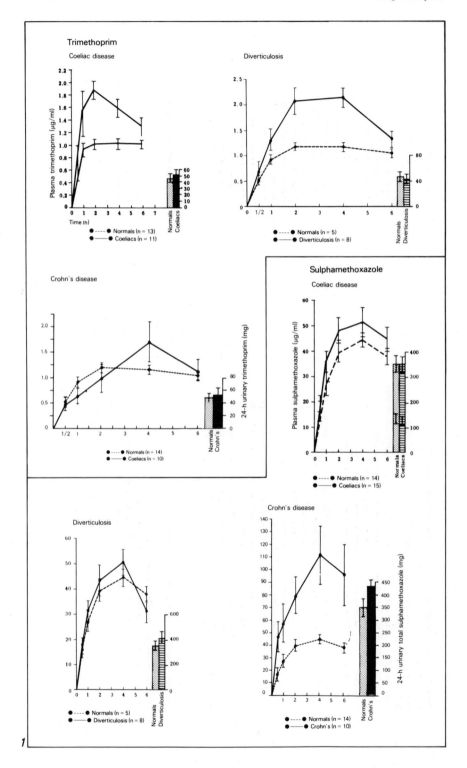

## 2. Chemical Structure, Physicochemical Properties and Drug Absorption in Gastrointestinal Disease

### 2.1 Active Transport

Most nutrients but few drugs are absorbed by active transport. Abnormal absorption of cyanocobalamin, tryptophan and thyroxine has been described in coeliac disease (Kowlessar et al., 1958; Elias et al., 1973; Vanderschueren-Lodeweyckz et al., 1977). However, the absorption of levodopa (fig. 5) and methyldopa (George et al., 1980) is not dramatically changed in this condition.

### 2.2 Passive Non-ionic Diffusion

Most drugs are absorbed by passive non-ionic diffusion (Shore et al., 1957; Brodie, 1964). This process is influenced by several factors including molecular weight, lipid- and water-solubility, and pH and pKa in the case of weak organic acids and bases. The relative importance of these factors for drug absorption in patients with gastrointestinal disease has not been established.

## 3. Clinical Relevance

Although plasma concentration-time curves following a single oral dose and steady-state plasma concentrations are widely used to evaluate drug absorption, such data may be a poor guide to therapeutic response. Some examples of clinically important changes in drug absorption in patients with gastrointestinal disease are given below.

### 3.1 Delayed Gastric Emptying

Delayed gastric emptying was responsible for therapeutic failure of levodopa in a patient with Parkinson's disease (Riviera-Calimlim et al., 1970). This may be less of a problem with the combined use of levodopa with decarboxylase inhibitors.

### 3.2 Achlorhydria

Achlorhydria occurs in pernicious anaemia and is common in the elderly (Baron and Lennard-Jones, 1971). The resulting changes in pH will influence drug dissolution and possibly gastric emptying rate and so alter the absorption of many drugs.

*Fig. 1.* Plasma concentration-time curves and urinary excretion of trimethoprim and sulphamethoxazole after oral administration of 160mg of trimethoprim and 800mg of sulphamethoxazole ('Bactrim', Roche) to healthy volunteers, adults with coeliac disease, small bowel diverticulosis or Crohn's disease, in the fasting state.

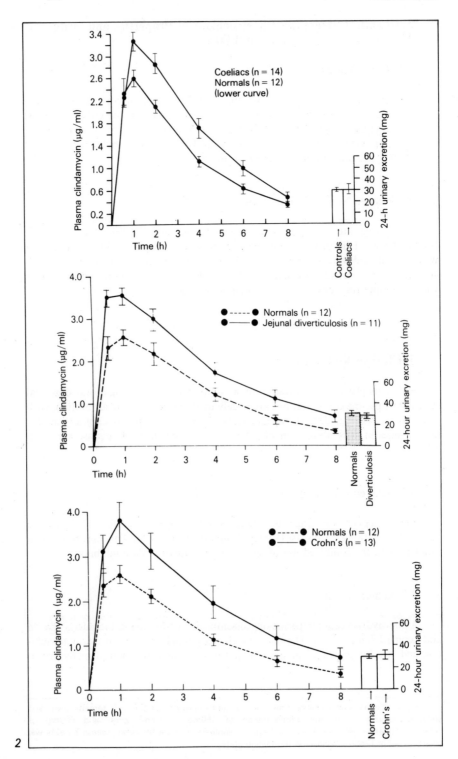

2

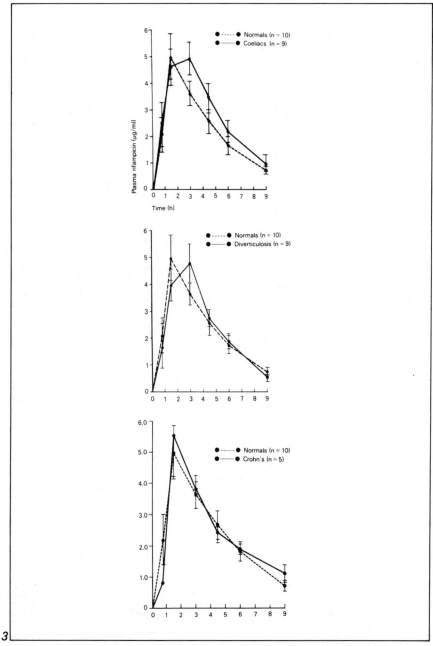

*Fig. 2.* Plasma concentration-time curves and urinary excretion of clindamycin after oral administration of 200mg to healthy volunteers, adults with coeliac disease, small bowel diverticulosis or Crohn's disease, in the fasting state.

*Fig. 3.* Plasma concentration-time curves after oral administration of 300mg of rifampicin ('Rimactane', Ciba) to healthy volunteers, adults with coeliac disease, small bowel diverticulosis or Crohn's disease, in the fasting state.

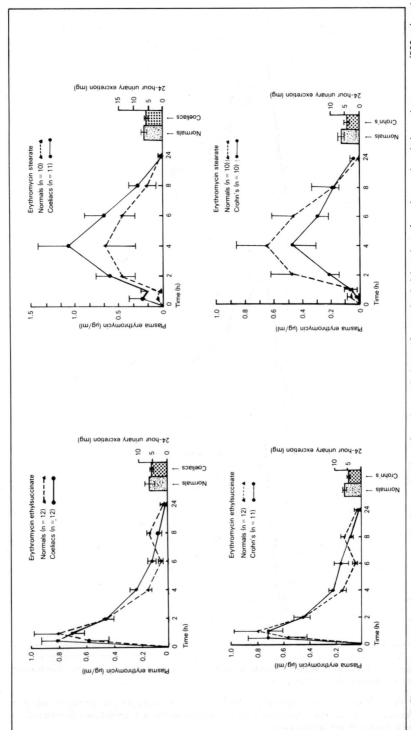

*Fig. 4.* Plasma concentration-time curves and urinary excretion of erythromycin base after oral administration of erythromycin ethyl succinate syrup (500mg) and erythromycin stearate tablets (500mg) to healthy subjects and adult patients with coeliac or Crohn's disease.

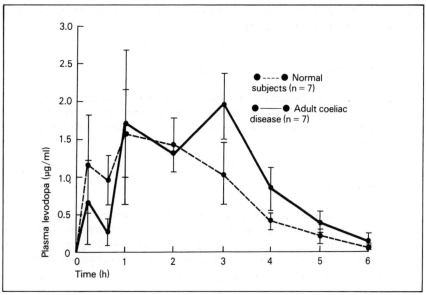

*Fig. 5.* Plasma concentration-time curves of levodopa after oral administration of 15mg/kg ('Larodopa', Roche) in healthy volunteers and adults with coeliac disease.

### 3.3 Gastric Surgery

Variable effects on drug absorption have been reported (table I).

### 3.4 Coeliac Disease

Hypothyroidism failing to respond to oral thyroxine or triiodothyronine is an important but rare complication of coeliac disease (Vanderschueren-Lodeweyckz et al., 1977). The risk of co-trimoxazole-induced aplastic anaemia is greatly increased in patients with coeliac disease and folate depletion (Chanarin and England, 1972) and osteomalacia is an important risk with prolonged anticonvulsant therapy in coeliac disease (Dent et al., 1970). The delayed absorption of many drugs in this condition (table I) is unlikely to be of therapeutic significance.

### 3.5 Effect of Gluten-free Diet on Drug Absorption in Coeliac Disease

Few patients with coeliac disease totally adhere to a gluten-free diet. However, we have found that the abnormal absorption pattern of propranolol and practolol in patients with coeliac disease improves with a gluten-free diet. In contrast, the abnormalities with cephalexin and fusidic acid become greater the longer the treatment.

### 3.6 Crohn's Disease

One possibly important consequence of altered drug absorption in patients with Crohn's disease is a change in the ratio of absorbed trimethoprim to sulphamethoxazole from the optimal ratio of 1:20 (Bushby and Hitchings, 1968). In Crohn's disease there is a relative excess of sulphamethoxazole in the plasma and the peak concentration of trimethoprim is delayed (fig. 1).

## 3.7 Diarrhoea

Diarrhoea with accelerated small intestinal transit may have important effects on drug absorption, particularly with slowly dissolving or slow release preparations. Indeed, diarrhoea has been held responsible for failure of oral contraception (John and Jones, 1975).

## 4. Conclusions

Drug absorption in patients with gastrointestinal disease is variable and unpredictable. This variation is often poorly correlated with the site and severity of disease, chemical structure and physicochemical properties of the drugs studies. Overall, the clinical significance of abnormal drug absorption is unknown, but there have been occasional reports of therapeutic failure attributed to this cause.

## References

Alexander, J.O'D.; Young, E.; McFadyen, T.; Fraser, N.G.; Duguid, W.P. and Meredith, E.M.: Absorption and excretion of $^{35}$S dapsone in dermatitis herpetiformis. British Journal of Dermatology 83: 620-631 (1970).

Back, D.J.; Breckenridge, A.M.; Crawford, F.E.; MacIver, M.; Orme, M.L'E.; Rowe, P.H., and Watts, M.J.: An investigation of the pharmacokinetics of ethinylestradiol in women using radioimmunoassay. Contraception 20: 263-274 (1979).

Baron, J.H. and Lennard-Jones, J.E.: Gastric secretion in health and disease. British Journal of Hospital Medicine 6: 303-306 (1971).

Beerman, B.; Hellstrom, K. and Rosen, A.: The gastrointestinal absorption of digoxin in 7 patients with gastric or small intestinal reconstructions. Acta Medica Scandinavica 193: 293-297 (1973).

Berndt, H.: Malabsorption due to cytostatics. Digestion 2: 358-361 (1969).

Brodie, B.B.: Physico-chemical factors in drug absorption; in Binns (Ed) Absorption and Distribution of Drugs, p.16-48 (Livingstone, Edinburgh 1964).

Bushby, S.R.M. and Hitchings, G.H.: Trimethoprim, a sulphonamide potentiator. British Journal of Pharmacology and Chemotherapy 33: 72-90 (1968).

Cerda, J.J.: Therapeutic considerations in the management of malabsorption syndromes; in Rabinowitz, and Myerson (Eds) Absorption Phenomena. Vol. 4, p.323-331 (Wiley-Interscience, New York 1974).

Chanarin, I. and England, J.M.: Toxicity of trimethoprim-sulphamethoxazole in patients with megaloblastic haemopoiesis. British Medical Journal 1: 651-653 (1972).

Compston, Juliet E. and Creamer, B.: Plasma levels and intestinal absorption of 25-hydroxyvitamin D in patients with small bowel resection. Gut 18: 171-175 (1977).

Cooper, B.T.; Cooke, W.T.; Lucas, M.L. and Blair, J.A.: Propranolol absorption in Crohn's disease and coeliac disease. British Medical Journal 4: 1135 (1976).

Cotton, P.B. and Walker, G.: Ethanol absorption after gastric operations and in the coeliac syndrome. Postgraduate Medical Journal 49: 27-28 (1973).

Davies, J.A.; Strangeways, J.E.M. and Holt, J.M.: Absorption of cephalexin from the gastrointestinal tract in diseased subjects. Postgraduate Medical Journal 46(Suppl.): 16-19 (Oct 1970).

Davies, J.A.: Absorption of cephalexin in diseased and aged subjects. Journal of Antimicrobial Chemotherapy 1(Suppl.): 69-70 (1975).

Davies, A.E. and Pirola, R.C.: Absorption of phenoxymethylpenicillin in patients with steatorrhoea. Australian Annals of Medicine 17: 63-65 (1968).

Dent, C.E.; Richens, A.; Rowe, D.J.F. and Stamp, T.C.B.: Osteomalacia with long term anticonvulsant therapy in epilepsy. British Medical Journal 4: 69-72 (1970).

Elias, E.; MacKinnon, A.M.; Short, M.D. and Dowling, R.H.: Factors controlling ileal adaptation after proximal small bowel resection and in coeliac disease. European Journal of Clinical Investigation 3: 226 (1973).

Elsborg, L.: Malabsorption of folic acid following partial gastrectomy. Scandinavian Journal of Gastroenterology 9: 271-274 (1974).

Elsborg, L.: Malabsorption in small intestinal diverticulosis treated with a low dosage sulphonamide-trimethoprim. Danish Medical Bulletin 24: 33-35 (1977).

George, C.F.; Higgins, V.; Power, K.J.; Renwick, A.G. and Smith, C.L.: Pharmacokinetics of methyldopa in gastrointestinal disease. British Journal of Clinical Pharmacology 9: 109-110 (1980).

Harris, F.C.: Pyloric stenosis. Hold-up of enteric coated aspirin tablets. British Journal of Surgery 60: 979-981 (1973).

Hartialia, K.; Kasanen, A. and Raussi, M.: The absorption of salicylamide in pernicious anaemia, gastric achylia and peptic ulcer. Annales Medicale Experimentale Fennae 41: 549-553 (1963).

Heinivaara, O. and Palva, I.P.: Malabsorption of vitamin $B_{12}$ during treatment with para-amino salicylic acid. A preliminary report. Acta Medica Scandinavica 175: 469-471 (1964).

Heizer, W.D.; Smith, T.W. and Goldfinger, S.E.: Absorption of digoxin in patients with malabsorption syndromes. New England Journal of Medicine 285: 257-259 (1971).

Holt, S.; Heading, R.C.; McLoughlin, G.P. and Prescott, L.F.: Paracetamol absorption in coeliac disease and Crohn's disease. Gut 20: A449 (1979).

John, A.H. and Jones, A.: Gastroenteritis causing failure of oral contraception. British Medical Journal 3: 207-208 (1975).

Jusko, W.J.; Mosovich, L.L.; Gerbarcht, L.M.; Mattar, M.E. and Yaffe, S.J.: Enhanced renal excretion of dicloxacillin in patients with cystic fibrosis. Pediatrics 56: 1038-1044 (1975).

Jussila, J.; Matilla, M.J. and Takki, S.: Drug absorption during lactose-induced intestinal symptoms in patients with selective lactose malabsorption. Annales Medicinae Experimentalis et Biologiae Fenniae 48: 33-37 (1970).

Keusch, G.T.; Troncale, F.J. and Buchanan, R.D.: Malabsorption due to paromomycin. Archives of Internal Medicine 125: 273-276 (1970).

Kitis, G.; Lucas, M.L.; Schneider, R.E.; Bishop, H.; Sargent, A.; Blair, J.A. and Allan, J.R.: Jejunal acid microclimate and its effect on absorption of folic acid and propranolol. Gut 20: A438 (1979).

Kowlessar, O.D.; Williams, R.C.; Law, D.H. and Sleisenger, M.H.: Urinary excretion of 5-hydroxyindoleacetic acid in diarrheal states, with special reference to nontropical sprue. New England Journal of Medicine 259: 340-341 (1958).

Kramer, P.A.; Chapron, D.J.; Benson, J. and Mercik, S.A.: Tetracycline absorption in elderly patients with achlorhydria. Clinical Pharmacology and Therapeutics 23: 467-472 (1978).

Lode, H.; Frisch, D. and Maumann, P.: Oral antibiotic therapy in patients with partial gastrectomy: in Daikas (Ed) Progress in Chemotherapy, vol.1 p.543-546 (Hellenic Society of Chemotherapy, Athens 1974).

Lupinsky, J. and Berthoud, S.: Absorption of penicillin V in relation to digestive disorders. Schweizerische Rundschau Fuer Medizinische (Praxis) 62: 959-963 (1973).

Matilla, M.J.; Friman, A.; Larmi, T.K.I. and Koskinen, R.: Absorption of ethionamide, isoniazid and aminosalicylic acid from the post-resection gastrointestinal tract. Annales Medicinae Experimentalis et Biologiae Fenniae 47: 209-212 (1969).

Matilla, M.J.; Jussila, J. and Takki, S.: Drug absorption in patients with intestinal villous atrophy. Arzneimittel-Forschung (Drug Research) 23: 583-585 (1973).

Mearrick, P.T.; Wade, D.N.; Birkett, D.J. and Morris, J.: Metoclopramide, gastric emptying and L-dopa absorption. Australian and New Zealand Journal of Medicine 4: 138-143 (1974).

Melander, A.; Kahlmeter, G.C. and Ursing, B.: Bioavailability of metronidazole in fasting and nonfasting healthy subjects and in patients with Crohn's disease. European Journal of Clinical Pharmacology 12: 69-72 (1977).

Mlynaryk, P. and Kirsner, J.B.: Absorption and excretion of $^{1,2}H^3$ hydrocortisone in regional enteritis and ulcerative colitis, with a note on hydrocortisone production rates. Gastroenterology 44: 257-60 (1963).

Moberg, S. and Carlberger, G.: Gastric emptying in healthy subjects and in patients with various malabsorptive states. Scandinavian Journal of Gastroenterology 9: 17-21 (1974).

Nelson, J.D.; Shelton, S.; Kusmiesz, H.T. and Haltalin, K.C.: Absorption of ampicillin and nalidixic acid by infants and children with actue shigellosis. Clinical Pharmacology and Therapeutics 13: 879-886 (1972).

O'Grady, F.; Dawson, A.M.; Dyer, N.H.; Hamilton, J.D. and Vince, A.: Patterns of disturbance of the gut microflora in gastrointestinal disease. Proceedings of the Eighth International Congress of Nutrition, Prague, p.438 (1971).

Palva, I.P.; Salokannel, S.J.; Timonen, T. and Palva, H.L.A.: Drug induced malabsorption of Vitamin $B_{12}$. Acta Medica Scandinavica 191: 355-357 (1972).

Parsons, R.L.; Bywaker, M.J. and Marshall, M.J.: The absorption of penicillins and cephalexin in adult coeliac disease; in Daikos (Ed). Progress in Chemotherapy, Athens, 1973, 1, p.534-542 (Hellenic Society for Chemotherapy, Athens 1974a).

Parsons, R.L.; Hossack, D.J.N.; Bywater, M.J.; Humphreys, D.M. and Hailey, D.M.: The absorption of trimethoprim, sulphamethoxazole, fucidin, lincomycin, clindamycin and rifampicin in adult coeliac disease; in Daikos (Ed). Progress in Chemotherapy: Proceedings of the 8th International Congress of Chemotherapy, Athens 1973, 1, p.499-506 (Hellenic Society for Chemotherapy, Athens 1974b).

Parsons, R.L.; Hossack, D.J.N.; Bywater, M.J.; Humphreys, D.M. and Hailey, D.M.: The absorption of antibiotics in small bowel diverticulosis; in Daikos (Ed) Progress in Chemotherapy vol.1, p.507-513 (Hellenic Society of Chemotherapy, Athens 1974c).

Parsons, R.L. and Kaye, C.M.: Plasma propranolol and practolol in adult coeliac disease. British Journal of Clinical Pharmacology 1: 348P (1974).

Parsons, R.L.; Hossack, G.A., and Paddock, G.M.: The absorption of antibiotics in adult patients with coeliac disease. Journal of Antimicrobial Chemotherapy 1: 39-50 (1975).

Parsons, R.L. and Paddock, G.M.: Absorption of two antibacterial drugs, cephalexin and co-trimoxazole in malabsorption syndromes. Journal of Antimicrobial Chemotherapy 1(Suppl.): 59-67 (1975).

Parsons, R.L.: Altered gastrointestinal function and the absorption of drugs. Drug and Therapeutic Bulletin 14: 57-58 (1976).

Parsons, R.L.; Kaye, C.M.; Raymond, K.; Trounce, J.R. and Turner, P.: Absorption of propranolol and practolol in coeliac disease. Gut 17: 139-143 (1976a).

Parsons, R.L.; Paddock, G.M.; Hossack, G.A., and Hailey, D.M.: Antibiotic absorption in Crohn's disease; in Williams and Geddes (Eds) Chemotherapy, Vol. 4, Pharmacology of Antibiotics, p.219-229 (Plenum Press, New York 1976b).

Parsons, R.L.; Jusko, W.J. and Lewis, G.P.: Pharmacokinetics of antibiotic absorption in coeliac disease. Journal of Antimicrobial Chemotherapy 2: 214-215 (1976c).

Parsons, R.L.; Paddock, G.M. and Kaye, C.M.: Drug absorption in malabsorption syndromes. Excerpta Medica International Congress Series No. 383. Proceedings of the Second International Meeting of Medical Advisers in the Pharmaceutical Industry, Florence, October 13-15, 1975. (Excerpta Medica, Amsterdam 1976d).

Parsons, R.L.: Drug absorption in gastrointestinal disease with particular reference to malabsorption syndromes. Clinical Pharmacokinetics 2: 45-60 (1977).

Parsons, R.L.; Kaye, C.M. and Raymond, K.: Pharmacokinetics of salicylate and indomethacin in coeliac disease. European Journal of Clinical Pharmacology 11: 473-477 (1977a).

Parsons, R.L.; Hossack, Gillian A. and Paddock, Gillian M.: Pharmacokinetics of pivmecillinam. British Journal of Clinical Pharmacology 4: 267-273 (1977b).

Parsons, R.L.; David, Jill A.; Paddock, Gillian M.; Raymond, K. and Kaye, C.M.: Pharmacokinetics or oral sodium fusidate and intravenous diethanolamine fusidate in normal subjects and coeliac disease: in Siegenthaler and Luthy (Eds) Current Chemotherapy. Proceedings of the 10th International Congress of Chemotherapy Zurich 18-23 Sept. 1977 vol.1, p.384-386 (American Society for Microbiology, Washington 1978).

Pottage, A.; Nimmo, J. and Prescott, L.F.: The absorption of aspirin and paracetamol in patients with achlorhydria. Journal of Pharmacy and Pharmacology 26: 144-145 (1974).

Race, T.F.; Paes, I.C. and Faloon, W.W.: Intestinal malabsorption induced by oral colchicine. Comparison with neomycin and cathartic agents. The American Journal of the Medical Sciences 259: 32-41 (1970).

Raeburn, J.A. and Devine, J.D.: Clindamycin levels in sputum in a patient with purulent chest disease due to cystic fibrosis. Postgraduate Medical Journal 47: 366-367 (1971).

Raeburn, J.A. and McCrae, W.M.: The management of chest infection in cystic fibrosis; in Daikos (Ed) Progress in Chemotherapy 2, p.730-734 (Hellenic Society for Chemotherapy, Athens 1974).

Rivera-Calimlim, L.; Dujovne, C.A.; Morgan, J.P.; Lasagna, L. and Bianchine, J.R.: L-dopa treatment failure: explanation and correction. British Medical Journal 4: 93-94 (1970).

Rivera-Calimlim, L.; Morgan, J.P.; Dujovne, C.A.; Bianchine, J.R. and Lasagna, L.: L-3, 4-dihydroxyphenylalanine metabolism by the gut in vitro. Biochemical Pharmacology 20: 3051-3057 (1971).

Saggers, B.A. and Lawson, D.: In vivo penetration of antibiotics into sputum in cystic fibrosis. Archives of Disease in Childhood 43: 404-409 (1968).

Schneider, R.E.; Babb, J.; Bishop, H.; Mitchard, M.; Hoare, A.M. and Hawkins, C.F.: Plasma levels of propranolol in treated patients with coeliac disease and patients with Crohn's disease. British Medical Journal 2: 794-795 (1976).

Schneider, R.E.; Bishop, H. and Hawkins, C.F.: Plasma propranolol concentrations and the erythrocyte sedimentation rate. British Journal of Clinical Pharmacology 8: 43-47 (1979).

Shore, P.A.; Brodie, B.B. and Hogben, C.A.M.: The gastric secretion of drugs. A pH partition hypothesis. Journal of Pharmacology and Experimental Therapeutics 119: 361-369 (1957).

Siurala, M.; Mustala, O. and Jussila, J.: Absorption of acetylsalicylic acid by a normal and an atrophic gastric mucosa. Scandinavian Journal of Gastroenterology 4: 269-273 (1969).

Sjoqvist, F.; Borga, O and Orme, M.L'E: Fundamentals of clinical pharmacology; in Avery (Ed) Drug Treatment, p.1-42 (ADIS Press, Sydney and Churchill Livingstone, Edinburgh 1976).

Smith, R.S.: Iron absorption in cystic fibrosis. British Medical Journal 1: 608-609 (1964).

Tomkin, G.H.; Hadden, D.R.; Weaver, J.A. and Montgomery, D.A.D.: Vitamin-$B_{12}$ status of patients on longterm metformin therapy. British Medical Journal 2: 685-687 (1971).

Toskes, P.P.; Hansell, J.; Cerda, J. and Deren, J.J.: Vitamin $B_{12}$ malabsorption in chronic pancreatic insufficiency. New England Journal of Medicine 284: 627-632 (1971).

Turnberg, L.A.: The absorption of iron after partial gastrectomy. Quarterly Journal of Medicine 25: 107-119 (1966).

Vanderschueren-Lodeweyckz, M.; Eggermont, E.; Cornette, C.; Beckers, C.; Malvaux, P. and Eeckels, C.: Decreased serum thyroid hormone levels and increased TSH response to TRH in infants with coeliac disease. Clinical Endocrinology 6: 361-367 (1977).

Venho, V.M.K.; Aukee, S.; Jussila, J. and Matilla, M.J.: Effect of gastric surgery on the gastrointestinal drug absorption in man. Scandinavian Journal of Gastroenterology 10: 43-47 (1975).

# Discussion

*D.W.T. Piercy* (Berkhamsted): You stressed the importance of maintaining the 1:20 ratio of trimethoprim to sulphonamide. This optimum ratio only refers to tests of *in vitro* minimum inhibitory concentration and bears no relationship to what happens in the patients.

*J. Urquhart* (Palo Alto): Could you comment on the prevalence of coeliac disease?

*R.L. Parsons*: It is quite a common condition and often goes undiagnosed. I would guess that it occurs in about 1 or 2 in every 2000.

*J. Urquhart*: To me, that is uncommon. In the context of the development of pharmaceutical products to be used for a wide variety of applications, one has to be cautious about the use of terminology with respect to prevalence. Product labelling gets more and more complex.

*R.L. Parsons*: Drug regulatory authorities increasingly are requesting pharmacokinetic information in patients with small bowel disease and malabsorption.

# 26

# Drug Absorption in 'Other Disease States'

*C.F. George, A.G. Renwick and D.G. Waller*

Clinical Pharmacology, Faculty of Medicine, University of Southampton

Drug absorption has been claimed to be abnormal in a variety of diseases (table I). Abnormalities which have been described involve the amount of drug absorbed, the absorption rate and bioavailability.

## 1. Limitations of Previous Studies

Methods of measuring the amount of drug absorbed include the recovery of $^3$H or $^{14}$C labels in the urine and breath. Although the recovery of a radiolabel in the urine provides good evidence that at least this amount has been absorbed, unless recovery is complete this technique may seriously underestimate the total absorption. For example, after the oral administration of $^{14}$C-acebutolol urinary recovery of the radiolabel varied between 26.3 and 35.3% of the dose (Collins and George, 1976). However, recovery of the remaining radioactivity in the faeces represents not only unabsorbed drug but also drug excreted in the bile and actively transported across the intestinal wall (George and Gruchy, 1979) [fig. 1]. Similarly, excretion of propranolol via the gut may account for up to 21.6% of a radiolabelled dose being recovered in the faeces of patients with renal failure (Thompson et al., 1972), compared with normal values of 0 to 4.6%.

Rates of drug absorption have often been estimated indirectly using serial measurements of blood concentrations. Usually absorption rate constants have been calculated by 'feathering' or stripping of the blood concentration-time curve (Wagner and Nelson, 1963). Many of the limitations of this method have been reviewed (Wagner, 1975), but it is invalid with extensive first-pass extraction and biotransformation. Under these circumstances the liver can act as a capacitor and calculated absorption rate constants may be wrong. For example, following the intraportal administration of propranolol in dogs, the apparent half-time of absorption using the feathering technique varied between < 5 and > 25 minutes when in reality half the dose was given in 5.4 minutes (fig. 2).

Bioavailability in disease has usually been estimated from the area under the concentration-time curve after oral administration ($AUC_o$). However, the $AUC_o$ does not provide an accurate estimate of either total absorption or bioavailability if the distribution volume (Vd) is altered.

Table I. 'Other disease states' in which drug absorption is claimed to be abnormal

| Disease state | Drug example(s) | Reference |
|---|---|---|
| Post-gastrectomy | Cephalexin | Lode et al. (1974) |
| Migraine attacks | Aspirin | Volans (1974) |
| Myocardial infarction | Procainamide | Koch-Weser (1971) |
| Heart failure | Quinidine | Bellet et al. (1971) |
| | | Crouthamel (1975) |
| | Metolazone | Tilstone et al. (1974) |
| *Inflammatory conditions* | | |
| Gut — Crohn's disease | Propranolol | Schneider et al. (1976) |
| Rheumatoid arthritis | Propranolol | Schneider (1979) |
| Renal disease | Propranolol | Thompson et al. (1972) |
| *Carcinoma* | | |
| Hepatic metastases | Pethidine | Bennett (pers. comm.) |
| Carcinostatic therapy | Phenobarbitone | Venho (1976) |
| (methotrexate) | and quinidine | |

## 2. d-Propranolol Concentrations After Myocardial Infarction

Considerable interest has centred on the prophylactic use of β-adrenoceptor antagonists after myocardial infarction since it was shown that alprenolol (Wilhelmsson et al., 1974) and practolol treatment (Multicentre International Study, 1975) started days or weeks after the event may reduce subsequent mortality.

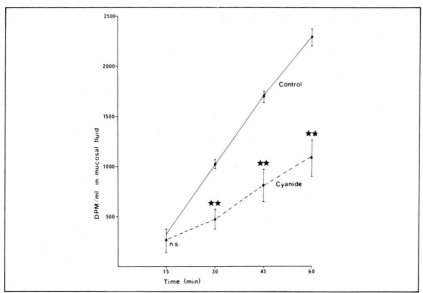

Fig. 1. The effect of cyanide $10^{-3}M$ on the *in vitro* transfer of $^{14}C$-acebutolol across isolated everted sacs of rat intestine. The 4 control sacs were incubated in Krebs solution at 37°C and bubbled with 5% $CO_2$ in oxygen. The experimental sacs were also exposed to cyanide (mean concentrations ± SE). **$p < 0.01$.

Although most deaths occur in the first 48 hours after myocardial infarction, clinical trials of propranolol given at this time failed to show any beneficial effect (Balcon et al., 1966; Clausen et al., 1966; Norris et al., 1968). One explanation for this failure of 'early' oral propranolol might be subtherapeutic blood concentrations due to poor absorption relating to low splanchnic blood flow (Maclean et al., 1978) following myocardial infarction. We have examined the plasma concentrations of propranolol given soon after infarction.

Nine patients without cardiac failure who fulfilled WHO criteria for acute myocardial infarction were studied between 18 and 36 hours after the event. By chance 2 were receiving phenytoin for epilepsy. After an overnight fast each received a single 50mg table of ( + )-propranolol and serial blood samples were drawn for measurement of plasma concentrations (Shand et al., 1970). Peak values and $AUC_0$'s were compared with values obtained in 8 control subjects.

Mean peak plasma propranolol concentrations were slightly higher in the patients with myocardial infarction than in the controls (fig. 3). Similarly, the mean AUC was larger in the infarction group. However, low plasma propranolol concentrations were seen in the 2 patients who were taking phenytoin.

## 3. Propranolol Bioavailability in Crohn's Disease and Rheumatoid Arthritis

Abnormal plasma propranolol concentrations in gastrointestinal disease were originally reported by Parsons et al. (1976) in patients with coeliac disease. Schneider et al. (1976) reported a significantly increased AUC for propranolol in Crohn's disease and subsequently in rheumatoid arthritis (Schneider et al., 1979). Several explanations have been advanced of which alterations in first-pass metabolism or distribution volume are the most plausible.

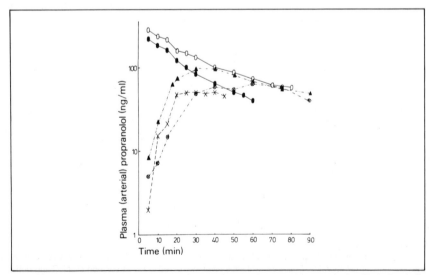

*Fig. 2.* Arterial propranolol concentrations in 5 dogs after portal venous dosing. Each dog, indicated by a different symbol, received 10.8mg propranolol, of which half was given in 5.4 minutes.

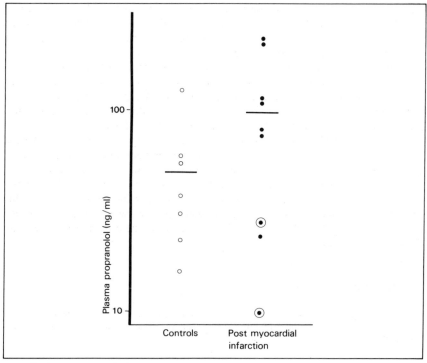

*Fig. 3.* Peak plasma ( + )-propranolol concentrations in 9 patients given 50mg orally within 36 hours of myocardial infarction. 2 patients (⊙) were receiving phenytoin.

Four patients with Crohn's disease and one with rheumatoid arthritis (ESR 100mm/h) have been studied so far, as described by Castleden and George (1979). Propranolol concentrations were measured by high pressure liquid chromatography (Nation et al., 1978).

In 3 of the 4 patients with Crohn's disease high plasma propranolol concentrations were found in the first hour after intravenous administration but beyond this time values fell to within our normal range. In contrast, in the single patient with rheumatoid arthritis, higher than normal values were seen throughout (fig. 4).

## 4. Discussion

It is well recognised that absorption of drugs from the subcutaneous and intramuscular sites is blood-flow-dependent but there are comparatively few data to show that splanchnic blood flow is of similar importance for drug absorption from the gut. Exceptions include various non-dissociable substances studied by Winne and Remischovsky (1970) in rat jejunal loops and cardiac glycosides in the guinea-pig (Haass et al., 1972). Nevertheless, the demonstration by computer simulation (Maclean et al., 1978) that splanchnic blood flow might affect bioavailability of orally administered propranolol, provided a potential explanation for the failure of 3 clinical trials to show any early benefit from this drug after myocardial infarction. However, in the present study on 9 patients therapeutic plasma concentrations were achieved in the majority after a 50mg oral dose of the dextro isomer. It is possible that the results would be different in the presence of heart failure. There is little published evidence that cardiac decompensation has any effect on drug absorption from the gut (Benet et al., 1976). However, significant abnormalities have been reported with hydrochlorothiazide (Anderson et al., 1961), procainamide (Koch-Weser, 1971), metolazone (Tilstone et al., 1974) and quinidine (Crouthamel, 1975). With most other drugs variation in plasma concentrations relates to differences in their distribution volume (Thomson et al., 1971; Ilett et al., 1979) or slow metabolism associated with diminished hepatic blood flow (Prescott et al., 1976; Jaillon et al., 1979).

Numerous explanations have been advanced for abnormalities of the plasma concentration-time curve for propranolol following oral administration in coeliac or Crohn's disease, and rheumatoid arthritis (Parsons et al., 1976; Schneider et al., 1979). Despite the small number of patients the present studies provide the first evidence of altered pharmacokinetics in the first hour after intravenous dosing. This probably reflects altered binding to plasma acid $\alpha_1$-glycoprotein (and other proteins) in both conditions (Piafsky et al., 1978). Collectively, these plasma proteins may delay the distribution of propranolol to the tissues.

## Acknowledgements

We are grateful to Mrs S. Evans for skilled technical assistance and to Mrs F.D. Lowman for typing the manuscript. We wish to thank ICI for the gift of the internal standards used in the propranolol assays and the British Heart Foundation for financial support.

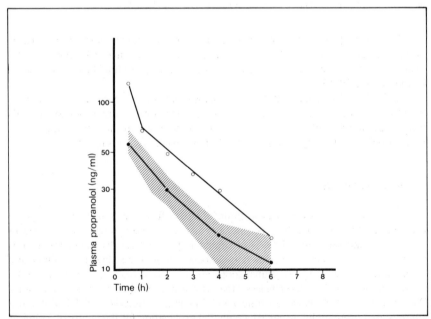

*Fig. 4.* Concentration-time curve for propranolol (0.15mg/kg intravenously) in a single patient with active rheumatoid arthritis. The shaded area represents our normal range of concentrations and the solid round symbols the mean values.

# References

Anderson, K.V.; Brettell, H.R. and Aikwa, J.K.: C$^{14}$-labelled hydrochlorothiazide in human beings. Archives of Internal Medicine 107: 168-174 (1961).

Balcon, R.; Jewitt, D.E.; Davies, J.P.H. and Oram, S.: A controlled trial of propranolol in acute myocardial infarction. Lancet 2: 917-920 (1966).

Bellet, S.; Roman, L.R. and Boza, A.: Relation between serum quinidine levels and renal function. American Journal of Cardiology 27: 368-371 (1971).

Benet, L.Z.; Greither, A. and Meister, W.: Gastrointestinal absorption of drugs in patients with cardiac failure; in Benet (Ed) The Effect of Disease States on Drug Pharmacokinetics, p.33-50 (American Pharmaceutical Association. Washington 1976).

Castleden, C.M. and George, C.F.: The effect of ageing on the hepatic clearance of propranolol. British Journal of Clinical Pharmacology 7: 49-54 (1979).

Clausen, J.; Felsby, M.; Schonau Jorgensen, F.; Lyager Nielsen, B.; Roin, J. and Strange, B.: Absence of prophylactic effect of propranolol in myocardial infarction. Lancet 2: 920-924 (1966).

Collins, R.F. and George, C.F.: Studies on the disposition and fate of [$^{14}$C]-acebutolol in man and dog. British Journal of Clinical Pharmacology 3: 346P (1976).

Crouthamel, W.G.: The effect of congestive heart failure on quinidine pharmacokinetics. American Heart Journal 90: 335-339 (1975).

George, C.F. and Gruchy, B.S.: Elimination of drugs by active intestinal transport. Journal of Pharmacy and Pharmacology 31: 643-644 (1979).

Haass, A.; Lullman, H. and Peters, Th.: Absorption rates of some cardiac glycosides and portal blood flow. European Journal of Pharmacology 19: 366-370 (1972).

Ilett, K.F.; Madsen, B.W. and Woods, J.D.: Pharmacokinetics of disopyramide in patients with acute myocardial infarction. Clinical Pharmacology and Therapeutics 26: 1-7 (1979).

Jaillon, P.; Rubin, P.; Yee, Y-G.; Ball, R.; Kates, R.; Harrison, D. and Blaschke, T.: Influence of congestive heart failure on prazosin kinetics. Clinical Pharmacology and Therapeutics 25: 792-794 (1979).

Koch-Weser, J.: Pharmacokinetics of procainamide in man. Annals of the New York Academy of Sciences 179: 370-382 (1971).

Lode, H.; Frisch, D. and Naumann, P.: Oral antibiotic therapy in patients with partial gastrectomy; in Daikos (Ed) Progress in Chemotherapy, vol. 1, p543-546 (Helenic Society of Chemotherapy, Athens 1974).

McLean, A.J.; McNamara, P.J.; du Souich, P.; Gibaldi, M. and Lalka, D.: Food, splanchnic blood flow and bioavailability of drugs subject to first-pass metabolism. Clinical Pharmacology and Therapeutics 24: 5-10 (1978).

Multicentre International Study: Improvement in prognosis of myocardial infarction by long term beta adrenoceptor blockade using practolol. British Medical Journal 3: 735-740 (1975).

Nation, R.L.; Peng, G.W. and Chiou, W.L.: High pressure liquid chromatographic method for the simultaneous quantitative analysis of propranolol and 4-hydroxy propranolol in plasma. Journal of Chromatography 145: 429-436 (1978).

Norris, R.M.; Caughey, D.E. and Scott, P.J.: Trial of propranolol in acute myocardial infarction. British Medical Journal, 2: 398-400 (1968).

Parsons, R.L.; Kaye, C.M.; Raymond, K.; Trounce, J.R. and Turner, P.: Absorption of propranolol and practolol in coeliac disease. Gut 17: 139-143 (1976).

Piafsky, K.M.; Borga, O.; Odar-Cederlof, I.; Johansson, C. and Sjoqvist, F.: Increased plasma protein binding of propranolol and chlorpromazine mediated by disease-induced elevations of plasma $\alpha_1$ acid glycoprotein. New England Journal of Medicine 299: 1435-1439 (1978).

Prescott, L.F.; Adjepon-Yamoah, K.K. and Talbot, R.G.: Impaired lignocaine metabolism in patients with myocardial infarction and cardiac failure. British Medical Journal 1: 939-941 (1976).

Schneider, R.E.; Babb, J.; Bishop, H.; Mitchard, M.; Hoare, A.M. and Hawkins, C.F.: Plasma levels of propranolol in treated patients with coeliac disease and patients with Crohn's disease. British Medical Journal 2: 794-795 (1976).

Schneider, R.E.; Bishop, H. and Hawkins, C.F.: Plasma propranolol concentrations and the erythrocyte sedimentation rate. British Journal of Clinical Pharmacology 8: 43-47 (1979).

Shand, D.G.; Nuckolls, E.M. and Oates, J.A.: Plasma propranolol levels in adults with observations in four children. Clinical Pharmacology and Therapeutics 11: 112-120 (1970).

Thompson, F.D.; Joekes, A.M. and Foulkes, D.M.: Pharmacodynamics of propranolol in renal failure. British Medical Journal 2: 434-436 (1972).

Thomson, P.D.; Rowland, M. and Melmon, K.L.: The influence of heart failure, liver disease, and renal failure on the disposition of lidocaine in man. American Heart Journal 82: 417-421 (1971).

Tilstone, W.J.; Dargie, H.; Dargie, E.N.; Morgan, H.G. and Kennedy, A.C.: Pharmacokinetics of metolazone in normal subjects and in patients with cardiac or renal failure. Clinical Pharmacology and Therapeutics 16: 322-329 (1974).

Venho, V.M.: Effect of methotrexate on drug absorption from the rat small intestine *in situ* and *in vitro*. Acta Pharmacologia et Toxicologia 38: 450-464 (1976).

Volans, G.N.: Absorption of effervescent aspirin during migraine. British Medical Journal 4: 265-268 (1974).

Wagner, J.G.: Fundamentals of Clinical Pharmacokinetics (Drug Intelligence Publications Inc., Hamilton 1975).

Wagner, J.G. and Nelson, E.: Percent absorbed time plots derived from blood level and/or urinary excretion data. Journal of Pharmaceutical Sciences 52: 610-611 (1963).

Wilhelmsson, C.; Vedin, J.A.; Wilhelsen, L.; Tibblin, G. and Werko, L.: Reduction of sudden deaths after myocardial infarction by treatment with alprenolol. Lancet 2: 1157-1159 (1974).

Winne, D. and Remischovsky, J.: Intestinal blood flow and absorption of non-dissociable substances. Journal of Pharmacy and Pharmacology 22: 640-641 (1970).

## Discussion

*R.C. Heading* (Chairman): I notice that you and Dr Parsons used fixed doses of drugs in your patients and control subjects. In my experience, patients with gastrectomy or untreated coeliac disease are often underweight and if given the standard dose, will obviously have different blood concentrations. Why did you not give doses adjusted for weight?

*C.F. George*: There were differences in the weights of our patients and our controls but nevertheless they were small and could not have accounted for the differences in concentration that we saw.

*J.A.J.H. Critchley* (Edinburgh): Can you comment on the belief that the absorption of oral frusemide is reduced in cardiac failure?

*C.F. George*: There are only 4 reasonably convincing studies of drug absorption in cardiac failure. The drugs were quinidine, metazolone, procainamide and hydrochlorothiazide. The pharmacokinetics after oral and intravenous administration have not been compared adequately. I am not totally convinced that there is any abnormality in the absorption of any drug in heart failure *per se*. It is extremely difficult to find a homogeneous population for such studies. Apart from the effects of disease, patients are often given other drugs which might for example, affect gastric emptying. Although more studies are needed, they are very difficult to do and I think I am going to abandon mine.

# 27

# Assessment of Drug Absorption: Pharmacokinetic Interpretation and Limitations

*Malcolm Rowland*

Department of Pharmacy, University of Manchester

Many of the preceding contributions have dealt with mechanisms of gastrointestinal absorption, factors that influence the process and the relevance of such factors to the administration of drugs to man. It has been tacitly assumed that our understanding of the process is relatively clear and that accurate methods exist for assessing both the rate and extent of absorption. While generally this is so, in specific instances it is not. I shall illustrate some difficulties in the assessment of absorption *in vivo* and indicate possible solutions.

## 1. A Definition

Part of the problem of the assessment of absorption lies in its definition. To some, absorption is the disappearance of drug from the gastrointestinal lumen, to many others it is the movement of drug across the gastrointestinal tract. Although techniques for sampling gastrointestinal fluids *in vivo* are available, difficulties arise in relating changes in the concentration of drug in the fluid sampled to rates of entry into the body, partly because of continuous changes in the volume of the gastrointestinal fluids and partly because of potential gastrointestinal destruction of drug. Causes of destruction include chemical instability and metabolism by gut wall enzymes or intestinal microflora (Mayersohn, 1979; Renwick, 1977; Rowland, 1973). Movement of drug across the intestinal epithelium can be measured *in vitro* (Barr, 1972), but this is difficult *in vivo* and virtually impossible in man, as it entails collecting blood immediately it leaves the gastrointestinal tract (Barr and Riegelman, 1970). Even then one cannot be sure that the rates of appearance of drug in the blood and transport across the intestinal epithelium are equal because of the possibility of metabolism by gut mucosal enzymes. Because of these inherent problems, assessment of absorption *in vivo* generally involves monitoring the drug, or sometimes its metabolite(s), at some site distant from the gastrointestinal tract.

Common sites of measurement are blood, usually taken from a peripheral (arm) vein, and urine; occasionally it may be a tissue in which the drug produces a response (Smolen and Weigand, 1973). Irrespective of the site monitored, however, drug must first dissolve and then traverse many sites such as the gut-wall, the liver, and the lungs (fig. 1). Incomplete dissolution or destruction at any of these sites will result in a loss of drug reaching the site of measurement. Most investigators use the intravenous route as a method to assess the 'absolute' amount of drug absorbed. Accordingly, absorption may be defined as the events that occur between drug administration and the appearance of drug at the site of measurement. Such a definition is compatible with inclusion of the pre-systemic first-pass effect, as a cause of decreased absorption (Gibaldi and Feldman, 1969; Rowland, 1973). The events beyond absorption, namely distribution and elimination, are generally referred to as disposition.

Given the above definition of absorption, rates and extents of the process can be assessed but since there are many events that can occur during absorption, interpretation of the results can sometimes be difficult. Incomplete absorption, for example, may be due to one or more of the events depicted in figure 1. Careful investigation is usually necessary to evaluate the relative contribution of any individual site of loss to an overall incomplete absorption. Moreover, elucidation of the mechanisms of absorption often involves the use of isolated organ or tissue preparations.

## 2. Assessment of Extent

The assessment of extent, F (often referred to as the bioavailability of the drug) follows from the fundamental relationship

$$F \cdot Dose = CL \cdot AUC \qquad \qquad Eq. \ 1$$

where CL, denotes the total clearance of the drug, and AUC the total area under the drug concentration-time profile from time zero to infinity.

An error in the assessment of availability immediately arises with the estimation of the AUC, partly due to the discrete nature of sampling and partly because sampling does not take place to infinite time. Several techniques are used to assess the area under the curve up to the last observation. The most common is the trapezoidal method, applied either to the observed data or to logarithmically transformed data. Yeh and Kwan (1978) have examined these two techniques and also the Lagrange and spline methods and found that under some circumstances the spline method leads to less error in the assessment of area. All methods introduce some error however. Estimation of the area beyond the last observation is generally predicated on the assumption that the kinetics that define the terminal part of the observed data can be extrapolated to time infinity. Unfortunately sometimes this is not so and generally one needs to sample for at least 4 to 5 elimination half-lives to minimise the problem.

A common practice is to compare the availability of the drug between 2 treatments, one being the drug preparation of interest and the other usually a reference treatment which may either be an intravenous dose or the most completely available extravascularly administered product. The corresponding equation defining the ratio of availability is

$$\frac{F_1}{F_2} = \frac{(CL_1 \cdot AUC_{1/Dose_1})}{(CL_2 \cdot AUC_{2/Dose_2})}$$                Eq. 2

Total clearance of the drug is generally assumed to be constant between treatments so that the ratio of availabilities is given by the ratio of the dose-normalised AUC values.

The use of urinary excretion data to assess the extent of absorption following a single dose of drug stems from the relationship that

$$F \cdot Dose = f_e \cdot Ae_\infty$$                Eq. 3

where $f_e$ is the fraction of the drug entering the general circulation which is excreted unchanged, and $Ae_\infty$ is the cumulative amount of drug excreted unchanged from time zero to time infinity. As before, one compares the ratio of the extents of absorption between 2 treatments. No matter whether plasma concentration or urinary excretion data are used, it is generally assumed that the values of the parameters such as clearance and fraction of drug excreted unchanged remain constant with both concentration and time. Unfortunately, this is not always the case.

### 2.1 Non-linear Clearance: Plasma Data

Salicylamide is a classic example of a drug with non-linear clearance, as shown by a disproportionate increase in AUC with increasing oral doses (fig. 2). The AUC-oral dose relationship is also said to be non-linear with propranolol (Shand and Rango, 1972; Walle et al., 1978) and alprenolol (Ablad et al., 1972). Shand and

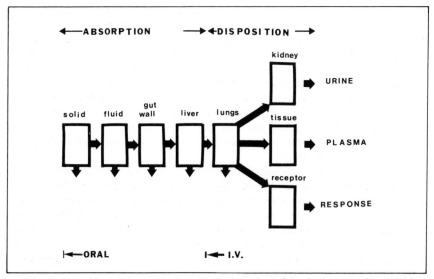

*Fig. 1.* Disposition encompasses all events within the body following intravascular administration. Absorption may be regarded as the additional events that occur as drug proceeds, for the first time, from site of administration to site of measurement; included are dissolution, transmembrane permeation, and passage through the liver.

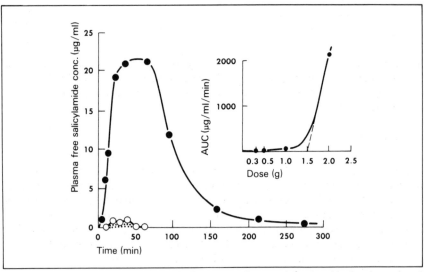

*Fig. 2.* Plasma concentration and AUC increase disproportionately with the dose of oral salicylamide (○ = 0.3 to 1.0g; ● = 2g). [Barr, 1969 with permission].

Rango (1972) gave propranolol intravenously and showed that within the concentration range studied, total clearance was constant. This observation supported their hypothesis that the disproportionate increase in AUC with oral dose is associated with an increase in availability due to saturation of hepatic metabolism during the first-pass of this highly cleared drug through the liver. Unfortunately, such clear cut statements cannot be made for salicylamide. This drug has a relatively small volume of distribution (Barr, 1969) and if an increase in availability is due to saturation of hepatic enzymes, then saturation should also occur following comparable intravenous doses (fig. 3). The resultant decrease in clearance with increasing plasma concentration, and hence dose, makes any quantitative estimation of availability, based on analysis of plasma concentration data, extremely difficult (Rowland, 1973). The absence of such a change in clearance with intravenous propranolol can be explained by its large volume of distribution so that systemically administered drug is so diluted before reaching the liver that the hepatic enzymes are not saturated. In contrast, the concentration of drug reaching the liver can be much higher when administered orally, as all absorbed drug must pass through the liver before being distributed systemically (Rowland, 1973).

The clearance of disopyramide increases with plasma concentration, making assessment of absorption based on plasma concentration data difficult. One solution to this problem is to base assessment on the unbound drug. Clearance increases because plasma binding decreases with increasing drug concentration, whereas clearance based on unbound drug remains constant (Meffin et al., 1979). Alternatively, assessment can be based on urinary excretion data as disopyramide is substantially excreted unchanged and the rate of excretion depends on the unbound rather than on the total drug concentration.

The clearance of phenytoin is also concentration dependent but in this case it is due to saturation of hepatic metabolic enzymes rather than altered protein binding. Recognising the difficulties created by saturable metabolism, Melikian et al. (1977)

compared the absorption of various commercial preparations of phenytoin by giving single small doses which, by not saturating the enzymes, permitted the use of dose-AUC comparisons to assess availability. Phenytoin, however, is intended for chronic use and because in therapeutic doses rates of administration approach the maximum rate of drug metabolism, the steady-state plasma concentration of this drug is extremely sensitive to small differences in the extent of absorption (fig. 4). Such small differences would be extremely difficult to detect from single low dose studies. Chronic dosing studies are necessary to assess the performance of preparations of phenytoin and similarly handled drugs, whether administered alone, with food, or with other drugs that may alter bioavailability. This extreme sensitivity of the steady-state plasma concentration of phenytoin to changes in extent of absorption may explain why the effects of changes in formulation by a manufacturer were detected only after clinical (chronic) use (Tyrer et al., 1970).

## 2.2 Non-linear Clearance: Excretion Data

Problems in the use of urinary excretion data to assess the extent of absorption exist when the value of $f_e$ is concentration and time dependent. $f_e$ is dependent upon the ratio of renal to total clearance; total clearance is the sum of renal and extra-renal clearance. If total clearance changes so generally does $f_e$. Renal clearance can also change with plasma concentration, generally due to saturation of the secretory

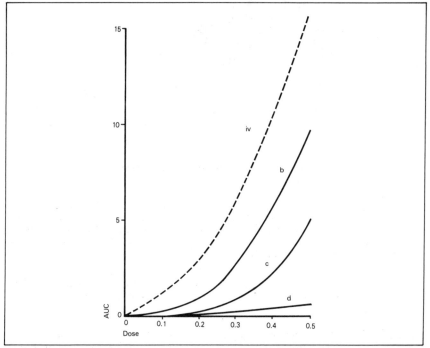

*Fig. 3.* Simulation showing disproportionate increase in AUC when hepatic drug metabolism is saturated after both oral (b, c and d) and intravenous (iv) administration. For a given dose, AUC is lower the slower the absorption (absorption rate b > c > d). [Rowland, 1973].

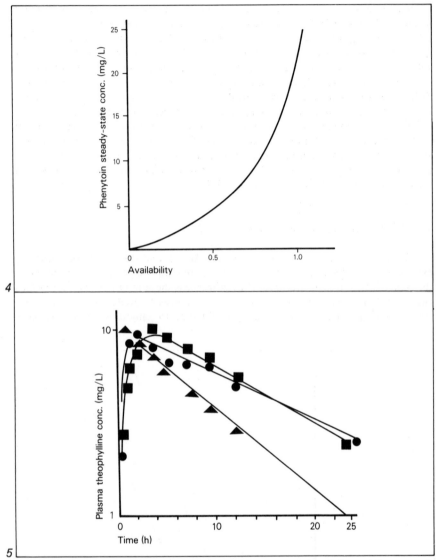

*Fig. 4.* Owing to saturation, the steady-state plasma concentration of phenytoin is very sensitive to differences in the extent of absorption as absorption approaches completeness. The calculation is based on the assumption that phenytoin is eliminated by a single enzyme system, that the daily dose = 300mg; that the maximum rate of metabolism = 400mg/day and that Michaelis-Menten constant = 8mg/litre.

*Fig. 5.* The terminal half-life of theophylline varies within the same individual when the drug is administered orally on different occasions (Upton et al., in press, with permission).

mechanisms, or it can change with time if renal clearance depends on urinary pH and flow (Weiner, 1973). When renal clearance is a large component of total clearance, changes in renal clearance are reflected by changes in total clearance making assessment from plasma concentration data also difficult. If extra-renal clearance is constant, however, a solution to this problem, of concentration and time dependence in renal clearance, consists of simultaneously measuring drug in plasma and in urine and applying mass balance equations (Rowland, 1973; Till et al., 1974). No problem in assessment exists with ampicillin (Jusko et al., 1973) and phenylpropanolamine (Beckett and Wilkinson, 1965), drugs that are excreted almost entirely unchanged. Here, of course, total urinary excretion is an accurate estimate of the extent of absorption.

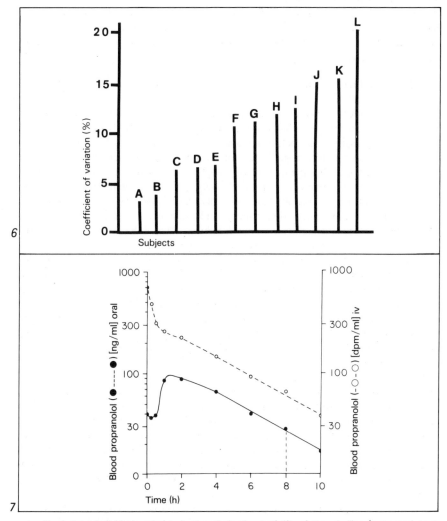

Fig. 6. Intra-individual variation in the elimination half-life of theophylline (expressed as a coefficient of variation) in 12 subjects (Upton et al., in press, with permission).

Fig. 7. Simultaneous determination of intravenous (disposition) and oral kinetics of propranolol in man. The solid circles represent the concentration of unlabelled propranolol in whole blood after chronic oral dosing. The open circles represent the concentration of tritiated propranolol after an intravenous tracer dose. The dotted line marks the end of the oral dosing interval of 8 hours (Kornhauser et al., 1978 with permission).

Urinary excretion data can sometimes be used to assess the extent of absorption even when metabolic clearance is non-linear. Non-linearity in the clearance of salicylic acid for example is partly due to saturation of the drug metabolism enzymes and partly to saturation of plasma protein binding sites. Such non-linearity makes assessment of absorption from plasma concentration data extremely difficult. Yet the problem becomes tractable through the analysis of unchanged drug and the metabolites in urine. The glycine conjugate (salicyluric acid) and 2 glucuronides account for almost the entire dose absorbed (Levy, 1965). By assaying all these species collectively (as total salicylate) assessment of absorption becomes simple. This procedure has also been applied to tolbutamide and griseofulvin (Riegelman et al., 1970), although with these 2 drugs non-linear disposition kinetics within the normal dose range has not been demonstrated.

## 2.3 Time Dependency

Intra-individual variability in the pharmacokinetic parameters of drugs occurs and the magnitude of the variability depends upon the drug (Alvares et al., 1979; Rowland, in press). Other factors include disease, other drugs, food and diet but variation can occur within an individual for no apparent reason. For example, Upton et al. (in press) found that the half-life of theophylline varied quite widely within individuals taking the same dose under relatively controlled conditions (fig. 5). The elimination half-life of theophylline, not only varied considerably within an individual but the degree of variation from one individual to another also varied (fig. 6). Using AUC as a bioavailability parameter, Schrogie et al. (1979), observed substantial intra-subject variability for methyldopa when the same dose was given orally to a panel of volunteers on 3 separate days. Such variation makes assessment of absorption difficult. Without replicate experiments it is difficult to separate intra-individual variability from the sensitivity of an individual to formulation effects.

One potential solution to the problem of intra-individual variability in disposition kinetics is to administer the drug orally and intravenously simultaneously. The common practice is to give the standard formulation of drug orally and either an intravenous radio-labelled tracer dose or a stable isotope intravenously. The use of this technique to assess the disposition kinetics of propranolol and its absorption after chronic oral administration is shown in figure 7. The assumption is made that the intravenous dose does not affect either the absorption or disposition kinetics of the orally administered drug. This situation is likely to be fulfilled with the radio-labelled tracer dose but would probably need to be tested when using stable isotopes. Generally the dose of stable isotope is of the same order as the oral dose and under these circumstances linearity in disposition kinetics would first need to be demonstrated. This technique can be particularly useful for the study of absorption of drugs in diseases which alter disposition kinetics and when the severity of the disease varies with time.

Simultaneous administration of a stable isotope solution and a standard drug formulation may reduce the number of subjects required to compare different formulations of the same drug (Heck et al., 1979). Because of both inter and intra-individual pharmacokinetic variability, relatively large numbers are required to assess with confidence whether any differences exist in the absorption of a drug from different formulations. By giving the stable isotope in solution simultaneously with the formulation, differences between drug and stable isotope can be assumed to reflect purely formulation effects. That is, once in solution, drug and stable isotope are handled identically. By adopting this approach, only 4 subjects were needed to compare 2 formulations of imipramine, whereas with the conventional bioavailability study 20 to 26 subjects would have been required to reach the same degree of confidence.

## 2.4 An Average Value

One assumption in the use of the stable isotope, given in solution orally is that absorption is similar to that of the solid drug once dissolved — a reasonable assumption when dealing with conventional dosage forms. A potential difficulty might arise with the evaluation of prolonged release formulations since the drug may be then released further down the gastrointestinal tract at sites that are not reached by the stable isotope given in solution. The absorption of drugs from these lower sites may be different from that at the upper part of the gastrointestinal tract. Several years ago Dr Sidney Riegelman and I found that the fractions of acetylsalicylic acid (aspirin) absorbed from a solution, a buffered preparation and a prolonged release formulation, compared to an intravenous dose, were 0.65, 0.65 and 0.48 respectively. The method of assessment was based on area comparisons using equation 2. Area measurements, however, give an estimate of the extent of absorption over all periods of time; that is, the estimate is an average value.

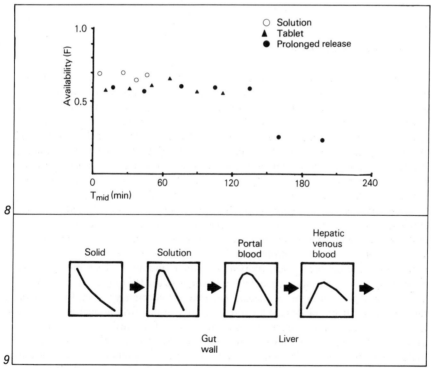

Fig. 8. Changes in the same subject, in the ratio of the rate of absorption of aspirin to that of aspirin plus salicylic acid with time, after aspirin is administered orally in solution (○), as a conventional tablet (▲) and as a prolonged release dosage form (●).

Fig. 9. The progressive dampening of the concentration-time profile of a drug (insets) as it proceeds through the various sites during systemic absorption.

The absorption of aspirin is incomplete because it is hydrolysed to salicylic acid in the gastrointestinal fluids, gut wall and liver. We measured both aspirin and salicylic acid in plasma and gave both drugs intravenously on separate occasions. Together, this information allowed an estimate of not only the extent of absorption of aspirin but also the rate of entry of aspirin and salicylic acid formed during absorption. It was therefore possible to estimate the fraction that was aspirin of the total mass absorbed at any time. For the first 2 hours, little difference in the extent of absorption of aspirin was seen between drug given as solution, tablet or as prolonged release form and the absorption of aspirin from the last formulation was reduced primarily because the fraction of released drug absorbed as aspirin diminished dramatically after 2 hours (fig. 8). Dawson and Pryse-Davies (1963) found that the distribution of gut wall esterase activity varies along the gastrointestinal tract, and a possible explanation for the results shown in figure 8 is that aspirin from the prolonged release formulation is released later and further down the gastrointestinal tract, where the mucosa may be richer in these hydrolytic enzymes. If this is the explanation it would suggest that there is little justification for prolonged release formulations of aspirin. For other drugs, differences in permeability characteristics in different parts of the small intestine may exist, as may differences in the dissolution profiles of drugs from solid particulate matter. Such differences potentially could be reflected in low and poor absorption from oral prolonged release formulations.

## 3. Assessment of Rate

Whatever problems exist in measurement of extent of absorption, they are compounded when assessing the rate. Assumptions of linearity and time-invariance in disposition kinetics are still necessary. In addition, numerical problems arise from the discrete nature of the observations. There are numerous methods for assessing the rate of absorption, assuming linear disposition pharmacokinetics including those of Wagner-Nelson (1964), Loo-Riegelman (1968) and various deconvolution techniques (Rescigno and Segre, 1966). The numerical problems associated with deconvolution have been explored by Cutler (1978a,b). Greater difficulties exist when the disposition kinetics of a drug are non-linear. Martis and Levy (1973), have suggested a method for assessing rates of absorption when elimination is by one saturable and one linear pathway, but the problems of multiple saturated pathways and changes in the volume of distribution with concentration remain to be solved. Even if these problems were surmountable, an additional problem still arises. Each barrier between the site of administration and the site of measurement is an impedance to the drug, distorting and dampening its concentration-time profile (George et al. 1976) [fig. 9]. Thus while 'rates of absorption' may be calculated, they may not accurately reflect, for example, rates of release from the dosage form, particularly in the early moments of absorption. These distortions are smaller the more dissolution becomes the rate-limiting step in the overall process. The problem can be minimised by using, for example, the technique described above in which stable isotope in solution is administered simultaneously with the solid drug, with the proviso about prolonged release formulations. Nonetheless, the difficulties involved in making these comparisons between rates *in vitro* and *in vivo* have led many investigators to simply compare different formulations based on the time to peak and the peak concentration (Westlake, 1973).

# References

Ablad, B.; Ervik, M.; Hallgren, J.; Johnsson, G. and Solvell, L.: Pharmacological effects and serum levels of orally administered alprenolol in man. European Journal of Clinical Pharmacology 5: 44-52 (1972).

Alvares, A.P.; Kappas, A.; Eiseman, J.L.; Anderson, K.E.; Pantuck, B.A.; Pantuck, E.J.; Hsiao, K-C.; Garland, W.A. and Conney, A.H.: Intra-individual variation in drug disposition. Clinical Pharmacology and Therapeutics 26: 407-429 (1979).

Barr, W.H.: Factors involved in the assessment of systemic or biologic availability of drug products. Drug Information Bulletin 3: 27-45 (1969).

Barr, W.H.: The use of physical and animal models to assess bioavailability. Pharmacology 8: 55-101 (1972).

Barr, W.H. and Riegelman, S.: Intestinal drug absorption and metabolism. I. Comparison of methods and models to study physiological factors of *in vitro* and *in vivo* intestinal absorption. Journal of Pharmaceutical Sciences 59: 154-163 (1970).

Beckett, A.H. and Wilkinson, G.R.: Urinary excretion of (-)-methylephedrine, (-)-ephedrine and (-)-norephedrine in man. Journal of Pharmacy and Pharmacology 17 (Suppl.): 107S-108S (1965).

Cutler, D.J.: Numerical deconvolution by least squares: use of prescribed input functions. Journal of Pharmacokinetics and Biopharmaceutics 6: 227-242 (1978a).

Cutler, D.J.: Numerical deconvolution by least squares: use of polynomials to represent the input function. Journal of Pharmacokinetics and Biopharmaceutics 6: 243-264 (1978b).

Dawson, I. and Pryse-Davies, J.: The distribution of certain enzyme systems in the normal human gastrointestinal tract. Gastroenterology 44: 745-760 (1963).

George, C.F.; Orme, M. L'E,; Buranapong, P.; Macerlean, D.; Breckenridge, A.M. and Dollery, C.T.: Contribution of the liver to overall elimination of propranolol. Journal of Pharmacokinetics and Biopharmaceutics 4: 17-28 (1976).

Gibaldi, M. and Feldman, S.: Pharmacokinetic basis for the influence of route of administration on the area under the plasma concentration-time curve. Journal of Pharmaeutical Sciences 58: 1477-1480 (1969).

Heck, H.d'A,; Buttrill, S.E.; Flynn, N.W.; Dryer, R.L.; Anbar, M.; Cairns, T.; Dighe, S. and Cabana, B.E.: Bioavailability of imipramine tablets relative to a stable isotope-labelled internal standard: increasing the power of bioavailability tests. Journal of Pharmacokinetics and Biopharmaceutics 7: 233-248 (1979).

Jusko, W.J.; Lewis, G.P. and Schmitt, G.W.: Ampicillin and hetacillin pharmacokinetics in normal and anephric subjects. Clinical Pharmacology and Therapeutics 14: 90-99 (1973).

Kornhauser, D.M.; Wood, A.J.J.; Vestal, R.E.; Wilkinson, G.R.; Branch, R.A. and Shand, D.G.: Biological determinants of propranolol disposition in man. Clinical Pharmacology and Therapeutics 23: 165-174 (1978).

Levy, G.: Pharmacokinetics of salicylic acid. Journal of Pharmaceutical Sciences 54: 959-966 (1965).

Loo, J.C.K. and Riegelman, S.: New method for calculating the intrinsic absorption rate of drugs. Journal of Pharmaceutical Sciences 57: 918-928 (1968).

Martis, L. and Levy, R.H.: Bioavailability calculations for drugs showing simultaneous first-order and capacity-limited elimination kinetics. Journal of Pharmacokinetics and Biopharmaceutics 1: 283-294 (1973).

Mayersohn, M.: Physiological factors that modify systemic drug availability and pharmacologic response in clinical practice; in Blanchard, Sawchuck and Brodie (Eds) Principles and Perspectives in Drug Bioavailability, p.211-273 (Karger, Basel 1979).

Meffin, P.J.; Rober, E.W.; Winkle, R.A.; Harapat, S.; Peters, F.A. and Harrison, D.C.: Role of concentration-dependent plasma protein binding in disopyramide disposition. Journal of Pharmacokinetics and Biopharmaceutics 7: 29-46 (1979).

Melikian, A.P.; Straughn, A.B.; Slywka, G.W.A.; Whyatt, P.L. and Meyer, M.C.: Bioavailability of 11 phenytoin products. Journal of Pharmacokinetics and Biopharmaceutics 5: 133-146 (1977).

Renwick, A.G.: Microbial metabolism of drugs; in Parke and Smith (Eds) Drug Metabolism. From Microbes to Man, p.167-189 (Taylor and Francis, London 1977).

Rescigno, A. and Segre, G.: in Drug and Tracer Kinetics, p.102-110 (Blaisdell Publishers, Waltham 1966).

Riegelman, S.; Rowland, M. and Epstein, W.L.: Griseofulvin-phenobarbital interaction in man. The Journal of the American Medical Association 213: 426-431 (1970).

Rowland, M.: Effect of some physiologic factors on bioavailability of oral dose forms; in Swarbrick (Ed) Current Concepts in the Pharmaceutical Sciences: Dosage Form Design and Bioavailability, p.181-222 (Lea and Febiger, Philadelphia 1973).

Rowland, M.: Intra-individual variability in pharmacokinetics; in Breimer (Ed) Safety of Drugs and Pharmaceutical Products (Elsevier, Holland, in press).

Schrogie, J.J.: Davies, R.O.; Hwang, S.S.; Hesney, M.; Breault, G.O.; Kwan, K.C.; Huber, P.B.; Feinberg, J.A.; Abrams, W.B. and Zinny, M.A.: Intrasubject variability in methyldopa bioavailability. Clinical Pharmacology and Therapeutics 25: 248 (1979).

Shand, D.G. and Rango, R.E.: The disposition of propranolol. I. Elimination during oral absorption in man. Pharmacology 7: 159-168 (1972).

Smolen, V.F. and Weigand, W.A.: Drug bioavailability and pharmacokinetic analysis from pharmacological data. Journal of Pharmacokinetics and Biopharmaceutics 1: 329-337 (1973).

Till, A.E.; Benet, L.Z. and Kwan, K.C.: An integrated approach to the pharmacokinetic analysis of drug absorption. Journal of Pharmacokinetics and Biopharmaceutics 2: 525-544 (1974).

Tyrer, J.H.; Eadie, M.J.; Sutherland, J.M. and Hooper, J.D.: Outbreak of anticonvulsant intoxication in an Australian city. British Medical Journal 4: 271-273 (1970).

Upton, R.A.; Thiercelin, J-F.; Guentert, T.W.; Wallace, S.M.; Powell, R.; Sansom, L. and Riegelman, S.: Intra-individual variability in theophylline pharmacokinetics: statistical verification in 39 of 60 healthy young adults. Journal of Pharmacokinetics and Biopharmaceutics. In press.

Wagner, J.G. and Nelson, E.: Kinetic analysis of blood levels and urinary excretion in the absorption phase after single doses of drug. Journal of Pharmaceutical Sciences 53: 1392-1403 (1964).

Walle, T.; Convadi, E.C.; Walle, K.; Fagan, T.C. and Gaffney, T.E.: The predictable relationship between plasma levels and dose during chronic propranolol therapy. Clinical Pharmacology and Therapeutics 24: 668-677 (1978).

Weiner, I.M.: Transport of weak acids and bases; in Handbook of Physiology: Renal Physiology, section 8, chapter 17 (American Physiological Society, Washington, DC 1973).

Westlake, W.J.: The design and analysis of comparative blood-level trials; in Swarbrick (Ed) Current Concepts in the Pharmaceutical Sciences: Dosage Form Design and Bioavailability, p.149-179 (Lea and Febiger, Philadelphia 1973).

Yeh, K.C. and Kwan, K.C.: A comparison of numerical integration logarithms by trapezoidal, Lagrange and spline approximation. Journal of Pharmacokinetics and Biopharmaceutics 6: 79-98 (1978).

## Discussion

*G. Levy* (Chairman): Can you give me your assessment of clearance as a source of variability relative to other sources when stable isotopes are used at the same time as an oral dosage form? You can control one source of variation, namely total clearance, but surely there are others.

*M. Rowland*: I have never seen a study in which the contribution of all possible parameters to total variance has been assessed. There is a problem with stable isotopes which may not be clearly recognised. The dose used can hardly be called a tracer and it should be established that the system is linear. Often, a single dose of both cold and stable isotope is given and it is assumed automatically that there is no interaction or non-linearity, and that their handling is identical.

# 28

# In-vitro and In-vivo Bioavailability Correlation

*Sidney Riegelman and Robert A. Upton*

School of Pharmacy, University of California

Many drug substances are available from a number of pharmaceutical manufacturers in seemingly identical dosage forms. Occasionally, inadequate clinical response has been noted with one or more. Such occurrences have led the US Food and Drug Administration (FDA) to screen the multi-source drugs to identify those products which have the potential for clinical failure (Gardner, 1977). The FDA has, for this purpose, established special criteria for production and quality control of each batch of these drug products. A large number of the products must comply with arbitrary *in vitro* dissolution test specifications and others must also undergo *in vivo* bioavailability studies.

*In vitro* dissolution tests are also increasingly important in drug dosage form development. They are required by regulatory agencies, particularly the FDA, in all New Drug Applications. The criteria for these release specifications are being closely examined and are often correlated with *in vivo* data.

To establish criteria for these tests, the FDA in the last decade has supported contract research to investigate the bioavailability of selected lots of commerically available tablets or capsules of a drug. Figure 1 represents dissolution profiles of different digitoxin tablets (Cabana, in press). These products exhibit marked differences in dissolution under the test conditions. Samples of 3 of these products were then administered to a panel of 12 subjects in a Latin square design and compared with the standard aqueous digitoxin solution (fig. 2). Many digitoxin products underwent both *in vitro* and *in vivo* testing and their relative bioavailability was compared with the oral solution using analysis of variance. The mean peak concentrations were similarly analysed. Figures 3 and 4 are plots of mean percent bioavailability and mean peak plasma concentration of digitoxin in relation to *in vitro* dissolution. Only slightly different results are obtained when the paddle method is substituted for the basket method.

The problems in extracting the correlation and defining the minimum criteria for *in vitro* dissolution tests in batch-to-batch quality control can be illustrated by noting the placement of the point representing product A in any of these graphs. It has good bioavailability and a high peak plasma concentration, but poor dissolution at 30 or 60 minutes. With an *in vitro* criterion for dissolution of 85% in 30 or 60 minutes, this product would be unacceptable even though bioavailability is acceptable.

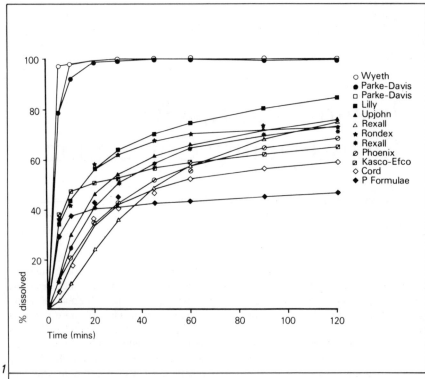

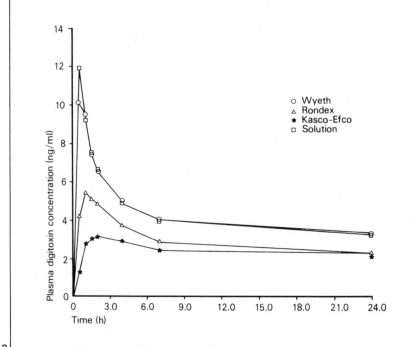

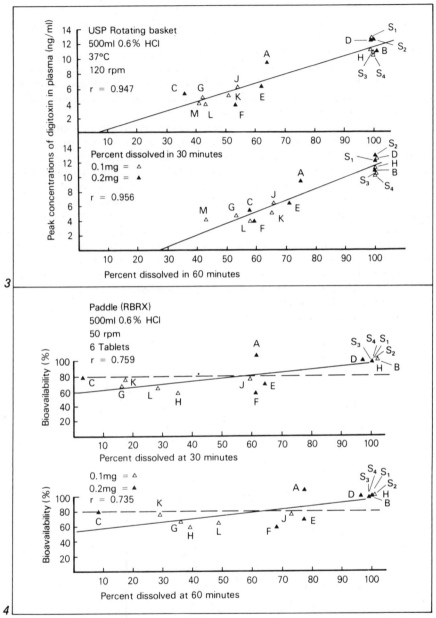

Fig. 1. Mean dissolution profile of 6 tablets for a series of commercially available digitoxin products. Data obtained using USP rotating basket method.

Fig. 2. Mean plasma concentration-time curves for 3 commercially available digitoxin tablets compared with a standard aqueous solution in 12 subjects.

Fig. 3. Mean peak plasma concentration for a series of commercially available digitoxin tablets *vs* the percent dissolved at 30 and 60 minutes using the USP rotating basket method.

Fig. 4. Mean bioavailability of a series of commercially available digitoxin tablets *vs* the percent dissolved at 30 or 60 minutes using the paddle method.

At least 3 problems are involved in the establishment of *in vitro* dissolution limits by the above procedures. A single dissolution test is usually based on studies of single lots of unique tablet formulations of different manufacturers. The correlations are drawn from mean data essentially ignoring the variance (along both coordinates). Finally and most importantly, great effort is involved in these single point estimates; literally hundreds of assays are performed to define the *in vitro* dissolution curves and an even larger number of plasma samples are assayed. Therefore, much abstractable information is not at present being utilised.

*In vitro* and *in vivo* drug release followed by absorption are complex kinetic processes. Information concerning each of these processes can be derived by more detailed analysis of the data. Figure 5 illustrates the processes that take place when a tablet or capsule is administered. The top part of the diagram, indicating dissolution in the gastric contents, includes many of the events taking place during *in vitro* dissolution studies. Initially, the tablet has to be wetted and if coated or a capsule, the shell must disintegrate so that the contents can dissolve. The overall process includes disintegration to the granules or aggregates and further de-aggregation to fine particles. The granules, aggregates and fine particles are all simultaneously dissolving. Thus, there is an increase of surface area and ultimate decrease in area as the product goes into solution. These processes depend on the stirring rate, temperature, and contents of the dissolution medium, as well as the specific design of the apparatus, and its hydrodynamic stability. Typical tablet dissolution is therefore far more complex than predicted by simple dissolution rate studies.

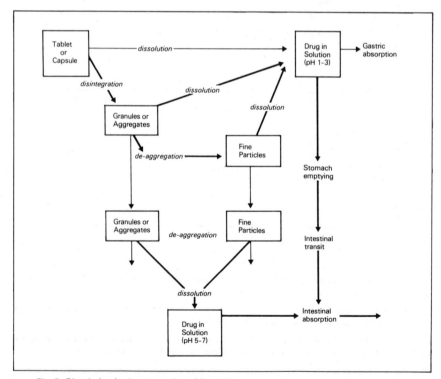

*Fig. 5.* Dissolution in the stomach and intestine.

Table I. Weibull function analysis dissolution data[1] for enteric coated tablets of aminophylline (CO)

| Product | $t_o$ | $t_D$ | $F, \infty$ | Beta |
|---|---|---|---|---|
| CO-1 | 73.1 (0.88)[2] | 33.2 (1) | 98.7 (0.45) | 1.42 (0.06) |
| CO-2 | 67.3 (0.73) | 31.6 (0.82) | 98.5 (0.35) | 1.17 (0.42) |
| CO-3 | 74.3 (0.46) | 33.3 (0.57) | 96.9 (0.33) | 1.25 (0.03) |
| CO-4 | 79.4 (0.36) | 20.1 (0.43) | 96.1 (0.15) | 1.18 (0.03) |
| CO-5 | 111 (1.8) | 38.5 (1.8) | 91.2 (0.59) | 1.86 (0.12) |
| CO-6 | 79.7 (1.2) | 30 (1.4) | 95.3 (0.55) | 1.36 (0.09) |
| Mean | 80.8 | 31.1 | 96.1 | 1.37 |
| CV% | (19%) | 19.6%) | (2.9%) | (18.7%) |

1　All fits show $R^2 > 0.9994$.
2　Asymptotic standard error of the estimate.

Disintegration and dissolution *in vivo* are further complicated. The tablet, capsule or micro encapsulated units may be lying in a mucous environment in the stomach; disintegration and dispersion into granules and primary particles are therefore influenced by surface tension, viscosity, pH, the volume of fluids, diffusion layer thickness and motility. The stomach contents also affect gastric emptying and delivery of the drug to the intestine, the principal absorption site. Stomach emptying is not instantaneous, as is required for the first-order absorption presumptions. The multiple granules or particles are possibly coated with a mucous film which may have changed the diffusion layer thickness. With all these complexities, it is illogical to presume that *in vitro* or *in vivo* dissolution should fit a zero- or first-order kinetic equation. A more general, possibly empirical approach to the kinetic analysis of the dissolution and absorption data may offer significant advantages.

Quantitative interpretation of dissolution rate data is greatly facilitated by the application of a general mathematical expression which describes the entire curve in terms of meaningful parameters. An idealised dissolution equation can be derived by theoretical treatment, e.g., the Hixson-Crowell equation (Hixson and Crowell 1931). However, in the most general cases of coated tablets, capsules or controlled release preparations, no such theoretical basis is available and the suitable function is only to be found empirically. Wagner (1969) suggested the probability approach. A more general function which may be applied successfully to almost all common types of dissolution curves was described by Weibull (Weibull, 1951) and applied by Langenbucher (1972, 1976). The Weibull function is shown in equation 1:

$$F = F^\infty \left[ 1 - e^{- \left( \dfrac{t-t_o}{t_d} \right)^\beta} \right]$$

Eq. 1

where the dependent variable F represents the fraction of the administered dose which is dissolved at time t; $F\infty$ is the amount dissolved at infinite time (theoretically labelled dose); t the time and $t_o$ the lag time for dissolution after disintegration. The mean dissolution time, $t_d$, is sometimes called a scaling factor. One can show mathematically that the mean dissolution time is the time required for 63.2% of the drug to dissolve. This is exactly the time when the ratio in the exponent of equa-

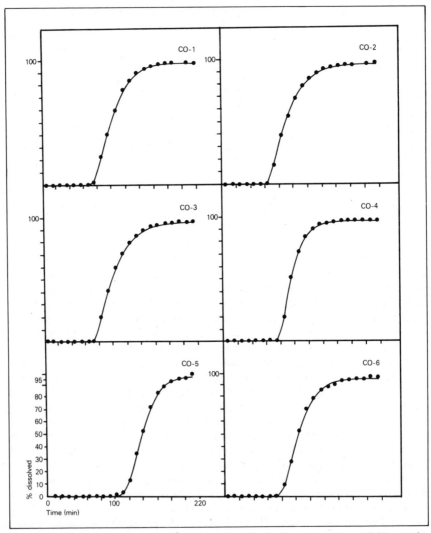

*Fig. 6.* Dissolution profiles and Weibull function fits for 6 commercially available enteric-coated tablets (Product-CO) [paddle method at 50rpm in 900ml of water].

tion 1 takes on a value 1. The exponent, $\beta$, is a unitless number ranging from 0 (when the system simulates zero-order dissolution) to 1 (when it simulates first-order dissolution) or values greater than 1 (when the curve takes on sigmoidal shape, increasing as sigmoidicity of the curve increases). The Weibull function allows us to define 4 parameters to describe the dissolution process, namely, a lag time for the disintegration, $t_0$ the drug content as defined by $F\infty$, the mean dissolution time, $t_d$ for 63 % of the drug to dissolve, and an exponent, $\beta$, which defines the shape of the dissolution curve. With suitable data, it is easy to estimate these 4 parameters by a non-linear regression procedure.

The Weibull function is by no means a universal dissolution equation.

Table II. Weibull function analysis dissolution data.[1] Means of the fitted parameters for 3 enteric-coated aminophylline products (CO, RO and WA)

|  | CO | RO | WA |
|---|---|---|---|
| $t_0$[1] | 80.8 (19%)[2] | 94 (5%) | 102 (27%) |
| $t_D$ | 31 (20%) | 14.3 (60%) | 150 (25%) |
| $F\infty$ | 96.1 (3%) | 107 (4%) | 97.5 (5%) |
| Beta | 1.37 (19%) | 2.25 (79%) | 2.70 (11%) |

1  Includes 60 minutes in simulated gastric fluid (pH = 1), then remainder in simulated intestinal fluid (pH 7.2).
2  Interindividual differences expressed as coefficients of variation.

Pedersen (1979) proposed an equation derived from physical chemical theory; however, it is extremely complicated and requires a special computer program for solution. In the limited trials where the Pedersen equation was compared with the Weibull function, both equations seemed to fit the data equally well (Pedersen and Myrick, 1978). Lippman (1974) has discussed several other empirical approaches for slowly disintegrating systems.

In this report we describe the application of this equation to dissolution rate data obtained from enteric-coated theophylline preparations. In addition we will show its applicability to absorption rate data following administration of these same dosage forms to a group of healthy adults.

## 1. Materials and Methods

Enteric-coated and rapidly released aminophylline preparations were selected for their *in vitro* release characteristics. Dissolution times were obtained by the USP paddle method (50rpm) involving exposure for 1 hour to simulated gastric fluid followed by transfer to simulated intestinal fluid. Samples were measured spectrophotometrically using a flow cell.

A 4-way Latin square design bioavailability study was run with 12 subjects in which a standard rapidly released aminophylline preparation (SE) was compared with the enteric-coated test products. The plasma concentration-time curve over 32 hours was determined using a specific high pressure liquid chromatographic method.

The Weibull function was fitted to the dissolution data utilising least squares minimisation. The initial estimates were obtained as described by Langenbucher (1976). It should be emphasised that all 4 parameters were fitted including $F\infty$, which in effect is the total dose in the tablet. In order to fit the *in vivo* data, the plasma concentration-time curves were analysed (Wagner and Nelson, 1963) to obtain the absorption rate plots which were subsequently fitted to the Weibull function as described below.

## 2. Results and Discussion

The dissolution-time profiles from 6 tablets each of the 3 enteric-coated preparations are represented in figure 6 (Product-CO), figure 7 (Product-RO) and figure 8 (Product-WA). The slopes of the curves decrease as one proceeds from figure 6 to 8

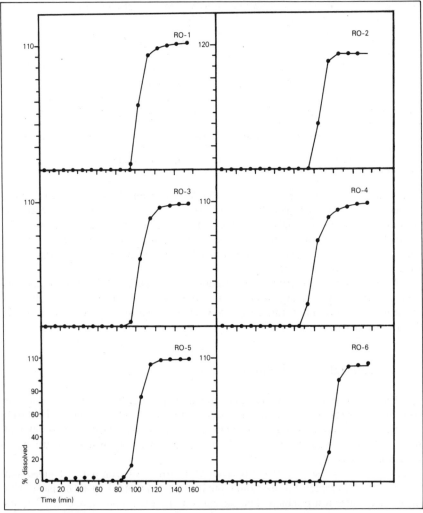

*Fig. 7.* Dissolution profiles and Weibull function fits for 6 commercially available enteric-coated tablets (Product-RO) [paddle method at 50rpm in 900ml of water].

and the differences would be greater with corrections for the time scales. In several of the tablets (figure 7, RO 1 and 2), the system appears to be following zero-order input. The curve approaches the exponential shape in RO-3, CO 1-3. Varying degrees of sigmoidicity are seen in RO 4-6, CO 5-6 and in all of the WA tablets. The intercept on the abscissa represents an estimate for the dissolution derived 'disintegration' time, $t_0$. The value of $t_d$ can be estimated by subtracting $t_0$ from the time at which the curve coincides with 63.2% dissolution. Every criteria used to define goodness of fit for these curves leads one to the conclusion that the fit is excellent. In all but one of the curves shown in figures 6 to 8, the coefficient of determination, $r^2$, is greater than 0.99.

The detailed data obtained from the Weibull function analysis of the enteric-coated product-CO, is summarised in table I. The estimated value for each of the 4 parameters in all 6 tablets are listed. The asymptotic standard error of the estimate represents the uncertainty of the parameter. Expressing these as relative standard errors, the first 3 columns show less than 5% deviation. The biggest variation in the estimate is shown in the fit to the exponent, beta. The mean values and the between-tablet coefficient of variation are listed in the bottom of each column and can be useful in maintaining quality control.

In order to contrast the fits, table II summarises *means* of the fitted parameters to the Weibull analysis for the 3 enteric-coated tablets. Unfortunately, the individual dissolution curves for the test product-SE were not available. The dissolution test includes a 60-minute exposure to gastric fluid followed by transfer to simulated intes-

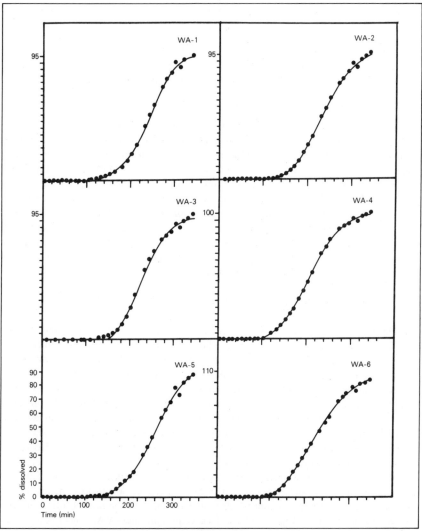

*Fig. 8.* Dissolution profiles and Weibull function fits for 6 commercially available enteric-coated tablets (Product-WA) [paddle method at 50rpm in 900ml of water].

*Table III.* Weibull function analysis of dissolution and absorption rate data expressed as means of the fitted parameters for 4 enteric-coated aminophylline products (CO, WA and RO, SE)

|  | SE | CO | WA | RO |
|---|---|---|---|---|
| $t_0$ |  |  |  |  |
| Dissolution | ≪ 1.0 | 80.8 (15.4)[1] | 102 (28) | 94 (4.9) |
| Absorption | 3.6 | 110 (8.5) | 146.4 (16) | 132 (42) |
| $t_D$ |  |  |  |  |
| Dissolution | 9.3 | 31.1 (6.1) | 150 (37) | 14 (8.6) |
| Absorption | 14.6 | 52.4 (8.3) | ˙182 (136) | 10 (16) |
| Beta |  |  |  |  |
| Dissolution | 1.59 | 1.37 (0.26) | 2.70 (0.30) | 2.25 (1.78) |
| Absorption | < 0.1 | 0.197 (0.26) | 1.49 (0.32) | 0.25 (0.15) |
| $F \infty$ |  |  |  |  |
| Dissolution | 99.6 | 96 (2.76) | 97.5 (5) | 107 (3.4) |
| Absorption | 96.6 | 109 (1.41) | 97.6 (2.3) | 100 (9.3) |

1   Interindividual differences expressed as coefficients of variation.

tinal fluid for the remainder of the test period. Product-CO shows 'disintegration', or lag-time ($t_0$) following transfer into intestinal fluids of approximately 20 minutes while RO and WA take longer. Comparison of the dissolution times ($t_d$) of the 3 products is very instructive. Under the test conditions product-RO underwent rapid dissolution requiring only on average 14 minutes for 63% dissolution. Product-CO required approximately 30 minutes while product-WA required 2.5 hours. Indeed, these results show that product-WA does not approach the ideal for an enteric-coated product, where rapid release of theophylline should occur after the tablet is exposed to the intestinal environment. The apparent content of all the products ($F \infty$), falls within the USP specification. The mean estimates of the beta exponents confirm the relative degrees of sigmoidicity as seen in figures 6 to 8.

## 2.1 Blood Concentration-Time Curves

Deconvolution of the plasma concentration-time curves to estimate the absorption rate profiles requires some understanding of the presumptions upon which these methods are based. This is discussed in appendix A, and the application of the Wagner-Nelson analysis to the present data is justified. Appropriate manipulation of the data results in a per cent absorbed versus time plot. These curves have similar shapes to the dissolution rate profiles. As discussed earlier, it is illogical to presume that these plots can be treated as either zero-order or first-order processes. The Weibull function was therefore applied to see if it has the same utility in describing the absorption rate process as shown above for the dissolution rate process. However, the Weibull analysis was applied retrospectively to data obtained for other purposes. Had the *in vivo* tests been designed specifically for this approach, a plasma sampling timetable would have been selected to delineate the absorption process better. Fig. 9 includes the data from the Wagner-Nelson analysis of the plasma concentration-time curves obtained from 5 subjects given enteric-coated product-WA. The crosses represent the points calculated from the Wagner-Nelson analyses of the plasma concentration-time data and the curves are the resultant fit to the Weibull function. Figure 10 includes representative curves from the 3 other preparations. Because of their more rapid absorption, fewer plasma samples were obtained during the absorption process. Nevertheless, it is still possible to describe the curves using the Weibull function, albeit with larger standard errors of estimates. Table III summarises the Weibull analysis for both the dissolution and absorption rate data, expressed in terms of the means of the fitted data. Only the average values were available for the dissolution process with preparation SE. It should be emphasised that the infinity value, $F^\infty$, obtained by the analysis of the absorption curves is not a true estimate of bioavailability since it is expressed relative to the area under the curve for that preparation. If it were standardised against an oral solution, this would indeed yield an estimate of bioavailability. It is interesting to note the rank order of the lag times and absorption or dissolution times as indicated in table III. These are further analysed in figure 12.

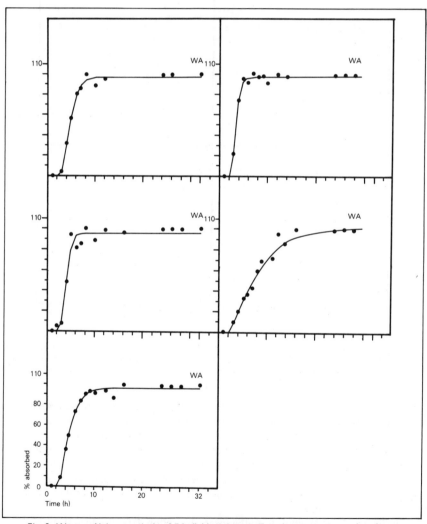

Fig. 9. Wagner-Nelson analysis of 5 individual theophylline plasma concentration-time curves after administering Product-WA. The solid curves represent the Weibull function fit to the data.

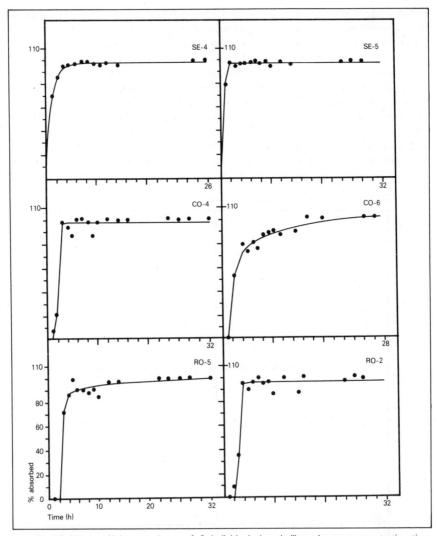

*Fig. 10.* Wagner-Nelson analyses of 2 individual theophylline plasma concentration-time curves obtained after administering 3 different commercially available theophylline preparations (Products SE, CO and RO). The solid curve represents the Weibull function fit to the data.

The estimates of the exponent, $\beta$, for the absorption plots are extremely small, indicating that absorption is approaching zero order. However, this may be an artifact due to the lack of sufficient data points during the absorption period.

The mean dissolution and mean concentration-time profiles for the preparations were also available. These were treated as above to determine the Weibull function parameters and an excellent fit was obtained with very small standard errors of estimate in each case. However, analysis of mean data can lead to a serious distortion due to the averaging process.

In figure 11 the Weibull fit to the mean absorption data (Product-WA) and also to the curve generated from the mean parameters obtained from 5 individual curves, is plotted. The curve generated from the mean of the fitted parameters begins to deviate above 60% absorption and indicates more rapid apparent absorption than is seen in the curve derived from the mean absorption data. This is seen with all averaged data, both *in vitro* and *in vivo*, and is a result of the averaging process.

Figure 12 represents an attempt to draw correlations from the data in table III. It is apparent that both correlations are excellent when utilising the parameters of the individually fitted data and are far superior to correlations obtained using fits to mean data. Some of the problems with standard procedures used by the FDA in attempting

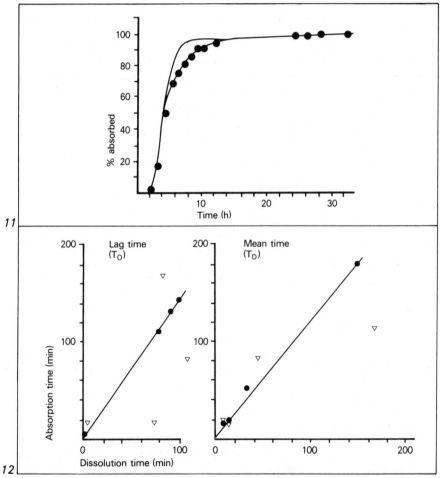

Fig. 11. Wagner-Nelson analyses of the theophylline plasma concentration-time curve obtained after administering Product-WA to a test panel. The closed circles represent the data from the analysis of the mean plasma concentration-time curve. The Weibull function fit to these data is indicated by the solid curves which follow the points. The curve which deviates represents the Weibull function curve drawn using the mean parameter estimates from individually fitted curves.

Fig. 12. Absorption and dissolution time data for 4 commercially available theophylline preparations. The left hand curve (A) illustrates the mean lag-time, and the right hand curve (B) the mean time, to absorb or dissolve 63% of the dose. The closed circles are from the mean parameter estimates to the fitted data and the triangles from the direct Weibull analyses of the mean data.

to draw correlations may be due to the use of mean data as well as the parameters selected for correlation.

The Weibull analysis of dissolution and absorption data can play an important function in product development and may lead to more rational quality control specifications. Dissolution rate data could be obtained by an appropriate methodology on the pure drug substance, after incorporating excipients and under various conditions of manufacture. Some European companies employ one or more of the estimated Weibull parameters as criteria for selecting the optimum formulation. Data from *in vitro* studies can be used to select a group of test formulations for *in vivo* studies.

This approach may be useful in the study of the *in vivo* release pattern from different dosage forms. Utilising the appropriate deconvolution procedure (see appendix) the resultant percent absorbed versus time plot can be fitted to the Weibull function. Comparison of the *in vitro* and *in vivo* parameters may allow the identification of critical steps in the process of *in vivo* drug release. The acceptable range of in-process specifications (e.g. tablet hardness) can be explored.

It may be necessary to re-investigate the specific conditions used in the *in vitro* dissolution (pH, composition, stirring rate). The advantage of the Weibull function analysis is that it allows the parameters from the *in vivo* drug release curves, not just the extent of bioavailability, to be used.

A note of caution is necessary. The bioavailability of the vast majority of drug substances is not limited by dissolution, unless they are specifically formulated to control release. While a dissolution test may be useful for quality control, detailed studies of the *in vivo* release from ordinary dosage forms of such drugs are probably not cost-effective or indeed necessary.

The Weibull parameter plots shown in figure 12 are drawn with reasonably similar scales. This is purely fortuitous. Some controlled release products are designed to release their dose over 8 to 12 hours. It is illogical and unnecessary to attempt to mimic the *in vivo* release when establishing the conditions for the *in vitro* dissolution test. The *in vitro* test should be designed so that dissolution is completed in 2 to 3 hours. Correlations such as shown in figure 12 can be equally well made with such data with much saving in quality control time.

Additional information can be obtained with appropriate analysis of *in vitro* as well as *in vivo* data. One should not be enamoured of the particular functions used in the analysis but rather of the value of the results in dosage form design and control.

## Appendix

Several systems for numerical deconvolution of plasma concentration-time curves have been proposed including the linear piecewise integration procedures of Wagner and Nelson (1963), and Loo and Riegelman, (1968). Both are model-dependent and based on a 1 or 2 compartment system. The goal of these analyses is to identify the input rate function independent of drug disposition. The Loo-Riegelman method utilises the micro constants obtained from the analysis of the concentration-time curve after administration of an intravenous (iv) dose. Cutler (1978a,b) described a numerical deconvolution procedure by least squares and Pedersen (1979) suggested a deconvolution procedure utilising a computer-derived least squares smoothed spline function of reference (e.g. intravenous) and test (oral) concentration-time curves. The latter method is model-independent and appears to have many advantages.

The Wagner-Nelson method can be used even in the absence of the intravenous data since all that is required is an estimate of the terminal elimination rate constant. Assuming first-order input and standard Laplace and compartmental notation, a 1-body compartment model can be written as

$$\overline{C} = \frac{FD/V\ ka}{(S + ka)(S + Kd)} \qquad\qquad \text{Eq. 1a}$$

The Wagner-Nelson data treatment is equivalent to letting $Kd = 0$, or

$$\overline{C}_{input} = \frac{(FD/V)ka}{(S + ka)s} \qquad\qquad \text{Eq. 2a}$$

The anti-Laplace of which is

$$C_{input} = \frac{FD}{V}\ (1 - e^{-kat}) \qquad\qquad \text{Eq. 3a}$$

Equation 3a has the form of an exponential curve with an asymptote at $FD/V$.

Presuming first-order input to a 2-body compartment model (2-BCM) and setting $\beta = 0$, results in

$$\overline{C}_{input} = \frac{FD/V\ (S + K_{21})}{(S + ka)(S + \beta)s} \qquad\qquad \text{Eq. 4a}$$

The anti-Laplace of which takes on the form

$$\frac{Ain}{V_1} = C_{input} = (1 - A\ e^{-\alpha t} - Ke^{-kat}) \qquad\qquad \text{Eq. 5a}$$

Thus when we analyse 2-BCM data using the Wagner-Nelson equation we obtain

$$\left(\frac{Ain}{V_1}\right)_t = (Cp)_t + AUC_t \qquad\qquad \text{Eq. 6a}$$

and at infinite time

$$\left(\frac{Ain}{V_1}\right)_\infty = \beta AUC_\infty \qquad\qquad \text{Eq.7a}$$

The fraction remaining to be absorbed plot will yield

$$\left(\frac{Ain}{V_1}\right)_\infty - \left(\frac{Ain}{V_1}\right)_t = A\ e^{-\alpha t} + K - e^{-kat} \qquad\qquad \text{Eq. 8a}$$

The contribution of the 2 exponentials to equations 5a to 8a are dependent on the values of the ka, $k_{21}$, and $\alpha$ rate constants. If ka $\ll k_{21} < \alpha$, the equation rapidly converges on the rate-limiting process involving the absorption rate. This appears to be the case for theophylline, particularly with controlled release dosage forms. If not, the percent absorbed plot may yield a hump and then fall to an asymptote.

The Wagner-Nelson numerical deconvolution procedure is utilised in the above test merely to exemplify the overall method of data processing. To yield less ambiguous results one could use one of the advanced methods of deconvolution such as the Pedersen procedure.

## Acknowledgements

We wish to acknowledge use of the digitoxin data reported in figures 1 to 4 obtained from Dr B. Cabana of the United States Food and Drug Administration. The dissolution data for the digitoxin and theophylline were obtained from Dr V. Shah and James W. Myrick of the US FDA. Dr T. Guentert and S. Vozeh were particularly helpful in the *in vivo* theophylline studies and the bioavailability analyses of the resultant data.

The PROPHET system is a specialised computer resource developed by the Chemical/Biological Information Handling Program of the National Institutes of Health. A detailed description of the system features appears in Proc. Nathl. Comput. Conf. Exposition, 43, 457 (1974).

The study was supported by contract 233-74-3145 funded by the Food and Drug Administration.

## References

Cabana, B.E.: The role of dissolution in new drug approval and assurance of drug bioavailability. Symposium on Biological Availability (in press).

Cutler, D.: Numerical deconvolution by least squares use of prescribed input function. Journal of Pharmacokinetics and Biopharmaceutics 6: 227-242 (1978a).

Cutler, D.: Numerical deconvolution by least squares: use of polynomials to represent the input function. Journal of Pharmacokinetics and Biopharmaceutics 6: 243-264 (1978b).

Garnder, S.: Bioavailability and bioequivalence requirements: procedures for establishing a bioequivalence requirement. Federal Register 42: 1624-1653 (1977).

Hixson, A. and Crowell, J.: Dependence of reaction velocity upon surface and agitation in theoretical consideration. Industrial and Engineering Chemistry 23: 923-931 (1931).

Langenbucher, F.: Linearization of dissolution rate curves by the Weibull function. Journal of Pharmacy and Pharmacology 24: 979-981 (1972).

Langenbucher, F.: Parametric representation of dissolution rate curves by the RRSW distribution. Pharmaceutical Industry 38: 472-477 (1976).

Lippman, I.: Curve fitting of dissolution data from solid dosage forms with the assistance of a digital computer; in Lieson and Carstensen (Eds) Dissolution Technolgoy, p.193-195 (American Pharmaceutical Association, Washington 1974).

Loo, J.C.K. and Riegelman, S.: New method for calculating the intrinsic absorption rate of drugs. Journal of Pharmaceutical Science 57: 918-928 (1968).

Pedersen, P.V.: New method of characterizing dissolution properties of drug powders. Journal of Pharmaceutical Science 66: 761-765 (1977).

Pedersen, P.V. and Myrick, J.W.: Versatile kinetic approach to analysis of dissolution data. Journal of Pharmaceutical Science 67: 1450-1455 (1978).

Pedersen, P.V.: Novel model independent method of input analysis and optimal drug control for linear pharmaceutical systems. Academy of Pharmaceutical Sciences Abstracts 8: 91 (1979).

Wagner, J. and Nelson, E.: Percent absorbed time plots derived from blood level and/or urinary excretion data. Journal of Pharmaceutical Science 52: 610-611 (1963).

Wagner, J.: Interpretation of percent dissolved time plots derived from *in vitro* testing of conventional tablets and capsules. Journal of Pharmaceutical Science 58: 1253-1257 (1969).

Weibull, W.: A statistical distribution function of wide applicability. Journal of Applied Mechanics 18: 293-297 (1951).

# 29

# Practical Problems in the Assessment of Drug Absorption in Man

*A. Karim and D.L. Azarnoff*

Research and Development Division, G.D. Searle and Company, Chicago

Many factors may complicate the assessment of drug absorption in man (table I). We have encountered several practical problems with investigation of the bioavailability of the anti-arrhythmic drug disopyramide, and these will be used as examples (Karim, 1975; Hinderling and Garrett, 1976; Cunningham et al., 1977; Cunningham et al., 1978; Meffin et al., 1979).

It is well recognised that metabolism during the first passage through the gut and liver may lead to incomplete systemic availability of an orally administered drug even though its absorption from the gastrointestinal tract is complete. However, it is not generally recognised that non-linear elimination kinetics can likewise lead to an apparent disparity between the amount of the drug absorbed and the amount appearing in the systemic circulation. In the case of disopyramide at least part of the non-linearity can be attributed to a concentration-related change in protein binding, a phenomenon which has also been reported with naproxen (Runkel et al., 1974). This characteristic can result in several practical problems in assessing bioavailability.

## 1. Materials and Methods

### 1.1 Clinical Studies

13 healthy males aged 20 to 35 years were studied as previously described (Karim, 1975; Cunningham et al., 1977, 1978).

*Study I. Radio-labelled Disopyramide*
3 subjects received 163mg of ($^{14}$C)-disopyramide phosphate and 3 received 326mg in 30ml of simple syrup. After 3 weeks, the dosing schedule was reversed. Blood samples were taken up to 36 hours, urine was collected up to 120 hours and

*Table I.* Factors influencing drug absorption and response

| *Dosage Form and Regimen* | *Dietry Factors* |
|---|---|
| | Effect on: |
| Drug form | drug absorption |
| Excipients | drug metabolism |
| Compounding | drug excretion |
| Coating | drug-receptor site interactions |
| Drug amount | *Pharmacological Factors* |
| Administration schedule | Effect of other drugs and |
| Route of administration | food constituents on: |
| *Physiological Factors* | enzyme induction |
| Age | enzyme inhibition |
| Sex | protein binding |
| Body weight | stomach emptying time |
| Genetic | intestinal motility |
| Nutritional state | biliary flow |
| Disease | local blood flow |
| Pregnancy | gut flora |
| Gut flora | urinary pH |
| Gastrointestinal motility | drug receptor interactions |
| Renal function | Tolerance |
| Physical activity | Environmental factors |

daily faecal collections were made for 5 days. Plasma, urine and faecal radioactivity was determined.

### Study II. Effect of Urine pH on Drug Excretion

2 subjects received 1.55mg of disopyramide intravenously over 2 to 3 minutes and 2 received 5mg/kg orally on 2 occasions at least 1 week apart. On the first occasion, the urine was made acidic with ammonium chloride and on the second occasion, alkaline with sodium bicarbonate (in each case 2g every 4 hours for 12 hours on the day prior to and during the study).

### Study III. Gastrointestinal Absorption and Systemic Availability

3 subjects received the drug both intravenously and orally on 2 separate occasions at least 1 week apart at the same doses and sampling schedules as in Study II.

## 1.2 Analytical Methods

Radioactivity in the plasma, urine and dry faeces was determined by previously described methods (Karim et al., 1972, 1977).

Plasma and urine concentrations of disopyramide and its mono-$N$-dealkylated metabolite (MND, fig. 1) were determined by gas-liquid chromatography (Cunningham et al., 1977).

Pooled, freshly drawn normal human plasma (total protein 7.5g/dl and albumin 4.1g/dl) was used for the protein binding study. Plasma was spiked with ($^{14}$C)-disopyramide phosphate to yield concentrations of 0.4 to 4µg/ml. Protein binding was determined by ultrafiltration (Borga et al., 1969). There was no significant adsorption to the cellophane membrane.

## 1.3 Pharmacokinetic Analysis

Plasma concentration-time data following oral dose in the radiolabelled Study I were analysed assuming a 1-compartment pharmacokinetic open model (Wagner, 1967) using the formula:

$$C = \frac{FD}{V} \left(\frac{K}{k_a - K}\right)\left(e^{-Kt} - e^{-k_a t}\right)$$

where C is the drug concentration ($\mu g/ml$) in the apparent volume of distribution V (ml). F is the fraction of the dose ($\mu g$) absorbed and $k_a$ and K ($hr^{-1}$) are first-order rate constants for absorption and elimination, respectively. Values of FD/V, $k_a$ and K were obtained by a least squares analysis using the NONLIN computer program (Metzler, 1969).

In Studies II and III, the $t_{1/2}\beta$ was calculated by least squares regression and the area under the plasma concentration-time curve (AUC) by the trapezoidal rule. Renal clearance ($Cl_r$) was calculated by dividing the amount excreted by the AUC for the corresponding time interval. Where appropriate renal clearance was corrected for plasma protein binding ($Clr^1$) using the AUC of the unbound plasma concentration.

Gastrointestinal absorption (F) was calculated by comparing the 72-hour cumulative urinary excretion of the unchanged drug following oral and intravenous administration. Apparent systemic availability ($\Theta$) was estimated from the 24-hour oral and intravenous AUC data corrected for dose.

This term $\Theta$, should be regarded merely as a measure of the relative plasma concentrations after oral and intravenous administration. It is not the fraction of the drug that escaped first-pass metabolism.

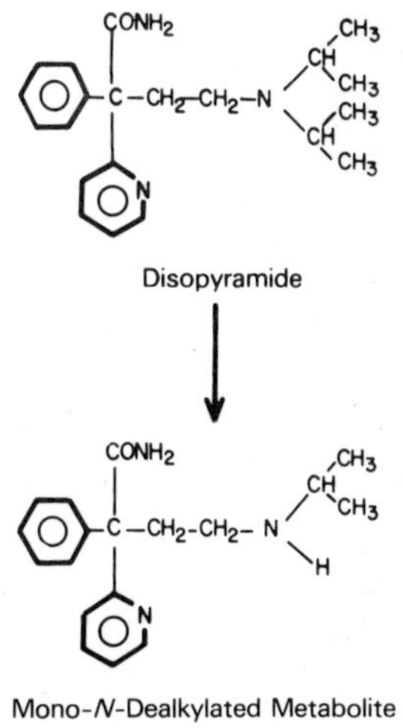

Fig. 1. Disopyramide and its mono-*N*-dealkylated metabolite (MND).

*Table II.* Absorption of total $^{14}C$ or disopyramide (DP) in 6 healthy volunteers given 163mg or 326mg of $^{14}C$-disopyramide orally as phosphate (all values mean ± SD)

| Dose | AUC µg h/ml 0–24 h | | $K_a$ h$^{-1}$ for absorption | | $t_{1/2}$ h$^{-1}$ for absorption | | Percent of dose excreted | | | | | | |
|---|---|---|---|---|---|---|---|---|---|---|---|---|---|
| | | | | | | | urine (0–24h) | | | urine (0–72h) | | | faeces (0–120h) |
| | total $^{14}C$ | DP | total $^{14}C$ | DP | total $^{14}C$ | DP | total $^{14}C$ | DP | MND[1] | total $^{14}C$ | DP | MND | total $^{14}C$ |
| 163mg | 25.5 ±5.4 | 12.0 ±2.9 | 1.60 ±1.08 | 1.64 ±0.89 | 0.57 ±0.27 | 0.54 ±0.28 | 62.3 ±5.2 | 31.7 ±5.1 | 13.0 ±1.8 | 69.9 ±7.1 | 34.1 ±5.6 | 15.0 ±1.8 | 5.7 ±2.3 |
| 326mg | 54.9 ±10.2 | 31.8 ±7.2 | 3.21 ±1.51 | 1.78 ±0.92 | 0.26 ±0.12 | 0.47 ±0.20 | 71.7 ±5.4 | 43.3 ±3.4 | 14.3 ±1.8 | 82.4 ±5.5 | 47.7 3.0 | 18.2 ±2.4 | 9.5 ±2.4 |

1   MND = mono-N-dealkylated metabolite.

The plasma protein binding data were analysed to yield maximum binding capacity and apparent association constant (Scatchard, 1949) and the theoretical unbound concentration of disopyramide was calculated (Coffey et al., 1971).

## 2. Results

### 2.1 Absorption of ($^{14}$C)-Disopyramide

($^{14}$C)-disopyramide phosphate was rapidly absorbed with an average $t_{1/2}$ of about 30 minutes (fig. 2). The kinetic absorption data are summarised in table II.

The average recovery of radioactivity in the urine plus faeces in 5 days was 97% of the high dose (range 90-110%) and 75.5% of the low dose (range 66-87%) [table II]. Urinary excretion of total -$^{14}$C, disopyramide and MND in 3 days constituted 82.4%, 47.7% and 18.2% of the high dose, respectively.

### 2.2 Effect of Urine pH on Disopyramide Excretion

The urine pH following ammonium chloride and sodium bicarbonate ranged from 5 to 5.5 and 7.6 to 8.1, respectively. The percentage of the dose excreted in the urine as disopyramide (46.9 to 67.0%), MND (11.2 to 37.0%) or the sum of these (64.5 to 95.8%) was not significantly different when the urine was made acid or alkaline and there were no noticeable differences in plasma concentrations or half-life.

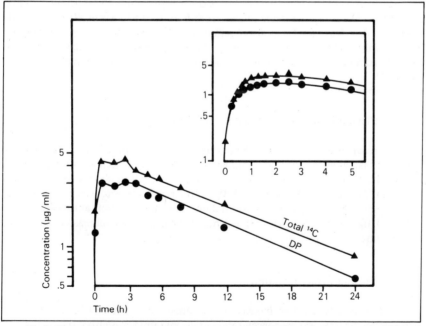

*Fig. 2.* Mean plasma concentration-time curves of total-$^{14}$C and disopyramide (DP) in 6 healthy men after 326mg of ($^{14}$C)-disopyramide given orally as the phosphate salt. The inset is an expanded time scale.

Table III. Apparent systemic availability (θ) and urinary excretion of disopyramide (DP) and its mono-N-dealkylated metabolite (MND) [adapted from Cunningham et al., 1978]

| Subject | Route | Plasma data | | | Urine data | | | |
|---------|-------|-------------|--------------|------|------------|------|-------|------|
| | | $T_{1/2\beta}$ (h) | (AUC/dose)[1] | $\theta$[2] | % of dose excreted | | | f[3] |
| | | | | | DP | MND | total | |
| EC | iv[4] | 6.94 | 10.2 | | 43.7 | 33.1 | 76.8 | |
| | po[5] | 7.35 | 4.66 | 0.457 | 40.0 | 40.5 | 80.5 | 0.92 |
| JM | iv | 6.73 | 10.6 | | —[6] | | — | |
| | po | 7.21 | 6.07 | 0.573 | 43.6 | 29.9 | 73.5 | — |
| WS | iv | 7.35 | 10.6 | | 40.2 | 46.9 | 87.1 | |
| | po | 6.74 | 5.47 | 0.516 | 35.4 | 36.6 | 72.0 | 0.88 |

1 $AUC_{0-24}$mg h/1/kg.
2 $(AUC/dose)_{po}/(AUC/dose)_{iv}$.
3 Oral bioavailability of disopyramide $= (f)_{po}/(f)_{iv}$ where f is the fraction excreted in urine unchanged.
4 2mg/kg of disopyramide phosphate = 1.55mg/kg of disopyramide.
5 5mg/kg of disopyramide.
6 Sample lost.

## 2.3 Gastrointestinal Absorption and Systemic Availability

Based on the AUC from 0 to 24 hours corrected for dose, the apparent systemic availability (Θ) of disopyramide ranged from 0.46 to 0.57. About 40% of the administered dose was excreted as disopyramide and 35% as MND after intravenous or oral administration. The total recovery in urine was about 75% regardless of the route of administration, indicating essentially complete gastrointestinal absorption (table III).

## 2.4 Plasma Concentration-dependent Renal Clearance

The renal clearance of both unbound and total disopyramide was always greater after oral than after intravenous administration and usually declined after the first 2 hours. This reduction in renal clearance paralleled the fall in plasma concentrations except during the first 2 hours (fig. 3). When the renal clearance was plotted against the corresponding total plasma concentration, there was a significant correlation (p < 0.001) [fig. 4] consistent with dependence of renal clearance on plasma concentration or time.

## 2.5 Plasma Protein Binding

Approximately a 2-fold increase in the unbound fraction (0.32 to 0.66) was found when the total plasma concentration of disopyramide rose from 0.4 to 4μg/ml. A Scatchard plot yielded a straight line (r = 0.97, p < 0.001), and suggested a single major binding site over the concentration range studied.

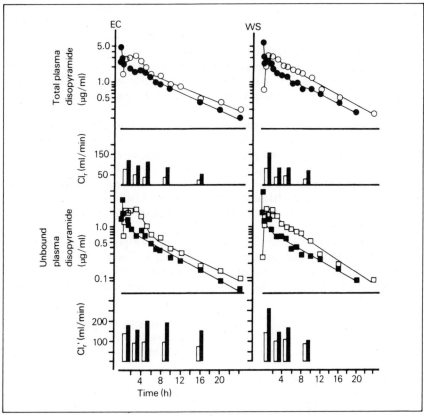

*Fig. 3.* Total plasma concentrations following intravenous (●) and oral (○) disopyramide in 2 subjects together with theoretical unbound concentrations in plasma [intravenous (■) and oral (□)]. The renal clearance based on total ($Cl_r$) and unbound ($Cl_r'$) concentrations after intravenous (□) and oral (■) administration is also shown (reproduced from Cunningham et al., 1978, with the permission of the publisher).

## 3. Discussion

Disopyramide was absorbed rapidly when given orally as the phosphate salt and peak plasma concentrations occurred between 0.5 and 3 hours. About 75% of the orally administered radioactive dose was excreted in the urine indicating that at least this much was absorbed. The total absorption was probably higher since less than half of the radioactive dose excreted in the faeces was unchanged drug. A small proportion of the absorbed disopyramide was therefore also excreted in the bile as metabolites.

In 3 subjects, the apparent systemic availability of disopyramide ranged from 0.46 to 0.57 when calculated from the plasma AUC data following 1.55mg/kg intravenously and 5mg/kg orally. However, the total recovery of disopyramide plus MND in urine was more than 70% regardless of the route of administration indicating essentially complete gastrointestinal absorption. The lower apparent systemic availability calculated from the plasma data cannot be entirely attributed to first-pass metabolism since the same fraction was metabolised to MND following oral and intravenous administration.

One possible explanation for the discrepancy might have been differences in urine pH during oral and intravenous administration. Although disopyramide is a basic drug (pKa 8.36) and its renal clearance might be expected to increase with decreased urine pH (Beckett et al., 1965), we found that its elimination was uninfluenced by alteration of urine pH. Similar results were noted by Ankier and Kay (1976).

However, the fact that the renal clearance of disopyramide varies with plasma concentration could be relevant. In Study III, the oral dose of disopyramide was 3.2 times the intravenous dose and plasma concentrations were higher following oral treatment. The unbound fraction in plasma varied from 0.32 to 0.66 as the concentration increased from 0.4 to 4.0µg/ml. Similar concentration-dependent protein binding has been reported (Hinderling et al., 1974; Meffin et al., 1979). Thus, changes in the fraction unbound could affect the amount of disopyramide filtered by the glomeruli.

The variation in renal clearance could only be partly explained by concentration-related protein binding since even when non-linearity in binding was taken into account, the renal clearance still varied with plasma concentration.

The method we used for determining protein binding had several limitations. These included:

a) Insensitivity of the GLC method for small volumes of ultrafiltrate
b) The specific activity of the ($^{14}$C)-disopyramide was too low for direct ultrafiltration measurements of *in vivo* samples

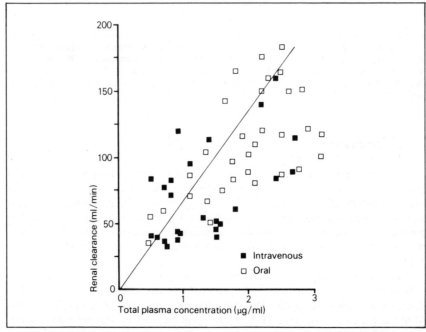

*Fig. 4.* Correlation between renal clearance of disopyramide and total plasma disopyramide concentration (adpated from Cunningham et al., 1977, with permission of the publisher).

c) *In vitro* plasma binding experiments were carried out using control plasma from 1 subject only

d) MND and other endogenous material *in vivo* may compete for the same binding sites as disopyramide

e) A single binding site for disopyramide was assumed and other binding sites may be important at low concentrations

f) Protein binding may have been affected by freezing the plasma and by the Vacutainer® stopper.

The route-dependent difference in renal clearance cannot be totally explained by plasma concentration-dependent renal clearance. A possible explanation for the lower clearance after intravenous disopyramide could be haemodynamic effects produced by rapid injection (Hillis et al., 1977).

Some of the above limitations were minimised in a recent study by Meffin et al., (1979) in which the role of concentration-dependent plasma protein binding in the disposition of disopyramide was confirmed in 12 patients who required the drug for suppression of their cardiac arrhythmias.

The clearance of disopyramide was dependent on the total plasma concentration but not on the unbound concentration. This finding presents a practical problem in the assessment of bioavailability of some drugs.


## Acknowledgement

The authors are indebted to Mrs Margaret Vargas for the preparation of this manuscript.


## References

Ankier, S.I. and Kaye, C.M.: The influence of pH on the buccal absorption and renal excretion of disopyramide in man. British Journal of Clinical Pharmacology 3: 672-673 (1976).

Beckett, A.H.; Rowland, M. and Turner, P.: Influence of urinary pH on excretion of amphetamine. Lancet 1:303 (1965).

Borga, O.; Azarnoff, D.L.; Plym-Forshell, G. and Sjoqvist, F.: Plasma protein binding of tricyclic antidepressants in man. Biochemical Pharmacology 18: 2135-2144 (1969).

Coffey, J.J.; Bullock, F.J. and Schoenemann, P.T.: Numerical solution of nonlinear pharmacokinetic equations: Effect of plasma protein binding on drug distribution and elimination. Journal of Pharmaceutical Sciences 60: 1623-1628 (1971).

Cunningham, J.L.; Shen, D.D.; Shudo, I. and Azarnoff, D.L.: The effects of urine pH and plasma protein binding on the renal clearance of disopyramide. Clinical Pharmacokinetics 2: 273-383 (1977).

Cunningham, J.L.; Shen, D.D.; Shudo, I. and Azarnoff, D.L.: The effect of non-linear disposition kinetics on the systemic availability of disopyramide. British Journal of Clinical Pharmacology 5: 343-346 (1978).

Hillis, W.S.; Bremmer, W.F.; Tweddel, A.; Lorimer, A.R. and Lawrie, T.D.V.: The effects of disopyramide on systolic time intervals. Proceedings of Disopyramide (Rythmodan) Seminar, St. John's College, Cambridge, March 24th and 25th, p.49 (1977).

Hinderling, P.H.; Bres, J. and Garrett, G.R.: Protein binding and erythrocyte partitioning of disopyramide and its monodealkylated metabolite. Journal of Pharmaceutical Sciences 63: 1684-1690 (1974).

Hinderling, P.H. and Garrett, E.R.: Pharmacokinetics of the antiarrhythmic disopyramide in healthy humans. Journal of Pharmacokinetics and Biopharmaceutics 4: 199-230 (1976).

Karim, A.; Ranney, R.E. and Kraychy, S.: Species differences in the biotransformation of a new antiarrhythmic agent: disopyramide phosphate. Journal of Pharmaceutical Sciences 61: 85-98 (1972).

Karim, A.: The pharmacokinetics of Norpace. Angiology 26: 85-98 (1975).

Karim, A.; Kook, C.; Campion, J. and Doherty, M.: Disopyramide phosphate: Tissue uptake and relationship between drug concentrations in the plasma and myocardium of rats. Archives Internationales de Pharmacodynamie et de Therapie 228: 222-236 (1977).

Meffin, P.J.; Robert, E.W.; Winkle, R.A.; Peters, F.A. and Harrison, D.D.: The role of concentration-de-
    pendent plasma protein binding in disopyramide disposition. Journal of Pharmacokinetics and
    Biopharmaceutics 7: 29-46 (1979).
Metzler, C.M.: Nonlin, a computer program for parameter estimation in nonlinear situations. Technical
    report 7292/69/7292/005 (Upjohn, Kalamazoo, 1969).
Runkel, R.; Forchielli, E.; Sevelius, H.; Chaplin, M. and Segre, E.: Nonlinear plasma level response to
    high doses of naproxen. Clinical Pharmacology and Therapeutics 15: 261-266 (1974).
Scatchard, G.: The attractions of protein for small molecules and ions. Annals of New York Academy of
    Sciences 51: 660-672 (1949).
Wagner, J.G.: Use of computers in pharmacokinetics. Clinical Pharmacology and Therapeutics 8:
    201-218 (1967).

## Discussion

*G. Leopold* (Darmstadt FDR): I would like to point out two additional practical
problems in the assessment of drug absorption in man.

The influence of psychic stress on the absorption of sulfaperine and indomethacin was studied in 16 healthy male volunteers, half of whom exhibited a high
level of neuroticism and the other half a low level. The complex psychic stress during
the absorption period consisted either of a concentration performance test (calculating
competition) under intermittent white noise of 90dB with financial motivation for the
best performance, or an acoustic vigilance test (signal recognition under white noise).

In both cases drug absorption was significantly delayed during stress. After
cessation of the stress, absorption returned to normal and finally, there was no difference in the extent of absorption (fig. 1).

The influence of smoking on the absorption of sulfaperine was investigated in 6
smokers and 6 non-smokers, smoking and non-smoking. When the smokers were
not allowed to smoke and the non-smokers were forced to smoke, the absorption of

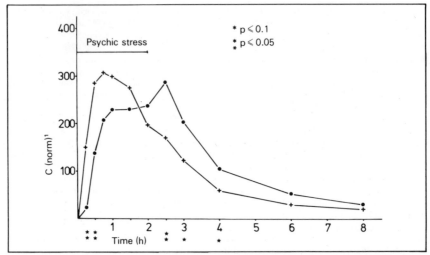

*Fig. 1.* Influence of psychic stress on the gastrointestinal absorption of indomethacin. Mean
plasma concentration time curves [c(norm)] after administration of 2 × 50mg capsules with ( ● ) and
without ( + ) psychic stress.

$$1 \quad c'(norm) = \frac{\text{serum concentration (mg/L)}}{\text{dose per kg (mg/kg)}} \times 100$$

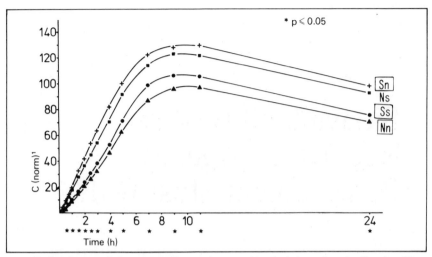

*Fig. 2.* Influence of cigarette smoking on the gastrointestinal absorption of sulfaperine. Mean serum concentration time curves after administration of 4 × 0.5g tablets 1/2 hour after a standard breakfast in smokers (S) and non-smokers (N) when smoking (s) and not smoking (n). Smoking: 6 cigarettes at 0.5 hour intervals starting after the administration of sulfaperine. (p ≤ 0.05 Ss vs. Sn and Nn vs. Ns).

1   See figure 1.

sulfaperine was faster and more complete. In these cases, gastrointestinal motility was enhanced as shown by endoradiopill studies (fig. 2).

Appropriate consideration of such factors is necessary in planning bioavailability studies.

*M. Rowland* (Manchester): I have always been concerned about the use of substances like ammonium chloride or sodium bicarbonate to alter the urinary pH without consideration of the potential effects of very high concentrations of electrolytes within the gastrointestinal tract influencing the dissolution of drug products. I know that you can alter gastrointestinal tract motility. By appropriate analysis, you can often get the information you want without the administration of ammonium chloride or sodium bicarbonate.

*A. Karim*: In some bioavailability studies, at least the urinary pH should be measured otherwise you could possibly get misleading data.

*G. Alvan* (Huddinge): Salicylate and naproxen also share this property of concentration-dependent protein binding. However, all drugs will show concentration-dependent protein binding at certain concentrations. What is important is whether protein binding is concentration-dependent at therapeutic concentrations.

*M. Balali* (Edinburgh): We investigated the effect of alkaline diuresis on the elimination of diflunisal and found the opposite effect — the lower the plasma concentration the higher the renal clearance. You mentioned concentration-dependent protein binding as a cause of non-linear pharmacokinetics. Do you think there could be another explanation?

*A. Karim*: Saturable re-absorption is a possibility.

*B.A. Beermann* (Stockholm): Disopyramide has anticholinergic effects. Do you think it could inhibit its own absorption?

*A. Karim*: It certainly has anticholinergic effects but we do not know if this delays absorption like propantheline.

# 30

# Bioavailability: Are Regulatory Agency Requirements Justified?

*Denys Cook*

Drug Research Laboratories, Health Protection Branch, Health and Welfare, Ottawa

In discussing the problem outlined in my title it is first necessary to know what the requirements are before the question of their justification can be discussed. It is evident that these requirements differ markedly in different countries. One country where a set of detailed proposals has been elaborated is the United States.

## 1. United States Requirements

The US Food and Drug Administration is concerned with regulations for the bioequivalence of prescription drugs. One reason for this concern is the development of drug benefit programs which are underwritten by Federal funds. The US Federal Government has initiated a scheme to control the cost of drugs paid for by Federal funds which is called the Maximum Allowable Cost Program (MAC). This is to establish, as a limit for reimbursement, the lowest cost at which the drug is generally available. Quality as well as cost is of concern and the FDA is responsible for standards such as bioavailability requirements. Since July 1975 only about 20 drugs have been through the MAC process.

The Therapeutic Equivalence List of 'Approved Drug Products with Proposed Therapeutic Equivalence Evaluations' is compiled by the FDA to aid the States in compiling formularies which are the keystone of 'adopted laws intended to encourage the substitution of one product of a particular drug entity for another with the intent of saving money for the consumer and containing costs in drug procurement and medical reimbursement programs'. It was published in January 1979 by the US Department of Health, Education and Welfare. The list is not comprehensive, but includes products which are considered either not to have bioequivalence problems or for which bioequivalence requirements have been met. A secondary category contains 'those products that the Food and Drug Administration is unable to recommend (at this time) as therapeutically equivalent'. Two sub-groups are described, one containing products with known bioequivalence problems for which adequate studies have not been submitted and another indicating products with potential problems.

The 1962 amendments to the US Federal Food, Drug and Cosmetic Act gave the authority for new drug approval before marketing and added a requirement for effectiveness as well as safety. Implementation included a retrospective survey of efficacy of drugs introduced between 1938 and 1962. This Drug Efficacy Study (DES) is important because where the drug has been termed effective, companies marketing or intending to market identical, relating or similar drug products must file a full New Drug Application (NDA) or an abbreviated NDA (ANDA).

The final Bioequivalence Regulations published in the Federal Register of January 7, 1977, list over 100 drugs and drug combinations for which a bioequivalence requirement is to be established by means of the following criteria:

a) Well controlled clinical trials or observations that such products do not give comparable therapeutic effects
b) Evidence from well controlled studies of non-bioequivalence
c) Narrow therapeutic ratio
d) Medical opinion that lack of bioequivalence would lead to serious adverse effect or treatment failure
e) Physicochemical evidence
f) Pharmacokinetic evidence.

These requirements are applicable to new drugs in NDAs and old drugs in ANDAs but may be waived when the drug does not meet the above criteria of bio-inequivalence.

Bioequivalence requirements for drugs not subject to the DES mechanism have been proposed in the Federal Register (e.g. Feb. 17, 1978 [43,6969] for tricyclic antidepressants). The notices include a literature review, evidence for potential bio-inequivalence, details of *in vitro* dissolution and bioavailability data required. Guidelines for bioavailability comparisons with the 'pioneer product' are available and differ according to the drug.

## 2. United Kingdom Requirements

In the United Kingdom there are not many official statements on bioavailability. However, at an international symposium held in 1975 in Ottawa on The Development of Use of Safe and Effective Drugs one of the objectives of the Committee on the Safety of Medicines was said to be 'to ensure the quality of the material which is marketed; that the formulations of the material do not interfere with the pharmacological actions or with bioavailability, and are suitable for the purpose and the method by which they are to be used'.

## 3. Dutch Requirements

In the Netherlands, the question of substitution is being examined and attempts will be made to list generic equivalents for the top 60 to 70 drugs (SCRIP No. 381, April 28, 1979).

## 4. Canadian Requirements

Responsibility for drug safety, efficacy and quality in Canada rests with the Federal Health Protection Branch. The Federal Food and Drugs Act is part of the Criminal Code and carries provisions for penalties against those who transgress. Devolving from the Act are the Food and Drug Regulations and essential to this legislation is the concept of a New Drug.

A New Drug is considered to be any chemical entity, dosage form or combination of 2 or more drugs that has not been sold as a drug in Canada for sufficient time and in sufficient quantity to establish in Canada its safety and effectiveness for use as a drug. New chemical entities are clearly New Drugs; extensive data to establish efficacy, safety and product quality are required in New Drug Submissions.

Prior to 1969, patent laws effectively ensured that only one manufacturer could market a new drug and exclusive sales were maintained during the protected 17 years. The legislation at that time did not preclude the granting of compulsory licences to other companies but they were rarely granted. Amendments to the Patent Act were enacted in June 1969 and considerably clarified the procedures for obtaining a compulsory licence. The objective was to reduce drug costs through stimulated competition. The requirements for New Drug Submissions in the Food and Drug Regulations are not modified because a product may be the subject of a compulsory licence. Any product which is determined to be a New Drug must be shown by the manufacturer to be safe and effective before it can be marketed.

Drugs marketed before 1963 are not usually considered to be New Drugs: thus important drugs such as warfarin, digoxin, quinidine and phenytoin are regarded as 'not New Drugs'. Semantically there are difficulties: when does a New Drug become an old drug? can an old drug become a New Drug? can an old drug for which new indications are uncovered become a New Drug just for that indication? can we have a special category for critical old drugs when there are special requirements? The answer to all these questions is 'yes', but with some strains developing in the semantic burden of the words New and Old.

The separation of Federal and Provincial responsibilities in Canada permits the 10 provinces to establish their own procedures whereby the health professionals may practise.

Many provinces are involved with drug reimbursement schemes, especially for the aged and the indigent and in some of these schemes formularies of permitted drugs and their cost were supported by regulations guiding professional practice. In some cases these regulations provided for substitution by the dispenser of another brand of the identical drug product provided no contrary instructions were given by the prescriber.

Information from the Health Protection Branch, from manufacturers, and from the literature is used by the Provincial Formulary Therapeutic Committees in making decisions on the acceptability of products for inclusion in the formularies.

A few drugs with bioavailability problems are listed in some of the formularies as 'non-interchangeable'. Drugs with steep dose/response curves such as warfarin and phenytoin are also listed as non-interchangeable since brand-switching is considered hazardous.

There is no unanimous view of the procedures necessary to prevent misadventure due to substitution. Some experts involved in provincial reimbursement plans have concluded that extensive programs to generate bioavailability data would be a waste of taxpayers' money and would increase the price of drugs. The solution as they see it would be an authoritative announcement that for most drugs there are no problems in permitting an alternative brand but in a few cases there are problems which can be dealt with by appropriate information to physicians and monitoring of their patients.

*Table I.* Comparative bioavailability in healthy volunteers of single doses of different brands of 16 drugs

| Drug | Number of products tested | Number unacceptable[1] |
|---|---|---|
| Paracetamol (acetaminophen) | 10 | 0 |
| Hydrochlorothiazide[2] | 36 | 0 |
| Chlorothiazide | 5 | 0 |
| Sulphamethizole | 5 | 0 |
| Nitrofurantoin[2] | 21 | 1 |
| Sulphafurazole (sulfisoxazole) | 17 | 2 |
| Tetracycline | 43 | 4 |
| Ampicillin | 8 | 1 |
| Erythromycin | 6 | 0 |
| Chlordiazepoxide | 21 | 1 |
| Diazepam | 2 | 0 |
| Warfarin | 4 | 0 |
| Metronidazole | 9 | 0 |
| Phenylbutazone | 22 | 5 |
| Digoxin | 17 | 6 |
| Isoniazid | 3 | 0 |
| Total | 229 | 20 |

1 Acceptability was defined as area under the plasma concentration-time curve within 80 to 125% of the innovator's product.
2 Acceptability based on urinary excretion comparisons.

## 5. Other Variable Factors

Much anxiety about bioequivalence stems from the presumed ease by which a patient can receive different brands during longterm treatment. To attempt to demonstrate that all brands are similar is, in the view of some, to ignore the realities of history since in the past there have been more problems from variation in the same manufacturer's product than from another manufacturer. Two examples are the digoxin episode and the Australian phenytoin incident.

According to Biron (1976) preoccupation with bioavailability has led to neglect of other factors which have equal if not greater significance, such as dosage and compliance, and the placebo effect, since he considers total therapeutic effect of a drug to be the sum of the pharmacological effect and the placebo effect.

The concluding paragraph of Biron's letter reads 'Compared with insufficient dosage and insufficient compliance, insufficient bioavailability is a marginal factor leading to insufficient blood concentrations of prescribed drugs. Much more energy and financial support should be directed towards educating physicians in prescribing the correct dosage and obtaining proper compliance, rather than towards increasing the number of sophisticated and costly bioavailability trials'.

Few will disagree that compliance and dosage are critical factors but there may be room for more debate on the relative importance of comparative bioavailability (Ruedy et al., 1977).

## 6. Bioavailability Studies

Prior to 1971, exploratory work had been carried out demonstrating that drug products having the identical active ingredient showed different absorption and bioavailability characteristics (Cook, 1973).

Between 1971 and 1975 all available brands of some 16 drug entities with a total of 229 products were examined. Comparative bioavailability was assessed in healthy volunteers following single dose administration. The main points are summarised in table I.

There were no reports of untoward effects from patients, physicians, pharmacists or adverse drug reaction reporting schemes nor did manufacturers report any problems.

Whether these differences have therapeutic implications is unknown. In the final analysis it is the clinical consequences of bioavailability differences that are of concern to the health professions and regulatory agencies. There are relatively few reports of clinical failure or increased adverse effects attributable to formulation changes as opposed to bioavailability inadequacies. Many are more anecdotal than scientific and few are adequately documented. Others are relatively inaccessible in government or company files.

### 6.1 Phenytoin and Carbamazepine

Phenytoin provides the best documented case of a formulation change resulting in clinical manifestations (Tyrer et al., 1970). Shortly after the excipient calcium sulphate was replaced by lactose, there was an increased incidence of phenytoin intoxication (nystagmus, dizziness, staggering and slurred speech). Subsequent comparisons of plasma concentrations following the 'old' and 'new' formulations revealed that with the lactose formulation, steady-state plasma concentrations of phenytoin were about doubled.

Our own studies of several phenytoin products showed only minor differences in absorption rate. Optimisation of formulation of the free acid can give a product of at least comparable bioavailability to sodium phenytoin.

Clinical problems have also arisen with non-equivalent formulations of carbamazepine. Kauko and Tammisto (1974) reported poor control of epilepsy with one brand of carbamazepine which gave lower steady-state plasma concentrations than another brand.

### 6.2 Digoxin

In late 1969 the Burroughs Wellcome Company in the UK altered its manufacturing process for digoxin with an inadvertent reduction in bioavailability. The original process was reintroduced in May 1972 yielding tablets of unknown but higher bioavailability. The clinical consequences of these changes are now well known and have been reviewed by Shaw (1974).

### 6.3 Corticosteroids

Apparent clinical failure has also been reported with prednisone tablets and this was associated with poor *in vitro* dissolution (Campagna et al., 1963, Levy et al.,

1964, Sullivan et al., 1975). Subsequently the FDA proposed an *in vitro* equivalence requirement for prednisone and other corticosteroids.

Two prednisone formulations of widely disparate dissolution properties were tested in a Health Protection Branch bioavailability study. Using the original paddle flask method *no* drug dissolved in 1 hour from one of the formulations. However, the bioavailabilities of the 2 formulations were not significantly different. Neither was any significant difference observed in absorption rate, although over the first hour the mean plasma concentrations from the faster dissolving form were higher. The dose-dependent pharmacokinetics of prednisone and prednisolone may complicate bioavailability assessment (Pickup et al., 1977; Loo et al., 1978). Dissolution tests are being introduced in attempts to standardise formulations, but if the correlations with *in vivo* data are poor the usefulness of such standards must be questioned.

### 6.4 Non-equivalence without Clinical Consequences

There have been many instances of significant differences in bioavailability without apparent therapeutic failure. A recent recall in Canada of a batch of phensuximide capsules is a case in point.

The problem first came to light during a routine examination of the capsules by the manufacturer when prolonged disintegration was noted. A subsequent bioavailability study showed impaired absorption but no untoward reports were made either to the company or to the Health Protection Branch.

Further tests were performed in our laboratory and on the basis of dissolution time alone, the bioavailability differences may not have been suspected.

Theophylline is eliminated more rapidly in children than in adults (Ellis et al., 1976) and attempts have been made to design formulations which would prolong the duration of action and maintain plasma theophylline concentrations above the minimum effective therapeutic level of $10\mu g/ml$. There have been conflicting reports on the performance of these sustained release forms. McKenzie and Baillie (1978) for example report wide inter- and intra-individual variations in plasma concentrations in children while Weinberger et al. (1978) found that in adults 3 slow-release forms of theophylline were absorbed consistently and more slowly than solution while with 3 other sustained release forms absorption was erratic and less complete.

Prolongation of effective plasma concentrations obtained with the sustained release forms may be advantageous (Sheen and Sly, 1978; Jones, 1979).

In a recent unreported study, conventional and slow-release combination products of theophylline, ephedrine and barbiturate were compared in 8 normal subjects. Compared with the conventional dosage form, the dose-corrected bioavailability of the slow-release product was 74.3% for theophylline and 73.4% for ephedrine. The uncorrected relative bioavailabilities of 1 slow-release tablet compared with 1 conventional tablet were 112 and 150% for theophylline and ephedrine respectively. 1 slow-release tablet containing 180mg theophylline and 48mg ephedrine HCl thus delivers inefficiently, similar amounts of theophylline and considerably more ephedrine than a conventional tablet containing 130mg theophylline and 24mg ephedrine.

## 7. Conclusions

Opinions differ on the clinical significance of variation in bioavailability and a commonsense balance must be sought between reduction of risks to the patient and the cost of that reduction.

# References

Biron, P. Dosage, compliance and bioavailability in perspective. Canadian Medical Association Journal 115: 102-103 (1976).

Campagna, F.A.; Cureton, G.; Mirigian, R.A. and Nelson, E.: Inactive prednisone tablets USP XVI. Journal of Pharmaceutical Sciences 52: 605-606 (1963).

Cook, D.: A history of bioavailability testing in the food and drug directorate. Revue Canadienne de Biologie 32: (Suppl.) 157-162 (1973).

Ellis, F.E.; Koysooka, R. and Levy, G.: Pharmacokinetics of theophylline in children with asthma. Pediatrics 58: 542-547 (1976).

Jones, R.W.: Comparative pharmacokinetics of two theophylline derivatives in asthmatic patients. Journal of International Medical Research 7: (Suppl. 1) 16-21 (1979).

Kauko, K. and Tammisto, P.: Comparison of two generically equivalent carbamazepine preparations. Annals of Clinical Research 6 (Suppl. 11) 21-25 (1974).

Levy, G.; Hall, N.A. and Nelson, E.: Studies on inactive prednisone tablets USP XVI. American Journal of Hospital Pharmacy 21: 402 (1964).

Loo, J.C.K.; McGilveray, I.J.; Jordan, N.; Moffatt, J. and Brien, R.: Dose-dependent pharmacokinetics of prednisone and prednisolone in man. Journal of Pharmacy and Pharmacology 30: 736 (1978).

McKenzie, S. and Baillie, E.: Serum theophylline levels in asthmatic children after oral administration of two slow-release theophylline preparations. Archives of Disease in Childhood 53: 943-946 (1978).

Pickup, M.E.; Lowe, J.R.; Leatham, P.A.; Rhind, V.M.; Wright, V. and Downie, W.W.: Dose-dependent pharmacokinetics of prednisolone. European Journal of Clinical Pharmacology 12: 213-219 (1977).

Ruedy, J.; Davies, R.O.; Gagnan, M.A.; McLean, W.M.; Thompson, W.G.; Vitti, T.G. and Wilson, T.W.: Dosage, compliance and bioavailability in perspective. Canadian Medical Association Journal 117: 323-324 (1977).

Shaw, T.R.D.: Non-equivalence of digoxin tablets in the UK and its clinical implications. Postgraduate Medical Journal 50 (Suppl. 6): 24-29 (1974).

Sheen, A. and Sly, R.M.: Serum theophylline concentrations in asthmatic children. Annals of Allergy 41: 327-328 (1978).

Sullivan, T.J.; Sakmar, E.; Albert, K.A.; Blair, D.C. and Wagner, J.G.: In vitro and in vivo availability of commerical prednisone tablets. Journal of Pharmaceutical Sciences 64: 1723-1725 (1975).

Tyrer, J.H.; Eadie, M.J.; Sutherland, J.M. and Hooper, W.D.: Outbreak of anticonvulsant intoxication in an Australian city. British Medical Journal 4: 271-273 (1970).

Weinberger, M.; Hendeles, L. and Bighley, L.: The relation of product formulation to absorption of oral theophylline. New England Journal of Medicine 299: 852-857 (1978).

# 31

# Drug Absorption and Bioavailability: the 1980's

## Current Therapeutic Problems

*Michael D. Rawlins*

Department of Pharmacological Sciences, The University, Newcastle-upon-Tyne

Drug absorption investigations carried out recently have emphasised the complexity of the processes involved. These pose considerable problems for prescribing doctors — and their patients — and special consideration will be given to those encountered in clinical practice.

## 1. Compliance

Numerous investigators (Sackett and Haynes, 1976; Mucklow, 1979) have demonstrated that many patients fail to take their drugs in the prescribed manner. Most studies have examined 'bulk' compliance — the proportion of the prescribed dose which has been consumed by the patient — and have expressed the results as a compliance index (ratio of observed to expected consumption). Poor communication between doctor and patient, particularly failure by the patient to understand the nature of his illness and the potential benefits of treatment, is an important cause of poor compliance. Other reasons include psychiatric illness, old age, social isolation and failing memory. In recent years, pharmaceutical manufacturers and doctors have assumed that drugs which need to be taken once daily promote greater compliance than those taken more frequently (Haynes et.al., 1977). There is a correlation between dosage interval and compliance (Gatley, 1968; Porter, 1969), but although compliance appears to be significantly worse when drugs are given thrice daily or more frequently, convincing evidence demonstrating advantages of once over twice-daily administration, is lacking.

Increasing the dosage interval for drugs with long half-lives presents no practical problems: for such drugs, there are usually only relatively small fluctuations in plasma concentration during a dosage interval, and no loss of efficacy results from changing the dosage frequency from 6-hourly or 8-hourly, to twice- or once-daily. For drugs with short half-lives, however, large changes in plasma concentration may occur between doses, particularly as the dosage interval is increased. Where there is poor correspondence between plasma concentration and effect during a dosage interval, such as between plasma labetalol levels and antihypertensive effect (Sanders et al., 1979), dosage intervals can be prolonged without compromising efficacy. However, where there appears to be benefit from maintaining 'therapeutic' plasma concentrations during a dosage interval then slow-release preparations are rational. However, slow-release forms may have disadvantages: erratic absorption, toxicity if absorption is rapid and incomplete absorption if there is increased gastrointestinal motility.

Although many studies have been undertaken of 'bulk' compliance, few investigators have examined 'strict' compliance — the patient's adherence to precise dosing instructions (e.g. times and relation to meals). The influence of food on the bioavailability of drugs such as hydrallazine and propranolol (Melander et al., 1977a,b) suggests that 'strict' compliance may be an important determinant of the therapeutic response.

*Problem 1.* For drugs which are to be given chronically, should we be encouraging the development, and use, of preparations which only need to be given twice daily?

*Problem 2.* Are sustained release preparations the best approach to increasing the dosage interval, or are these temporary measures which should be supplanted by compounds with longer half-lives?

*Problem 3.* Is it reasonable to expect patients to take drugs at specific times of the day, and in relation to meals? Or should we avoid the use of drugs which interact with food?

*Problem 4.* What data requirements should drug regulatory agencies need, before giving marketing approval to sustained release formulations?


## 2. Small Intestinal Absorption

Despite its limitations, the oral route remains the most convenient way of administering drugs. Because of its large absorption surface area and relatively high blood flow, most drugs are absorbed predominantly from the small intestine after oral administration.


### 2.1 Rate of Absorption

Although many factors influence the rate of drug absorption, pharmaceutical formulation and the rate of gastric emptying are major sources of individual variation. Such variability, though largely irrelevant during chronic therapy, is important for drugs given acutely (e.g. analgesics, hypnotics) or when rapid initiation of therapy is needed (e.g. prevention of febrile convulsions with antipyretics, anti-arrhythmic prophylaxis).

The influence of pharmaceutical formulation on the absorption of 2 brands of paracetamol (which had similar *in vitro* disintegration rates) is shown in figure 1. Peak plasma concentrations were higher, and occurred earlier, with one brand of tablets than with the other.

The rate-limiting effect of gastric emptying on drug absorption is probably a more formidable problem. Delayed gastric emptying occurs after food, in association

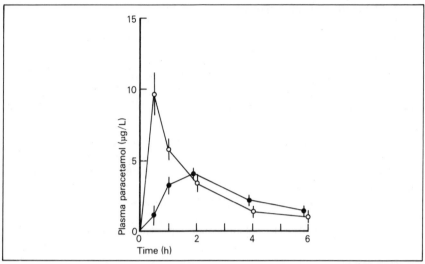

*Fig. 1.* Mean plasma paracetamol concentrations in 6 fasting healthy volunteers after ingestion of 500mg of 2 different brands of the drug.

with fear, anxiety, pain and nausea, as well as after the administration of anticholinergics or opiates. Thus in many of the circumstances when rapid absorption is desired, it is compromised by physiological, pathological or pharmacological influences.

*Problem 5.* What data requirements on the rate of absorption, should drug regulatory bodies need in considering a marketing application?

*Problem 6.* Is delayed gastric emptying a sufficiently serious problem that we should be encouraging the development, and use, of compounds which are rapidly absorbed from the stomach; and/or should we be encouraging the use of alternative routes of administration?

## 2.2 Extent of Absorption

Incomplete absorption of drugs across the gastrointestinal mucosa, or first-pass elimination by the gut wall or liver, diminishes systemic availability.

Drugs which are poorly absorbed tend to have common features: their systemic availability is subject both to formulation differences, and to inter- and intra-individual differences within formulations; absorption is subject to alterations in small bowel motility; and small bowel mucosal disease may further impair bioavailability. First-pass elimination is also variable within, and between, individuals, is affected by other drugs, and is altered by liver disease.

*Problem 7.* Should we eschew drugs which are incompletely absorbed from the gastrointestinal tract?

*Problem 8.* Does first-pass metabolism represent such an important source of variation that we should be encouraging the development of compounds which do not undergo extensive metabolism by the gut wall or liver?

*Problem 9.* What data requirements should drug regulatory agencies demand in considering the bioavailability of new compounds and formulations?

## 3. Other Routes of Absorption

Problems associated with oral drug administration suggest that other routes may have substantial advantages:

1) By eliminating the rate-limiting effect of gastric emptying on absorption
2) By ensuring complete bioavailability
3) By allowing drugs to reach their target organs without causing widespread toxicity.

*Problem 10.* Is it likely that bulk transfer of drugs across the buccal and rectal mucosa can be improved by chemical and pharmaceutical advances?

*Problem 11.* Can target-organ selectivity be achieved by means other than local administration?

*Problem 12.* Does the rectal route offer advantages which we are currently ignoring?

*Problem 13.* Does transdermal absorption represent a practicable alternative?

## References

Gatley, M.S. To be taken as directed. Journal of the Royal College of General Practitioners 16: 39-44 (1968).

Haynes, R.B.; Sackett, D.L.; Taylor, D.W.; Roberts, R.S. and Johnson, A.L.: Manipulation of the therapeutic regimen to improve compliance: conceptions and misconceptions. Clinical Pharmacology and Therapeutics 22: 125-130 (1977).

Melander, A.; Danielson, K.; Hanson, A.; Rudell, B.; Schersten, B.; Thulin, T. and Wahlen, E.: Enhancement of hydrallazine bioavailability by food. Clinical Pharmacology and Therapeutics 22: 104-107 (1977a).

Melander, A.; Danielson, K.; Schersten, B. and Wahlen, E.: Enhancement of the bioavailability of propranolol and metoprolol by food. Clinical Pharmacology and Therapeutics 22: 108-112 (1977b).

Mucklow, J.C.: Compliance; in Davies and Rawlins (Eds) Topics in Therapeutics — 5, p.47-55 (Pitman, London 1979).

Porter, A.M.W.: Drug defaulting in general practice. British Medical Journal, 1: 218-222 (1969).

Sackett, D.L. and Haynes, R.B. (Eds): Compliance with Therapeutic Regimens (Johns Hopkins University Press, Baltimore 1976).

Sanders, G.L.; Murray, A. and Rawlins, M.D.: Interdose control of β-blockade and arterial blood pressure during chronic oral labetaolol treatment. British Journal of Clinical Pharmacology 8: 1255-1275 (1979).

# Drug Regulatory Agency Attitudes to Bioavailability Studies

*J.P. Griffin*

Medicines Division, Department of Health and Social Security, London

Several questions have been directed to the requirements of regulatory authorities by Professor Rawlins.

# 1. What Are the Regulatory Requirements For Bioavailability Studies?

In the United Kingdom the regulatory authorities have not issued any formal guidelines. In this area, therefore, I intend to refer to two sets of guidelines — the proposed EEC Guidelines from the Committee on Proprietary Medicinal Products (CPMP) and those of the Australian Authority published in June 1977. Both these documents cover only the general problems, and special problems need special studies designed to meet the circumstances.

## 1.1 Definition of Bioavailability

The CPMP Guidelines define their scope as follows:

'Bioavailability may be considered as comprising data on the rate and extent of delivery to the site of action of a medicinal substance when administered in a *particular pharmaceutical form*. Bioavailability is a characteristic of this form and does not necessarily run parallel to particular pharmacological or therapeutic effects. Bioavailability is generally determined by the degree and rate of *absorption* of a drug from its pharmaceutical form, but there may be other important determinants such as first-pass metabolism and intestinal degradation. It may be useful to distinguish between the *'absolute'* bioavailability of a given pharmaceutical form when compared with that (100%) following intravenous administration, and the *'relative'* bioavailability as compared with another form administered by the same route (e.g. tablets vs capsules).

'Questions of bioavailability most commonly arise with products administered by the oral route. In these cases, the most convenient measure of bioavailability is as a rule the concentration-time curve in the blood of the active component or its active moiety or metabolites, since this will presumably reflect the concentration attained at the site of action. However, administration by other routes will obviously sometimes raise analogous problems, requiring a comparable (though different) approach. Studies of blood concentration are sometimes not feasible, and in other instances they are not directly relevant to the effects of the drug, in such cases the measurement of concentrations elsewhere (e.g. urine), of pharmacological effect, or therapeutic efficacy using sensitive and reproducible methods may be acceptable and occasionally more realistic.'

## 1.2 When Are Bioavailability Studies Required?

The Australian Notes for Guidance state that bioavailability studies will be required for products in one or more of the following categories:

1) Those containing drugs which require close control and which are used in the treatment of serious or life-threatening disease
2) Those containing drugs which show poor or variable absorption during animal trials
3) Those containing drugs whose physicochemical properties make it likely that a change in formulation will alter bioavailability
4) Those for which special claims are made in relation to absorption properties, e.g. sustained release products

5) Those for which there is evidence of problems with bioavailability of existing formulations of the same drug

6) Those containing more than one drug where any component may behave as described above

7) Those containing more than one drug where there is evidence that one may affect the bioavailability of the other.

The Australian Guidelines give the following additional advice:

'A suitable *in vitro* method of testing should be established for use as a routine quality control measure to ensure batch to batch uniformity. For solid formulations, dissolution profiles should be determined under various conditions for use both as a basis for a quality control measure and as a possible reference should problems of bioavailability arise subsequently. The degree of correlation between *in vitro* and *in vivo* data should be ascertained.

Dissolution profiles should be obtained on a number of samples of each solid formulation used in the bioavailability trial, the samples being taken from the same batches as were used in the trial. The results should be reported both as individual and averaged data and should include measures of variation for each point. A number of points should be determined at appropriate intervals for each graph.'

This recommendation by the Australians that 'data on bioavailability should be correlated with dissolution or other appropriate *in vitro* studies' is a sound one, but it does not appear in the CPMP document.

## 1.3 When Are Bioavailability Studies Not Required?

It is useful to have a clear statement of when bioavailability studies need not be conducted and this is given in the proposed CPMP Notes for Guidance on Bioavailability Studies.

1) When the drug is intended solely for intravenous use.

2) When the drug is destined for local therapeutic use (though this does not necessarily exclude the need for studies of its passage into the general circulation).

3) When the drug is an oral product not required to be absorbed (though this does not necessarily exclude the need for studies of its passage into the general circulation).

4) When the drug differs only as regards the quantity of active substance from another having the same pharmaceutical form, the same proportion of active component and excipients, made by the same manufacturer, provided the bioavailability of the latter has been demonstrated and the two products meet the requirements of an *in vitro* dissolution test.

5) When the drug has been reformulated but remains identical (except as regards the colorant, sweetener or preservative), to the drug previously prepared by the same manufacturer, provided the bioavailability of the latter is known and the two versions meet the requirements of an *in vitro* dissolution test.

6) When it can be shown that there is no analytical method for the determination of the active principle, or where the existing method is not satisfactory, in such a situation, it may be possible to obtain an indirect estimate by careful measurement of a relevant pharmacological or therapeutic effect.

The above circumstances are generalisations and probably most of us could think of exceptions. For example, sodium cyclamate markedly reduced the absorption of lincomycin from a syrup formulation compared with absorption from capsules. Under the Guidelines from the CPMP, bioavailability studies would have been exempted.

### 1.4 Particular Problems in Guidelines on Bioavailability

Both the Australian Guideline and the draft CPMP Guidelines comment on between patient variability with respect to bioavailability and strongly recommended cross-over studies when marking comparisons between preparations.

The CPMP Guidelines recommend that the effect of food on drug absorption should be considered.

Neither Guideline covers the problem of bioavailability changing as the tablet is stored.

## 2. Rate of Absorption

In reply to the question on what data requirements on rate of absorption should regulatory authorities request, both the Australian and the draft CPMP Guidelines specifically indicate a strong preference for studies to cover rate of absorption as opposed to total absorption as might be determined by a 24-hour urine collection. The Australian Guideline states explicitly 'Data on blood levels and/or urinary excretion of the drug or its active metabolite should be reported as a function of time for individual subjects.'

Neither Guideline refers to the special problem of prodrugs and this is an area where useful guidance could be incorporated in the future.

## 3. Incomplete Absorption

The drug that is completely absorbed is the exception. It is important to ensure that absorption is predictable and as far as possible constant for a particular product, bearing in mind the considerable individual variability in absorption in man by both the oral and rectal routes. With generic products such as digoxin BP, tetracycline BP, prednisolone BP it is essential that the bioavailability of all formulations is identical.

Differences in the bioavailability of tetracycline products and digoxin products as have occurred in the past should not be allowed to recur and it is hoped that the specifications laid down in the British Pharmacopoeia (BP) and European Pharmacopeia (EP) for generic products are adequate to ensure uniformity.

## 4. Sustained Release Products

Sustained release preparations are justifiable when they give a sustained therapeutic effect and therefore advantages to the patient in terms of:

a) Convenience and improved compliance
b) Therapeutic advantage
c) Reduced side effects.

*Table I. In vivo* release of prednisolone from sustained release tablets as indicated by percentage of initial prednisolone content retained

| Formulation | Percentage prednisolone left in sustained release tablet matrix (number of tablets analysed) | | | |
|---|---|---|---|---|
| | subject 1 | subject 2 | subject 3 | subject 4 |
| A | 4.0 (8) | 8.7 (6) | 12.5 (6) | 23.2 (6) |
| B | 14.4 (12) | 22.0 (2) | 34.3 (8) | 53.1 (5) |
| C | — | — | — | 72.5 (4) |

In many cases sustained release preparations are impaired release gimmickery and do not provide any therapeutic advantage. On the other hand there have been some very elegant pharmaceutical devices for providing sustained release by routes other than oral administration that provide definite therapeutic advances (e.g.) 'Ocusert'[1]).

Where different commerical sustained release preparations of the same substance are available, comparable release rates are highly desirable. At present there are various sustained release lithium carbonate dosage forms available with different nominal tablet content and non-equivalent release rates. In practical terms this may not be as undesirable as it appears since lithium has a long half-life and it may be unnecessary to have sustained release preparations anyway. In any case, plasma lithium concentrations should be monitored regularly. Nevertheless, change from one sustained release lithium carbonate preparation to another could possibly create clinical problems.

## 5. Data Required for Sustained Release Products

Ideally the data required for sustained release preparations should include the following as illustrated by a comparative study on 3 sustained release prednisolone preparations based on an inert plastic matrix (D'Arcy et al., 1971).

1) *In vitro release rates* were measured for all 3 sustained release preparations.

2) *Plasma concentration-time curves* were determined for all 3 sustained release preparations and for the same dose of prednisolone BP in compressed tablets in a cross-over study in which subjects received all 4 formulations.

3) *Availability of the drug from the matrix and individual variability.* 4 subjects undertook to recover the undissolved plastic matrices from their faeces so that these matrices could be analysed for residual prednisolone.

The variation between subjects was nearly as great as the variation between products (table I), and the subjects were ranked in the same order with respect to elution of the drugs from the different plastic matrix formulations.

4) *Biological effect.* Suppression of plasma cortisol provided a suitable measurement of effect and 24 hours after dosing with sustained release preparations concentrations were lower than with the same dose of prednisolone BP in compressed tablets.

1 'Ocusert' (Alza).

## 6. What Methods Can Be Exploited to Achieve Greater Organ Selectivity of Drug Action?

The function of regulatory authorities is to ensure that studies are conducted according to the optimum scientific standards of the day. As to the likely future developments in terms of improving delivery of the active drug substance to the target organ our crystal ball is no better than anybody else's. All that can be said is that improvements will occur and that guidelines issued by regulatory authorities will have to change to keep pace.

### Reference

D'Arcy, P.F.; Griffin, J.P.; Jenkins, J.S.; Kirk, W.F. and Peacock, A.W.C.: Sustained release formulation of prednisolone administered orally to man. Journal of Pharmaceutical Sciences 60: 1028-1033 (1971).

# Clinical Pharmacology

*C.T. Dollery*

Royal Postgraduate Medical School, London

I shall deal with the questions posed by Professor Rawlins very briefly and then go on to debate some of the relevant issues raised during the meeting. My response to the question concerning the desirability of achieving no more than twice-daily dosing is affirmative. It is more convenient for the patient and omission of lunch-time doses is very common. I suspect that few patients take note of very precise instructions concerning the timing of doses in relation to meals. Possibly they would do so if there were an immediate adverse consequence if they did not but I cannot think of a good example.

The concept that a drug should be deliberately designed to be absorbed from the stomach to overcome the problem of delay in gastric emptying is an interesting one but I believe that it is impracticable. The surface area available for absorption in the stomach is too small for this to be a general approach. First-pass metabolism is an important problem but there are relatively few drugs that cannot be used by the oral route because of it. I shall return to this issue when I consider the question of drug design. The transdermal route is promising for a small number of drugs that are given in small doses and which are very lipid soluble but I do not see it as a route that has general application.

## 1. How Important Are the Kinetic Properties of a Drug?

Pharmacokinetic characteristics are of great fascination and substantial importance but they should not be over emphasised. Efficacy and safety are of much greater significance. Insulin was not discarded because it had difficult pharmacokinetic properties neither were benzlypenicillin or hexamethonium. Hexamethonium was eventually superceded by ganglion blocking drugs such as mecamylamine and pempidine which had superior kinetic properties but these in their turn were displaced by guanethidine and methyldopa which had pharmacodynamic advantages. Propranolol is a very useful drug despite its high first-pass clearance. Indeed a whole industry has sprung up dedicated to the study of that property. Pharmacokinetic properties only become a determinant of therapeutic choice when there are a range of structures with similar therapeutic efficacy and safety from which to choose. This is usually a relatively late stage in the maturation of a field of drug therapy. By that time the accumulated experience of safety and mode of use may suggest that the innovator compound remains the best choice even if there are alternatives with some advantages in their pharmacokinetic profile. There is a danger of only viewing therapeutics through a keyhole labelled kinetics.

## 2. Concentration-effect Relationships

Drug absorption is important because it is one of the main determinants of the concentration at the site of action. But, looking at the concentration alone may be misleading and a clinical pharmacologist must give thought to the shape of the concentration-effect curve. Propranolol provides an excellent example. In a study we carried out in volunteers the half-life of a single 200mg dose was about 3.2 hours. The time to half-offset the blockade of exercise tachycardia in the same individuals was almost 12 hours. Other studies we have made of the hypotensive effect of a single dose in hypertensive patients show that the duration of effect exceeds 24 hours. It would have been easy to conclude from the half-life measurement that the drug ought to be administered every 4 to 6 hours but the conclusion would have been wrong. Special formulations to maintain the effect are scarcely needed if the action of the normal formulation is prolonged. The same argument applies to the unedifying 'battles of the blood levels' with many antibiotics. Leaving on one side the question of the advantages of a pulse versus a maintained concentration, the main question is whether the concentration achieved is high enough to inhibit growth of the target organism. Whether this is overdone by a factor of 6 or 10 may be relatively unimportant from the therapeutic standpoint.

## 3. Ingenious Devices

Some of the ideas that we have discussed here are very, very ingenious. I am thinking of Dr Shaw's appliances that stick to the skin behind the ear and Dr Banker's hydrated polymer pills that swell to the size of a ping-pong ball in the stomach. My niggling doubts gave rise to some irreverent thoughts. What happens when a patient wearing one of Dr Shaw's capsules goes for a swim or washes behind his ears? What might happen to Dr Banker's pills in a patient with stomach outflow obstruction? Can I see in my mind's eye a case report in the Lancet entitled, 'Intestinal Obstruction due to Ping-Pong Pills'? Joking apart I see a need for extensive field testing of such devices in the type of elderly multiply sick patient who seems to form a large part of the practice of a specialist in internal medicine. Blood level endpoints in motivated normal volunteers are not enough.

## 4. Role of Special Formulations

My expectations from special formulations are modest but I believe that they have a place. They can minimise local irritation of the gastrointestinal tract e.g. Slow-K[1]. They can smooth out the peak concentration following an oral dose and so minimise side effects, especially on the central nervous system e.g. phenytoin or clonidine. Obviously with a drug that must have a rapid onset of action such as a hypnotic or an analgesic the situation is reversed. Very occasionally a sustained release preparation will stretch the duration of action of a drug with a short half-life, to an extent that is clinically useful e.g. quinidine. More often sustained release means delayed release, variable bioavailability and no discernible advantage.

Special formulations, particularly combined preparations, may have a role in simplifying treatment. Simplification of the number of tablets and frequency of ingestion is a great convenience, especially to elderly patients. I prefer to think of convenience rather than compliance as the latter is a rather arrogant, physician-centred, concept. How dare the patient not 'comply' with the orders of his god-like medical attendant!

## 5. Commercial versus Therapeutic Arguments

Emphatically there is no need for a mass of special formulations whose main justification is commercial rather than therapeutic. There are disturbing signs that, as innovation becomes more difficult, greater thought is given to prolonging product life by reformulation. I understand the reasons. Patent life is too short in relation to the long cycle of drug development. But do not expect me to applaud the results which are often more expensive than the original product without any proven therapeutic advantage.

## 6. Regulations Made by Governments

This is an area in which it would be wise to make haste slowly. Simple bioavailability standards will be needed to protect the public against poorly made generic products. It is not difficult to define those which ought to be given priority e.g. steroids, digitalis glycosides and some antibiotics. One benefit of wider use of plasma concentration measurements may be readier detection of inadequate formulations. But, it would be to put the kinetic cart before the dynamic horse if the introduction of promising new drug entities were to be further delayed by the need to reach some general bioavailability standard. On the other hand, governments may have to play a role in restraining the growth of useless special formulations by limiting the reimbursement of their cost under national health insurance plans.

1 'Slow-K' (Ciba).

# A View From the Pharmaceutical Industry

*P. Johnson*

Hoechst Pharmaceutical Research Laboratories, Milton Keynes

I have been asked to comment on some of the questions raised by Professor Rawlins.

## 1. Compliance

Dosing once or twice a day as an ideal situation would probably meet with general agreement. There is apparently some evidence that dosing twice a day may in fact lead to greater compliance than once a day, and in some situations a missed single daily dose might be more of a problem than omission with more frequent dosage regimens. Once a day dosing, of course, implies the use of a drug with a fairly long half-life or a sustained release preparation.

The following points should be considered with respect to drugs with long half-lives:

1) There is a greater chance of problems arising from accumulation and possible saturation of binding sites
2) The problem of toxic metabolites with long half-lives may be accentuated
3) Close control of the clinical situation is lost, so that problems of termination of drug effect, treatment of overdose and impaired elimination become more acute.

In contrast to these points, which tend to mitigate against the use of drugs with long half-lives, there are several possible advantages of controlled release preparations:

1) They reduce both local and systemic peak concentrations of drug (and metabolites) and hence minimise local and systemic adverse effects
2) They minimise the problem of drug accumulation
3) Greater control can be achieved through the maintenance of constant drug levels with minimal fluctuation
4) A more economic use of drug may be achieved (although this is not necessarily reflected in the price of the dose).

A number of points apply equally to both long half-life and controlled release preparations:

1) There is an implicit assumption that efficacy is related to the maintenance of drug level in a broadly defined 'window' and that no pulse effect is required.

2) There may be advantages in special circumstances, such as the maintenance of overnight levels of drug.

3) Less frequent dosing *might* aid compliance through convenience.

Table I. Some compounds known to show or suspected of showing a first-pass effect[1]

| Drug | Species | Drug | Species |
|------|---------|------|---------|
| Acetylsalicylic acid | Dog, man | Nortriptyline | Man, rat |
| Aldosterone | Man | Organic nitrates | Rat |
| Alprenolol | Man | Paracetamol | Rat |
| Beclomethasone | Rat, dog, man | Pentazocine | Man |
| Chlorpromazine | Rat, man | Pethidine | Man |
| Cortisone | Dog | Propoxyphene | Rat, man |
| Desmethylimipramine | Rat | Propranolol | Rat, dog, man |
| γ-Hydroxybutyric acid | Dog | Salbutamol | Man |
| Imipramine | Man | Salicylamide | Man, dog |
| Lidocaine | Dog, man, rat monkey | Sulphisoxazole | Rat |
| Morphine | Man | Terbutaline | Rat, man |

1    Modified from Rowland, 1977.

The major problem in this area is the lack of good clinical data. In general, long half-life preparations may cause more problems than they solve, but controlled release preparations, if proven to be clinically effective and reproducible in their release properties, come closer to the ideal.

## 2. Small Intestinal Absorption

We should not be encouraging the development of compounds which are rapidly absorbed from the stomach. Even if there are sufficient studies in man to prove that effects on gastric emptying are such a big problem, which is doubtful, many potential difficulties remain, e.g. local irritation, residence time, the local pH and food. The stomach is also relatively poorly perfused and has at least 300 times less absorptive surface area than the small intestine if the microvilli are taken into account.

The general assumption that food tends to delay gastric emptying and thus delays drug absorption, can be misleading. The use of the gamma camera and labelled technetium allows a detailed examination of the dynamic situation *in vivo*, and recent work has shown that a capsule with rapid *in vitro* disintegration left the stomach much more quickly after a meal than in the fasted state (Hunter et al., in press). This contrasted with a capsule with slow disintegration characteristics *in vitro*, and the capsule which emptied rapidly after food was further shown to disintegrate much more rapidly in the stomach contents after food than in fasted subjects.

The relationship between gastric emptying, food and formulation warrants further investigation, and it is evident that attempts to promote drug absorption from the stomach would be fraught with difficulties.

It is obviously impracticable to make 100% absorption a prerequisite of any drug dosage form. At least, we should not make such an aim a limitation on chemical structure; pharmacological activity is still the prime goal in drug research. However, we can and should strive to maximise absorption to reduce patient variability and increase clinical control, and more attention could be paid to extent of absorption and to metabolic clearance at an early stage in the process of drug design. Absorption, may be improved by the use of surface active agents, ion pair formulations, liposomes, emulsions and medium chain length glycerides, quite apart from the improvements with some ester prodrugs.

## 3. First-pass Metabolism

The ideal drug would have a low clearance and avoid first-pass effects altogether, but again, making this a prerequisite of chemical structure is an enormous problem. Not only are first-pass effects known to occur with so many different chemical types (table I) that easy prediction is impossible, but even trial experiments in animals do not necessarily reflect the human situation and the sites available for first-pass effects are certainly not restricted to the liver and gut wall (Johnson, 1979). Nevertheless, some attempts have been made at modifying chemical structure to retain pharmacological activity but reduce metabolic lability and improve pharmacokinetics (Nelson, 1977; Notari, 1977). The idea of using a second molecule to inhibit metabolic enzymes has been used in the case of β-lactamase inhibitors, and a self-inhibiting prodrug has also been reported (Lipper et al., 1978). The use of an inactive optical isomer as a competitive inhibitor of metabolism may also be worthy of exploration.

## 4. Other Routes of Administration

I am sure that other routes of administration are of growing importance. Sublingual administration may not be acceptable to patients, the route is not suitable for all drugs, appropriate formulations can be difficult to achieve, and the problem of compliance is the same as for an oral dose. Possibly of even greater interest are the transdermal devices as described by Dr Shaw. There are now slow release prepara-

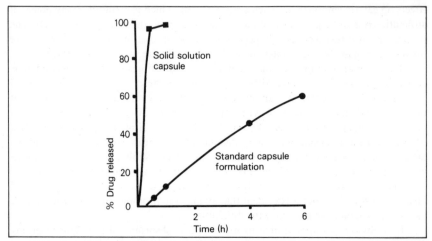

*Fig. 1.* Comparison of a solid solution capsule with a standard capsule in release of drug by the USP Dissolution Test.

tions for cattle which use a nose-clamp to hold the dose in the nasal cavity. These may be of limited application in man!

The rectal route is not acceptable to patients in some countries, and could lead to even greater problems of compliance. But is the route, as effective as some would have us believe? Dr Breimer has shown that rectal dosing can be less than ideal in avoiding portal absorption in man, giving variability comparable with that from the oral route. Additional problems may arise from premature defaecation and bacterial metabolism, but information is scant.

However, advances in pharmaceutical technology will continue, and Dr Banker has described how it may be possible to anchor a formulation in a desired position, which could overcome some of the problems with rectal administration, for example. The potential of transdermal devices has not been fully explored, and the buccal route has yet to be fully exploited.

An interesting recent advance from our own laboratory is the use of solid solution technology to improve absorption (Walker et al., 1980). Although solid solutions or eutectic mixtures have been available for many years, the technology required for pharmaceutical formulations has been achieved only recently. Capsules can now be formulated with a dramatic improvement in dissolution properties (fig. 1).

In summary, oral dosing will remain the preferred route for the immediate future, but other routes may also come into prominence with advances in chemical and pharmaceutical technology. An ideal preparation would be highly absorbed with minimal first-pass loss. Sustained release preparations have an important part to play but long half-life drugs are to be avoided and absorption from the stomach is not a good proposition.

## References

Hunter, E.; Fell, J.T.; Calvert, R.T. and Sharma, H.: *In vivo* disintegration of hard gelatin capsules in fasting and non-fasting subjects. International Journal of Pharmaceutics (in press).

Johnson, P.: First pass elimination of drugs, in Proceedings of the VIth International Symposium on Medicinal Chemistry, Brighton, U.K., September 1978, p.203-213 (Cotswold Press, Oxford 1979).

Lipper, R.A.; Mackovech, S.M.; Drach, J.C. and Higuchi, W.I.: Inhibition of drug metabolism by a prodrug; 9-β-D-arabinofuranosyladenine 5'-valerate as an inhibitor of adenosine deaminase. Molecular Pharmacology 14: 366-369 (1978).

Nelson, S.D.: Alteration of drug metabolism through structural modification, in Roche (Ed) Design of Biopharmaceutical Properties through Prodrugs and Analogs, p.316-343 (American Pharmaceutical Association, Washington 1977).

Notari, R.E.: Alteration of pharmacokinetics through structural modification, ibid., p.68-97.

Rowland, M.: Pharmacokinetics, in Parke and Smith (Eds) Drug Metabolism from Microbe to Man, p.123-145 (Taylor and Francis, London 1977).

Walker, S.E.; Ganley, J.A.; Bedford, K. and Eaves, T.: The filling of molten and thixotropic formulations into hard gelatin capsules. Journal of Pharmacy and Pharmacology 32: 389-393 (1980).

## Discussion

*J.E. Shaw* (Palo Alto): In the time that was allotted to me, it was not possible to review all the clinical studies with the transdermal system. Adhesion is very important and clinical studies have shown that the system stays in place for 3 days. Some systems under development have to stay in place only for 1 day and we have others which remain for 7 days. In California, the active population is ideal for testing these systems since we have people who jog, play tennis, sit in saunas and swim. I can assure you that this system has been designed to remain in place for the 3 days.

*D.D. Breimer* (Leiden): I agree with Dr Johnson that rectal administration is not just an alternative to the oral route. There are certain conditions in which it might be preferred, for example in small children and in patients who feel sick.

*M. Rowland* (Manchester): Would the panel comment on bioavailability testing where one product is evaluated against another in a cross-over design and statements are made on their relative performance in that particular sample? If the patient is already stabilised on one preparation, could the other be safely substituted on the basis of bioequivalence data published by the regulatory authorities?

*C.T. Dollery*: The decision rests not with us but with those who pay at Government level for drugs. It is clear that substitution will take place whether we like it or not when health budgets come under pressure. If money were no object, there would be many reasons for keeping the patient on the same preparation. For example, when bulk supplies change and the physical appearance of pills changes, even if they are bioequivalent, patients often lose confidence because they have become accustomed to a particular formulation. As long as preparations are broadly equivalent, I think that is all we can ask for. If you have tablets of identical appearance containing 40 and 80mg propranolol, I bet it would take quite a long time before you could tell which was which using them in ordinary clinical practice.

*P. Goldman* (Boston): We all agree with Professor Dollery that drugs should primarily be safe and effective and therefore it is very good that the Food and Drug Administration has actually incorporated this into their statutes. If the efficacy of a drug is established on the basis of clinical trials, then in a sense, the clinical trial becomes the standard for these statutes. If formulations are changed, all the assumptions discussed at this Conference must be introduced and this would clearly be very difficult to justify. We must be very cautious about trying to extrapolate to other formulations which may or may not be equivalent depending on these assumptions.

*R.C. Heading* (Edinburgh): Gastric emptying seems to be regarded as a rate-limiting step in many aspects of drug absorption, but Dr Johnson's comments remind us that it is not a simple phenomenon. A full stomach, be it filled with fluid, with food or whatever, is totally different from the stomach which only has a little pill and a small amount of water in it. It seems to be widely accepted here that age has a major effect on gastric emptying but I do not think that this is accepted by gastroenterologists. Occasionally, abnormalities of gastric emptying and gastrointestinal transit can be a problem for drug absorption and our job is to identify such situations.

*M.D. Rawlins*: An example of a problem with gastric emptying is the prophylaxis of febrile convulsions in children who are nauseated. It is difficult to persuade them to take paracetamol by mouth and even if they do swallow it, absorption may be so slow that it does not have any beneficial effect.

## Concluding Remarks

*L.F. Prescott*

Many important aspects of drug absorption from the gastrointestinal tract have been discussed here over the last 3 days. We have looked at the physiological and physicochemical basis of absorption and the influence of common sources of variation such as formulation, disease, food and other drugs. Acknowledging the limitations of conventional oral dosage forms, we have explored other approaches such as rectal and transdermal absorption and the use of novel oral drug delivery systems to obtain controlled release and absorption.

Drug absorption has become increasingly important in drug development and in preclinical pharmacology and toxicology studies. There are also formidable legal problems with regulatory agency requirements and the whole question of bio-availability.

Many important questions remain unanswered. What are the ideal absorption characteristics for a particular drug to be used for a particular disease and can complete and reliable absorption be obtained through advances in pharmaceutical technology? What are sensible and practicable standards for bioavailability testing and regulatory agency requirements? Is there really a glittering prize in the form of zero-order pharmacology to be obtained with controlled release formulations? What simple practical advice can we give to our clinical colleagues?

The interest shown in this meeting is both revealing and encouraging. Perhaps we should meet again soon to discuss further these important and unresolved issues.

# Subject Index